32-43
51-62

W9-AZK-306

David Commins is Benjamin Rush Distinguished Chair in Liberal Arts and Sciences and Professor of History at Dickinson College, Pennsylvania. His publications include *The Wahhabi Mission and Saudi Arabia* (I.B.Tauris, 2006), *Historical Dictionary of Syria* (1996, revised edition 2004) and *Islamic Reform: Politics and Social Change in Late Ottoman Syria* (1990).

p.304- Jeff Mancris article
-p.4 Author's thesis - Gulf states linked to rise & fall of Port towns

THE GULF
STATES
A MODERN
HISTORY

David Commins

I.B. TAURIS
LONDON · NEW YORK

Published in 2012 by I.B.Tauris & Co Ltd
6 Salem Road, London W2 4BU
175 Fifth Avenue, New York NY 10010
www.ibtauris.com

Distributed in the United States and Canada
Exclusively by Palgrave Macmillan
175 Fifth Avenue, New York NY 10010

Copyright © 2012 David Commins

The right of David Commins to be identified as the author of this
work has been asserted by him in accordance with the
Copyright, Designs and Patent Act 1988.

All rights reserved. Except for brief quotations in a review, this book,
or any part thereof, may not be reproduced, stored in or introduced
into a retrieval system, or transmitted, in any form or by any means,
electronic, mechanical, photocopying, recording or otherwise,
without the prior written permission of the publisher.

ISBN: 978 1 84885 278 5

A full CIP record for this book is available from the British Library
A full CIP record is available from the Library of Congress

Library of Congress Catalog Card Number: available

Printed and bound by CPI Group (UK) Ltd, Croydon, CR0 4YY

For Rosemarie Swanson Goodbody

CONTENTS

List of Illustrations   viii
A Note on Naming the Gulf   ix
Maps by Kerstin Martin and James Ciarrocca   x
Acknowledgments   xii

1 Introduction to the Gulf   1
2 Historical Patterns to 1500   13
3 Muslim and European Empires, 1500–1720   32
4 An Era of Political Turbulence, 1720–1820   51
5 The Era of British Supremacy, 1820–1920   76
6 The Formation of Modern States, 1920–56   120
7 The Gulf in the Era of Arab Nationalism, 1956–71   164
8 Affluence, Revolution and War, 1971–91   197
9 Years of Deepening American Intervention   250

   Conclusion   292
   Notes   300
   Bibliography   301
   Index   308

ILLUSTRATIONS

1 Fishermen and Dhow in Oman (Tor Eigeland,
  Saudi Aramco World PADIA)   5
2 Making a Fish Trap in Bahrain (Wendy Levine,
  Saudi Aramco World PADIA)   6
3 Bedouin Children in Saudi Arabia
  (Dorothy Miller, *Saudi Aramco World* PADIA)   8
4 Ashar Creek Basra (A. Kerim, Courtesy
  of Special Collections, Fine Arts Library,
  Harvard College Library)   44
5 Exploring for Oil in Saudi Arabia
  (Saudi Aramco Archives, *Saudi Aramco World* PADIA)   137
6 Khobar Aramco Petrol Station (T.F. Walters,
  Saudi Aramco World PADIA)   138
7 Dubai Creek (Susan Lindt)   190
8 The Conquest of Scarcity: Kuwait's Water
  Towers (Tor Eigeland, *Saudi Aramco World* PADIA)   201
9 Abu Dhabi Skyline (Susan Lindt)   288
10 The Suq al Dijaj in Basra City (A. Kerim,
  Courtesy of Special Collections, Fine Arts Library,
  Harvard College Library)   293
11 Mall of the Pharaohs in Dubai (Susan Lindt)   293
12 Arabian Transport, Past and Present (Susan Lindt)   294

A NOTE ON NAMING THE GULF

Place names are a matter of convention rather than nature, and therefore naming the body of water between Iran and Arabia either the Persian Gulf or the Arabian Gulf is rooted in convention. Ancient Greek works on navigation and geography used the name Persian Gulf. That name passed into Arabic at the hands of early Muslim geographers, from whom Portuguese mariners of the sixteenth century absorbed it into European languages. Naming the gulf Arabian as opposed to Persian became a matter of dispute in the second half of the twentieth century with the rise of Arab nationalism, whereas in ancient Greek and medieval Arabic works, the 'Arabian Gulf' commonly referred to the Red Sea.

Of course, we find variants for place names elsewhere, such as the Malvinas/Falkland Islands and the English Channel/La Manche. By adopting the convention of Persian Gulf, I follow common practice, not endorsing a nationalist agenda. Nor would I argue that writers who refer to the body of water as the Arabian Gulf are incorrect, only making a different choice. In this work, I use 'the Gulf' even if it makes nobody happy.[1]

By Kerstin Martin and James Ciarrocca, ESRI Data & Maps. Redlands, California: Environmental Systems Research Institute Inc., 2008

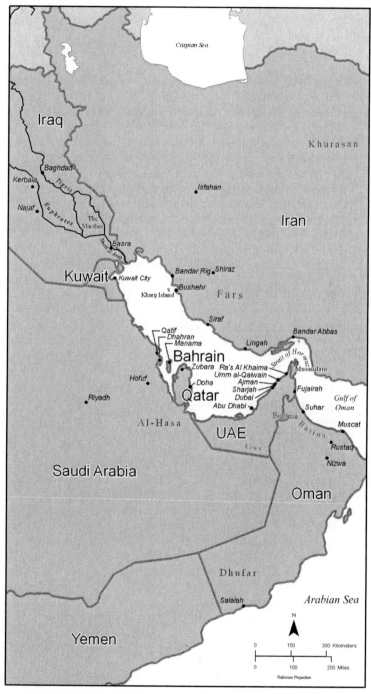

By Kerstin Martin and James Ciarrocca, ESRI Data & Maps. Redlands, California: Environmental Systems Research Institute Inc., 2008

ACKNOWLEDGMENTS

It is a pleasure to express my gratitude to all who contributed to this book. I would not have undertaken it were it not for Dr. Lester Crook at I.B.Tauris, who suggested the project and then lent it a discerning eye and steady hand. I am indebted to the three anonymous reviewers for taking the time to read the manuscript and for their valuable suggestions to improve it. I appreciate the expertise that Joanna Godfrey and Cecile Rault at I.B.Tauris brought to moving this work through final stages. The production manager at Integra, Priya Venkat, was a prompt collaborator on copyediting.

In collecting material on the history of the Gulf, I have benefited from the labours of dozens of scholars who have scoured archives, pored over chronicles, excavated archaeological sites, and devoted years of their lives to acquire deep familiarity with the region. I have tried to distil their research into a compact survey that honours their contributions to our understanding the Gulf and shares their insights with the reader.

For the precious gift of time for research and writing, I am grateful to The Kalaris Faculty Fellowship Fund and to John and Ann Curley's support for The Dickinson Faculty Excellence Fund. Provost Neil Weissman and the Faculty Personnel Committee supported my work with a Dickinson College Sabbatical Supplement Grant. I thank my esteemed colleague and friend Stephen Weinberger for letting me bend his ear with episodes in the history of the Gulf. Tina Maresco and Sandra Gority at the Waidner-Spahr Library's interlibrary loan department kept the supply of books and articles flowing. Elaine Mellen cheerfully assisted me with miscellaneous tasks in the preparation of the manuscript. James Ciarrocca GIS Specialist at Dickinson College and Kerstin Martin exhibited technical skill and aesthetic taste in producing the maps. For the historical photographs, it is a pleasure to acknowledge Joanne Bloom's assistance in steering me through the steps to obtain permission to reproduce photographs from the Special Collections of the Fine Arts Library of the Harvard College Library; and Saudi Aramco World kindly granted permission to reproduce historical photographs from its Public Affairs Digital Image Archive.

I owe a great deal to my family. My dear wife Susan Lindt provided the contemporary photographs, buoyed my spirits with her lively wit and abiding love, and mediated between Oliver and me. My mother Marcia Faye Swanson Commins discovered and nurtured my interest in history long before I had any inkling it would become my profession. My aunt Rosemarie Swanson Goodbody has always been generous in support and affection. My daughter Marcia Zakeeya Commins along with my brothers Stephen, Gary, and Neil Commins have a much appreciated knack for keeping me humble.

1 Introduction to the Gulf

The Gulf conjures images of fabulous wealth. A thousand years ago, the legend of Sinbad told of intrepid sailors making fortunes from treasures and trade in the Indian Ocean. A century ago, Gulf waters were famed for yielding splendid pearls that bedecked royalty and rich bourgeois. In the petroleum era, the Arabian shore's drab ports underwent rapid transformation into cosmopolitan hubs renowned for sleek architecture. Each era's affluence accrued to a handful of fortunate merchants and rulers while most men and women have had to toil for basic necessities, whether by fishing, pearling, trading, farming or pasturing herds of camels.

In the span of history, the amount of wealth flowing to the Gulf due to oil exports is exceptional. The attention paid to the region by powerful external forces is typical of the modern era. In the 1600s, Britain and the Netherlands challenged the Portuguese; in the 1800s, Britain, France, Germany and Russia jockeyed for spheres of influence. Early in the twenty-first century, the Gulf was the scene of an extraordinary concentration of military power due to global dependence on oil and political rifts that threatened its flow through the Strait of Hormuz. The United States now maintains a string of military bases along the Arabian shore from Kuwait to Oman. The military budgets of the Gulf Cooperation Council states are vast for countries with such small populations. Iran's Islamic Republic possesses an array of ballistic missiles and its nuclear power programme may result in its joining the ranks of nuclear states. In the current situation, we can see the recurrence of a historical pattern whose elements include geostrategic rivalry, military confrontation and a pivotal economic role for outside powers. Before delving into the history of the Gulf, let us consider the natural resources for economic activity and the forms of social and political organization that constitute the foundations for the sheikhs, kings and sultans who have sought to harness the Gulf's potential.

While the Gulf has witnessed a parade of empires, it has never spawned its own major power. In fact, throughout history no local force has ever unified the Gulf. The dispersion of power and the role of external forces present a challenge to the task of framing a historical survey because the standard narrative approach is to define eras according to the rise, development and fall of dynasties and nations. But here we have to deal with a different kind of history, not the story of kingdoms and empires, for the region typically lay at the edge of empires forming a frontier and a passageway between them. Therefore, while this history says a great deal about the succession of powers that struggled to dominate the Gulf, it is important also to pay attention to the durable rhythms of economy and society that persisted whether Persians, Arabs or Europeans had the upper hand in one era or another. Those rhythms owed much to limits imposed and possibilities offered by climate and natural resources.

A survey of geography illustrates the environmental constraints on economic production, social organization and political development. Meagre freshwater supplies and extreme aridity account for low population density, making it difficult to marshal economic and material resources for a powerful state. The ancient civilizations of the Middle East evolved along the banks of the Nile and the Tigris and Euphrates Rivers: South Asian civilization arose along the Indus River; Persian kingdoms and empires developed on the far side of the Zagros range whose spring run-off feeds fertile lands. Along the shores of the Gulf, human settlement was concentrated at the few locations with freshwater sources.

The northern end of the Gulf is the outlet for the Shatt al-Arab, the river formed by the confluence of the Tigris and Euphrates. The Shatt irrigates fertile gardens and carries goods from the Gulf upriver for distribution in the Mesopotamian valley and for transport across the desert to Mediterranean destinations, and sends goods downstream for shipment to Gulf ports and beyond. South of the Shatt on the Arabian side the land is barren until one reaches the fertile aquifer-fed oases of al-Hasa, scene of densest settlement on either coast. Four to five dozen artesian springs flow into irrigation canals and channels watering date groves and vegetable gardens.

Across a shallow bay from al-Hasa lies the Bahrain archipelago, blessed with abundant springs. Its largest island, in medieval times known as Awal, more recently as Bahrain, is about 30 miles long and ten miles wide at its broadest point. The two other primary islands are Muharraq and Sitra. The entire archipelago is located in the midst of pearl beds. The Qatar peninsula marks the southern end of this relatively wet (for Arabia) region before the

[margin notes: gulf- frontier; geographic constraints of the Gulf; Bahrain archipelago]

[bottom margin: Mtns, archipelagos, desserts in Middle East]

coast bends northward through the United Arab Emirates (UAE) to the tip of the Omani peninsula, which straddles four zones: on the west, the northern stretch of the peninsula forms part of the Gulf shore; the eastern side faces the Indian Ocean; along the central spine of the peninsula and bending southeast runs the mountain range called Jabal Akhdar; to the south is the edge of Arabia's most barren desert, the Empty Quarter. At the feet of Oman's mountains a string of aquifers supply water to oasis settlements. The northernmost extremity of Oman, the Musandam peninsula overlooks the Strait of Hormuz, across which lies Iran. From Hormuz to the Gulf's northern end is nearly 600 miles. The Strait itself is about thirty miles wide.

While the Arabian shore is a long stretch of flatlands from the Shatt al-Arab to the mountains that rise some miles south of Musandam, the Iranian side is a narrow coastal plain between 15 and 40 miles wide behind which rise the Zagros Mountains. This range impedes communication between the coast and the interior, funnelling trade through a handful of passes and shielding coastal towns from easy domination by interior powers. By contrast, the lack of any physical barrier between the coast and the interior on the Arabian side facilitated trade and political domination by nomadic tribes over the coastal peoples. The Iranian shore is dotted by ports that trade between the sea and the interior plateau. Bandar Abbas was developed by a seventeenth-century Persian shah to serve as a point of exchange with European traders. Half a millennium earlier, the port was known as Hormuz. It had the advantage of proximity to a relatively lush region watered by a small river. The name Hormuz later became attached to an island in the mouth of the strait. A short distance away is Qeshm Island, where the British established a naval headquarters in 1820 to suppress piracy, only to abandon it after a few years due to the intolerable heat. Further up the coast are a string of historic ports: Lingah, Kish/Qais Island, Bushehr and Siraf.

The interior region served by these ports is Fars, the historical centre of Persian culture and civilization. A few miles from the sea, the land rises sharply, creating three distinct climatic zones, each offering distinct resources and opportunities for varieties of production and exchange. The coastal plain is a narrow band of sandy, barren land on which little besides date palms can grow. Further inland foothills are cut by fertile valleys and meadows watered by small streams coursing from high peaks. Here decent soil and careful use of water made possible cultivation of orchards yielding a variety of fruits. Towering over the foothills the peaks of the Zagros range forms a forbidding obstacle to human traffic except through narrow passes leading to the Iranian plateau

which taps mountain run-off diverted to a maze of underground
channels leading water to fields, villages and towns.

Sea offers prosperity

Compared to the rugged Iranian and arid Arabian shores,
the sea offers a variety of riches. Its warm waters teem with
animal life: fish, crustaceans and the dugong, a large aquatic
mammal belonging to the manatee family hunted for its meat.
For centuries divers retrieved pearl-bearing molluscs in shallow waters. Since the seabed on the Arabian side is generally
shallow, pearling has been most intensive there, especially on
either side of the Qatar peninsula, north to Bahrain and south
to the Musandam peninsula. Less extensive pearl beds lie off
the coast of Kuwait and in the shallow waters around Kish and
Kharg Islands near the Iranian shore. To obtain pearls, divers
scour the seabed at depths of 15–20 yards wearing stone weights
to keep them submerged until they tug a rope to signal the crew
to pull them to the surface. Water temperature varies by season, and the optimal time for divers is the warm months from
May to October. Providing and provisioning a boat required a
capital outlay normally provided as an interest-bearing loan by
rich merchants. The captain, crew and divers hoped to recover
enough pearls to pay back the loan, but frequently fell short and
consequently carried their debt forward to the next year. Divers
might bequeath their debts to their children, creating a form of
debt bondage from which it was difficult to ever escape.

Before modern times, the best opportunity for accumulating
wealth was by controlling ports to tax the flow of goods. The
Iranian shore has an edge over the Arabian side because the deep-
est parts of the Gulf, for the most part a shallow body of water, lie
close by. That explains the concentration of a succession of major
port towns until modern times on the Iranian shore. Along that
shore, no single location has the advantage of a superior natural
harbour. Therefore, several ports and islands serve roughly equally
well as points of exchange. The upshot is that Gulf history is
marked by the rise and fall of port towns, influenced by changing
trade patterns and the fortunes of external powers.

thesis

As a matter of broad historical conception, the shifting fortunes
of Gulf ports make most sense when the region is viewed as part
of a larger economic system encompassing the Indian Ocean basin
and two types of exchange networks. In local networks, small vessels hugging the coast carried goods between Arabia and the Indus
River delta. In long-distance networks, large ships connected the
main ports in the Gulf, India, East Africa, Southeast Asia and China.
Traders from all parts of the basin exchanged raw materials and
manufactures with each other's ports, and each port also looked
to its own hinterland for exchange. No single zone – be it India,

China, Africa or the Gulf – had a natural advantage over another, and no port within a particular zone had a natural advantage over another; therefore trade patterns constantly recalibrated according to market conditions and prices. Parity in access to goods and the sea lanes meant that no single location could monopolize trade without resorting to force, an element that was not introduced until the advent of the Portuguese in the sixteenth century. In other words, the economy of the Gulf and Indian Ocean had no

1. Fishermen and Dhow in Oman.

mobile like marine corps

natural centre. It consisted of networks that adapted to economic fluctuations arising from political disturbances.

Maritime trade is a mobile mode of existence

The suitability of different sites for ports combined with the scarcity of water for cultivation and consumption to produce one of the distinctive features of the Gulf's peoples, namely their mobility. Maritime trade is in its nature a mobile mode of existence, bringing sailors and merchants from different regions into contact. Because ports had roughly equal access to inland trade routes, it was possible for upstarts to challenge dominant centres. In the early 1600s, Hormuz Island lost its paramount standing in trade because Portuguese governors tried to exact too heavy a tax from merchants, who chose to relocate. In the early 1900s, Dubai lured traders from the Persian port of Lingah with low tax rates and cheap real estate.

Mobility is key → Bedouins for example

Mobility was also part of the fishing and pearling economy, the latter drawing divers from the settled population for the five-month season. For the region's purely terrestrial residents, mobility is the byword for raising livestock. Arabia is the land of Bedouin, whose very survival required seasonal migration with their flocks in pursuit of pasture. A political by-product of the population's penchant for migration was the difficulty of establishing and sustaining control over people and resources. If fishermen, pearlers, traders or nomads found a local strongman oppressive, they moved with their boats, goods and animals to a more amenable place.

2. Making a Fish Trap in Bahrain.

The people of the Gulf inhabited three kinds of environment: coastal towns, oasis settlements and the desert. Coastal towns lived off the sea. Fishermen plied the waters in boats and cast nets from shore. Pearlers on the Arabian side dived for treasures during the warm months. Traders participated in exchange networks in the Gulf and the Indian Ocean world, benefitting from the regularity of the seasonal monsoon whose winds propel ships from Arabia to India during summer months and in the other direction during winter months. All three activities converged on shipbuilding, represented by the famous dhow. The margin of subsistence in all these fields of production and exchange was narrow. The surplus yielded by scattered populations was insufficient for the construction of large palaces or religious monuments. The thin bounty did not fund patronage for writers to produce literary testaments to a ruler's grandeur. Therefore, the historical record is spotty, usually rendered by travellers passing through: Greeks, Arabs, Persians and Europeans. As a result, in speaking of how Gulf peoples organized their daily lives of production and exchange, we assume stability and continuity to fill gaps in written testimony that stretch for centuries.

Oasis settlements occurred where underground aquifers are close enough to the surface for cultivators to irrigate date palms. The date palm was more than a source of food for human nourishment. In an illustration of maximum utilization of the natural environment, Arabians used palm branches in the construction of homes and beds, fronds to make brooms, leaves to weave mats and baskets, and date kernels to feed animals. A variety of grains and vegetables was also grown in oases and supplied to traders and sailors residing in ports. The largest concentration of oases naturally occurred above the region's most abundant aquifers: along the bases of the mountainous Oman peninsula and in al-Hasa.

On the Iranian side of the Gulf, cultivators confronted the same dearth of rain and surface water as their counterparts in Arabia. They excavated tunnels to channel snow melt from mountain slopes to the plains. This hydrological innovation called the qanat system minimized evaporation in a hot climate and enhanced storage capacity in a line of wells that tap the subterranean channels. The first qanats were excavated in Iran during the tenth to eighth centuries BCE. During the Achaemenid era (c. 550 BCE–330 BCE), Persian settlers introduced qanats to Oman, where the mountainous topography resembled that across the Strait of Hormuz. They made possible the spread of cultivation in the Omani interior and were the cause of the increase in population and number of towns, each based on a local qanat system. It is no exaggeration to say that qanats made it possible for *bedouins relations w/ sedentary Kingdu.*

Qanat irrigation extremely important

Oman to develop strong states in different eras. Qanat irrigation supported a much larger population than would otherwise have been sustainable and that population supplied the manpower for a succession of Omani dynasties. Qanats were also excavated in Bahrain and al-Hasa during the Sasanian era (240–630) and helped account for their perennial prosperity.

The Bedouin of the desert raised livestock, primarily camels and goats, in a terrain that requires movement over a broad swathe of territory. Their migrations followed a seasonal rhythm according to the location of grazing sufficient to keep their hardy flocks alive. During long dry spells that could kill off a tribe's animals, Bedouins would raid oases and coastal towns rather than starve. Even in flush years, settled populations normally paid tribute to powerful Bedouin tribes, the *khuwwa* or brotherhood payment, in reality a form of protection or extortion. The coercive dimension of Bedouin relations with sedentary folk was tempered by symbiotic relations. The Bedouin exchanged animal products for grain and riding equipment. They also served as guides and escorts for overland caravans, and supplied camels

3. Bedouin Children in Saudi Arabia.

dispersion of power in Gulf

Islam: most enduring Legacy of Gulf

to bear loads of merchandise. In that capacity, they played a critical part in connecting the Gulf to centres of production and consumption in Syria and the Mediterranean lands.

The dispersed, local scale of economic production and social organization, roughly equal up and down the length of the Gulf's shores, obstructed the accumulation of power and its concentration in a single location able to dominate the region. In political terms, this meant two things. First, any single port, oasis or Bedouin tribe possessed a high degree of autonomy. Second, the dispersion of local power made the region vulnerable to domination by ambitious external powers. If we compare political patterns along northern and southern shores, we find variation due to their respective hinterlands. The northern shore forms a natural boundary for land-based kingdoms and empires with centres in the Iranian plateau. The first Middle Eastern empire, founded in the sixth century BCE by the Achaemenid dynasty near present-day Shiraz, inaugurated a history of Persian power in the Gulf, including periods of domination over much of the southern shore.

The Arabian side of the waters did not generate a comparable political force because the peninsula's extreme aridity barred the development of economic foundations for empire. This is not to say that Arabia's interior dynamics did not impact the Gulf. The most enduring legacy is, of course, the dominant religion, Islam, formed on the far western side of the peninsula in the seventh century. Apart from that singular event for world history, the movements of Arabian Bedouin tribes from time to time departed from customary migratory circuits to form waves crossing from south-west to north-east. In the early 1700s, such a wave of tribal movement brought to Arabian shores today's ruling clans of Kuwait, Bahrain and Qatar.

Political history, then, is in large measure a record of the advent and recession of external powers (unless we view the northern shore as a natural part of the Persian realm; in that case, we would speak of the strengthening and weakening of central control over its southern periphery). During times of imperial assertion, the historical record is fuller due to the coins struck by royal mints and narratives penned by court chroniclers. At times of imperial weakness, the record is sketchy and we are left with the occasional traveller's description and the assumption that the basic building blocks of society, economy, and local politics carried on.

At the local level, kinship is the governing principle of social relations as well as the conceptual core of the tribe, defined here as a collection of clans that recognize descent from a common

disperse economic power be maritime trade prevent central power

Empires keep good records

kinship: governing principle social relation

ancestor and that is governed by custom and ties of mutual obligation. Anthropologists remind us that the kinship basis of tribes is fictive, a necessary political construction in the absence of a state that protects members from enemies and avenges harm done to its members. The relevant unit for daily life is the clan or lineage, many of which together comprise a tribe. Determining the precise boundary of a tribe in terms of territory is elusive because of the absence of natural barriers between neighbouring tribal domains although the desert is not nearly as barren of features in Bedouin eyes as it appears to the townsman. Variation in vegetation, colour of sand, mountain ridges and other natural features are obvious to the denizen of the desert. Based on them tribesmen have a well-defined sense of their territory, their *dira*, that others trespass on peril of retaliation.

Arabian tribes frequently dominated the Gulf's southern shore because of their martial qualities. As skilled camel riders, the Bedouin were adept at mounted combat, a military skill reinforced by their ethos where the mounted warrior represented the ideal of manliness. While the tribe may have spent most of the year as a dispersed set of clans, when it was summoned to battle, kinship ties mobilized a larger pool of manpower than could scattered oases and coastal towns. This explains why powerful political formations tended to arise on the foundation of tribal ties even though according to the usual scale of civilized life, this meant the technically advanced sedentary population came under the rule of 'backward' nomads.

As for the internal dynamics of tribes, their titular chief was the sheikh belonging to a ruling lineage, something like a dynasty. Two differences distinguish the sheikhly lineage from the dynasties of settled rulers. First, succession in the sheikhly lineage seldom passes directly from one generation to the next, from father to son. Rather, succession is transferred laterally to a brother, nephew, uncle or cousin because the sheikh's authority is a function of the entire lineage. And that leads to the second difference: the sheikh does not wield power in the way a powerful king does. Rather, the sheikh wields influence. He does not command an army; he may rally a tribal force if the leaders of other lineages agree with his judgment that fighting is warranted or necessary. He does not collect taxes from fellow tribesmen; and if he attempts to tax traders too heavily, they may move with their goods to another port. He does collect protection or *khuwwa* from oasis dwellers, but he is obliged to share it with poor clans, for generosity is a fundamental virtue that requires frequent demonstration to justify a claim to be the sheikh. Rare is the sheikh who accumulates a treasury that can long withstand the rightful claims of the poor. Furthermore, the sheikh does not issue decrees or laws. Rather, he arbitrates disputes among tribesmen on the basis of unwritten customs. The goal of arbitration is to find a solution that addresses a grievance or a dispute in accordance with tribal custom without unduly offending the clansmen of one found to have violated custom. The sheikh's role in adjudicating disputes is more akin to a wise man than a judge. On the whole, the power of the sheikh is variable. It depends on the degree to which he manages to embody intangible values of courage, wisdom and generosity as much as on tangible foundations of oasis production, the size of herds and secure trade routes. In material terms, little might separate the sheikh from the ordinary tribesman.

This is not to say that Gulf societies were egalitarian. There were wealthy merchants and poor fishermen, powerful sheikhs and weak cultivators. Gender inequality was embedded in patriarchal norms that allocated authority to men and in patrilineal customs that determined the generational transfer of power and wealth through the male line. Men dominated public spaces and women observed rules of modesty. Fighting, diplomacy and deliberating on matters of common interest fell into the male sphere. Men also handled long-distance trade, be it overland or maritime. Women pitched tents, gathered wood and brought water from wells. In some locations, they could sell in local markets. Livelihoods such as fishing and pearling belonged to the male realm. In oasis settlements, women shared the chores of cultivation and harvest. Likewise, in the Bedouin economy they bore the burdens of tending the needs of livestock and processing animal products for consumption and exchange.

Apart from gender, the other major categorical distinction was between the free and slaves. All ancient societies of the Mediterranean and Indian Ocean worlds sanctioned slavery, and the Gulf was no different. Slaves from East Africa were put to work as household servants, armed retainers and concubines. When Islam was introduced to the region, its legal framework provided for the offspring of masters and concubines to be free but allowed the enslavement of non-Muslims. Slavery lasted well into the twentieth century on the Arabian side of the Gulf.

The Gulf's intermediate location accounts for the diverse population that has inhabited and frequented coastal regions since antiquity, giving the ports a cosmopolitan quality. Residents on both shores easily cross the shallow waters to trade and occasionally to emigrate for the sake of either greater security or to seek better livelihoods. The Gulf was not an obstacle

Gulf States always very diverse

to interaction but a passageway to folk living along the coast, rendering efforts to characterize it as Persian or Arab moot. Merchants and seamen from the Indian Ocean basin speaking a variety of African and South Asian tongues also flocked to the Gulf. The polyglot character of modern Gulf cities is the historical norm, not an effect of oil wealth pulling in cheap unskilled and expensive technical labour although today's high proportion of expatriate workers is exceptional. To find a purely Arab or Persian town is to find one that was marginal to broader circuits of exchange. The local tapestry naturally exhibited variety in religion, with Muslims of different sects alongside Hindus, Christians and Jews. In the typical marketplace before modern times, one would hear Gujarati, Baluchi, Swahili and one or two South Indian tongues. In the modern era, Portuguese, Dutch, English and French became part of the mix as well.

2 Historical Patterns to 1500

FROM ANCIENT MESOPOTAMIA
TO THE RISE OF ISLAM

Beneath the sands of the Gulf coast lie the remains of ancient human settlement. The labours of archaeologists, patiently excavating sites from Oman to Kuwait, yield evidence for the social and economic development of Gulf peoples long before the first written records bore testimony about them. Caches of stone tools, shells and the bones of marine and terrestrial animals attest to the rise of agriculture, domesticated livestock and maritime trade some 7,000–8,000 years ago. One of the signature features of the region's economy, pearling, is evident in finds dating from around 5000 BCE in Kuwait and Sharjah. Contacts with early Mesopotamian and Indus civilizations during the fourth and third millennia BCE are evident in ceramic and sculpture fragments at several dozen locations between al-Hasa and Oman.

The first identifiable centre of long-distance trade emerged around 3000–2500 BCE at Dilmun. Its exact location has not been identified, but it was in the vicinity of Bahrain and al-Hasa. More than 4,000 years ago, its traders and sailors were laying foundations of an integrated economy of production, manufacture and exchange. They transported timber, tin and copper from the southern end of the Gulf to Mesopotamia. Ceramic finds indicate contacts as distant as the Indus Valley. Dilmun flourished for well over half a millennium before entering a period of decline around 1750 BCE, owing to troubles in the two civilizations it connected, the Indus and Mesopotamian.

The Gulf entered Mesopotamia's political orbit when an Akkadian king (r. 2269–2255 BCE) invaded Oman, perhaps to secure supplies of copper, an important material in manufacturing

Gulf under domination of empire much of its history

Def of Empire

weapons. External cultural influence on the people of 'the Lower Sea', as the Gulf was called in Mesopotamian sources, began to appear in this period, e.g., a temple dedicated to a Sumerian deity in Bahrain. In the next five centuries, Dilmun developed trade with new partners in western Iran (at Susa) and in the Syrian desert metropolis of Mari via overland caravan. To summarize early economic developments, coastal dwellers turned the waters into a highway for transporting goods up and down the Gulf, tapping sea and land routes that connected India, Iran, Arabia, Mesopotamia and Syria. Along with trade came political and cultural influences from centres of power in Mesopotamia.

from start sea is key

① Kassites

The first Mesopotamian power to truly rule in the Gulf were the Kassites, who conquered Bahrain in the fifteenth century BCE and held it for 400 years. In the same period, the Elamite kingdom of western Iran extended its power over the northern shore of the Gulf. The Kassite–Elamite era may be considered the dawn of competition between Mesopotamian and Iranian powers in the Gulf region. The next episode of external domination came in the eighth century BCE with the rise of the Assyrian Empire, which exacted tribute from Bahrain. Two centuries later, the great Persian Achaemenid Empire incorporated the northern shore and conquered Oman.

basis of empire that dominate gulf

nature of empires

↓ similar how important = map game

For much of its history, the Gulf region has been under the domination of either one empire or another, or on the periphery of empires. In order to make sense of the succession of empires through the ages, it is worthwhile to consider the nature of empires and the dynamics that explain both rapid ascent and collapse. An empire is based on a central power, say a Persian or Arab dynasty, with a store of wealth and population under its command that it uses to conquer and control a large territory. Unlike modern governments which wield effective, direct authority over their lands and people through a uniform system of laws and institutions, empires exercise indirect rule through variable arrangements with each region. Arrangements between centre and province vary because empires grow through military conquest of existing political entities and typically make alliances with local potentates to govern on their behalf. Instead of building institutions in newly absorbed zones, empires take over existing ones, allowing for rapid incorporation but weak integration.

In each region, a local agent is responsible for keeping order and for collecting and remitting taxes. As long as the agent fulfils those tasks as signs of loyalty to the centre, he is free to rule his region as he wishes. Working through existing political and administrative structures makes empires low-cost polities that expend minimal resources to monitor their provinces. Weak administrative integration allows for rapid expansion but also makes empires vulnerable to sudden collapse. Local agents may build up their power and break away; or dynastic disputes, ineffective rulers and economic disruptions may generate weakness at the centre, which emboldens ambitious provincial figures and external enemies.

The Persian Achaemenid Empire (550–330 BCE) founded by Cyrus the Great was the first power to rule the entire Middle East, from Egypt in the west, to Asia Minor in the north, across Mesopotamia and Iran to the borders of western Central Asia and India in the east. The events surrounding its rise and expansion are shrouded in obscurity because the Achaemenids did not have a tradition of writing history. Much of our knowledge comes from the histories composed by one of their subject peoples, the Greeks, who coined the term 'the Persian Gulf' around 500 BCE. Herodotus, the 'father of history', lived during the early phase of Achaemenid power. In addition to Greek accounts, royal inscriptions and archaeological remains shed light on facets of imperial organization.

Persian Empire

The Achaemenids divided their empire into provinces called satrapies. Each satrapy was headed by a viceroy responsible for administrative, military and fiscal affairs. The viceroy's court formed the centre for Persian officials assigned to provincial duties. Implementing uniform procedures and regulations throughout the far-flung empire was not feasible. The scanty record indicates that the roles of Persian officials and local notables differed from one region to another and did not remain constant in any given location. The vacillation between autonomous and centralizing impulses typical of empires appears in the fragmentary record of provincial Achaemenid history. The patchy record tells us little about a peripheral region like the Gulf. It appears that Oman was annexed in 519 BCE, but what the Achaemenids and their agents were up to there and in other parts of the Gulf in any given year is beyond the historian's reach. The significant point is that this empire marked the beginning of the Gulf's integration into Iran's political orbit.

In the fourth century BCE, the armies of Alexander of Macedon vanquished the Achaemenid Empire. This event marked the first direct political encounter of a Mediterranean power with the Gulf region, heralded a period of intensive commercial interaction, and made possible deeper familiarity. The first detailed observations of the Gulf were set down by three naval expeditions dispatched by Alexander to survey the coast from the Indus River to Mesopotamia. The original works – surveys of tribes,

Alexander the Great surveys the Gulf

towns, flora, fauna and pearling – are lost but they survived in the works of later Greek geographers who cited from them extensively. Their descriptions outlived Alexander's empire, which fragmented among his generals. One of them, Seleucus, carved out a realm from Alexander's western Asian possessions, from Asia Minor through Mesopotamia and Iran to India. In the Gulf, his successors established a colony near Rishahr on the Persian shore as well as others whose locations have not been determined. The largest trading centre of the era was Gerrha, which handled goods from India to Mesopotamia. Its location is not known but historians believe it was in the al-Hasa region. Before the Seleucid Empire collapsed in the first century BCE, it boosted overland trade between the Gulf and the Mediterranean lands via the Syrian caravan town of Palmyra.

The fall of the Seleucids opened the way in southern Iran for the Parthians to assert themselves in the first two centuries of the Common Era, bringing the Gulf into their sphere of influence. It was the Sasanian Empire (224–642 CE) that turned the Gulf into a Persian domain. The dynasty's official religion, Zoroastrianism, had a geographical conception of empire, *iranshahr*, which included both shores of the Gulf. In accord with that conception, the first Sasanian shah, Ardashir I, conquered the Gulf region. In north-east Arabia, the Sasanians exercised authority through the Lakhmids, a vassal Arab dynasty with a capital on the Euphrates at Hira. For at least part of the Sasanian era, Bahrain was ruled through a military governor. In Oman, the Sasanians maintained garrisons that reinforced an older Persian element of the population. A new element in the Gulf during the Sasanian era was the advent of Christianity. A centre for the Nestorian church was set up at Rev-Ardashir (near Bushehr). Proselytizing led to the establishment of churches in Bahrain, Jubail and Failaka Island off the coast of Kuwait while monasteries were constructed in Qatar and on islands off the coast of Abu Dhabi.

Before and during the Sasanian period, Oman's Arab population grew as successive waves of tribes arrived from the west and the north. To manage the Arabs of the interior, the Sasanians designated a chief known as the Julanda. While some Arabs continued their nomadic ways in the interior regions, others settled on the coast where they became fishermen, traders and sailors, while yet others crossed the Strait to Iran, where the main tribe, the Bani Salima, controlled the land along the straits until the tenth century. The point is worth noting for it underlines the long history of demographic mixing on both shores. Thus, in the fourth century, the Abd al-Qays tribe moved from the vicinity of Bahrain to the coast of Fars, apparently in defiance of the Sasanian emperor, who ordered a punitive expedition. Upon defeating the Arabian tribes, around 350 CE, Shapur II forcibly resettled segments of Arabian tribes in Kerman and Ahvaz.

Due to the duration and affluence of the Sasanian Empire, new ports emerged on the Iranian shore. Bushehr became the main outlet for Fars. Siraf was a second outpost on the Gulf, later to become a major port during the Islamic period. Further down the coast, maritime exchange picked up at Hormuz and other sites. The concentration of political power and economic activity in ancient Iran from the Achaemenid through Sasanian eras accounts for the domination of trade by ports on the Iranian shore. This does not mean that the Sasanians neglected the Arabian shore. Telltale signs of Persian activity such as qanats and archaeological remains show up in al-Hasa. Moreover, the Sasanians maintained military outposts overlooking the Strait of Hormuz and the Gulf of Oman. The density of strongholds along both shores went in tandem with the spread of Persian merchants in the Indian Ocean, from East Africa to India, Ceylon and the Malay peninsula.

[margin note: Empire Sasanians brings new wealth]

To summarize pre-Islamic political patterns, relations between Mesopotamian and Persian powers and the Gulf fluctuated between periods of subordination to Kassites, Elamites, Achaemenids, Parthians and Sasanians, and periods when external forces were absent. Although it was costly to mount military expeditions to subjugate the Gulf's scattered population, external powers gained a dominant role in trade with the Indian Ocean basin. Over the long term a dense web of commercial networks connected the Gulf to the Indian Ocean rim, a vast pool of diverse resources from China, India and Africa to the Gulf, Iran, Mesopotamia and the Mediterranean lands. The Gulf did not give rise to its own independent civilization, but it did become a permanent and essential part of the growing Eurasian world economy.

ISLAM: ORIGINS AND BELIEFS

The emergence of Islam in western Arabia and the Arab conquests marked a new era for the entire Middle East, including the Gulf. Because Islam and its sectarian divisions have played significant roles in Gulf politics, society and culture, it is important not only to understand the general shape of its early development, but also to pay particular attention to internal struggles that revolved around the right to lead the Muslim community.

The youngest monotheistic religion appeared in Mecca, the site of a shrine, called the Ka'ba. In Muslim belief, the patriarch Abraham had founded the Ka'ba as a site for worshipping the one God. Subsequently, polytheism took hold among the area's townsmen and Bedouin. Given its remote location in a rugged mountain valley, Mecca was independent of the Byzantine and Sasanid Empires, but its merchants came into contact with both powers to the north, Yemen to the south, and Arabia's scattered oases. In 610, a Meccan trader, Muhammad ibn Abdullah, had a revelation commanding him to 'recite' divine messages warning his fellow townsmen to forsake their idols and reminding them of their duty to worship God alone. The Arabic word for 'recitation' is Qur'an, hence the name for the collection of revelations that Muhammad intermittently received for 22 years until he died in 632. Muhammad's preaching gradually attracted followers in spite of opposition from the town's leading clan, Quraish. As Mecca's social order hinged on clans, he obtained protection from persecution from his clan elder, an uncle named Abu Talib. This man's son Ali, some 30 years younger than the Prophet, became an early convert and a steadfast champion of the new religion.

When Abu Talib died in 619, Muhammad lost his protector and began to search for a more receptive milieu than firmly polytheistic Mecca. Some two hundred miles north lay Yathrib, a cluster of settlements divided between polytheist Arab and Jewish clans. The town had long been divided between feuding factions, each one comprised of Jews and polytheists. Clan leaders hoped that Muhammad's sound judgment and character would make him a suitable arbiter to settle disputes. In addition, his new religion was gaining ground among Yathrib's polytheists. Muhammad and a delegation from Yathrib agreed on a pact to govern relations between the clans and his following, termed the umma, the community of believers. This pact is known as the Constitution of Medina. It marks the emergence of the Muslims as a distinct body bound by ties of belief rather than kinship. In 622, Muhammad and the believers undertook a hijra, or emigration, to Yathrib, which became known as Medina. The believers who accompanied him became known as 'the Emigrants' and the Medinans who assisted with their resettlement became known as 'the Helpers'.

Muhammad's departure from Mecca did not end his conflict with Quraish. In 624, a band of Muslims waylaid a Meccan caravan at a site called Badr, where they prevailed in a skirmish against the Meccans. The *jihad*, or holy war, in God's path against His enemies had begun. The following year, Mecca retaliated with an attack on Medina that inflicted many casualties on the Muslims, honoured as martyrs for jihad. The punitive expedition, however, did not persuade Muhammad to abandon raids on Meccan caravans. The Meccans mobilized tribal allies for a second, larger campaign against Medina, but were stymied by a deep trench dug at the suggestion of a Persian convert. At the same time that Muhammad was demonstrating his ability as a military leader, he was consolidating his position against rivals in Medina. One group pretended to embrace Islam but secretly strove to undermine Muhammad and the believers. They were known as the Hypocrites.

Opposition to Muhammad's religious message came from Jews who voiced doubts about it, especially the claim to represent the line of prophets from Abraham, Noah and Moses. After the first Meccan attack, he ordered the expulsion of a Jewish clan. Following the next Meccan attack, he had male members of a second Jewish clan slain for their alleged collusion with the Meccans. At that point, Muhammad was the undisputed leader of Medina and he turned his attention to subduing Mecca, achieved in 630. Rather than return to his home town, he continued to reside in Medina, which became the Muslim capital for the next three decades. Diplomacy and proselytizing soon resulted in nearly all Arabia's tribes embracing Islam. The Prophet died in 632. His tomb in Medina became the second holiest site in Islam after the Ka'ba in Mecca.

The basic tenets of Islam are belief in God, the angels, the books, the messengers, the day of judgement and divine decree. The books are the revelations sent down to previous messengers: the Torah revealed to Moses, the Psalms revealed to David and the Gospel revealed to Jesus. The Qur'an is part of the series of books and therefore is not Muhammad's teaching but God's word revealed to him. The day of judgement will follow the last day, when God destroys all creation, resurrects all humans, and judges each one on the basis of their deeds. A garden of paradise is the reward for those whose good deeds outweigh the bad; the fire of hell is the punishment for those whose bad deeds outweigh the good. Belief in divine decree means that God is the source for all outcomes in natural and human affairs.

The fundamental religious duties of Muslims are the five pillars of Islam. The profession of faith is the declaration that there is no god but the one God and that Muhammad is the messenger of God. Muslims are to pray five times each day, at dawn, noon, afternoon, sunset and dusk. A tax on wealth is a reminder

of God's bounty and expresses charity towards the less fortunate. During the month of Ramadan, Muslims fast during day-
light hours. Pilgrimage to Mecca includes the completion of a
set of rituals at the Ka'ba and nearby sites; the believer is to perform it once in a lifetime. The five pillars of Islam are the profession of faith, daily prayers, charity, fasting during Ramadan, and
pilgrimage to Mecca. In addition, Muslims have a duty to obey
God and His messenger in their daily life, making adherence
to Islam a matter expressed in the believer's everyday manners
and conduct. For belief, religious duties and personal conduct,
Muslims recognize the Qur'an and the Prophet's Sunna, his
exemplary practice, as authoritative sources.

THE SEEDS OF SCHISM IN ISLAM

During Muhammad's lifetime, believers could turn to him for
guidance on details and questions in all spheres of life: worship,
belief, manners, morality, crime and punishment, politics and
warfare. When he died, the *umma* (the community of believers)
lost its prophet and its leader in worldly affairs. There was no
question of succession to his apostleship. As for leadership of
the community, his companions selected a respected emigrant,
Abu Bakr, to assume a commanding role, inaugurating the office
of the caliph, or deputy to God's messenger. He immediately
confronted the challenge of holding the *umma* together. Some
Arabian tribesmen considered recognition of Muhammad's
authority a matter of fealty to him alone rather than a pact binding them to membership in the *umma* and obliging them to obey
his deputy in Medina. Abu Bakr and his associates, however,
regarded refusal to accept his authority not merely as a political act but apostasy demanding a military campaign to return
rebellious tribesmen to the fold. For two years, he commanded
Muslim forces in the Ridda (apostasy) Wars, restoring the umma's
unity and consolidating Medina's power over Arabia.

Upon Abu Bakr's death, Muslim elders selected Umar to
become the next caliph. He presided over the first burst of Arab
expansion into Syria, Egypt and Iraq. The central lands of the
Middle East had certainly seen their share of warfare between
empires, but never before had they been overrun by mounted
warriors from Arabia. Byzantine-ruled towns in Syria and Egypt
fell one by one in less than a decade; Sasanian forces in Iraq gave
way in roughly the same span. In Eastern Arabia, tribal leaders

embraced Islam towards the end of the Prophet's life and participated in battles to expel Persian garrisons. In Oman, the Julanda
chiefs, formerly Sasanian vassals, converted to Islam and gave
allegiance to Medina, ending four centuries of Persian rule.

Medina rapidly emerged as the centre of a new Middle Eastern
empire. When Umar died of knife wounds inflicted by a Persian
captive in 644, a council of elders convened to select the next
caliph. They narrowed the field of candidates to two men, the
Prophet's cousin Ali and his close companion Uthman. In choosing the latter, it seems the council was swayed by his pledge to
lead on the basis of the Qur'an, the Sunna, and the precedents
established by Abu Bakr and Umar, whereas Ali had agreed
to regard only the Qur'an and the Sunna as binding. Under
Uthman's caliphate from 644 to 656, Arab armies completed
the conquest of Iran, toppling the Sasanian dynasty. Military
success, however, did not bring political harmony. Uthman's
policies, especially his appointment to provincial and military
posts of kinsmen from his clan, the Umayyads, fostered resentment. His fiscal policies likewise upset fellow Muslims. A band
of disgruntled believers attacked him at the mosque in Medina
and assassinated him, whereupon they proclaimed Ali the new
caliph. This act set the stage for the first *fitna* or civil war and a
permanent schism among Muslims. Their division into Sunni,
Shi'i and Kharijite sects stemmed from that schism.

Uthman's kinsmen in the Umayyad clan refused to recognize
Ali as caliph unless he brought the assassins to justice. Sentiment
for Ali was rooted in the view that the *umma* was in danger of
straying from its ideals. The conquests had yielded vast boun-
ties of war booty and control over the ancient centres of Middle
East civilization. The influx of wealth to Medina created social
fissures unimaginable when it was a collection of date palm gardens. Ali embodied two qualities that attracted Muslims alarmed
at the prospect of moral corruption. On one hand, he was one
of the earliest converts to Islam, known for his courage in early
battles and for his personal piety. In that respect, he represented
the notion that piety rather than customary Arabian criteria of
affiliation with a prestigious clan determined one's standing. On
the other hand, Ali belonged to *ahl al-bait*, the people of the
house, that is, the family of the Prophet. Muhammad had died
without male heir, but he was survived by his daughter Fatima,
who had married Ali, and together they had two sons, Hussein
and Hasan. Apostleship may have ended with Muhammad, but
the charismatic quality of his authority could be ascribed to his
closest heirs and their descendants. Ali's coalition, then, rested
on a single impulse to restore moral leadership but there was no

consensus on whether piety or kinship with the Prophet was the principal criterion for deciding exactly who deserved the caliphate. In the course of Ali's struggle for power, that fault line would be exposed and his following would split.

The leader of the Umayyad clan was Uthman's kinsman Muawiya, the governor of Syria, where he commanded a powerful army. The Muslim garrison towns in Iraq leaned towards Ali, and if he was going to assert his claim to the caliphate, he had to rally his backers there rather than try to rule from Medina. From Iraq, Ali led his troops towards Syria. In 657, two Muslim armies met in the desert at Siffin. Before the fighting reached a conclusive outcome, the two sides agreed to a truce and an arbitration of political differences. In some accounts, Ali's soldiers had the upper hand in the fighting and it was Muawiya who sued for a cessation of hostilities to avoid a rout. The section of Ali's supporters dedicated to his cause on grounds that he was the most pious candidate for the caliphate was furious with him for not pushing the fight to the end and they abandoned his camp. They became known as the Kharijites and henceforth regarded both Ali and Muawiya as enemies. The arbitration dragged on, Muawiya held fast in Syria, and Ali confronted Kharijite rebellion in Iraq. In 661, he was assassinated by a Kharijite in Iraq at Najaf, where his grave would become the site of a holy place for Shi'i Muslims. At that point, Muawiya proclaimed his caliphate in Damascus. The centre of Muslim power moved from Arabia to Syria, marking the end of Medina's brief spell as an imperial capital.

Ali's assassination brought to a close the first Muslim civil war, but it did not heal the schism opened by Uthman's murder. Loyalty to the Prophet's Family remained a principle for many Muslims who viewed Muawiya as a usurper. For nearly two decades, however, he ruled with a blend of tact and force while resuming military campaigns to extend the bounds of Arab rule across North Africa and beyond Iran into the Caucasus. Towards the end of his reign he provoked new controversy when he designated his son Yazid to be his successor, instituting the dynastic principle for the first time. By the time of Muawiya's death in 680, Ali's older son Hasan had died in Medina, leaving Hussein as the natural candidate of the Prophet's Family to make a bid for leadership. Supporters in Iraq urged him to challenge Yazid. His departure for Iraq marked the onset of the second Muslim civil war. Yazid's troops intercepted Hussein on his journey at Kerbala, where the Prophet's grandson was killed on the tenth of the Muslim month of Muharram in 680. In Arabic, the tenth is *ashura*, and over time, Shi'i Muslims developed religious ceremonies to commemorate Hussein's martyrdom on that date at Kerbala, the site of a shrine at his grave.

The line of the Prophet's Family survived Hussein's death, as did its political cause. It served as a rallying cry for the revolutionary movement that overthrew the Umayyad caliphate in 750. The leaders of that movement descended from a different line of the Prophet's Family, from Muhammad's uncle Abbas rather than from Ali, but their propaganda played on sympathy for Ali's descendants and mobilized many partisans of Ali, or *Shi'at Ali*. The Abbasids also succeeded in tapping the discontent of the swelling ranks of non-Arab converts to Islam upset at Umayyad Arab chauvinism, which was at odds with Islamic ideals of piety and disregard for descent. In 747, the Abbasids launched a revolt in north-east Iran's Khurasan province. Their forces swept westward, capturing one town after another, and inflicted a crushing defeat on the Umayyads in 750. The Abbasids hunted down members of the clan, almost extinguishing it completely, but for a single prince who escaped to North Africa and made his way to Spain, where he established an Umayyad principality.

Muslims expecting the Abbasid victory to bring a descendant of Ali to the caliphate were disappointed. Instead, the Abbasids set themselves up as the new caliphs. The Shi'at Ali were again in the political wilderness and soon faced new challenges in maintaining unity in their own ranks. They had developed a distinctive conception of leadership, the imamate, which combined religious and political authority. This conception held that a single living member of Ali's line, an imam, possessed unique qualities that made him the sole suitable candidate for leadership of the *umma*. Furthermore, the imam knew which of his sons possessed those qualities and publicly designated him as the next imam. Such designation would remove any doubt about leadership, unless the designated successor predeceased the imam. And that is exactly what happened not long after the Abbasids came to power. The Sixth Imam, Jafar al-Sadiq, designated his son Ismail to be his successor, but he died before his father. Jafar then designated another son, Musa al-Kazim, to be his successor and Seventh Imam. Upon Jafar's death, the Shi'at Ali divided between followers of Musa and followers of Ismail's son Muhammad. That schism gradually hardened into two rival streams of Shi'ism. The stream that was loyal to Musa became known as Imami or Twelver Shi'ism. Over time, it became firmly established in Iraq, parts of Lebanon, Iran and the Gulf. In the short run, however, Ismaili Shi'ism was the more dynamic stream, even though it splintered into rival sects. From the

ninth through thirteenth centuries, Ismaili movements challenged Sunni power in the central Middle East.

Although the Kharijites dwindled in number and significance
on the broad canvas of Islamic history, their success in securing an enduring foothold in Oman makes them an important
factor in the history of the Gulf. As Umayyad rulers suppressed
a series of Kharijite uprisings, the implications of political failure led to divisions in their ranks. The essential problem was
whether to live under the rule of an illegitimate imam or to emigrate in order to establish a community of believers, in imitation
of the Prophet's transfer from Mecca to Medina. In the ninth
century, a pocket of Kharijite scholars and merchants known as
the Ibadis formed in Basra, which served as a springboard for
missionary work. The Basran Ibadi scholars adopted a doctrine
allowing quiet coexistence in the midst of other Muslims by permitting the believer to conceal his true belief. Ibadi missionaries
found receptive audiences among Omani tribes, and when
the Umayyads fell, they established an independent imamate,
the first of several Ibadi principalities that rose and fell until the
mid-twentieth century.

In the history of the Gulf, the pattern of regional dynasties
rooted in a particular religious view of political authority is peculiar to Oman, so it bears some explanation. First, Oman is well
insulated against invasion by virtue of geography, surrounded
by the seas and the impenetrable Empty Quarter. The rugged
terrain of the Hajar Mountains makes the region impervious
to long-term subjugation by external powers. Second, Oman
possessed the economic foundations for a state – a sizable
population, extensive territory and diverse economic resources.
Qanat-based agriculture dispersed in every village and town in
the Hajar Mountains supported a denser population than possible elsewhere in the Gulf, with the exception of al-Hasa.

Along the Gulf of Oman, there stretches the 150 mile-long
coastal plain, the Batina, whose merchants participated in the
littoral world of the Indian Ocean. Oman's tribal population
is largely settled at small towns and oases rather than roaming
through the desert with flocks of sheep, goats and camels. The
challenge to would-be dynasts was unifying independent tribal
leaders and commercial ports under a single authority. Ibadi
doctrine was the ideological glue binding Oman's disparate
population together. The cohesion and survival of the imamate
depended on the ruler's ability to retain the loyalty of tribal leaders, who commanded tribal warriors. The meshing of religious
ideology with tribal social structure made the Ibadi imamate a
volatile institution, capable of sudden ascent and collapse. Thus,

the first imamate gained power in the 790s and ruled for about a century before disintegrating in succession struggles.

FROM UNITY TO FRAGMENTATION

The Abbasid overthrow of the Umayyads shifted the geographical centre of the Arab empire from Syria to Iraq. In 762, the Abbasid caliph al-Mansur decided to build a new imperial capital on the site of a small town on the Tigris River called Baghdad. The new city attracted thousands of artisans and workers to construct palaces and barracks for the rulers. Traders flocked to Baghdad to supply the royal court with luxury goods. Poets, theologians and scientists arrived seeking royal patronage. Baghdad was soon teeming with tens of thousands of residents. The concentration of wealth and population stimulated demand for goods from the Indian Ocean rim. The ninth century was the heyday for sailors to set out from Basra and Siraf to seek fortunes by trading with India, China and Africa, giving rise to the legend of Sinbad.

At the height of their power, the Abbasid caliphs ruled an empire extending from Tunisia to Afghanistan. A complex mix of political, economic and religious forces presented insurmountable challenges to the talents and resources of the caliphs and their advisers. The first major cracks broke open with a four-year civil war (809–813) between the sons of Caliph Harun al-Rashid, revealing a struggle for control over manpower and wealth between the capital and the provinces. An attempt to strengthen Baghdad's grip with a specialized corps of slave soldiers proved effective for some decades before rebellious slave captains seized power for themselves, setting off a decade of anarchy in the 860s, when provincial governors exploited the opportunity to withhold annual tribute in order to build up their own local bases of wealth and power. Such behaviour was part of the pattern of imperial fragmentation. The outbreak of revolt in the fields of southern Iraq around Basra was something entirely new.

The Zanj Revolt erupted in 869 and ravaged southern Iraq for 14 years. Its leader, Ali ibn Muhammad, came from an Arab family that had settled in Iran. After failing to establish himself in the caliph's literary circle, he dedicated his energies to undermining Abbasid power. He settled in Basra, where he found favourable conditions for rebellion due to the unique form that slavery had assumed in the marshes of southern Iraq. The Zanj were East African slaves tasked with draining the marshes for cultivation. Only in this region of the Middle East were large numbers of slaves put to toilsome labour under such miserable conditions. Ali ibn Muhammad found the slaves a receptive audience for revolutionary messages and incited them to revolt against their masters. The slave rebels overran Basra and the garrison town of Wasit. The fighting against Abbasid forces was ferocious and the chronicles are filled with tales of massacres and destruction of mosques by former slaves enraged by the harsh treatment they had endured. The revolt had enduring consequences for the region's history. Much of southern Iraq's intricate network of irrigation canals, which required annual upkeep, either fell into disrepair or was damaged to such an extent that the region's agricultural productivity never recovered. Basra in particular suffered terrible damage from the initial fighting and then from the Abbasid campaign to recover it in 883. During the revolt, merchants trading between the Indian Ocean and the Mediterranean diverted commerce from the Gulf to the Red Sea. After the revolt, maritime traffic resumed but never regained its earlier prosperity.

Baghdad's preoccupation with the Zanj Revolt gave opportunities to regional governors in Egypt, Syria and Iran to loosen their ties to the caliph and set up autonomous dynasties. It also gave religious dissidents an opening to spread their influence and establish an independent realm in Eastern Arabia. In the late ninth century, Ismaili Shi'is circulated anti-Abbasid propaganda. One of the distinctive tenets of their propaganda was a call to social justice rooted in scathing criticism of Abbasid rulers for betraying Islam's egalitarian values. Ismaili preaching held that the Seventh Imam, Muhammad ibn Ismail, had not actually died in the mid-eighth century. He was absent and would return as the *mahdi*, the 'rightly guided' one, a messianic figure who will wipe out injustice and usher in the reign of justice and equality. Such teaching had broad appeal for poor townsmen, peasants and Bedouins. Disagreement over the identity of the Mahdi split Ismaili ranks. In the 870s, a preacher named Hamdan Qarmat attracted a following that broke with fellow Ismailis drawn to Ubayd Allah, who claimed to be the rightful imam. Hamdan's disciples came to be known as Qarmatis, or more commonly in English, Carmathians. They believed that the line of imams descended from Ali had come to an end and that the Seventh Imam would return as the Mahdi. Other Ismailis accepted Ubayd Allah's claim to be the Mahdi, and his movement took root in Tunisia, where it became known as the Fatimid movement (named for Ali's wife, the Prophet's daughter

Fatima). Bedouin tribesmen loyal to Hamdan Qarmat occupied the main Syrian towns in 902, but Abbasid forces expelled them a few years later.

The Carmathians were more successful in Eastern Arabia, where they established the most remarkable Gulf common-wealth of the medieval period. In 894, Hamdan Qarmat sent an agent to the Eastern Arabian province of Hajar, which consisted of Bahrain, the ports of Uqair and Qatif, and the fertile oases of al-Hasa. The Carmathian agent won over a powerful Arab clan that provided military backing for the Ismaili movement to take over the region. In 930, the Carmathians launched their most daring exploit. At the time, they believed that the Mahdi's return was imminent and that it was necessary to suspend ritual observ-ances, including the annual pilgrimage, in preparation for him. The millennial scenario inspired them to attack Mecca during the pilgrimage, massacre pilgrims, pluck the famous Black Stone from its resting place in the Ka'ba, and retreat with it to Bahrain. The next year, the Carmathians proclaimed the return of the Mahdi, elevating a captive to that divine standing, and carry-ing out his commands to ignore Islamic law. Meanwhile, for 20 years, pilgrims to Mecca could not perform the ritual rubbing of the Black Stone. The Carmathians finally accepted a ransom payment to restore it. The combination of attacks on pilgrims and violation of Mecca's sanctuary blackened the Carmathians' reputation. False tales circulated by Sunni authors found a ready audience, so it became widely believed that the Carmathians practised a form of communalism involving not just sharing wealth, which they apparently did, but wives as well, a matter of sheer invention.

Not long after restoring the Black Stone, the Carmathians set their sights on Egypt and Syria. In 968, they occupied Damascus. It was for them an unfortunate historical coinci-dence that the very next year, their Ismaili rivals, the Fatimids, conquered Egypt from their base in North Africa, setting up a collision between the Ismaili powers. For a decade, and uniquely in the history of the Middle East, a political force cen-tred in the Gulf challenged an Egyptian power for control over Syria. Twice, in 971 and 974, Carmathian forces laid siege to Cairo, the newly founded Fatimid capital. But their Bedouin troops were unwilling to serve as a permanent garrison, making it impossible to keep Damascus for long. In 978, the Fatimids inflicted a decisive defeat, routing them from Syria once and for all. Henceforth, the Carmathians were confined to their base in Eastern Arabia.

By the time the Fatimids conquered Egypt, the Abbasid caliphate had succumbed to domination by the Buyids, a clan of military chiefs who first rose to influence in northern Iran and then wrested control over cities from rulers who had broken from the Abbasid caliphate. In 945, Buyid forces occupied Baghdad. Although they declared themselves Twelver Shiʻis, they left the Sunni Abbasid caliph in place as a figurehead. At their height, the Buyids ruled Iraq, Iran and Oman, but they were not able to uproot the Carmathians. By restoring secure travel conditions between central Iran and Gulf ports, they gave a needed boost to maritime trade during their century in power (945–1055). Their most lasting impact stemmed from their support for such Shiʻi rituals as mourning to mark Imam Hussein's martyrdom on Ashura. This ritual and others marked the development of Twelver Shiʻism customs that revolved around the graves of the imams and that set it apart from Ismaili Shiʻism as well as Sunni Islam.

Early in the eleventh century, Buyid power began to slip, largely because the confederation lacked internal cohesion, but also due to the arrival of a new force on the stage of Middle East history in the form of massive waves of Central Asian pastoral nomads. The largest segment of the migration consisted of Turks of the Oghuz confederation. In the 1040s, one of the Oghuz clans, the Saljuks, conquered northern and central Iran. The Buyids were helpless before the hardy Central Asian horsemen. In 1055, the Saljuk sultan expelled them from Baghdad and offered allegiance to the Abbasid caliph, promising to restore Sunni power. As staunch Sunnis, the Saljuks strove to undermine the Carmathians. In 1070, an Arab tribal chieftain, Abdullah ibn Ali al-ʻUyuni, initiated a series of raids on al-Hasa. With backing from Baghdad, Sheikh Abdullah brought down the Ismaili Shiʻi commonwealth in 1077 and founded the Uyunid tribal dynasty that ruled over Bahrain and al-Hasa for about a century. In Oman, the Saljuks conquered the main ports, while in the interior Ibadi tribesmen revived the imamate at Nizwa.

Sources for the history of Gulf ports in this period are spotty, but we do have enough written records to complement archaeological findings for a glimpse of conditions in Siraf during the Buyid and Saljuk centuries. Situated on a narrow band of lowlands between the Gulf and the Zagros Range, Siraf became the first in a series of trading towns that prospered in spite of the dearth of nearby natural resources, feeding on the appetite of the Abbasid imperial capital Baghdad for goods from China, India and East Africa. Siraf's legendary wealth rose and fell with the fortunes of Iraq's economy, which prospered in the late eighth and ninth centuries before tailing off in the tenth century and finally plunging in the later eleventh century due to political strife. As commercial activity diminished, affluent residents, primarily ship owners and wealthy merchants, relocated to other Gulf ports. Residences were abandoned; palaces became dilapidated; debris filled streets on the outskirts; the inhabited area shrank by more than half over the course of a century, from the early 900s to the early 1000s.

Contraction, however, was not the same as general impoverishment. In the first decades of the twelfth century, a wealthy merchant accumulated an immense fortune. Ramisht was a Persian trader famous in his day for religious philanthropy, paying for the construction and maintenance of a hospice in Mecca, and the purchase of a covering for the Ka'ba woven from Chinese cloth, an expensive gesture ordinarily made by royal personalities. Nevertheless, by the early thirteenth century, Siraf was a minor town with a poor population and abandoned buildings. On the other hand, down the coast, Kish Island began its ascent in the eleventh century under the Arab Banu Qaisar tribesmen, and would surpass Siraf as the leading port. In its heyday, roughly 1100–1330, it exhibited the cosmopolitanism that was the hallmark of Gulf emporia: a population of traders from Iraq and Iran, Yemen and India exchanging cloths and spices.

The Saljuk sultans proved no more effective at laying lasting foundations for rule than the Buyids. By the early twelfth century, the region began to fragment once again. The next major development was the arrival of Mongol invaders from Central Asia in the early 1200s. Between 1219 and 1223, Mongol horsemen overran northern Iran, laying waste to cities that had survived centuries of intermittent warfare. In the 1250s, the Mongols launched a second wave of invasions that conquered the central lands of the Middle East, crowned by the sack of Baghdad and the extermination of the Abbasid caliphate in 1258. Their leader Hulegu established his capital in north-west Iran at Tabriz, which became the seat of the Il-Khan dynasty. Southern Iran was spared Mongol devastation because its mountainous terrain was not suitable for the Central Asian herders. Moreover, as rulers of a vast Eurasian land mass, they profited from overland trade, the renowned silk route. Consequently, they showed no interest in mastering maritime routes running through the Gulf.

Around the same time that Mongols were overrunning Iran, a new kingdom was rising along the southern Iranian Gulf shore at Hormuz, present-day Bandar Abbas. Refugees from the Abbasid conquest of Oman had settled there and around

900 established an independent principality. The Saljuk sultans managed to exercise loose authority over Hormuz, but its emirs asserted their independence in the political turmoil that accompanied the disintegration of the Saljuk sultanate.

Towards the end of the 1200s, Emir Rukn al-Din Mahmud Qalhati turned Hormuz into a regional power. He gained control over ports on the Arabian shore up to Bahrain, along Oman's coastline, and on the Iranian shore from the Makran coast to Sind. Territorial expansion inspired the rulers to adopt the title of king rather than emir. Around 1300, King Baha al-Din Ayaz moved his court to Jarun Island, about four miles offshore, primarily to put some water between him and the Mongols. He constructed a city and a port, initially dubbed New Hormuz. Over time, both the port and the island became known as Hormuz while the original coastal town of that name became known as Gombroon, later as Bandar Abbas. Security was its chief advantage; nearly complete lack of freshwater its chief defect; its saline soil made it impossible to grow anything. Nearby Qeshm Island was the main source of water and food, supporting a population as large as 40,000. The island's location near the mouth of the Hormuz Strait allowed its kings to control maritime trade to and from the Indian Ocean. Two centuries later, that strategic perch made Hormuz the target of the first European conquest in the Gulf.

The kings of Hormuz turned the island into the hinge of Indo–Iranian commerce, exporting Iranian goods and Arabian horses, importing spices and herbs from Gujarat and the Deccan. The kings embellished their reputations by patronizing Sunni institutions, paying for the construction of a mosque, a religious school and a hospital. They did not, however, allow their particular religious allegiance to interfere with the pursuit of profit. Shi'i residents freely observed their distinctive ceremonies just as Hindus from Gujarat, Christians of several denominations and Jews all enjoyed religious freedom.

In three respects, the Gulf exhibited continuity throughout the ancient, classical and Islamic periods. First, its location made it a channel for maritime trade and contact between south-west Asia and the Indian Ocean rim. Second, the population along its shores was mobile in pursuing livelihoods and occasionally migrating to escape instability. Both short-term travel for trade and long-term migration contributed to the rise and fall of ports. Third, the Gulf was not a boundary between the two shores but a maritime highway for constant traffic, exchange and movement. As a result, littoral society was a mixture of local and exogenous peoples.

Within the contours of these continuities, Islam and Islamic dynasties left permanent imprints on the Gulf. The majority of the population converted to the new religion, leaving little trace of either Zoroastrianism or Christianity. For three centuries, political power was in the hands of Arab Muslim caliphs and their commanders. The Gulf shared the wider Muslim world's political patterns, including the rise and fall of dynasties, the contest for supremacy among Sunni, Shi'i and Kharijite sects, and the impact of Central Asian migrations. During the early Islamic centuries, three significant political formations arose in the Gulf. The first was the Ibadi imamate in Oman, which would surface, vanish and resurface for a millennium. The second was the Carmathian commonwealth of al-Hasa and Bahrain. The third was the Kingdom of Hormuz, founded in the shadow of Mongol power and destined to survive, albeit in weakened form, until the seventeenth century.

① Dynasties Gulf

① location = maritime trade

② mobile society along shores; political instability

③ Gulf not boundary but maritime highway for constant traffic exchange, and movement.

3 Muslim and European Empires, 1500–1720

Abbasid

After the decline of Abbasid power in the late ninth century, the Gulf lay beyond the horizon of major Middle Eastern powers for more than half a millennium. Apart from a brief revival in the early eleventh century, the Baghdad caliphate ruled little more than nearby portions of Iraq. Turkish military and political power in Iran rested on migrating tribesmen grazing their flocks on the rich pastures of the northern regions. Turkish tribesmen trickled into Fars, but the centre of Turkish dynasties was located in the north. The absence of major empires did not harm the fortunes of the Gulf. On the contrary, petty rulers and rich merchants prospered as long as supplies and markets in the Middle East and the Indian Ocean rim held up.

The political picture completely changed in the early 1500s when the Gulf became the intersection between three new empires. The Portuguese maritime empire encompassed the east and west coasts of Africa, the Indian Ocean rim, the western Pacific and Brazil. Iran emerged from a long phase of instability with the rise of the Safavid dynasty which unified the country for two centuries. The Ottoman Empire pushed into the Arab lands, conquered Iraq and established a foothold in Eastern Arabia. The new powers absorbed the Gulf's existing polities, such as the Kingdom of Hormuz, into their spheres as regional governors and vassals. Given the expansionist character of empires, frontier zones like the Gulf turned into arenas for competition, warfare and uneasy coexistence between Portuguese, Ottomans and Safavids.

The picture was further complicated in the seventeenth century by the appearance of three new actors: the Dutch East India Company, the English East India Company and the Yariba Imamate in Oman. All these players sought a share in the Indian Ocean economy that encompassed South-east Asia's Spice Islands, India's rich textile, spice and pepper supplies, Persian silk, and East African ivory and slaves. Apart from the initial burst of Portuguese aggression, the Europeans forged symbiotic relationships with Asian powers. The Safavids, the Ottomans and the Mughal dynasty of India based their imperial power on control over land – agrarian surpluses, manufactures, raw materials and trade. None of them possessed or developed maritime forces in the Indian Ocean (the Ottomans did have a formidable Mediterranean fleet). They found it convenient to allow the establishment of European trading posts, or factories, on their coasts in order to augment trade and revenues from customs duties. At times, they tapped the Europeans' naval power to deal with fractious subjects. The Europeans preferred to stay out of political and military conflicts, but if threatened with the closure of their factories, they would lease ships and lend sailors to the Muslim empires.

Tracing the course of politics, war and diplomacy in any detail reveals a complex sequence of events. Struggles over strategic ports, towns and regions between evenly matched foes seldom resulted in substantial changes in the balance of forces. The Portuguese dream of a trade monopoly proved elusive but they held a dominant position for 100 years. As a land-based power in north-west Iran, the Safavids were too busy at first defending against external threats and overcoming civil wars to have much interest in the Gulf. Military pressure from the Ottoman Empire twice caused them to move their capital south, but it was not until they came to regard the Gulf as a secure outlet for the lucrative silk crop that they concentrated on exercising direct rule over the coast and Bahrain. Even then, their lack of a navy meant that they could not oust the Portuguese from their stronghold at Hormuz without the assistance of an English fleet.

The Ottomans were yet more removed from the Gulf, well over a thousand miles from Istanbul. Strategic considerations drew the Ottomans to Iraq in order to shore up their flank against the Safavids. Basra and Eastern Arabia were frontier outposts, offering neither economic resources nor manpower to offset the cost of keeping them secure. After some clashes with the Portuguese, they settled into a long undeclared truce. The Dutch and English trading companies arrived on the scene at the same time in the early 1600s. Their pursuit of profit was hindered by Portugal's grip on trade through Hormuz, so while they were rivals in other parts of the Indian Ocean, they cooperated to undermine the Portuguese. Oman remained divided between the tribal interior and port cities under Portuguese rule until the mid-1600s. The Ibadi imamate's revival coincided with Portugal's expulsion from Hormuz. For the remainder of the century, Oman's rulers undertook an aggressive campaign against Portuguese bases on the Omani coast, the Gulf, India and East Africa.

THE PORTUGUESE

The rise of the Portuguese seaborne empire unfolded over the course of the fifteenth and sixteenth centuries. In 1415, an expedition captured the Moroccan port of Ceuta, situated inside the Gibraltar Strait. In the next 80 years, Lisbon's navigators crept down the Atlantic coast of Africa, establishing trading posts and colonies. Vasco da Gama's 1497–8 circumnavigation of Africa extended Portugal's reach into the Indian Ocean. At the end of a ten-month voyage, he reached India's Malabar Coast, bought a load of spices, and returned home with his precious cargo. In the next half-century, Portuguese navigators founded trading posts and forts along the African, Arabian and Asian shores of the Indian Ocean. The promise of profit lured them into the Pacific Ocean, where they set up posts to trade with China and Japan. In the same period, Lisbon's fleets traversed the Atlantic Ocean and landed on the coast of Brazil. The far-flung Portuguese Empire reached its zenith by 1600. Then Dutch and English traders entered the Indian Ocean and in 50 years of intermittent warfare expelled the Portuguese from most of their Indian Ocean strongholds.

Portugal laid down the basic framework for organizing its far-flung empire in 1504. The king appointed a viceroy to oversee military and administrative affairs from headquarters in India (Goa became the vice-regal seat in 1530). Due to the long time it took to complete a round-trip voyage to Lisbon, the viceroy operated as a semi-independent authority. His immediate entourage included a captain of the fortress, a vice-regal council and a financial council. With advice from these officials, the viceroy had responsibility for diplomacy and war, finance and trade. His capacity to command fortress-captains at remote locations, however, was limited.

The Portuguese established fortresses and trading posts in locations to profit from the Indian Ocean trade in pepper and spices. At the time of their arrival in the region, merchandise passed westward along two primary routes, through the Gulf and the Red Sea. Imposing a monopoly required shutting off those two waterways in order to divert all traffic to Portuguese

Gulf appendage Portugal

vessels sailing around Africa. The strategy threatened to disrupt the ancient habit for trade in the vast Indian Ocean basin to circulate according to prices and supplies rather than pressures applied through military force. Regional powers customarily skimmed customs dues from maritime commerce by offering security and facilities to merchants. Failure to maintain stability or efforts to raise customs rates caused traders to migrate to other ports, whose rulers were glad to welcome them. For the Portuguese to monopolize trade, they would have to use their gunships to force merchant vessels to ports under their control. It was the impulse to monopoly that led them to covet Hormuz and its possessions in the Gulf and Oman.

European visitors to Hormuz were impressed by its prosperity: mats covered the dusty streets; vendors sold water borne by camels to thirsty pedestrians; homes were adorned with aromatic plants and flowers; even Persian wine was easily available. Beneath the prosperous veneer ran turbulent political currents. In 1505, the son of the ruler murdered his father, only to be killed himself by the head of the royal bodyguard. A court eunuch then seized power and installed a young boy on the throne. It was a propitious moment for the Portuguese to arrive, but they were divided about how to subordinate Hormuz. The first viceroy of India, Dom Francisco de Almeida, preferred imposing indirect rule whereby the king of Hormuz would pay tribute. A more aggressive policy of conquest was preferred by Afonso de Albuquerque, commander of a squadron dispatched to block Muslim ships from entering the Red Sea. Albuquerque's first invasion of Hormuz in 1507 fizzled out when some of his own sailors deserted. His second expedition eight years later was a success. King Turanshah IV accepted Portuguese suzerainty, but in 1522 he plotted a rebellion to oust the Portuguese. The Portuguese gathered forces to crush the rebellion, execute King Turanshah IV, and put his 13-year-old son on the throne. To prevent a recurrence of rebellion, the Portuguese banned Muslims from bearing arms.

Hormuz remained an outpost of Portugal's vast maritime empire, Estado da India, for a century. Its institutions and arrangements varied widely according to negotiations with local powers. At some locations, such as Goa, the Portuguese ruled directly and therefore required a large number of administrators and soldiers. By contrast, at Hormuz, where they retained the local dynasty, they never exceeded a few hundred soldiers and settlers. The most powerful Portuguese official was the fortress captain, who commanded 400 soldiers manning the garrison and a fleet of ships patrolling the sea lanes. The civilian administration included a court magistrate and customs officials. The Catholic Church sent priests to serve the Portuguese colony and to proselytize. They introduced an intolerant mood by persuading the Portuguese governor to shut down Jewish synagogues and Hindu temples, which the Muslim rulers had previously allowed in order to facilitate trade.

As for relations with the Hormuz dynasty, Portuguese officials manipulated the historic rivalry between kings and viziers. At moments of succession, candidates for the throne jockeyed to win Portuguese favour, obtained with gifts and tax concessions. Even though the kings had little power, they were useful to the Portuguese for endowing their domination with a patina of Muslim legitimacy. The Hormuz dynasty retained the authority to appoint its own officials on the island and to collect tribute from vassals in the Gulf and Oman. The system of indirect rule meant that vassals did not have to interact with Portuguese captains, just with a handful of traders. In such reduced circumstances, the 300-year-old Hormuz kingdom lived on, its fortunes entwined with the Portuguese Empire's ability to hold the island.

The Portuguese sought to monopolize the spice trade by blocking traffic through the Gulf to Iraq and the Red Sea to Egypt. Their initial success at shutting off the Red Sea diverted traffic to the Gulf. Albuquerque wanted to close off shipping through the Gulf as well but interference with the Red Sea route drove prices up so high that it was more profitable to sell spices in the Gulf than in Lisbon. It did not take long for the Portuguese to realize that it was impossible to monopolize trade because merchants simply relocated to other ports, reducing the volume of trade passing through Hormuz. Moreover, the trade route leading through the Gulf to Basra and then overland to the Mediterranean became immensely lucrative for Portuguese customs coffers and officials engaging in trade for personal gain. As a substitute for monopoly, Portugal regulated commerce with a system of passes whereby merchants paid a fee to obtain a pass allowing them to trade in the Portuguese domain. If a Portuguese ship encountered a crew lacking the pass, its merchandise would be confiscated. In sum, after an initial period of disruption and adjustment, Indian Ocean trade assimilated the Portuguese as a new political, military and commercial player profiting from perennial patterns of production and exchange.

Once the Portuguese had a foothold at the southern end of the Gulf they looked northward for opportunities to extend their sway, first to Bahrain and then to Basra, where they played on local rivalries. The prospects for extending Estado da India's reach to the northern end of the Gulf, however, dimmed with the arrival of a powerful Muslim dynasty in Iraq.

Sultan Sweim an I, 1520 -greatest otbn

THE OTTOMAN EMPIRE

Ottom̃arts defeated at Ankara 1402

The Ottoman Empire arose in what is now north-west Turkey in the early fourteenth century. By 1400, Ottoman territory stretched from the Balkans to eastern Asia Minor. The first phase of expansion came to a sudden halt when the Ottomans collided with the mighty Central Asian conqueror Timur Leng (Tamerlane) at a calamitous battle at Ankara in 1402. It took two decades for the Ottomans to recover from that defeat and regain their former domains. In 1453, they realized the ancient Muslim ambition of capturing Constantinople, putting an end to the Byzantine Empire. Fifty years later, the sudden rise of the Safavids in Iran alarmed the Ottomans and they mounted an attack that shattered Safavid forces at the Battle of Chaldiran in 1514, the first of many military clashes between the two Muslim powers. Two years later, Istanbul turned its attention to the Mamluk Sultanate, which had ruled Syria, Egypt and Hijaz since 1260. The Ottoman army crushed the Mamluks and added the central Arab lands to Istanbul's possessions.

In 1520, Sultan Suleiman I, the greatest ruler in the history of the Ottoman dynasty, ascended the throne. The early years of his reign were occupied with consolidating control over Syria and Egypt. He then launched a military campaign against Hungary, culminating in the unsuccessful siege of Vienna. Next, Suleiman turned his attention to the Safavids. In 1534, his forces occupied their capital at Tabriz, marched through central Iran, and seized Baghdad from a Safavid garrison. The rulers of Basra and Bahrain declared their allegiance to Suleiman. By establishing a presence at the northern end of the Gulf, the Ottomans were encroaching on the Portuguese at Hormuz, but the first *Port in* clash between the Muslim and Christian powers took place far *Gulf 34* away, off the shore of India. In 1538, Sultan Suleiman received *o ttomanr* a request from a Muslim prince in Gujarat for assistance to expel the Portuguese from a port they had recently seized. The Ottoman fleet at Suez headed east, but by the time the fleet reached India, the Portuguese had killed the prince who reached out to Istanbul and replaced him with a compliant Muslim vassal. Without a local ally, the Ottomans returned to Egypt after a brief, fruitless siege.

In 1546, the Ottomans drew closer to the Portuguese in the Gulf by asserting direct control over Basra. The Arab tribal sheikh in control of the town appealed to the Portuguese for assistance to repel the invaders, but before Goa could respond, the Ottomans occupied the city. Possessing an outpost on the Gulf, the Ottomans pondered how to secure it against Portuguese attack. Strategic logic suggested annexation of the Eastern Arabian shore at al-Hasa, which they conquered in 1552. Istanbul's bid to advance further down the Gulf by seizing Bahrain, a possession of Hormuz, was thwarted by the Portuguese. Further efforts by the two powers to gain decisive advantage over one another ended in stalemate. In the early 1560s, they concluded a truce that divided the Arab shore of the Gulf, with the Portuguese maintaining their hold on Bahrain, Hormuz and the Omani ports while the Ottomans kept al-Hasa and Basra.

When it came to ruling al-Hasa, Istanbul relied more on diplomacy than force, as it could never spare more than several hundred troops for the sparsely populated region. The major local power, the Banu Khalid tribe, shifted between loyalty and revolt. Deft manoeuvring on the part of the tribe's sheikhs enabled them to regain power in the 1670s when Istanbul had to concentrate forces on the European frontier. The Ottoman position in Basra was just as shaky. The Marsh Arabs to the city's north-west rejected Istanbul's authority and plundered vulnerable caravans travelling to and from Baghdad. In the other landward direction, the Arab chiefs of Huwaiza paid allegiance to the Safavids and intermittently put the city under siege. The Ottoman position on the Gulf, therefore, was essentially defensive, intended to contain the Portuguese and guard the frontier against the Safavids.

SAFAVID IRAN

The Safavid dynasty founded the second major Middle Eastern power of the era. During its 200-year reign (1501–1722), it wrought the most significant change in Iran's history since the Muslim conquests by converting the population to Twelver Shi'ism. In addition, the Safavids asserted central control over the Gulf in their pursuit of profit from the silk trade. They first appeared as a Sufi order – a popular mystical brotherhood – in the north-western Iranian region of Azerbaijan during the

Mongol Il-Khanid dynasty's rule. When the Il-Khan ruler converted to Islam around 1300, he patronized religious personalities, including the head of the Safavid Sufi order, with gifts and land grants. During the political turbulence that engulfed Iran in the later 1300s and 1400s, the Safavids retained influence in Azerbaijan and formed an alliance that a powerful tribal leader sealed by marriage. They also developed a militant streak with raids against neighbouring Muslim and Christian principalities.

The Safavids became the rulers of Iran under their leader Ismail, a charismatic figure who raised a following among Turcoman tribesmen in north-west Iran and eastern Anatolia. His preaching, often expressed in mystical poetry, asserted that he possessed semi-divine qualities as heir of the Shi'i Imams. He enjoyed the backing of tribesmen organized into a special military order known as the Qizilbash, or 'red heads', named after their distinctive red turbans. In 1501, Ismail's Qizilbash forces conquered Tabriz, the former Il-Khan capital, and in the next ten years, they overran the rest of Iran, eastern Anatolia and central Iraq. He then turned to propagating a blend of messianic and mystical doctrines that represented a heterodox form of Shi'ism at odds with the outlook of Twelver Shi'i religious scholars, who based their teachings on traditions passed down from the Imams. In the early years of Safavid rule, conversion to Shi'ism entailed exalting Ali and pronouncing a ritual curse on the first three caliphs for usurping Ali's rightful leadership. Shah Ismail did not use force to convert all of Iran's Sunnis, who formed the majority of the population, but he did attack specific Sunni groups. Such episodes arose from the desire to eliminate powerful religious leaders, especially Sufi sheikhs whose charismatic reputations could detract from his authority.

Shah Ismail's ambitions were not limited to Iran. In eastern Anatolia, thousands of Turcoman tribesmen regarded him as a divine figure. Naturally, the staunchly Sunni Ottomans considered the presence of so many followers of a rival ruler a threat, and in 1512, Sultan Selim determined to crush both the Shi'i Turcomen and Shah Ismail. His forces carried out a brutal massacre of Ismail's followers in eastern Anatolia (hence his nickname, Selim 'the Grim'). Two years later, he led the powerful Ottoman army for a showdown with Ismail. At the Battle of Chaldiran, less than 100 miles from Tabriz, Ottoman artillery shattered the Safavid cavalry. Shah Ismail's rule survived, however, because the supply line from Istanbul to Tabriz was too long for the Ottomans to sustain, so they withdrew after a brief occupation.

A greater threat to Safavid rule came when Ismail died in 1524 and his eight-year-old son Tahmasp succeeded him. Civil war erupted between rival Qizilbash chieftains to determine who would gain the lion's share of power under the next shah. With Iran in disarray for 12 years, Ottoman armies conquered Iraq and briefly reoccupied Tabriz. After the fighting subsided, Shah Tahmasp bolstered the institutional foundations of the more orthodox expression of Twelver Shi'ism favoured by learned clerics. He appointed a Shi'i theologian to supervise religious institutions, appointing prayer leaders and preachers to lay the foundation for a national clerical hierarchy. The chief theologian also presided over properties dedicated to religious purposes (*evqaf*), a valuable source of income that paid stipends to religious pupils, teachers and mosque personnel. Safavid patronage attracted religious scholars from Iraq and southern Lebanon, knitting together previously scattered pockets of Shi'i religious scholars. For a time, the Ottomans in al-Hasa and the Hormuz governors in Bahrain stood in the way of interaction between their Shi'i subjects and the vibrant religious institution taking shape in Iran, but the Safavids did eventually project their influence to the Arabian shore and integrate its Shi'i communities into a regional network of clerics.

After four decades of calm, Shah Tahmasp's death in 1576 was the occasion for a new outbreak of civil war among Qizilbash chieftains. The turmoil subsided in 1587, when a grandson of Tahmasp was crowned as Shah Abbas. A talented, energetic and ruthless leader, the new Safavid ruler broadened the base of dynastic power with an expanded corps of royal slaves he assigned to military and civilian posts. In the 1590s, he relocated the capital away from the Ottoman frontier to Isfahan, where he ordered the construction of one of the world's most dazzling array of palaces, mosques and markets around a vast rectangular plaza. Shah Abbas's 40-year reign marked the high point of Safavid splendour, in part because he paid close attention to developing long-distance trade as a lucrative source of customs taxes for his coffers. Measures to promote commerce included the construction of markets and caravanserais, which were combinations of inns and warehouses. He took special care to promote and profit from Iran's most valuable export – silk. Shah Abbas asserted control over supplies by designating the primary areas of cultivation in the Caspian provinces as crown lands. In addition, he aspired to control the main route for sending Persian silk to Ottoman and European factories, which passed from the Caspian provinces through Asia Minor to Bursa, the centre of the Ottoman silk industry. From there, silk products were exported to European markets. On previous occasions, the Ottomans had exploited their position on the

silk route to inflict economic harm on the Safavids, and in the
1590s, they invaded and briefly occupied Shirvan, an important
silk-producing region. The silk trade was too valuable for Shah
Abbas to leave in so vulnerable a position, so he sought an alternative route to European markets. To do so, he had to divert silk
supplies from the Ottoman frontier and develop direct ties with
European merchants.

In the late 1500s, an Armenian town in Azerbaijan called Julfa
emerged as a prosperous distribution point. To tap its trade, in
1605 the shah ordered the Julfa Armenians to relocate to a new
settlement that he constructed on the outskirts of Isfahan, aptly
named New Julfa. The Armenian traders had agents dispersed
across Eurasia at locations in Holland, Venice, Russia, India and
the Ottoman Empire, so they were ideal conduits for distributing
Iran's precious silk cargoes. While relocation from Azerbaijan to
Isfahan was enormously disruptive, Shah Abbas compensated
the Armenians with land grants for the construction of new
churches. The Armenians were not the only non-Muslim traders
benefiting from Shah Abbas's hunger for tax revenues. Isfahan
hosted around 10,000 Indian traders, known as *banians*, in the
later 1600s. At the capital and at the major outlet in the Gulf,
Bandar Abbas, the banians handled the valuable trade in Indian
cloth and acted as moneylenders. Shah Abbas was the kind of
ruler who would also do business with European traders.

THE EAST INDIA COMPANIES

The shah's drive for direct trade with Europeans coincided
with the rise of a new kind of commercial venture in the early
seventeenth century. The rulers of the Netherlands and England
issued charters to private investors and merchants authorizing
them to form companies for the purpose of developing trade
with the East Indies. The English East India Company formed
in 1600 and the Dutch East India Company in 1602. The Dutch
charter empowered the Company to wage war and negotiate
treaties, endowing it with the attributes of a private state. It is
a peculiarity of the era that private commercial ventures developed into powerful political actors.

The Dutch Company's leadership consisted of a board
of directors, known as 'the Seventeen' for the number of its
members. The directors appointed a governor-general to execute policy and oversee a string of local directorates at trading

stations. In 1619, the Company established headquarters at Batavia (modern-day Jakarta) on the island of Java, weakening the Portuguese grip on the East Indies spice trade. The upstart Dutch merchants soon gained a dominant share of the trade and edged out the Portuguese. The English East Company also set up factories in the East Indies, but the Dutch forced them out, and the English wound up concentrating on India, where in 1613 they had established a trading post on the coast of Gujarat at Surat.

Whereas Portugal's maritime empire was an extension of royal power and remained under the authority of the crown, the Dutch empire was built by merchants independent of the ruler. Apart from that difference, they used the same means to build empire: the Dutch relied on military force to grab a share of the spice trade, just as the Portuguese had done a century earlier. Competition between the Dutch and the Portuguese had a political dimension that went back to the early 1500s when the Habsburg dynasty ruled Austria, Spain and the Netherlands. In 1568, the Dutch tried to break away from Habsburg rule, initiating the Eighty Years War, a conflict that smouldered and flared for two generations. In 1580, King Philip II annexed Portugal to Spain. Forty years later, the Dutch reignited their fight for independence. Since Portuguese possessions were held under the Spanish flag, the Dutch Company took the fight to the enemy's holdings around the globe, from Brazil to the Gulf.

The arrival of the Dutch and the English in the Indian Ocean and the consolidation of Safavid power augured the end of the Portuguese rule at Hormuz. In 1601, Shah Abbas strengthened his grip on the Gulf coast, putting his forces in striking range of Bahrain and its valuable pearl beds. In 1602, the Safavids occupied Bahrain, killed the Hormuz governor, and turned back a Portuguese fleet sent to retake the island. Shah Abbas's next goal was to expel the Portuguese from Hormuz. He blockaded supplies from the mainland to the Portuguese garrison, but he lacked a naval force for a conclusive assault on Hormuz. The English and the Dutch, however, possessed the requisite naval forces as well as the desire to defeat Portugal. The shah offered them trade concessions if they supplied naval support for a Persian assault on Hormuz. In 1622, English East India Company ships conveyed a Safavid force to expel the Portuguese, but losing Hormuz did not spell the end of their role in the Gulf. They merely did what so many other traders had done throughout the region's history by relocating headquarters to a nearby trading post and retaining agents at Basra and Muscat. As for the king of Hormuz, the Safavids took him to Shiraz, where he died along with the 400-year-old dynasty in 1635.

Cooperation against the Portuguese did not pave the way to easy relations between the Safavids and European traders because of friction over the terms of trade. Eager to maximize income from the silk trade, operated as a royal monopoly, Shah Abbas required the European companies to purchase a set quantity at a high price. In return, he granted Dutch and English traders the right to trade freely in his realm and exemption from taxes. Frustrated with the shah's insistence on forced purchase, the English abandoned the enterprise in 1642, leaving the field entirely to the Dutch. In the next few decades, the value of silk fell and political tensions disrupted Dutch–Iranian relations. In 1645, they fought an inconclusive war over prices, and a second war erupted in 1680 when the Safavids tried to impose forced purchases. By that time, less expensive Chinese silk was lowering demand for the Iranian product. The Dutch Company nevertheless persevered because its consent to disadvantageous terms on silk was outweighed by profits on other goods. Only in the final years of the Safavid dynasty did the silk trade lapse due to falling production and waning Dutch interest.

IRAQ UNDER LOCAL RULE

Political and economic dynamics at the northern end of the Gulf turned on the balance between imperial Ottoman troops and local forces around Basra. It was the largest town in the region, even though it was not ideally located for Gulf traders (one must sail up the Shatt al-Arab about 70 miles and then navigate a narrow canal to the Euphrates River in order to reach it), and the harsh climate restricted trade to a few months a year. Nevertheless, Basra was the gateway to Baghdad and a staging point for Iranian pilgrims on their way to Mecca or the Shi'i holy places at Kerbala and Najaf. It lay in the midst of a productive agricultural region, criss-crossed by dozens of irrigation canals that fed date palm groves, fruit orchards and vegetable gardens. The advent of the Portuguese in the Indian Ocean stimulated Basra's growth because their efforts to close shipping through the Red Sea drove traders to transport goods on caravans that made their way from Basra upriver to Baghdad then across the desert to Aleppo and Damascus. In the seventeenth century it

4. Ashar Creek Basra.

was the largest port in the Gulf, with an estimated population of 50,000 prospering from its position as the entrepot for goods moving between the Indian Ocean and the Middle East.

The main challenges to Ottoman authority around Basra came from Arab tribesmen inhabiting the dense marshes upriver and from desert tribes below the Euphrates. Both groups frequently interfered with trade and communication to Baghdad. On the Iranian side of the Shatt al-Arab, the Arab sheikh of Huwaiza, a Safavid vassal, extended his sway over the borderlands. The Ottomans lacked the capacity to secure Basra and its hinterland, so in 1596 a local strongman, Afrasiyab Pasha, paid the governor of Baghdad for the right to govern the town. He and his descendants wound up ruling Basra for 70 years.

As nominal vassals of Istanbul, the pashas of Basra had to be on guard against the Safavids. To ward off that threat, Afrasiyab Pasha welcomed a Portuguese trading post after their expulsion from Hormuz in 1622. When Shah Abbas invaded Iraq to conquer Baghdad the next year, a Portuguese squadron helped keep Safavid forces at bay. English merchants frustrated with Dutch domination at Bandar Abbas explored the possibility of setting up a factory in Basra and began to trade there in 1643. The Dutch showed up the following year due to their dispute over silk prices with the Safavids. Early European trade to Basra was an offshoot of commerce in the lower Gulf, but it paved the way for later growth when political conditions settled down. In the

first half of the seventeenth century, the pashas of Basra illus-
trated one of the enduring truths of Gulf history: that imperial
rule is not a requirement for prosperity.

The third Afrasiyab ruler, Hussein Pasha, alienated Basrans
with a greedy streak he exhibited by confiscating the property of merchants upon their deaths. As a result, local support
diminished. Unfortunately for the Basrans, in the course of
three Ottoman attempts to remove Hussein Pasha, Istanbul's
military commanders proved just as greedy and cruel. The first
Ottoman expedition in 1654 forced Hussein Pasha to flee but
the commander's harsh measures in Basra squandered local support. Hussein Pasha returned to lead a rising of townsmen and
tribesmen that put the city back in his hands. Rather than being
chastened, he then made a bid to seize al-Hasa from its Ottoman
governor. In 1665, Istanbul sent a second expedition to remove
him, but the wily governor built up massive fortifications at the
strategic town of Qurna, where the Euphrates and Tigris Rivers
converge to form the Shatt al-Arab. A nine-month siege ended in
a deal whereby he resigned his position and Istanbul appointed
his son Yahya governor. Once back in Basra, he reneged on the
deal. The Ottomans then gathered a larger, better equipped
force to do away with him for good. Hussein Pasha escaped first
to Iran and then further east to Mughal India where Emperor
Aurangzeb integrated him into his massive military machine
as a mid-level commander. According to some reports, Hussein
Pasha fell foul of the powerful emperor, who ordered that he be
put to death in 1673.

After Hussein Pasha had fled, the Ottomans had appointed
his son Yahya Pasha to govern Basra, but when he tried to
shake off the sultan's authority, they restored direct rule, ending the era of local autonomy. Ottoman governors proved effective at keeping order for about 20 years until the 1690s, when
Istanbul's long war against the Habsburgs (1683–99) took its
toll of military and financial resources, leaving little for remote
provinces. Basra was soon engulfed in a complex power struggle
involving the Ottomans, the Muntafiq tribe, the Huwaiza Arabs,
and the Safavids. The city changed hands several times before
the Ottomans, having ended their war against the Habsburgs,
were able to consolidate control in 1701. Overall, the end of the
seventeenth century was a dark time for Basra. The first blow
was a terrible plague in 1690, followed by political instability
and a seemingly endless series of sieges.

In Baghdad, the Ottoman grip began to slacken around the
same time as the rise of Afrasiyab Pasha in Basra. The fundamental problem in Baghdad, however, was not so much the

threats posed by unruly Arab tribesmen but friction between military factions that were supposed to keep order in the city and protect caravan routes. Two revolts against Istanbul broke out in the early 1600s. The second one was in full throttle when Shah Abbas seized the city in 1623. After his death, Istanbul twice tried and failed to retake Baghdad before succeeding in 1638. The Treaty of Zuhab ended the Ottoman-Safavid wars for the rest of the century, but Baghdad remained a difficult possession due to ongoing clashes between rival military factions and harassment by Arab tribes.

A new chapter opened with the governorship of Hasan Pasha (r. 1704–23). He had risen through the provincial ranks to become governor. By dint of his familiarity with tribal and factional politics, he stabilized the province and added Basra to his domain. Unlike most Ottoman governors assigned to three-year posts, Hasan Pasha ruled for nearly two decades, auguring a more stable era for the key Ottoman possession in Iraq. The fundamental problem for Ottoman rule in Iraq throughout the period lay in Istanbul's fiscal deficits. Lacking the means to pay janissaries (imperial infantry) their salaries and Arab tribesmen the subsidies they demanded, one governor after another resorted to extorting townsmen, to the detriment of trade, or letting pay to janissaries lapse, at risk of their desertion and disorder, or withholding subsidies from tribesmen, at risk of their ravaging caravans.

OMAN

The silence of Arabic and Persian sources on inner Oman from the early 1200s to the early 1400s suggests the region was isolated from coastal city-states and kingdoms, perhaps divided among small chieftaincies strewn over the rugged mountains and plateaus. Omani chronicles resume with reports on attempts at reviving the Ibadi imamate at Nizwa in the 1430s. In spite of support from powerful tribal chiefs, these initiatives ended in failure. The new political dispensation of the early 1500s in the Gulf, with Safavids, Portuguese and Ottomans jostling for dominance, barely made a ripple in inner Oman. The Portuguese had absorbed the Kingdom of Hormuz's coastal possessions, but the mountain valleys and desert plains of the interior remained divided into numerous small chieftaincies and tribal domains.

The conditions for launching a new imamate after an 800-year hiatus did not appear promising. But in 1624, a powerful tribal combination heeded the call of an Ibadi scholar from Rustaq to support Nasir ibn Murshid of the Yariba clan as the new Ibadi imam. Soon, his realm was prospering, in large measure thanks to taxes imposed on European traders at Muscat. The Yariba imams invested tax revenues to repair old forts, construct new ones and expand trading activities. Maritime commerce was largely handled by Indian merchants, who oversaw trade on ships owned by the imam and tribal chiefs. India was an essential source for rice, lumber (to build ships) and cotton. Omani traders also established posts on the East African coast, where they purchased and exported slaves to toil on agricultural lands around inner Oman's villages. The gruelling task of rehabilitating the ancient network of subterranean irrigation canals, the qanats, fell to African slaves and defeated tribesmen. Omani agricultural production achieved its highest levels since the early Islamic period.

Oman's commercial expansion in the Indian Ocean put the Yariba Imamate on a collision course with the Portuguese. The first step in 1650 was to expel them from Muscat. Omani warships then raided Portuguese outposts in the Gulf, India and East Africa, in addition to plundering merchant vessels on the high seas. The Portuguese reciprocated with seizures of Omani trading ships and by shelling Muscat and other Omani ports. They each sought advantage by allying with their rivals' adversaries. Hence, the Yariba imams reached out to the Dutch and English while the Portuguese formed ties with Arab sheikhs opposed to the imam. The prospect of loot fuelled the conflict with such intensity that European traders avoided Muscat throughout most of the seventeenth century.

At the turn of the eighteenth century, Imam Saif ibn Sultan (r. 1692–1711) extended his power down the coast of East Africa, seizing Mombasa from the Portuguese in 1698, pushing as far south as Kilwa in the early 1700s, and establishing garrisons at Pemba and Zanzibar. For the next 150 years, Omani traders in East Africa profited from growing demand for slaves and ivory. The last effective Yariba imam, Sultan ibn Saif II (r. 1711–19), exploited Safavid weakness to seize control of Bahrain and islands close to the Iranian shore (Qeshm and Larak). With a flourishing agricultural base and bustling trading posts stretching from Mozambique to Bahrain, the Yariba Imamate demonstrated Oman's potential for empire building given the right alignment of religious and tribal forces. The alignment, however, was fragile and susceptible to rapid disintegration.

TWELVER SHI'ISM

The most significant historical development in this period had nothing to do with imperial rivalries or European trade. It was the consolidation of Twelver Shi'ism as the dominant religion in Iran. Some facets of that development are essential for understanding later historical events. The Safavid dynasty presented opportunity to Shi'i scholars and a challenge to one of their major intellectual traditions. Centuries of Sunni rule had strengthened the Shi'i doctrine that there was no legitimate political authority in the absence of the imam. Consequently, the congregational Friday prayer had to be suspended, there was no legal basis for a ruler to collect taxes, and scholars could not accept appointments to official positions. According to this doctrine, called Akhbarism, the religious scholars acted as deputies to the only legitimate public authority, the imams, preserving and transmitting their lore down the generations until the reappearance of the Twelfth Imam as the messianic figure of the Mahdi. In issuing legal rulings, the Akhbari jurist would restrict himself to the Qur'an, the Prophetic Tradition and the teachings of the imams.

The Safavid shahs, however, constructed a powerful infrastructure of clerical authority that some Shi'i scholars justified in the name of a legal doctrine called Usulism. Its proponents concurred with the Akhbaris on the primacy of the Qur'an, the Prophetic Tradition and the teachings of the imams in Islamic law. But they also argued that when those sources did not yield a solution to legal questions, then a legal expert, a *mujtahid*, had the right to use his reason to deduce rulings. Furthermore, the Usuli doctrine asserted that ordinary believers had a duty to abide by the rulings of a living mujtahid. The effect of the Usuli doctrine was to magnify the authority of religious jurists. While the Safavids encouraged the Usuli doctrine, the Akhbari doctrine remained the dominant strain among Shi'i scholars living under Sunni rule in Ottoman Iraq and Hormuzi Bahrain, where there was no prospect of a Friday prayer in the Shi'i formula, with its denunciation of caliphs revered by Sunnis. When the Safavid dynasty fell, the Akhbari tendency became ascendant once more. The doctrinal controversies remained deeply embedded in Twelver Shi'ism through modern times, and later political conditions would summon new splits.

The debates over legal doctrine preoccupied circles of jurists and their pupils but did not inform the religious outlook of common folk. During the Safavid era, popular Shi'i beliefs and rituals gradually took root in towns and villages. The countryside was dotted with shrines dedicated to mystics and saints considered to emanate divine grace to visitors seeking solace. Preachers tapped popular attachment to holy places with tales that associated shrines with the imams and their descendants (*imamzadeh*s). Visits to the major shrines of the imams and imamzadehs in Iran and Iraq were accorded spiritual value on a par with the hajj to Mecca, which was intermittently disrupted by the outbreak of Ottoman–Safavid hostilities. Imperial patronage for Shi'i clerics provided the foundation for the elaboration of popular beliefs that enhanced their authority. They claimed that because of their dedication to the imams the Hidden Imam would visit them in dreams, and that insulting a cleric could incur divine wrath. The clerics augmented their religious standing with control over influential spheres of social authority, including civil and commercial law. In addition to supervising religious foundations, they collected religious taxes, the so-called Hidden Imam's share that they spent to keep mosques in good repair and to pay stipends to religious students.

The concentration of material and symbolic resources in clerical hands was a strikingly novel development and an enduring legacy of Safavid rule for later Iranian history. Furthermore, isolated pockets of Twelver Shi'is in Lebanon, Iraq and Eastern Arabia formed strong connections with Iran. The Safavid conquest of Bahrain in 1602 reinvigorated its scholarly Shi'i tradition that had developed under a local dynasty in the fourteenth century as the old Carmathian Ismaili sect faded. The Safavids patronized Shi'i ulama in Bahrain, funded mosques and revived the Shi'i Friday prayer. Shi'i judges presided over courts and royal funds financed wealthy religious endowments. Shi'i ulama from Bahrain immigrated to Iran to take up posts as judges and teachers. Indeed, one of the hallmarks of Twelver Shi'ism since the Safavid era has been mobility, expressed in the circulation of scholars and students, facilitated by long-distance trade. At times of insecurity or persecution, migration was an option, just as it had been for merchants, sailors and fishermen in the Gulf for centuries.

SAFAVID COLLAPSE

It is conventional to observe that after Shah Abbas died in 1629, the Safavid dynasty entered a period of prolonged decline culminating in its overthrow by upstart Afghan tribesmen in 1722. That picture is complicated by a number of facts about the later

Safavid period. First, the bloody civil wars that broke out after the first two shahs died never recurred. Second, after Shah Safi (r. 1629–42) signed the Treaty of Zuhab with the Ottomans, ceding Iraq to Istanbul, Iran enjoyed a long period of peace and security along its borders. Third, Safavid cultural achievements in the arts remained vibrant. One chronic problem that bedevilled the Safavids was the unfavourable balance of trade with India, which drained silver from the Safavid domain. The shahs tried to siphon trade through Bandar Abbas and negotiated agreements with Dutch traders in the Gulf stipulating that they purchase fixed quantities of silk at fixed prices, but they proved impossible to enforce, especially when Bengali and Chinese silk flooded the market. In addition to global economic trends, nature played havoc with Iran in the late seventeenth century when it was struck by a series of devastating plagues and famines. Whether the Safavids were doomed by bad rulers or insurmountable circumstances, their achievement was remarkable. In Iran's long history in the Islamic era, they were the most durable dynasty; they left a brilliant artistic and architectural imprint; and their religious policy turned Iran into the largest majority Shi'i country in the Muslim world.

The fall of the Safavids in 1722 threw Iran into chaos. The political underpinnings of the silk trade disintegrated as Afghan invaders took over Bandar Abbas and ended the tax exemption on silk exports. The port's bustling activity had already diminished, so the Safavid collapse merely accelerated its decline. Given the Dutch Company's focus on South-east Asian trade and spice supplies, the Gulf had always been a matter of opportunity rather than priority. The directors in Amsterdam were ready to pull out well before its agents on the scene, who tried different locations and combinations of merchandise to sustain company activities. Now they shifted headquarters to Basra, leaving behind a minor station at Bandar Abbas.

In the early 1720s, the constellation of Muslim powers in the Gulf was in transition. The fall of the Safavid and Yariba dynasties plunged Iran and Oman into civil wars while the Ottoman Empire was struggling to cope with the emergence of more threatening neighbours in Russia and central Europe. The Ottoman hold in Baghdad and Basra was tenuous, its foothold in al-Hasa lost to the Banu Khalid. The Portuguese were routed from the Gulf by Safavid, English, Dutch and Omani assaults on their last strongholds. The Dutch and English trading companies adapted to shifting political patterns by keeping their focus on commerce and staying out of political and military entanglements to avoid alienating local powers.

Nadir Shah
Najd
Ibad

4   An Era of Political Turbulence, 1720–1820

In the eighteenth century, a new enduring constellation of forces took shape in and around the Gulf. The English edged out the Dutch, fended off a French effort to enter the region, and slowly became the dominant European power in the region. Iran fluctuated between fragmentation and consolidation, swinging between asserting power in the Gulf and receding from its shores. When a stable dynasty did emerge, its northern base of power (like the early Safavids) kept it from exercising authority over the Gulf's Iranian shore. For much of this period, the Ottoman Empire was consumed with European wars, so it rested its attenuated authority in Iraq on the shoulders of autonomous governors. The weakness of Muslim imperial powers left a vacuum filled by Arab sheikhdoms. Central Arabia had always been beyond the reach of external rulers. In this period, the first Saudi emirate represented a political–religious force that unified much of Arabia and introduced a novel historical situation where a Central Arabian power exercised influence over the lower Gulf. At Muscat, a new dynasty arose to become the major Muslim power in the Western Indian Ocean. Up and down the Gulf, endemic warfare among evenly matched rulers fostered insecure conditions that hurt trade. The era of warfare began to wind down in 1820 with a decisive English military intervention that froze in place political arrangements in the lower Gulf, from Bahrain to Oman.

IRAN

The political history of Iran after the Safavids saw periods of order and interludes of tribal anarchy. The swings in fortune reflected the country's mix of pastoral tribesmen and settled

Iran rise power Nadir Shah

Iran dominated by a few tribal leaders

folk – cultivators, merchants and artisans. Ever since the Saljuk era, tribesmen dominated war and politics. The reservoir of tribal warriors offered gifted military leaders the means to carry out expansionist initiatives that made Iran an influential regional power. But the warrior base came from fractious Turcoman tribes led by khans whose loyalties were fluid. The settled population provided rulers the fiscal resources and administrative talent necessary to achieve the political stability they sought for protection from predatory khans. For much of the eighteenth century, two tribal leaders dominated the political scene. They ruled in very different ways, pointing to the critical role of individual leadership in mobilizing and taming unruly tribesmen. At the end of the century, a third powerful khan emerged to unite the country. There was no reason to suppose that he or his successors would sustain that achievement, but they ruled Iran into the twentieth century.

Iran falls Afghan invaders

The fall of Isfahan to Afghan invaders in 1722 was the opening to a decade of civil war. As soon as word of the Safavid dynasty's collapse spread, the Ottoman Empire and Russia invaded the border regions while tribal warlords plunged into a flurry of raids and attacks that ravaged cities and countryside. The eventual victor, Nadir Khan, came from the Afshar tribal confederation in the north-east. On his rise to power he defeated the formidable Qajar confederation, expelled the Afghans, and chased Ottoman and Russian forces off Iranian soil. In March 1736, Nadir convened the major tribal leaders for his coronation. At the grand assembly on the plain of Mughan in Azerbaijan, that crowned him shah, he announced a bold religious policy that apparently aimed to tamp down sectarian tensions in Iran and remove a cause of hostility with the Ottoman Empire. Nadir Shah proclaimed Iran's adherence to what he called Jafari doctrine, retaining the distinctive legal tradition of Twelver Shi'ism but eschewing the ritual cursing of the first three caliphs. When a prominent Shi'i cleric expressed outrage at the doctrine, Nadir had him put to death on the spot, cowing the rest of the Shi'i clerics into acquiescence.

Nadir Shah = Warmonger

Nadir Shah possessed an insatiable appetite for conquest but no vision for constructing the foundations of stable rule. Consequently, the annals of his decade in power consist of ambitious military campaigns that overran neighbouring lands followed by abrupt withdrawals as he set off in another direction. His first and most spectacular invasion targeted India's Mughal dynasty, long past its prime but still fabulously wealthy. After overcoming stubborn Afghan resistance at Kandahar he led his triumphant army into the Indus Delta. Even before his forces arrived at Delhi in March 1739, the Mughal emperor realized it would be futile, even foolish, to mount resistance, so he went out to pay homage to Nadir Shah. His troops then emptied Mughal coffers of so much treasure, gold and silver that he declared a three-year tax holiday for Iran. Having impoverished the once mighty Indian Muslim dynasty, Nadir Shah put the Mughal emperor back on his diminished throne and marched back to Iran.

Turning to the Gulf, he aimed to re-establish control over Bahrain, conquer Oman, and seize Basra from the Ottomans. He confronted a fundamental problem, however, in that he did not have a navy, nor did he manage to construct one. Instead, he resorted to *ad hoc* measures to address the current military necessity. He assembled a naval force for the invasion of Bahrain by purchasing ships from the English and commissioning the construction of some vessels. He apparently decided it was not worth stationing a large garrison in Bahrain, so he withdrew after one year to turn his attention to Oman. It took some time to put together a naval force, this time through various means: borrowing a ship from the Dutch, purchasing and occasionally seizing ships from the English and the French. An attempt to construct a shipbuilding yard on the Gulf failed for a lack of carpenters. A propitious moment for invading Oman arose when the Ibadi imam solicited his support against dynastic rivals. The expedition was a success, but as in the case of Bahrain, Nadir Shah shortly withdrew the bulk of his forces for other adventures.

[margin: wants Gulf Ottomans]

In 1743, he invaded Iraq and became bogged down in a stalemate that exhausted both sides and led to a series of diplomatic exchanges. Nadir proposed normalizing Sunni–Shi'i relations by having Istanbul recognize Jafari doctrine as a fifth religious legal school at Mecca, alongside the four Sunni schools. However, the Ottomans were disinclined to compromise their adherence to the integrity of Sunnism for the sake of satisfying Nadir Shah. The outcome was an Ottoman–Iranian treaty in 1746 that did not bring up the matter of the Jafari doctrine, but did satisfy Nadir Shah's demand that the Ottomans guarantee safe passage for Iranian pilgrims to Mecca and to the Shi'i shrines in Iraq in exchange for abolishing the ritual curse of the first caliphs.

Nadir Shah was a tireless military campaigner but he failed to develop institutions that would make his rule more than a matter of applying brute force. Erecting towers of skulls as reminders of the consequences of defiance ensured obedience but not loyalty. Moreover, his unquenchable appetite for taxes and confiscations

[margin: power = universal virtue M.E.]

[handwritten: Karim Khan = accessible ruler to subjects just, trade flourishes]

to fund constant warfare undermined economic recovery from the wars that tore Iran apart after the Safavids. In 1747, he met his death at the hands of members of his own bodyguard. The military chieftains who had served under his banner marched off with their troops to fight for power, making Iran once again the arena for civil war.

One of the contenders for power came from the Zand tribe, whose homeland lay in the Zagros Mountains of south-west Iran. The Zand leader, Karim Khan, plunged into a maze of skirmishes and battles that raged for over a decade. In addition to seeking military advantage and territory, the warring parties sought the legitimacy afforded by members of the Safavid clan. Thus, in 1750 Karim Khan put a Safavid puppet on the throne in Isfahan and adopted the humble title of regent (*vakil*). Once Karim Khan definitively cleared the central and south-west of rivals in 1763, his stable rule gave a boost to urban life after decades of predatory domination by tribesmen and Nadir Shah. Merchants benefitted from his interest in promoting trade with the Gulf and India. Shiraz in particular flourished under his benign rule and his expenditures to repair and renovate the city's walls and monuments. In the later years of Karim Khan's reign, clashes along the Ottoman–Iranian border reverberated in the northern Gulf as he put Basra under siege in 1775. The Ottoman garrison held out for a year before surrendering and retreating to Baghdad. The Iranian occupation turned into a brutal season of plunder and extortion, compelling European traders to relocate to Kuwait, which was just emerging as an entrepot. Karim Khan may have been on the verge of abandoning Basra when he died in 1779 because his forces departed shortly afterward. Even though he failed to establish the foundation for a sustainable polity, his reign became a byword for a just ruler accessible to his subjects.

Iran again fell into a phase of tumultuous tribal warfare. The eventual victor was Agha Muhammad Khan, the chieftain of the Qajar tribe. The Qajars had been one of the Turcoman tribes that formed the Qizilbash during the Safavid era and their khans served the dynasty in high military offices and as provincial governors. After Nadir Shah, an energetic Qajar chieftain, Muhammad Hasan Khan, gained power in several northern districts where he was the dominant figure for nearly a decade before Karim Khan killed him in battle in 1757. To ensure good behaviour on the part of Qajar tribesmen, Karim Khan took Muhammad Hasan Khan's son Agha Muhammad back to Shiraz where he was kept hostage. When Karim Khan died in 1779, Agha Muhammad escaped captivity and made his way north to fight for supremacy against rival Qajar khans. In 1785, he emerged victorious and established his capital at Tehran, located near the Qajar tribe's historic grazing lands in Azerbaijan and Mazandaran. In the next ten years, he embarked on campaigns against rival khans for mastery in Iran. He had himself proclaimed shah in 1796, but he was not to enjoy his new title for long: he was murdered by two slaves in June 1797. He had previously arranged for succession by his nephew Fath Ali to prevent the sort of destructive dynastic struggles that doomed would-be rulers after Nadir Shah and Karim Khan. The chief challenge facing Fath Ali Shah was not internal unrest – he ensured stability by placating powerful kinsmen with posts as provincial governors – but external aggression. In the early 1800s, the Qajars became embroiled in rivalry among the European powers. To the north, Russia was expanding down the shore of the Caspian Sea. To the south and east, the British were strengthening their position in the Gulf and India. During the Napoleonic Wars, Britain and France jostled for advantage in Iran. Between 1801 and 1814, the Qajars signed four treaties, first with Britain, then with France, and then again with Britain. In each instance, the Qajars' primary interest was to find an ally that would help them in their struggle with Russia for control over Georgia. Despite their efforts to navigate the rapid turns in European diplomacy that characterized the Napoleonic era, the Qajars suffered a major defeat in 1812 to the Russians. In its aftermath, Russia extracted extensive territorial concessions in the Caucasus under the Treaty of Gulistan (1813), the first time a European country imposed harsh terms on Iran, auguring a new phase in the history of relations between Iran and the West.

Ch.1 difference Shah + other rulers

turn internal probs outward

THE OTTOMAN EMPIRE

Historians have long framed Ottoman history in the eighteenth century as a story of decadence and decline. The decline scenario depicts an empire ruled by weak sultans, ridden with decaying military and administrative institutions, plagued by provincial insubordination, and beset by aggressive European neighbours bent on territorial expansion at Istanbul's expense. In the last 20 years, historians digging in Ottoman archives have challenged the image of an empire in decline. Instead, they note that land-based empires in general – the Habsburgs and the Romanovs as much as the Ottomans – suffered chronic

Otto decline? specific vs general

fiscal shortfalls that diminished their capacity to pay for essential military and security operations that guarded borders
and ensured domestic tranquillity. Imperial rulers, statesmen
and administrators responded by experimenting with institutional modifications and by adjusting relations between centre
and provinces. Moreover, the image of Ottoman might in the
fifteenth and sixteenth centuries may have been exaggerated.
Istanbul never firmly controlled remote and dispersed
communities inhabiting deserts and mountains: the costs of
mounting military expeditions and maintaining garrisons
outweighed the benefits of direct rule over territory on the mar-
gins. From Istanbul's vantage point, Baghdad was a remote,
frontier capital, more than a thousand miles away, holding
the line against Iran. It did not offer abundant agricultural
revenues or a pool of manpower, resources that the Ottomans
found closer at hand in their European and Anatolian domains.
European aggressiveness and the value of Ottoman possessions
in the Balkans and Danubian provinces made defence of the
empire's north-west frontiers a priority.

Between 1715 and 1792, Istanbul fought four major wars
against Russia and Austria. The concentration of manpower and
treasure on those wars meant less attention to the Arab provinces like Iraq, where the mountain redoubts of the Kurds and
the desert and marsh retreats of Arab tribes lay beyond the reach
of firm Ottoman control. At most, Istanbul expected occasional
payment of tribute and security for travellers and outlying villages. When Istanbul was distracted by war or political distur-
bance, these populations refused to pay tribute, asserted power
over trade routes, extorted protection payments from merchants
and towns, plundered caravans and cities, and at times seized
control. In the eighteenth century, Istanbul's frequent wars with
Europe and fiscal weakness, exacerbated by those wars, eroded
its capacity to keep unruly tribesmen at bay by direct means.
Consequently, indirect rule became a sufficient instrument to
maintain some degree of authority to guard frontiers, keep trade
routes open (usually), and extract taxes or tribute, however
sporadically. From Istanbul's perspective, indirect rule was not
ideal, but it was preferable to losing a province altogether, either
through secession or foreign conquest.

In the first two decades of the eighteenth century, Iraq was
firmly in the hands of Hasan Pasha, an experienced administra-
tor trained at Istanbul's palace. Ottoman authority in Iraq had
been on shaky ground in the decades since the Safavid occupation of 1624–38 and the Afrasiyab clan's rule in Basra. Hasan
Pasha shored up his power by purchasing and training a corps

of slaves, Mamluks, from Georgia. Military slavery in Muslim politics went back to early ninth-century Abbasid Baghdad. It was a proven method of creating an effective corps of soldiers dependent on and loyal to their master. The Saljuks had shifted from depending on tribesmen to military slaves (*ghilman*) in thirteenth-century Anatolia. The early Ottoman emirs likewise included military slaves in their armies.

Hasan Pasha's corps of Mamluks closely resembled early Ottoman practice, whereby tutors gave young slaves a broad education to prepare them for filling administrative roles, in addition to training in military arts. Istanbul was satisfied with the stability he achieved, leaving him in his post until he died in 1723 in the course of leading an Ottoman invasion of Iran. Such a long tenure as provincial governor was a sign of Istanbul's willingness to depart from the custom of two or three year rotations. Another departure from custom was Istanbul's recognition of Hasan Pasha's son Ahmad as the new governor. Hereditary governorship also worked for a time in Mosul and Damascus during this period. In Ahmad Pasha's case, he had already served as deputy governor in Basra, and he remained the governor of Baghdad for an eventful quarter century that witnessed a revival of Ottoman–Iranian warfare following the collapse of the Safavids and the rise of Nadir Shah.

The period of hereditary governorship ended with Ahmad Pasha's death in 1747, but not in a way that Istanbul expected. The Ottomans tried to restore central control by appointing an imperial official as governor of Baghdad, but Ahmad Pasha's Mamluks were determined to maintain their autonomy and they rallied to the governor of Basra, the Georgian Mamluk Suleiman Abu Laila. He led a coalition of Mamluks and Arab tribesmen to occupy Baghdad and forced Istanbul to recognize him as governor. Mamluk governors ruled Iraq from that point until 1831. While providing continuity in Baghdad, the Mamluk regime faced a variety of challenges. The Muntafiq tribe alternated between cooperation and rebellion, sometimes cutting communications and trade routes. The Banu Ka'b tribe east of Basra frequently strained the deputy governor's military resources in the south. The Mamluks themselves formed rival factions that disputed leadership at times of succession. Perhaps the worst circumstances to confront the Mamluks struck Basra in the 1770s. A devastating plague in 1773 killed thousands and brought trade to a halt. Before normal life could resume, Basra underwent a long siege and occupation by Karim Khan's unruly forces. The Zand ruler's death in 1779 opened the way for the Ottoman Mamluks to restore stability to Basra.

Suleiman the Great

Mamluk Factio

The most illustrious Mamluk was Suleiman the Great, appointed by Istanbul to govern three provinces Baghdad, Basra and the Kurdish region of Shahrizor. For twenty years, he maintained order on the Iranian frontier and along the caravan routes in the face of the perennial challenge of restless nomadic tribes. After Suleiman the Great, quarrels among Mamluk factions led to a series of short-lived governorships. Four Mamluk governors came and went in 14 years before Daud Pasha restored stability in 1816. He faced a major challenge when the Qajars invaded Iraq in 1821. A two-year war ensued that ended in stalemate and confirmation of borders set by the 1639 Treaty of Zuhab. Daud Pasha's satisfactory defence of imperial territory underscored the efficacy of the Mamluk regime in Iraq in spite of spells of instability.

Twelve Shi'ism

While political conditions never really settled down in this period, a lasting change did take place far from Ottoman provincial capitals in the countryside around the Shi'i shrine cities, Najaf and Kerbala: the conversion of many tribesmen in southern Iraq to Twelver Shi'ism. Tribal migrations from Arabia in the 1700s had a billiard-ball effect on patterns of tribal distribution in the Iraqi desert south of the Euphrates. Sections of tribes began to settle in villages and towns near the shrine cities, presenting opportunities for Shi'i clerics to proselytize.

Southern Iraq goes Shi'i

Conversion to Shi'ism was a gradual process, occurring through developing the custom of visiting the imams' shrines and participating in Ashura celebrations. Shi'i teachers welcomed tribal boys to their study circles and their former pupils became conduits for strengthening ties to communities scattered throughout the countryside. By the mid-1800s, the combination of demographic trends – migration and settlement – and Shi'i proselytizing resulted in southern Iraq's transformation into a primarily Shi'i region.

EUROPEAN COMPANIES AND ARAB SHEIKHS

The disorder that engulfed Iran after the Safavid dynasty's collapse presented challenges to European traders at Bandar Abbas. The Iranian market for Asian and European goods contracted, erratic security constricted overland trade, and supplies of raw materials for export dwindled. Traders hoped that political conditions would improve; therefore they were willing to endure short-term losses because of the expense of re-establishing

[handwritten annotations: "English relocate when shit hits fan / overtake Dutch", "↪ also Barter, Dutch only cash"]

trading posts if they withdrew. Furthermore, rivalry between the Dutch and English spurred them to persevere in order to prevent one another from gaining advantage. Only when conditions deteriorated rapidly after Nadir Shah did the Companies search for alternative bases. They found Arab sheikhs at the northern end of the Gulf eager for European traders to set up factories in order to increase commercial traffic at their ports. In 1753, the Dutch established a factory on Kharg Island off the coast of Bandar Rig, paving the way for withdrawal from Bandar Abbas six years later. In 1763, the English transferred Gulf headquarters from Bandar Abbas to Basra and established a trading post at Bushehr. In essence, by relocating operations, the European Companies followed the practice of so many Gulf merchants through the ages when confronted with intolerable conditions. But hopes for stability at their new posts foundered on rivalry between the Arab sheikhs and the failure of Ottoman and Iranian rulers to establish secure conditions.

In the short run, the relocation of European operations from Bandar Abbas to northern ports did two things. First, it put the Companies on firmer footing to continue their competition with one another. In that contest, the Dutch began to fall behind. By the mid-1700s, the English Company was in a stronger financial position than the Dutch to cope with annual fluctuations in political and economic conditions. For one thing, its traders found that English woollen goods fared quite well in the Iranian market. Furthermore, the English Company's willingness to negotiate barter deals and to extend credit to Gulf traders gave them an edge over the Dutch, who dealt only in cash. Finally, the Dutch Company's directors in Amsterdam showed little inclination to expend scarce resources on forts to maintain its position in a market where profitability was so uncertain. *[handwritten: "Dutch w/draw"]*

The second effect of transferring Company operations was to shift the centre of commercial activity to the sphere of Arab sheikhdoms at Bushehr and Bandar Rig. Al Madhkur, the rulers of Bushehr, migrated from Oman in the 1600s. The Banu Sa'b, also originally from Oman, controlled nearby Bandar Rig, where they served the Safavids as tax collectors. In the broad sweep of Gulf history, these sheikhdoms came and went without making much impact, but for roughly half a century, their mastery of local terrain and small warfare tactics meant that European merchants and Muslim rulers had to deal with them. It is an important point to keep in mind in order to avoid the mistake of reading into the eighteenth century the completely different power balance of the nineteenth century when Europeans possessed superior military and technological resources. In

Handwritten annotations:
Arabia not profitable Dutch leave
Eng stay bc India + France - Micro colonialism
w/out firm empire - local Sheiks dominate

fact, the eighteenth century chronicles are filled with accounts of skirmishes between coastal sheikhs, European (English and Dutch) forces, and Ottoman and Iranian authorities. Lacking the means to sustain large garrisons on the coast, the Muslim powers resorted to sporadic military expeditions that the sheikhs eluded by escaping to islands or into the desert and marshes. Inevitably, military demands elsewhere led the Ottomans and Iranians to either reduce or withdraw garrisons, opening the way for fugitive sheikhs to return. The English and the Dutch tried as much as possible to stay out of local conflicts but were sometimes drawn in, either by the threat of losing permission to trade or by attacks on their ships and factories. In the end, the Dutch calculated that the Gulf trade was not worthwhile and pulled out. Neither did the English prosper, but they stayed in order to protect communications with India and to keep out the French.

Bushehr began its rise from obscurity in 1734 as Nadir Shah's choice for a naval base due to its proximity to Basra and Bahrain. The Dutch established a small trading post and soon found themselves courted by Arab sheikhs hungry for the customs revenues that followed shifts in the flow of goods. Local rivalry heated up in the 1750s when the sheikh of Bandar Rig, Mir Nasir, had a falling out with Bushehr's Sheikh Nasir ibn Madhkur over the share of revenue from Bahrain, which they had conquered in tandem. The Dutch trade, while quite small from Amsterdam's perspective, was a prize for the Arab sheikhs, and Mir Nasir invited the Dutch Company to set up a factory on Kharg Island, a few miles off the coast of Bandar Rig. Soon after the Dutch arrived, dynastic strife erupted at Bandar Rig. Mir Nasir's son Mir Muhanna murdered him and then expelled European traders from the port, but left the Dutch island outpost alone.

The Dutch soon found themselves embroiled in a protracted contest between Mir Muhanna and Karim Khan. In 1757, Karim Khan sent a force to capture the Arab sheikh, but he escaped to a small island whence he raided the shipping of the Dutch and other traders. Unable to reach the Arab sheikh's island redoubt, Karim Khan withdrew his forces, whereupon Mir Muhanna returned to Bandar Rig and took to robbing caravans plying the route between the coast and Shiraz. Karim Khan made a second attempt against the troublesome sheikh in 1765, but once again the sheikh escaped. Karim Khan then leaned on the Dutch to lend naval assistance for an attack on the sheikh's island retreat, threatening to ban Dutch imports if they refused. The Dutch complied, but their joint assault with Karim Khan's men was routed by Mir Muhanna. He then punished the Dutch by expelling them from Kharg Island. He now dominated the northern Gulf, imposing tolls on shipping and plundering caravans. He met his end in 1769 when members of his own clan rebelled against him, forcing him to flee to Basra where an Ottoman patrol picked him up and delivered him to the deputy-governor of Basra, who put him to death by strangling.

Compared to the travails that afflicted the Dutch Company, the English Company's fortunes at Basra were only slightly better. The difficulties of pursuing profits and avoiding political entanglement emerge from the twists and turns in a minor war along the Ottoman–Iranian frontier. The Banu Ka'b were nominal subjects of Iran who roamed the marshlands east of Basra, preyed on merchant vessels, and occasionally raided the outskirts of Basra. Their depredations were a regular nuisance tolerated by English traders. In 1765, however, Banu Ka'b tribesmen seized three Company ships, prompting the East India Company's Bombay Presidency to dispatch a naval force with the mission either to retrieve the ships or crush the tribe. The expedition turned into a fiasco for the English. For one thing, the Company depended on the Ottomans to supply its land forces but it proved impossible to coordinate operations with them. For another, the Banu Ka'b's mastery of terrain and tactics made them a more formidable enemy than the English expected. Their familiarity with the multitude of tiny creeks and hideouts in marshes enabled them to escape when outnumbered; their small vessels gave them superior mobility to manoeuvre around the larger, slower English ships; and the English troops were too few to hold onto villages and strongholds abandoned by the Banu Ka'b. Moreover, when the English finally did corner them, the Arab warriors mounted stiff resistance and forced the English to retreat.

The Banu Ka'b also proved masters of political manipulation. They invoked Karim Khan's protection, and he insisted that the Ottomans and the English withdraw from his territory, promising that the Banu Ka'b would pay restitution to the English Company, which never materialized. Finally, the Ottoman governor of Basra was forced to appeal to the Banu Ka'b for aid against an imminent attack from another powerful Arab tribe. Since the English Company's priority was the security of Basra, it agreed to the Ottoman governor's request that it cease operations against the Banu Ka'b. The whole affair was symptomatic of the European traders' precarious position during this era.

THE FIRST SAUDI EMIRATE

Before the rise of the first Saudi state in the mid-1700s, Central Arabian politics rarely impinged on the Gulf. In fact, the Banu Khalid tribal confederation of al-Hasa dominated the towns and tribes of the interior, exacting tribute and loyalty. The balance of power between Najd and the Gulf shifted with the rise of the Saudi emirate in the second half of the eighteenth century. Before then, the Al Saud rulers of al-Dir'iyya were part of a patch-work of petty chieftaincies. The turning point in their politi-cal fortunes was their embrace of the teachings of a reformist preacher in 1744. The preacher, Muhammad ibn Abd al-Wahhab (1703–92), had suffered expulsion from two other towns before finding refuge with Al Saud. The native of a nearby town, Ibn Abd al-Wahhab came from an extended family renowned for religious expertise. After early studies with his father and uncle, he travelled to the holy cities, as was common for ambitious religious pupils in Najd. He then went to study with sheikhs in Basra, where he began his vocation of calling for the revival of correct worship untarnished by innovations. When he returned to Najd, he settled in a town where his father was the religious judge. Ibn Abd al-Wahhab refrained from launching a campaign for religious purification as long as his father was living, appar-ently in deference to him. In 1740, though, his father died and Ibn Abd al-Wahhab began attacking beliefs and practices he con-sidered idolatrous violations of believers' duty to worship God alone.

Reformist preachers had appeared in many times and places in the course of Islamic history. Few created so much contro-versy as did Muhammad ibn Abd al-Wahhab because of his view that the Muslims of his era were not merely lax or misguided but, in fact, unbelievers. Were his views a matter of debate confined to the realm of religious teachers, they would not have spilled into the political realm. But Ibn Abd al-Wahhab was determined to secure the support of a ruler to enforce his views. Consequently, prominent religious scholars in the holy cities, al-Hasa and Basra, composed epistles denouncing him and condemning his ideas as heretical, indicating their peculiar-ity by calling his teachings 'Wahhabi', a name that would stick through the ages in spite of his and his followers' protestations that they merely called to pure worship of God, untainted by intercession or exalting any creature but God.

The religious controversy that unfolded in exchanges of epis-tles continues to the present. It centres on Ibn Abd al-Wahhab's insistence that proclaiming belief in one God and Muhammad as his prophet along with performing the ritual duties of prayer and pilgrimage, alms and fasting do not suffice to make someone a Muslim. If one did not refrain from practices that imply worshipping a being other than God, then one was an idolater whose blood could be shed and property plundered. The practical effect of this doctrine was to make his political enemies infidels rather than Muslim foes. This may have injected a more effective sense of esprit de corps in the first Saudi state than was possible under customary chieftainships built on ties of kinship and personal loyalty, but it also engendered lasting enmity in the hearts of Muslims attached to the customs that Ibn Abd al-Wahhab denounced as polytheism. Thus, by so sharply defining political boundaries in terms of adherence to a doctrine and loyalty to a ruling lineage, the Wahhabi mission strengthened the internal cohesion of its members and alienated Muslims standing against it.

The alliance between Muhammad ibn Abd al-Wahhab and the Saudi chieftains of al-Dir'iyya came about as a result of the preacher's expulsion from al-Uyaina. In 1744, the Banu Khalid sheikh of al-Hasa, whose sway extended to a number of Najdi settlements, ordered the sheikh of al-Uyaina to expel Ibn Abd al-Wahhab. By then he had attracted supporters in several towns, including al-Dir'iyya, so he went there to see if he might find a secure base for his mission. Exactly why Emir Muhammad ibn Saud made his pact with Muhammad ibn Abd al-Wahhab is impossible to say with certainty. The earliest Saudi sources indicate that members of Al Saud had already embraced the reformer's teachings. In any event, the chieftain and the preacher agreed to support each other: wherever Al Saud ruled, they would establish Ibn Abd al-Wahhab's teachings; and whoever supported those teachings would back the Saudi political enterprise. The pact had the effect of converting skirmishes between minor Arabian powers into an expansionist jihad in the path of God against the forces of idolatry.

The first phases of Saudi expansion through conquest were slow: it took nearly three decades to consolidate power in southern Najd. Throughout Muhammad ibn Saud's reign, his forces did not have an advantage over nearby chieftains like Riyadh's Dahham ibn Dawwas. Resistance to the Wahhabi mission was just as hard to overcome, as religious scholars bolstered chieftains to reject calls from al-Dir'iyya for alliance or subordination. One of the most determined adversaries to Ibn Abd al-Wahhab's teachings was his own brother, Suleiman, who composed an early polemic condemning the reformist doctrine. It was under Emir Abdulaziz ibn Muhammad (r. 1765–1803) that the Saudi polity expanded beyond the immediate vicinity of al-Dir'iyya.

Expansion was slow, in part because defenders of well-stocked fortified towns could outlast the will of attacking forces. A patient Saudi strategy of frequent raids wore down one settlement after another. Wherever the Saudis ruled, religious teachers who refused to embrace Wahhabi doctrine departed, finding refuge with like-minded Muslims in the holy cities and Iraq. Ibn Abd al-Wahhab appointed judges and teachers loyal to his views, thereby planting the seeds of doctrinal domination that last to the present. A turning point in Saudi fortunes occurred in 1773 when Riyadh fell, removing a nearby enemy that had prevented Saudi forces from straying too far from their home base.

The next major adversary was the Banu Khalid sheikhs of al-Hasa. They had warily tracked Saudi expansion in Najd as a potential threat but they lacked the military capability to overcome well-fortified strongholds. Starting in 1784, Saudi raids probed the borders of al-Hasa, encroaching on the Gulf for the first time. Emir Abdulaziz took advantage of feuds among Banu Khalid sheikhs. In alliance with a dissident faction, he launched an attack in 1789 that swept his enemy's warriors from the battlefield, but the Saudis did not have the means to conquer fortified strongholds in al-Hasa. Further raids gave the Saudis a foothold in the regions' smaller towns, an essential step to final conquest, which they achieved in 1795.

Saudi forces now controlled Eastern Arabia's richest agricultural zone and a strategic position on the Arabian shore. When they launched raids into southern and central Iraq, the Mamluk governor Suleiman Pasha responded with counteroffensives, but they failed to expel the Saudis from al-Hasa. In 1802, the Saudis carried out a devastating attack on the Shi'i shrine city of Kerbala, left defenceless when its Mamluk garrison fled. Sectarian enmity turned the raid into a massacre, as Saudi forces killed around 5,000 inhabitants, sparing neither women nor children. In addition, they looted treasures from Imam Hussein's shrine. Apart from poisoning Shi'i attitudes towards the Wahhabis, the Kerbala raid fuelled a revenge attack: in 1803, a survivor of the massacre assassinated Saudi Emir Abdulaziz ibn Muhammad.

In the first years of the nineteenth century, Saudi warriors continued to advance on all fronts, from the outskirts of Damascus to Muscat. The high point of Saudi expansion came with the conquest of Mecca and Medina in 1806. The advent of Wahhabi power meant a strict regime of moral and ritual propriety. The Saudis razed domes over the graves of saints and imposed compulsory attendance at congregational prayer; tobacco consumption was prohibited in public places. Their handling of the annual pilgrimage became a matter of broad controversy among Muslims. The Saudis declared they would not interfere with Muslims conforming to their conception of correct pilgrimage rites. Hence, the Moroccan caravan passed muster, but the Saudis blocked the Ottomans when their commander refused to recognize the upstart Arabians' authority to dictate performance of the ancient custom.

The loss of Mecca and Medina was a huge blow to Ottoman prestige, but the sultan was in no position to recover the distant province, no matter how symbolically important. In 1807, the janissaries in Istanbul mutinied and overthrew Sultan Selim III in response to his innovations aimed to strengthen the military. If Hijaz were to be recovered, the task would fall to a provincial warlord, the customary Ottoman tactic for coping with secession and rebellion in Arab possessions. In 1811, Istanbul asked the governor of Egypt, Muhammad Ali Pasha, to recover the holy cities. The Pasha had arrived in Egypt with an Anglo–Ottoman expedition to expel the French, who had invaded in 1798. He then prevailed in a furious power struggle against rival military factions. His ambition impelled him to look to European military advisers to help construct the Middle East's first modern army. Arabia was to be his first military adventure. By early 1813, Egyptian forces chased the Saudis from Medina and Mecca. They took two years to prepare for an invasion of Central Arabia that fizzled out, and then negotiated a truce. The Egyptians used the interlude to reinforce troops and materiel before launching a well-equipped invasion of the Saudi heartland. Their advance was slow but methodical. In April 1818, the invaders arrived at the Saudi capital and put it under siege. The defenders held out for five months before al-Dir'iyya fell in September 1818.

Members of Al Saud and the Wahhabi religious leadership were taken prisoner and transported to Egypt, where Muhammad Ali kept them under close watch. The Saudi ruler, Emir Abdullah ibn Abdulaziz, was sent to Istanbul, where the sultan had him decapitated and his corpse displayed to illustrate the fate of rebels. But a small number of Saudi emirs and Wahhabi preachers escaped into the desert beyond the reach of Egyptian garrisons. The Saudi–Wahhabi Empire that had taken more than half a century to build up through raiding and proselytizing dissolved in less than a decade. In 1820, it appeared to be a spent force.

THE UTUB SHEIKHDOMS IN
KUWAIT AND BAHRAIN

Three of today's Arab Gulf states – Kuwait, Bahrain and Qatar –
can be traced to the migration of a collection of Central Arabian
tribes, known as the Utub, to the Gulf in the seventeenth century. The causes and course of Arabian migrations in different
historical eras are matters of speculation. Drought and pressure
from neighbouring tribes are the usual causes mentioned in the
chronicles. During the seventeenth and eighteenth centuries,
sections of the large Anaza confederation migrated to the Gulf
and the Syrian Desert. The Utub were part of that human wave,
settling at a fishing village named Grane, that later became
known as Kuwait.

By the early 1750s, the Utub at Kuwait had selected Sheikh
Sabah ibn Jabir as their leader, establishing the custom of rule
by Al Sabah that has now continued without interruption for
two-and-a-half centuries. When Sheikh Sabah died in 1762, his
son Abdullah succeeded him and steered Kuwait through a half
century of regional turmoil. The dynastic tradition continued
with his son Jabir's succession in 1812. Kuwait owed its growth
to the penchant for merchants to seek stable, convenient and
inexpensive ports. Its location made it a logical alternative to
Basra, about eighty miles to the north, at times of instability or
difficulty with the local authorities. For example, in 1793, the
English East India Company moved its factory to Kuwait due
to a dispute with the Ottoman deputy governor. This is not to
say that Kuwait was always free of problems: Saudi raids caused
alarm and caravans to Baghdad had to negotiate protection with
Bedouin tribes.

In 1766, when Kuwait was still in the early stages of growth, a
section of the Utub tribe led by Sheikh Muhammad ibn Khalifah
migrated to the lightly populated Qatar peninsula. At the time,
there were a handful of small fishing villages at the northern tip.
Otherwise, Qatar's population consisted of seasonal and year-
round nomads belonging to half-a-dozen tribal sections. Sheikh
Muhammad chose a site close to one of the area's few fresh water
sources for the construction of a new settlement called Zubara
and made it a port for trade in the Bay of Bahrain.

Starting in the 1770s, Kuwait and Qatar grew and prospered,
thanks to instability in other parts of the region. Al-Hasa was a
battleground for Saudi and Banu Khalid forces; during Karim
Khan's siege of Basra, Arab merchants migrated to Kuwait and
Zubara. In Qatar, Al Khalifah drew pearl traders to Zubara with

low taxes. Kuwait's Sheikh Abdullah ibn Sabah viewed the refugees from Basra as resources for expanding commercial networks and he turned Kuwait into a staging point for caravans between the Gulf and Baghdad and Aleppo as well as an entrepot for maritime traffic coming from India. Karim Khan's occupation of Basra led to the first contacts between Kuwait and the English East India Company. Sheikh Abdullah ibn Sabah encouraged the Company to use Kuwait as a staging point for couriers carrying mail between London and Bombay.

When Karim Khan died in 1779, fighting broke out among sheikhdoms on both shores of the Gulf. On the Arabian side of the water, the most consequential development was Al Khalifah's conquest of Bahrain, prized for its pearls and fertile oases. Since 1753, Bushehr's Al Madhkur ruled it on behalf of Karim Khan. From the perspective of Al Madhkur's Sheikh Nasir, the rise of Zubara represented a potential threat to his control over Bahrain. He banded together with the Banu Ka'b and the sheikh of Bandar Rig to conquer Zubara, but Al Khalifah drove them off. Sheikh Ahmad ibn Khalifah then allied with Qatari tribesmen for a counter-attack on Bahrain. In 1783, Sheikh Ahmad's forces took control of the island's two forts and drove off Al Madhkur. It is notable that Bahrainis themselves took little part, if any, in the fighting. Sheikh Ahmad continued to reside for most of the year at Zubara, treating Bahrain as a dependency in a manner similar to the tributary relationship maintained for centuries by outside rulers dating to the Kingdom of Hormuz. While the conquest of Bahrain was a triumph for Al Khalifah, it came at the price of severe internal dissent when the Jalahima clan seceded, perhaps dissatisfied with its share of the spoils. The Jalahima leader, Sheikh Rahma ibn Jabir, settled at Khor Hasan, a tiny fishing village up the coast from Zubara. For the next 40 years, Sheikh Rahma waged war against Al Khalifah and earned a reputation as one of the Gulf's most fearsome naval warriors.

While Kuwait's distance from Najd spared it the full weight of Saudi power, Qatar abuts al-Hasa and Bahrain's proximity to the coast made it vulnerable to invasion. For about 20 years, Al Khalifah struggled to maintain independence in the face of Saudi and Omani efforts to absorb Bahrain into their realms. The difficulties began in 1796, when the Saudis invaded Qatar and overwhelmed Al Khalifah forces. Rather than surrender, the sheikhs and their tribal allies abandoned Zubara and sailed across the bay to Bahrain. Having escaped the Saudis, Al Khalifah confronted a new threat in the shape of the rising power of Oman, whose ruler demanded tribute for the right to pass through the Hormuz Strait, echoing the Portuguese system of passes. Al

Khalifah refused to pay and Omani forces invaded in 1800, forcing Al Khalifah to return to Zubara. Now they approached the Saudis for help against a common enemy. The Saudis considered the request an opportunity to turn Al Khalifah into vassals. A joint expedition in 1801 expelled the Omanis from Bahrain and restored Al Khalifah, who found Saudi rule bearable as long as it was indirect. In 1810, however, the Saudis tightened their grip, and at that point Al Khalifah invited Oman to help expel Saudi forces in exchange for annual tribute. Once the Saudi threat receded due to the Egyptian invasion, Al Khalifah stopped paying tribute and then expelled the Omanis altogether.

OMAN AND THE ORIGINS
OF THE TRUCIAL STATES

Three of today's ruling families in the southern Gulf trace their ascendance to this period: the Al Bu Said of Oman, the Qasimi clan of Sharjah and Ra's al-Khaima, and the Bani Yas of Abu Dhabi. In general, the Qasimi sheikhs and the Al Bu Said sayyids were rivals engaged in a struggle for domination of the Oman peninsula. The Bani Yas sheikhs had their roots in the interior. Because their domain was adjacent to that of the Qasimis, they tended to side with Al Bu Said. The Saudis too played a role in the early 1800s, forging strong ties with the Qasimi sheikhs. The balance of forces was even enough to prevent one power or combination of powers from achieving definitive supremacy, and as a result, the region became the scene of raids and invasions until two external powers entered the scene to impose their wills.

From 1720 to 1750, Oman suffered incessant civil war and foreign conquest before it emerged under a new dynasty – the Al Bu Said – that has endured to the present. The early Al Bu Said rulers confronted the same set of challenges as the Yariba imams: satisfying the expectations of Ibadi ulama, retaining the allegiance of fractious tribes and navigating the shifting shoals of regional power relations. By the early 1800s, Oman's rulers had made the most of opportunities for maritime expansion to emerge as the major Muslim power of the Western Indian Ocean.

The Yariba imamate disintegrated after the death of Sultan ibn Saif II in 1719. A powerful tribal faction backed the late imam's young son, Saif ibn Sultan, while Ibadi purists supported a candidate who vowed to abolish non-canonical taxes imposed by later Yariba imams. Tribal rivalry between Hinawi and Ghafiri tribal confederations intensified the dispute. Civil war tore the country apart for a decade before Saif ibn Sultan II consolidated his position on the coast while the Ibadi ulama and inner Omani tribes set up their own imam at Nizwa. In 1737, Saif ibn Sultan II reached out to Nadir Shah to help defeat the rival imam. A first intervention failed, but a second in 1743 conquered Muscat. Nadir Shah shortly withdrew most of his troops in order to confront the Ottomans in Iraq, leaving behind a small force at Muscat. Opposition to Nadir Shah coalesced around the governor of Sohar, Sayyid Ahmad ibn Said, who expelled the invaders shortly after Nadir Shah's death in 1747. Once he had dealt with the foreign threat, Sayyid Ahmad conquered Nizwa. The Ibadi ulama acknowledged his fitness to rule by electing him imam around 1750. Sayyid Ahmad and his descendants, the Al Bu Said dynasty, have ruled Muscat ever since.

We know little about the Al Bu Said or Sayyid Ahmad's background. He may have been a merchant before the Yariba imam appointed him governor of Sohar. The early years of his rule were consumed with pacifying inner Oman's powerful tribal leaders and defeating rival claimants to the imamate. He then embarked on military campaigns to expand his realm. In the early 1760s, he annexed Oman's Arabian shore, but was unable to subjugate the Qasimi sheikhs of Ra's al-Khaima. For the next half-century, the Qasimis and the Al Bu Said rulers engaged in intermittent warfare to control the ports overlooking the passage between the Gulf and the Indian Ocean.

The last years of Sayyid Ahmad's reign were plagued by dynastic quarrels. He designated his son Said as his successor but two other sons, Sultan and Saif, refused to recognize him and they seized Muscat in 1781. Sayyid Ahmad forced them out and they fled to the Makran coast, which straddles present-day Iran and Pakistan, where they found protection under a Baluchi khan and waited for an opportunity to return to Oman. When Sayyid Ahmad died in 1783, the ulama elected Said to the imamate, as the late ruler had wished, but dynastic rivalries continued to divide the country. While Sayyid Said held the historical seat of the imamate at Rustaq, his own son Sayyid Hamad made a grab for power at Muscat. Yet another member of the Al Bu Said, Sayyid Qais ibn Ahmad, governor of Sohar during Sayyid Ahmad's reign, dug in and staked a claim to the imamate. Of the three sayyids, Hamad was in the strongest position, thanks to Muscat's rising prosperity. Instability at Basra and Bushehr and low customs duties at Muscat drew more merchants to his port. In addition, he expanded his commercial fleet by investing profits in new vessels constructed at shipyards in India.

Sayyid Hamad also laid the foundations for Al Bu Said power in East Africa by controlling Zanzibar and Kilwa. With a foothold on the mainland and a defensible island port, Muscat merchants became the major suppliers of slaves to France's colony at Mauritius (then known as Ile de France), where there were extensive sugar plantations.

The prospect of a new bout of dynastic strife loomed when Sayyid Hamad died in 1792. Sayyid Sultan returned from exile in Makran to seize Muscat, but rather than plunge the country into civil war, he negotiated a division of the realm at a meeting with Said and Qais. They agreed that Said would remain the nominal imam with his seat at Rustaq, that Qais would retain his post as governor of Sohar, and that Sultan would keep Muscat. When Sayyid Said died around 1811, his brothers made no attempt to claim the imamate, leaving it vacant. Sayyid Sultan continued Hamad's focus on turning Muscat into a commercial centre and a regional power. During his time in Makran, he had developed friendly relations with the Baluchis that allowed him to gain possession of the port town of Gwadar. He soon added a second Makran port along with Hormuz and Qeshm to his realm. He rounded out his gains by obtaining from the Qajars of Iran the right to administer Bandar Abbas in return for paying an annual sum. All that stood in the way of Sayyid Sultan's ambition to establish Muscat's domination over the southern end of the Gulf was the Qasimi sheikhdom at Ra's al-Khaima, holding sway from Dubai to the eastern shore of the Musandam peninsula.

The first Qasimi ruler of note was Sheikh Rahma ibn Matar, who developed Ra's al-Khaima in the 1720s. Sheikh Rahma's brother Rashid augmented Qasimi possessions in the 1760s by acquiring ports on Qeshm Island and the Iranian shore. A collision with the Al Bu Said was inevitable because they both sought to dominate the Omani peninsula and the Hormuz Strait. War broke out in the late 1770s, with clashes on land and at sea. Qasimi forces attacked and seized merchant ships bearing cargoes bound for and leaving Muscat, whether the ships belonged to Muscat merchants or others. The rules and conduct of maritime warfare were fluid, resulting in attacks on vessels belonging to non-combatants. For instance, in 1778, a Qasimi squadron captured a British vessel that had been flying the flag of Muscat in order to evade French warships. The Qasimi sheikh sent a message to the English at Bushehr declaring that he had not meant to attack them. It was an isolated incident at the time, but it was the sort of aggression that would lead the English to refer to Ra's al-Khaima's domain as 'the Pirate Coast'. At its height, the Qasimi domain consisted of about two dozen towns and villages stretching from Dubai to Ra's al-Khaima, in addition to a handful of ports on the northern shore.

The development that would tip the balance against the Qasimi sheikhs was the signing of a treaty between Oman and Britain, the first of several diplomatic agreements that put Oman firmly in Britain's sphere of influence. The chief impetus for the Treaty of 1798 was Britain's desire to curtail French influence in the Indian Ocean. Up to that point, Sayyid Sultan had no reason to refrain from trading with any European power. With regard to France, he turned a good profit by exporting slaves from Omani-controlled ports in East Africa to sugar planters at Reunion and Mauritius, French possessions off the coast of Madagascar. The outbreak of war between revolutionary France and England in 1793 turned the Indian Ocean into a European battleground and political chessboard. The English suspected the French of seeking Sayyid Sultan's permission to establish a trading post at Muscat. In order to deny France a foothold at the strategic port, the English Company threatened to close Surat and Bombay to Omani traders. Sayyid Sultan needed to preserve access to his primary markets, so he signed the Treaty of 1798, pledging to bar French ships from Muscat. A second treaty two years later granted the Company permission to post an agent at Muscat.

The establishment of formal ties with Britain momentarily strengthened Sayyid Sultan's position against the Qasimi sheikhs. In 1800, however, the tide turned with the Saudi occupation of the Buraimi Oasis, a collection of half-a-dozen villages straddling the political frontiers of the Saudi Emirate, Muscat and Ra's al-Khaima. The Saudis made the oasis headquarters for political and military activities intended to bring the Oman coast under their dominion. The alignment of Arabian powers now had the Saudis, the Qasimis and Al Khalifah on one side and the Al Bu Said on the other. The Saudis organized a two-pronged attack against Oman on land and sea by combining with Al Khalifah and Qasimi sheikhs. To get some breathing space, Sayyid Sultan agreed to pay tribute to the Saudis. He was on the defensive but not defeated when he was killed in an ambush by marauders in waters off Qeshm Island in 1804. The Qasimis then quickly overran Muscat's possessions of Hormuz and Bandar Abbas, putting their ships in position to attack and seize Muscat's vessels heading for Bushehr and Basra.

Meanwhile, Sayyid Sultan's nephew Badr ibn Saif solicited Saudi backing in his bid to win the succession struggle in Muscat. He held power for three years before Sayyid Sultan's son Said assassinated him in 1807. Sayyid Said would go on to rule for nearly half a century and lead Oman to its imperial height with possessions in East Africa, Oman and the Gulf. The Egyptian invasion of Arabia in 1811 drew Saudi forces away from the Gulf, giving Sayyid Said the opportunity to attack Bahrain and expel the rump Saudi garrison. Closer to home, however, he was unable to gain decisive advantage over the Qasimi sheikhs, and the perennial rivals took to raiding one another's ports on either side of the Hormuz Strait, in what appeared likely to turn into long-term, chronic warfare.

THE ASSERTION OF BRITISH POWER

The Egyptian assault on the Saudi Emirate altered the balance of power in the Gulf, but there was no immediate indication that the new alignment would bring a conclusion to the seemingly endless state of war between equally matched powers. The catalyst for the pacification of the entire Gulf was an 1819 British naval expedition against the Qasimi sheikhs. The ferocity and thoroughness of Britain's attack on Ra's al-Khaima and other Qasimi ports were surprising because Gulf sheikhs had become accustomed to European warships plying the waters for 300 years without their having a definitive impact on local power struggles. The British naval campaign of 1819 was something entirely new. To make sense of it requires a detour to developments in Bengal 60 years earlier.

The story of England's rise to a dominant role in the Gulf begins in India. In the mid-1700s, England and France were competing for markets and influence around the globe, including India's Coromandel Coast and Bengal. As they jostled for footholds on the subcontinent, an official in the French East India Company, Joseph Francois Dupleix, developed an effective two-part strategy for advancing his firm's commercial interests. First, he put together a small but disciplined military force comprising French officers and Indian soldiers that bested the larger but less cohesive forces of Indian rulers. Second, he used financial inducements and coercion to wield influence over Indian allies, Hindu rajas and Muslim emirs who maintained the symbols and ceremonies of political authority while Dupleix operated behind the scenes to profit from trade concessions.

The English Company learned Dupleix's methods and applied them in Bengal, India's most populous and productive region. In 1756, the Muslim ruler of Bengal, apprehensive about the East India Company's rising influence, mounted an attack on its factory in Calcutta and stuffed 66 men into a dungeon. Forty-two of the prisoners perished overnight in the Black Hole of Calcutta. In response, the Company summoned Robert Clive to restore the Company factory. Taking a leaf out of Dupleix's book, he colluded with disgruntled local bankers and notables to pave the way for a decisive victory over the Muslim ruler at the Battle of Plassey on 23 June 1757.

Afterward, the new Muslim ruler found himself dependent on the Company's military forces, so he allocated tax revenues to cover their expenses. The English used the income to build a larger army that intervened in local power struggles in order to increase trade and gain access to more land revenues. As the Company augmented the scope of its revenue collection, its complement of native soldiers, or *sepoys*, grew from 25,000 in 1768 to 65,000 in 1814. The sepoy units provided the Company with a mass of well-trained troops known for their discipline under fire and loyalty to their English officers. In addition to building a large military force, the Company created a substantial naval force in 1754, the Bombay Marine. Although the impetus for establishing the new fleet came from the need to ward off attacks by a Hindu warlord, the Bombay Marine, along with sepoys, would become the Company's instrument for pacifying the Gulf.

These developments in India were at most dimly perceived in the Gulf. The first sign of Britain's new power came in 1808, when Qasimi sheikhs attacked English merchant ships. The English responded by teaming up with Oman to carry out a punitive attack on Qasimi ports on the Arabian and Persian shores, destroying dozens of vessels and pummelling Ra's al-Khaima with naval bombardment. The retaliation inflicted a painful but not mortal blow to the Qasimis, in part because the Company's Bombay military resources were concentrated on reducing the Maratha confederacy in India.

The British raid of 1808 coincided with a change in Qasimi leadership. The Saudis had imposed their authority over the Qasimi realm and decided to depose Sheikh Sultan ibn Saqr and replace him with a cousin, Sheikh Hasan ibn Rahma. Sheikh Sultan was transported to al-Dir'iyya while the Saudis helped Sheikh Hasan rebuild Ra's al-Khaima. By 1813, Sheikh Hasan was sending ships into the Gulf and the Indian Ocean on expeditions to plunder commercial vessels. The Qasimi fleet was indiscriminate in its attacks, striking ships from Yemen to Zanzibar. In 1816, they seized and plundered three Indian merchant ships from Surat, assaults that boomeranged because they made the English determined to completely destroy Qasimi power.

Moreover, the entire political landscape of Arabia shifted dramatically in September 1818 when Egyptian forces vanquished the Saudis. Bereft of his primary ally, Sheikh Hasan was helpless in the face of a second, larger Anglo–Omani force that appeared offshore in December 1819. By that time, the Company had defeated the Marathas, so it could afford to assemble a much larger force than before. Sir William Keir commanded a fleet of 11 warships and 3,500 men. The British assault on Ra's al-Khaima began on 3 December 1819. Sheikh Hasan ibn Rahma's forces mounted stiff resistance before surrendering on 9 December.

The destruction of Qasimi sea power was the beginning of Britain's definitive ascent in Gulf affairs. At Ra's al-Khaima, Keir deposed Sheikh Hasan and reinstalled Sheikh Sultan ibn Saqr. In January 1820, the sheikhs of Sharjah, Abu Dhabi, Ajman and Umm al-Qaiwain came to meet with Commander Keir at Ra's al-Khaima, where they signed the General Treaty of Peace with the Arab Tribes. The Treaty bound them to refrain from acts of piracy and to establish registers for their ships that British naval patrols could examine to ensure their peaceful purposes. In February, Bahrain too acceded to the General Treaty of Peace. In spite of its official name, the Treaty prohibited piracy but not maritime warfare altogether. It would take another three decades before the British were able to pacify the lower Gulf.

PIRATES AND GREAT POWERS

Before leaving behind this century of constant sieges, skirmishes, thrusts and parries between petty sheikhdoms, short-lived dynasts and exasperated European commanders, it is worth observing for the sake of comparative political typology that the era's dynamics call to mind a famous passage from a distant era and culture. The fourth-century Christian theologian, St Augustine, wrote in his treatise *The City of God*:

> Justice being taken away, then, what are kingdoms but great robberies? For what are robberies themselves, but little kingdoms? The band itself is made up of men; it is ruled by the authority of a prince, it is knit together by the pact of the confederacy; the booty is divided by the law agreed on. If, by the admittance of abandoned men, this evil increases to such a degree that it holds places, fixes abodes, takes possession of cities, and subdues peoples, it assumes the more plainly the name of a kingdom, because the reality is now manifestly conferred on it, not by the

removal of covetousness, but by the addition of impunity. Indeed, that was an apt and true reply which was given to Alexander the Great by a pirate who had been seized. For when that king had asked the man what he meant by keeping hostile possession of the sea, he answered with bold pride, 'What thou meanest by seizing the whole earth; but because I do it with a petty ship, I am called a robber, whilst thou who dost it with a great fleet art styled emperor.'[1]

5 The Era of British Supremacy, 1820–1920

If the eighteenth century was the age of weak empires and chronic disorder, the nineteenth century was the era of reviving empires and the emergence of a stable political order. The British, the Ottomans and the Qajars strengthened their authority over the Gulf. This is not to say that regional conflicts and dynastic strife disappeared, but they were increasingly contained, largely as a consequence of Britain's construction of informal empire governed by a network of treaties that by 1916 encompassed the entire Arabian shore of the Gulf. The period was also notable for two developments in regional political structures and dynamics. First, the Ottoman Empire initiated and pursued measures designed to strengthen its internal coherence by increasing the capacity of the state – specialized government bureaus, uniform regulations and faster communications – and redefining membership in the imperial political community as a matter of horizontal bonds among the sultan's subjects on equal footing. In so doing, the Ottomans pioneered the transformation of Middle Eastern politics from the era of empires, sultans and subjects to one of nations and citizens, a process that was incomplete when the empire was destroyed in the First World War.

The second notable development was the emergence of political contestation between rulers and organized segments of the population. Before the late nineteenth century, politics was a matter of dynastic strife, conflict and negotiation between rulers and populations they sought to control, and fluctuating relations of war, truce and alliance between powers. Around 1900, both the Ottoman Empire and Qajar Iran saw the first modern political movements making demands on rulers for constitutions to set clear limits on their power. The Gulf's distance from Tehran and Istanbul meant that these political changes did not immediately take root, but it was not long before they appeared in a number of Arab sheikhdoms in the 1930s.

The nineteenth century is also the era when economic activity showed a definitive shift to the Arabian side of the Gulf. For centuries, the locus of trade shifted from one location to another along the Iranian shoreline, among some islands at the Strait of Hormuz, and in the al-Hasa oasis. That pattern made sense given the distribution of natural resources (fresh water supplies and arable land) and Iran's pre-eminence in politics and economy: merchants coming to the Gulf sought markets for their wares, and those markets lay in Iran's interior to far greater extent than in Arabia's. But if we look at the present distribution of population and wealth in the Gulf, Iran's coastal centres occupy second place to a string of wealthy cities from Kuwait to Saudi Arabia's Khobar–Dhahran–Dammam conurbation, Bahrain's capital Manama, Qatar's capital Doha, and Abu Dhabi and Dubai in the UAE.

Until the 1700s, the sites of Doha, Abu Dhabi and Dubai were uninhabited; Kuwait was a fishing village; the Saudi cities were small towns; Manama was a regional port. Their settlement and rise to prominence stemmed from growing global demand for one of the region's most valuable natural products, not petroleum, but pearls. Abu Dhabi and its surrounding islands show no evidence of permanent, year-round settlement before the 1700s. Like Dubai, Sharjah and Doha, it lacked sufficient fresh water and arable soil to sustain a sizable population. While rich pearl banks lay offshore, they were harvested by fleets organized by merchants based in Bahrain and Ra's al-Khaima, which possessed sufficient local water and food supplies to support modest-sized towns. During the nineteenth century, the world's appetite for pearls grew so much that the volume and value of Gulf exports made it worthwhile to establish permanent settlements near the pearl banks, even if it meant transporting food and water.

The pearl merchants plugged into perennial trade to India, where Bombay emerged as the global distribution centre, re-exporting the Gulf's gems to Europe and North America. By the early 1900s, the populations of Abu Dhabi and Dubai each exceeded 10,000; small towns by today's standards, but sizable considering their natural resources. It is no exaggeration to state that without pearls, neither town would have evolved at that time. In the later twentieth century, the petroleum boom dwarfed the scale of wealth, population growth and construction that the pearl trade generated. But the basic pattern of concentrating wealth and population in some of the Gulf's most barren stretches is the same, with external demand for a local product yielding enormous riches.

BRITAIN'S INFORMAL EMPIRE

The General Treaty of Peace in 1820 was the beginning of closer engagement between Great Britain and the Gulf. British policy and tactics were governed by strategic and economic considerations that had crystallized at the turn of the century. The British sought to exclude rival European powers from the Gulf, particularly France and Russia, in order to assure communications between India and England. As the British constructed a network of alliances with Arab rulers, they acquired an interest in preserving their independence of the regional powers – Saudi Arabia, Qajar Iran and the Ottoman Empire. They also wanted to guarantee the safety of British merchants and British-protected Indian subjects. To achieve these ends, the British resolved to pacify the Gulf. A third goal of British policy in the Gulf emerged from the abolitionist movement in England. In that instance, one of the earliest Western humanitarian campaigns succeeded at determining foreign policy. Consequently, British diplomats used their influence to nudge the minor sheikhs, the Ottomans and the Qajars to sign treaties for the constriction and abolition of the slave trade.

Implementation of British policy rested in the hands of the Resident at Bushehr and native agents – Indian, Persian and Arab – at Muscat, Sharjah, Bahrain and Lingah. The Resident answered to the East India Company Governor of Bombay, who in turn came under the head of the Government of India, the Viceroy at Calcutta. It was therefore to be expected that London viewed Gulf affairs through the prism of imperial interests in India. Officials in Calcutta regarded the Gulf as a buffer zone, similar to Burma, Afghanistan and Iran, that cushioned India against threats from rival powers. In general, officials in London and Calcutta seldom paid attention to Gulf affairs, leaving them to the Resident and his agents.

To enforce the General Treaty of Peace, the Bombay Marine deployed a squadron to conduct regular patrols from a base on Qeshm Island. One of the challenges before British commanders was distinguishing between piracy, which the treaty banned, and maritime warfare, which was not covered. In dealing with captured pirates, commanders made another distinction, governed by the Treaty, between incidents that targeted vessels under the British flag and those belonging to other parties. In the first instance, they dispatched arrested pirates to Bombay for trial. In the latter, they returned pirates to their sheikhs and obtained compensation for their victims.

The frequency of incidents was tolerable until an outbreak of maritime violence in 1835 precipitated by dynastic strife in Oman. The sheikhs of Abu Dhabi, Sharjah, Ra's al-Khaima and Ajman went on a spree in the Gulf of Oman, attacking vessels belonging to one of the factions in Oman's civil war before broadening the scope of plunder to just about any merchant ship that passed their way. Abu Dhabi's warships in particular seized and plundered nearly twenty merchant vessels, two of them bearing British flags. The Bombay Marine responded by dispatching a fleet to suppress the violence. In a decisive battle on 16 April 1835, the British put Abu Dhabi's war boats to flight. The British then landed at Abu Dhabi and exacted restitution from its leader, Sheikh Khalifah ibn Shakhbut.

It had become clear that the General Treaty of Peace was not a sufficient instrument for pacifying the Gulf. The British tried a different approach reflecting the assumption that a fundamental cause of piracy was the disruptive effect of maritime violence on pearling and trade. Essentially, it boiled down to viewing piracy as a response to economic hardship. To test that supposition, the British proposed a comprehensive six-month truce during the pearling season, banning all maritime hostilities. In addition, the signatories agreed to keep their war boats out of the primary merchant shipping lanes that ran close to the Iranian shore. Not only did the six months pass without incident, but there were no incidents the rest of the year. The sheikhs willingly renewed the truce in 1836 for eight months instead of six. At the end of the second truce, Sharjah's Sheikh Sultan ibn Saqr suggested that Britain sponsor a permanent truce, but the British considered it premature, preferring to take small steps that were likely to succeed rather than an ambitious leap that might fail. As an alternative, they proposed turning the seasonal truce into a renewable, full-year pact. Apart from a few scuffles between pearlers from Dubai and Abu Dhabi, who resented Dubai's secession in 1833, the new arrangement worked well, probably because of the economic benefits that peace brought to the sheikhdoms. In 1843, Britain proposed and the sheikhs signed a ten-year truce. The climate had calmed to the point that the Bombay Marine cut the Gulf squadron to just three ships.

When the end of the ten-year truce approached, the British canvassed the sheikhs to see if they would endorse a permanent peace treaty. In May 1853, the sheikhs of Abu Dhabi, Dubai, Sharjah, Ra's al-Khaima, Ajman and Umm al-Qaiwain signed the Treaty of Maritime Peace in Perpetuity. The Treaty committed them to punish violations by their subjects and to refrain from retaliation against violators from other sheikhdoms, delegating the task of recovering losses to the British Resident. In addition to the economic benefits of maritime peace, the signatories obtained a tacit guarantee that the British would defend them against aggression.

The trucial system represented a new kind of political relationship among littoral rulers, and between them and a dominant power. For centuries, external powers had imposed either tributary relations or direct rule, Local power-holders chafed at outside domination, withheld tribute if they could get away with it, or rose up in revolt. Through trial and error, the British devised a system that combined formal treaty commitments, regular port visits by warships and officials, and non-intervention in mainland politics. Instead of creating pressures for secession and revolt, it stimulated the gradual calming of the Gulf through consensus, not force. Moreover, the trucial system's implicit promise of British protection for the independence of its sheikhs made it attractive to sheikhs still on the outside. Bahrain, Kuwait and Qatar eventually entered Britain's informal protectorate to preserve their independence from what they viewed as more demanding external powers – Saudi Arabia, the Ottoman Empire and Qajar Iran. By freezing conflicts between littoral rulers and preventing conquest by the larger regional powers, Britain's informal protectorate laid the foundations for the contemporary political map of the Arabian shore of the Gulf.

Starting in the 1820s, Government of India officials had to contend with pressures from the abolitionist movement in England. For 20 years, the Viceroy in Calcutta and the Resident in Bushehr maintained that only a gradual approach to abolition would achieve both humanitarian aims and preservation of Britain's imperial interests. The Government of India felt that a comprehensive ban would destabilize the delicate political balance in the Gulf. In 1842, however, the abolitionist Foreign Secretary Lord Palmerston wrested control over the issue. He pushed for total abolition, considering the humanitarian dimension too important to compromise for the sake of the political convenience.

The practical and political obstacles to either gradual or immediate abolition were formidable. Slavery and the slave trade had been part of the fabric of Muslim societies, and the Indian Ocean and Gulf economies for a millennium. Under Islamic law, slavery was a legitimate institution regulated by principles embedded in the Qur'an and Prophetic Tradition. In the early nineteenth century, slavery in the Indian Ocean and Gulf was pervasive. Most slaves were captured in wars and raids on the African interior and transported to East African ports, from Somalia to Mozambique. Buyers from Arabia and India purchased slaves at the ports and shipped them across the waters to a multitude of destinations.

In the Gulf itself, slaves worked on the coast as pearl divers, servants, soldiers, sailors and dock workers. In addition, they laboured in date groves and agricultural fields, especially in inner Oman, and also in Basra, Bahrain and towns on the Iranian coast. To abolish the institution would disrupt economic production, diminish the profits of traders, and reduce the customs revenues of rulers. It would also mark the imposition of Western humanitarian ideals, recently articulated and embraced, at the expense of well-established Islamic principles. Given the complexity and sensitivity of the matter, it was natural that Britain's assault on the slave trade unfolded over the course of decades, and while it did succeed in effecting legal abolition, the pursuit of profit and cultural habit pushed the trade into illicit channels that lasted into the twentieth century.

The British were fortunate that the major stakeholder in the slave trade was their ally Sayyid Said of Muscat. When Al Bu Said Sayyids developed their strongholds on the East African littoral, Omani traders developed contacts with African suppliers to purchase slaves for export to Arabia, Persia and India. In 1822, the British persuaded Sayyid Said to sign the Treaty of Moresby banning the sale of slaves at Zanzibar to Christian (European and American) merchants, and the export of slaves to territories under European control such as the French colony at Mauritius. The treaty also traced a line in the Indian Ocean, known as the Moresby Line, extending from Zanzibar to the north-west coast of India. Vessels with slave cargoes were prohibited east of that line in order to keep African slaves out of British-ruled India.

By signing the treaty, Sayyid Said sacrificed customs revenues and jeopardized his legitimacy by placing relations with a Christian power above a practice sanctioned by Islamic law. When the British came back to him seeking a broader prohibition, he suggested that he should be compensated in some way, with either a guarantee of British military support against enemy attack on his possessions in Oman and Africa or a financial settlement that would enable him to permanently resettle in Zanzibar and renounce his rule in Oman. The British balked at those terms. In 1839, however, they persuaded him to sign a new treaty that moved the Moresby Line westward in order to completely outlaw slave traffic between his possessions in Oman and Africa on one side, and Indian ports on the other.

He also ceded to the British the right to search and seize vessels suspected of violating the ban.

The British understood that if Sayyid Said were the only ruler committed to suppressing the slave trade, it would move to other locations. Thus, in 1839 they prevailed upon the Trucial sheikhs to sign the treaty. The slave trade then shifted to merchants based in Kuwait, Bahrain, Basra and Bushehr. The British then negotiated treaties with Istanbul in 1847 and Tehran in 1848 to suppress the trade. For Istanbul it was a trivial concession, since few Ottoman merchants were active in the region; but the Qajar shah dragged out negotiations, on the grounds that he could not simply banish a practice that Islamic scholars deemed completely legitimate, before consenting to sign a treaty.

Slave traders found diverse ways to elude the ban. Neither Sayyid Said nor the British possessed the means to patrol all ports and sea lanes. Muscat traders shifted operations to Sur, where Al Bu Said authority was weak, and from there sent their human cargoes overland to the Gulf. Furthermore, the treaties only affected ports under Sayyid Said's rule, leaving Somali and Ethiopian ports free to continue exporting slaves. Finally, slave ships took to flying the Persian flag upon approaching Hormuz because the Anglo–Persian Treaty did not grant the British the right to search and seize suspected Persian vessels. In the early 1850s, British envoys urged the Qajars to allow the British navy to search ships and seize slaves found on board. The shah withheld consent for two years before accepting a compromise whereby a Qajar official accompanied a British patrol of Persian ports, thereby affirming the shah's legal authority to enforce the treaty. The tactic proved effective at detecting and fining slave traders.

In spite of cooperation from the Qajars and treaties with all the Gulf Arab rulers, the slave trade did not diminish; this was because of a huge loophole in the treaty with Sayyid Said permitting traffic in slaves between Zanzibar and African ports under his rule. Consequently, Zanzibar became a conduit for Arabian slavers. Its ruler in the early 1870s, Sultan Barghash, resisted closing the loophole because of the economic damage that Zanzibar would suffer. When the British threatened to impose a blockade, he relented and in 1873 signed a treaty that completely outlawed the slave trade in his dominion. To counter the ban's effect on Sultan Barghash's treasury, the treaty included a provision for paying him an annual subsidy.

Slave traders then resorted to yet another tactic to evade the ban by cooperating with France, which was seeking to expand its influence in the Gulf and Africa. The French were courting Oman because it was not part of the trucial system. Allowing Omani traders to fly the French flag to avoid search by British patrols was a tactic intended to undermine London's pre-eminence in the region. That stratagem worked until London and Paris reached an entente in 1904 that resolved their differences, whereupon France stopped allowing slave ships to hide behind its flag.

Calculating abolition's exact impact on the slave trade is difficult because estimates of annual traffic by contemporary observers range widely. One close study suggests that annual traffic between Africa and Arabia peaked between 1840 and 1870 at 2,000–3,000 slaves per year. By 1900, annual numbers fell to under one hundred. It is notable that contrary to the concerns expressed by Government of India officials, the triumph of abolitionism did not harm Britain's political standing in the Gulf.

In the last three decades of the century, Britain responded to assertions by regional and European powers in the Gulf by entering into exclusive and non-alienation treaties with Oman, Bahrain and the Trucial sheikhdoms. The first such treaty stemmed from London's apprehensions about Ottoman designs on Bahrain. After Istanbul had reoccupied al-Hasa in 1871, it asserted claims to Kuwait, Bahrain and Qatar. In the late 1870s, the Ottomans appeared to be intriguing with the sheikh of Qatar and dissident members of Al Khalifah to incorporate Bahrain into their realm. In December 1880, Bahrain's Sheikh Isa ibn Ali firmed up Britain's commitment to his rule by signing an exclusive treaty that obliged him to obtain Britain's consent before having contact with another foreign power. In August 1887, the Trucial sheikhs were the next to enter an exclusive arrangement, in response to Iran's proposal to post an agent in Dubai. The push for signing non-alienation clauses came after a French agent acquired property in Umm al-Qaiwain in September 1891. According to those clauses, signed in March 1892, the Trucial sheikhdoms and Bahrain pledged not to cede, sell or mortgage territory to any foreign power but Britain. When Kuwait signed similar treaties in 1899 and 1904, the British had effectively sealed much of the Arabian shore against foreign rivals and also committed their prestige and power to the integrity of the sheikhdoms.

THE TRUCIAL STATES

The emergence of the trucial system limited but by no means ended political and military conflicts in the Trucial States. Dynastic strife within ruling clans, rivalry between sheikhdoms, and battles with neighbouring rulers (Oman, Saudi Arabia and Bahrain) persisted. By the early 1900s, the sheikhly clans had not settled on rules for succession, or even on respecting the authority of living sheikhs.

The roots of Abu Dhabi's ruling tribe, the Bani Yas, lay in Liwa, a band of oases stretching for about 50 miles in Dhafrah, a region about 60 miles inland. Members of the tribe cultivated date palms at Liwa and roamed the surrounding desert with their herds. According to local lore, some wandering tribesmen discovered extensive subterranean fresh water springs on an island that became known as Abu Dhabi. In the 1760s, their leader, Sheikh Dhiyab ibn Isa, began to settle tribesmen on the island and had a watch tower constructed to defend the new settlement. Bani Yas clans also colonized nearby Dalma Island, which was well situated for fishing and pearling. Around 1800, Sheikh Dhiyab's son and successor, Sheikh Shakhbut, moved from Liwa to Abu Dhabi. In the early nineteenth century, the Bani Yas were rising, thanks not only to their new coastal enclave but also to their close ties to the Dhawahir tribe in Buraimi and the Manasir tribe in Liwa. The Bani Yas thus drew on coastal and interior resources that offered a mix of date production, animal husbandry, fishing, pearling and trade.

For most of the nineteenth century, the Bani Yas and the Qasimi confederacy were the two major sheikhdoms on the Trucial Coast. In the mid-1820s, the Qasimis tried to seize control of Dubai from Abu Dhabi, but the Bani Yas were able to hold on to what was then a minor port. In the following decade, however, dynastic strife among the Bani Yas resulted in the establishment of Dubai as an independent sheikhdom. In 1833, Abu Dhabi's sheikh was murdered by his two brothers Khalifah and Sultan ibn Shakhbut, and the Bani Yas divided into feuding factions. During the fighting, Maktum ibn Buti, leader of the Al-Bu Falasa section, refused to accept Sheikh Khalifah's leadership and migrated with his clan to Dubai. Sheikh Maktum deftly cultivated Qasimi support, which was gladly given in order to weaken the rival Bani Yas. Even more importantly, Maktum persuaded the British to recognize his independence, sealed by his signing of the Maritime Truce of 1835. Nevertheless, Sheikh Khalifah attempted to regain control over Dubai. When the Qasimis blocked his first attempt in 1838, he offered to partition Dubai with them, but Sheikh Maktum was able to break up the budding alliance by intriguing with a dissident Bani Yas sheikh.

Sheikh Khalifah was more successful at strengthening Abu Dhabi's position in Buraimi. The strategic location of the oasis and its rich harvests made it the focus of tribal diplomacy and intermittent warfare among Abu Dhabi, Sharjah, Oman and Saudi Arabia. Abu Dhabi's claim evolved through economic integration in the early 1800s. As its trade and pearling industry grew, it attracted tribesmen from Buraimi for seasonal labour and merchants exchanging dates for dried fish and Gulf imports. The next step in tightening relations came when Bani Yas sheikhs began purchasing date groves in the oasis. In 1839, Sheikh Khalifah attained political influence with strategic intervention in a conflict between two of Buraimi's major tribes, the Dhawahir and the Naim. In return for his support, Dhawahir tribesmen gave him their allegiance, and with that, a foothold. By the time of his assassination in 1845, most of Buraimi's tribes recognized his authority, although tribal allegiance was never a reliable foundation for territorial claims because tribes could easily shift loyalty to another sheikh.

Sheikh Khalifah's murder sparked a new round of dynastic strife. Bani Yas leaders decided the issue by supporting Sheikh Said ibn Tahnun (whose father Sheikh Khalifah had murdered to gain power in 1833). Sheikh Said's maladroit initiatives undermined his predecessor's gains. First, he tried to retake Dubai but again firm Qasimi opposition forced him to retreat. Then, he attacked Buraimi villages under Saudi authority. Riyadh dispatched an expedition to expel him and cement its hold on Buraimi. In 1855, Bani Yas tribal leaders decided that Said was too rash and ousted him, installing in his place Sheikh Zayid ibn Khalifah. As it turned out, Sheikh Zayid would rule for the next half-century until he died of natural causes in 1909.

Sheikh Zayid led Abu Dhabi to the peak of its influence. Through a series of strategic marriages, he cemented alliances with the major clans of Liwa as well as with neighbouring Dubai's Al Maktum. When the Saudis waged a prolonged succession struggle in the 1870s, Zayid seized the opportunity to reassert Bani Yas power in Buraimi, where he again used marriage to political advantage, taking a bride from the Naim tribe that had historically opposed Abu Dhabi. He also deputized the Naim sheikh to collect taxes and ensure security. The centre of Zayid's power in Buraimi was the village of al-Ain, which he captured in 1891 and developed after purchasing land and water rights. For the next few decades, the oasis was divided between Abu Dhabi, Oman and local tribes.

One factor behind Sheikh Zayid's success was the decline of Qasimi power. In the early 1820s, the Qasimi sheikhs still possessed Lingah and Qeshm Island, as well as Sharjah and Ra's al-Khaima, which never fully recovered from the 1819 British assault. But the trucial system eroded the bases of Qasimi power by putting an end to maritime warfare as a way to dominate the southern Gulf. Sharjah's Sheikh Sultan ibn Saqr spent three decades fighting Muscat for control over ports on the Gulf of Oman before a final resolution in 1850 placed the tip of the Musandam peninsula under Muscat and confirmed Qasimi rule over Kalba and Fujaira, enclaves on the Arabian Sea side of the peninsula.

The issue that most weakened the Qasimis, however, was the habit of its sheikhs to plot against one another. Even the venerable Sheikh Sultan ibn Saqr (r. 1820–66) was unable to rein in his own sons, who insisted on governing Sharjah as autonomous sheikhs. Upon his death in 1866, Sharjah came under the joint rule of two half-brothers while Ra's al-Khaima became virtually independent for three decades under their nephew. It became exceptional for the two main Qasimi towns to be under the authority of a single sheikh. With frequent feuds sapping Qasimi power, the way was clear for Abu Dhabi's Bani Yas sheikhs to expand their influence.

In the 1880s, Sheikh Zayid of Abu Dhabi became embroiled in a conflict with Qatar's Sheikh Qasim for control over Khor al-Udaid, a settlement at the base of the Qatar peninsula. Sheikh Zayid's tribal allies, the Manasir, carried out raids on Qatar; Sheikh Qasim retaliated against inland areas of Abu Dhabi. In an attempt to restore calm, the British Resident dissuaded Sheikh Qasim from pursuing efforts to seize Khor al-Udaid. Nevertheless, clashes in the desert continued and reached their climax in 1889 when Sheikh Qasim invited the Saudis and the Rashidis (a rising Central Arabian power) to join an attack on the Liwa oases, massacring villagers and cutting down date palms. Sheikh Zayid rallied tribal allies to force the invaders to retreat. Taxes on Liwa's date palms accounted for a tiny portion of the sheikh's annual revenues, most of which came from pearling and fishing activities, but his power base rested on domination of a broad swathe of the desert that tribal allies frequented, so he could not afford to cede authority to neighbouring sheikhs.

When Sheikh Zayid died in 1909, Abu Dhabi's population was around 15,000 and it was the leading site for pearling in the Lower Gulf. The sheikhdom's tense political situation after Sheikh Zayid threatened to harm commercial interests. The eldest son, Khalifah (d. 1945), was considered the most likely successor, due to his extensive experience in tribal affairs and the wide respect that he enjoyed. But he chose to assume the king-maker role and supported his brother Tahnun as the next sheikh. Tahnun ruled for just three years before dying of illness. Sheikh

Khalifah managed the succession of another brother, Sheikh Hamdan, who ruled Abu Dhabi during the First World War.

While Abu Dhabi enjoyed its ascendancy under Sheikh Zayid, Dubai was beginning in the 1880s and 1890s its rise to influence as a trading post. The ruling Al Maktum clan turned the former possession of Abu Dhabi into a centre for free trade, luring a wave of merchants from the Persian coast when the Qajar government consolidated control at Bandar Abbas and other ports. For instance, when the Qasimi chief at Lingah resisted Qajar rule, Tehran had him arrested and transported to the capital. Dubai's Sheikh Rashid ibn Maktum and then his nephew Sheikh Maktum ibn Hasher offered land for shops and homes to Lingah's Arab, Persian and Indian traders. Their section of Dubai, known as al-Bastakiyyah, added to the sheikhdom's commercial prosperity and foreshadowed the town's later flourishing as a free port.

OMAN

While the trucial system did not incorporate Oman, the implied guarantees to the sheikhs in treaty relations with Britain curtailed Al Bu Said's expansionist designs in the Gulf and redirected them to East Africa. As Sayyid Said spent more time in Zanzibar and devoted less attention to Oman's affairs, the process of dynastic splintering that plagued his predecessors, and the earlier Yariba imamate, threatened to fragment Oman. British officials intervened in Omani politics on several occasions, mediating tensions between the ruler of Muscat and rebellious members of Al Bu Said, and neutralizing the threat that interior tribes posed to the coast with a combination of carrots (subsidies) and sticks (taxing their exports). In the long term, Britain's determination to preserve stability in the Western Indian Ocean and the Gulf had the dual effect of ensuring the continuity of Al Bu Said rule and weakening the foundations of legitimacy due to its close relations with a Christian power. By the time of the First World War, Oman was further partitioned between the Al Bu Said regime on the coast and the Ibadi imamate in the interior.

Britain's 1819 destruction of Ra's al-Khaima cut Oman's major adversary down to size, allowing Sayyid Said to concentrate on building a maritime empire that he envisioned stretching from Bahrain to East Africa. After Bahrain's Al Khalifah sheikhs staved off a series of attacks, the last one in 1828. Sayyid Said

turned to Zanzibar and East Africa. Starting in 1830, he undertook a series of military expeditions to recapture Mombasa from
a dissident Omani clan. Each time he left Arabia, the political
cohesion of his realm frayed under internal and external pressures. Regarding the latter, Sharjah's Sheikh Sultan ibn Saqr
seized some of the ports of northern Oman, and in 1833 forces
from the second Saudi emirate reoccupied Buraimi. The internal
challenges came from two quarters. First, a dissident Al Bu Said
Sayyid, Hamud ibn Azan, carved out an independent niche at
Sohar. Second, Ibadi ulama of the interior fostered a religious
renaissance led by Sheikh Said ibn Khalfan al-Khalili, who supported Sayyid Hamud's claim to the imamate. They joined
forces in a campaign to seize the Batinah coast after Sayyid Said
transferred his court to Zanzibar. He was not eager to deal with
the Ibadi movement, but the British were concerned about the
security of shipping around Muscat and they pressed him to
lead an expedition that forced Hamud to retreat to the interior.

Zanzibar's economy prospered as a result of Sayyid Said's
attention to its clove and coconut plantations. The island's traders also profited from the slave trade. Ships from Europe, India,
Arabia and even the United States called on Zanzibar, making it
the primary source of wealth in Said's maritime empire. Muscat
profited from its standing as the political centre of the empire
and its population swelled to over 50,000. Zanzibar's economic
heyday, however, was brief because of Britain's campaign against
the slave trade.

Soon after Sayyid Said died in 1856, dynastic rivalry led to
the division of his realm between his sons Sayyid Thuwaini
(r. 1856–66) and Sayyid Majid. The former had governed Oman
since his father's transfer to Zanzibar. Sayyid Majid was left in
charge of Zanzibar when Said departed to lead a fatal expedition to the Gulf in 1854. When news of Said's death reached
Zanzibar, Majid refused to acknowledge Thuwaini's authority, so
Thuwaini prepared a naval expedition to assert his claim to the
empire's wealthier half. Before his fleet reached its destination,
British naval forces intercepted it. Lord Canning, Viceroy of
India, presided over negotiations between the rivals that resulted
in the Omani empire's formal partition. To soften the blow of
losing the primary source of revenue for Muscat's treasury, the
agreement stipulated that Zanzibar would render annual tribute to Muscat, a payment known as the Canning Award (1861).
The Award also referred to the rulers of Oman and Zanzibar as
'sultans', not sayyids. Around the same time, Muscat's economy
was further undermined by the growth of British steamship traffic, which replaced Omani merchant ships as the leading carriers

of Western Indian Ocean trade. Oman then fell into a prolonged period of economic decline.

Sayyid Thuwaini's truncated realm suffered not only economic disruption but also political turmoil. He was able to survive threats from the Saudi emirate and the Ibadi imamate because British officials in the Gulf and India preferred Al Bu Said rule at Muscat. When the Saudis had regained control over Buraimi in the early 1850s, the British were concerned that they would raid towns on the Omani coast and they decided to send a naval force to deter them. When Sayyid Thuwaini first came to power, he agreed to pay tribute to the Saudis in return for their refraining from raids against the coast. In 1865, however, the Saudis raised their demand for tribute to take advantage of Sayyid Thuwaini's vulnerability while he was under attack by a rival member of Al Bu Said (Sayyid Azzan ibn Qais). When Thuwaini rejected their demand, a Saudi force plundered the port city of Sur, killing an Indian trader under British protection. A second Saudi raid on other coastal towns resulted in the death of a second British Indian subject. At that point, the British Resident ordered a retaliatory bombardment on the Saudis' main Gulf ports Dammam and Qatif. That put an end to Saudi attacks on Oman.

Shortly after the Saudi threat receded, Thuwaini's son Sayyid Salim assassinated him in 1868. Before he was able to consolidate his position, Ibadi and tribal forces overran the coast and he went into exile. The Ibadi imamate briefly reunified Oman by blending three strands of power: the Qais branch of Al Bu Said, the Hinawi tribal confederation and Ibadi religious leadership. Azzan ibn Qais (r. 1868–71) became the imam with support from the Ibadi scholar Sheikh Said ibn Khalfan al-Khalili. The Ibadi divine then became the chief religious judge and the governor of Muscat, where he imposed a puritanical moral order. The imamate relied on the military strength of the Hinawi confederacy's dynamic sheikh, Salih ibn Ali. Imam Azzan succeeded in recovering Buraimi (thanks to a civil war that erupted among Saudi emirs) and establishing his authority over both the coast and the interior, but his religious–tribal coalition lasted only three years. The imamate suffered a blow when Iranian Qajar forces overran the Omani garrison at Bandar Abbas. Moreover, Muscat residents resented the austere moral regime guided by Ibadi religious leaders, and its Hindu merchants, a small but influential community, some of whom were British subjects, endured beatings, confiscations of property and restrictions on their religious customs. The British refused to recognize the imamate and therefore withheld the Zanzibar subsidy. To compensate for the loss of the subsidy and customs revenues from Bandar Abbas, the imamate attempted to enforce new taxes on the tribes, but that resulted in alienating one of its major props. The British allowed an exiled Al Bu Said Sayyid, Turki ibn Said, to leave India to rally tribes opposed to the imamate. In addition, Zanzibar's Sayyid Majid helped pay for Turki's expedition, which seized Muscat in February 1871 and abolished the imamate (Imam Azzan was killed in the fighting).

During Sayyid Turki's reign (1871–88), British domination over Oman reached new levels. Sayyid Turki faced challenges from Azzan's brother Ibrahim ibn Qais, ensconced at Sohar, Hinawi tribes, Ibadi stalwarts and Sayyid Salim. A turning point in Turki's fortunes came about as a result of his signing a treaty with Britain pledging to ban the slave trade. The British then restored the Zanzibar subsidy, no longer paid by Zanzibar but from the Indian government's treasury. Turki used the injection of funds to mount military expeditions in 1873 to conquer Sohar and the surrounding al-Batinah region. His consolidation of power was interrupted by illness and he departed to Gwadar (an Omani enclave in Baluchistan from 1794 to 1958) to recover, leaving his half-brother Sayyid Abdulaziz as regent. In 1875, Turki was well enough to resume his duties, but Abdulaziz made a bid for power by blocking his return to Muscat. The British, however, backed Turki and forced Abdulaziz to retreat to the interior, where he spent years plotting with tribal leaders for a chance to regain power.

Dynastic intrigue remained a chronic problem for Sayyid Turki. Two of his sons proved loyal governors, but other members of Al Bu Said joined plots against him, and he responded by strengthening bonds with the British. On three occasions (1874, 1877 and 1883), British gunboats helped Turki turn back offensives by Ibadi tribal forces. In 1886, the British made an open declaration that they would counter any effort to depose the ruler, effectively guaranteeing his power, which was limited to the main coastal towns between Sohar and Salalah. The latter was the major port in Dhufar that Turki annexed in 1879 when he installed a governor there. In the context of Al Bu Said's stormy dynastic history, perhaps Turki's most notable success was the unchallenged succession of his son Sayyid Faisal (r. 1888–1913).

Sayyid Faisal began his reign with the ambition of ending dependence on the British and imposing direct authority over the interior. His expedition to seize Rustaq, historical centre of the imamate, was a costly failure and forced him to abandon his quest for more robust rule. To demonstrate independence of

Britain, in part to gain the support of conservative sentiment, he ceased enforcing the ban on the slave trade. British officials, however, were determined to retain paramount influence and they persuaded Faisal to sign the Anglo–Omani Commercial Treaty in 1891, which included a 'non-alienation' codicil against Oman's ceding territory to another power without first consulting Britain, which considered such a codicil necessary to block attempts by European rivals to interfere in what Britain regarded as its exclusive sphere of influence.

Notwithstanding the restrictive clauses in the treaty, Faisal welcomed the establishment in 1894 of a French consulate at Muscat. For the next four years, French influence eclipsed that of Britain. Since the 1860s, French ships had allowed Omani captains from Sur to trade under the French flag, a tactic that accounted for the continuation of the slave trade even after the 1873 ban. Anglo–French rivalry stemmed from the rise of more assertive statesmen in Paris willing to challenge British supremacy in the Indian Ocean, Africa and South-east Asia. Muscat was thus a sub-plot in a broader diplomatic game. In 1898, Faisal agreed to a French proposal to set up a coaling station at a port near Muscat (Bandar Jissah). Lord Curzon, the viceroy of India and an ardent proponent of a vigorous imperial policy, demanded that Faisal revoke the agreement with France. To back up his words, Curzon sent a fleet of gunboats to Muscat and threatened to shell the port. To defuse the crisis, British and French diplomats worked out a compromise whereby the coaling station would serve ships of both powers. Unable to impose his authority over the interior or to loosen Britain's grip on the coast, Faisal became amenable to accepting the necessity of close relations with Britain. A new political agent at Muscat, Percy Cox, arrived in 1899 and proved adept at restoring amicable relations.

In the early 1900s, British officials in the Gulf and India fretted about Oman's role as a transit point in illegal arms trade. A large supply of modern rifles from Oman reached Afghanistan and north-west India, perennial sources of unrest and instability for the Government of India. Likewise, Omani tribesmen became equipped with deadlier weapons than before, tilting the balance of force in their favour. In 1912, Faisal agreed to ban the arms trade in return for a large sum from the British. Many Omanis viewed this measure in the same light as the 1873 ban on the slave trade, namely, as a sign that the ruler was subservient to a Christian power.

A new alliance of tribesmen and Ibadi ulama formed in 1913 to mobilize for an attack on Muscat. In May, a council of ulama

and tribal leaders elected Sheikh Salim al-Kharusi to the imamate, and the ulama announced Faisal's deposition. The imam's
forces unified the interior and seized the passes to Muscat. Britain
responded by sending reinforcements from India to deter an
attack. In the midst of the crisis, Faisal died on 4 October 1913.
His son Taimur succeeded him. The tense stand-off combusted
in January 1915, when the imam's forces attacked Muscat; but
British Indian forces held their ground. With Britain's political
and military energies consumed by the war in Europe, Sayyid
Taimur maintained a tenuous grip on Oman's coastal districts
while the Ibadi Imamate ruled the interior.

SAUDI ARABIA

The Egyptian invasion of Arabia in 1818 crushed the first Saudi
Emirate but not the political forces behind it. First of all, the
Egyptians did not kill or capture all of the Saudi emirs and
Wahhabi ulama. The survivors found refuge with tribal allies as
far afield as Ra's al-Khaima. Second, Central Arabia held no value
for Muhammad Ali Pasha, so the Egyptian garrison withdrew
from al-Dir'iyya after a brief occupation. A Saudi emir, Turki ibn
Abdullah, then appeared from the desert and took over Riyadh.
Muhammad Ali was compelled to send back his forces to chase
him away and set up several garrisons to pre-empt Saudi initiatives. But Emir Turki waged a campaign of harassment that wore
down the Egyptians by raising the cost of stationing and provisioning troops. In 1824, Muhammad Ali gave up and pulled
his forces back to Hijaz. Emir Turki then established himself at
Riyadh, a few miles south of al-Dir'iyya, which the Egyptians
had razed to the ground.

Emir Turki embarked on military campaigns to re-establish Saudi rule over the Gulf coast, but conditions there had
changed since the fall of the first emirate. The English East India
Company – and its naval forces – had transformed political and
military affairs by imposing a maritime truce and by guaranteeing the position of sheikhs with whom it had treaty relations.
Therefore Saudi encroachment on the Gulf would create friction, if not a collision, with the British. At the same time, the
British expressed no interest in hinterland politics or the fates of
sheikhs outside the treaty system. In 1830, Emir Turki conquered
al-Hasa and imposed tribute on Bahrain. And in 1832, he sent
an expedition to reoccupy Buraimi and exact tribute from the

Oman's Sayyid Said. Turki's revival of Saudi political power gave new life to the Wahhabi mission. A grandson of Muhammad ibn Abd al-Wahhab who had been exiled to Cairo was allowed to return to Arabia. Sheikh Abd al-Rahman ibn Hasan presided over the reborn religious estate, appointing judges and teachers to enforce conformity to Wahhabi norms.

Emir Turki's political career was cut short in 1834 when a Saudi cousin, Mishari ibn Abd al-Rahman, assassinated him and seized Riyadh. Turki's son Faisal was leading a military expedition against Bahrain when he got word of the murder. He turned around to march on Riyadh, captured Mishari, and put him to death. Emir Faisal then concentrated on strengthening Saudi rule in Najd, al-Hasa and Buraimi, refraining from any westward thrust towards the Holy Cities that were under firm Egyptian control. He appeared to have a clear path to stability but Egypt's Muhammad Ali Pasha decided in 1837 to invade Arabia once again. This time, he was not serving Istanbul's purpose, for he was in open rebellion against the Ottoman Empire, having conquered the Syrian provinces in 1831. The second invasion of Arabia was part of an ambitious vision to expand his power all the way to the Gulf. Rather than try to subject the oasis settlements and tribes to direct rule from Cairo, Muhammad Ali recruited a Saudi emir, Khalid ibn Saud, to serve as his deputy in Riyadh. At the approach of the Egyptian army, Emir Faisal retreated south, but Egyptian forces caught up with him and captured him. He was then transported to captivity in Cairo.

While Faisal languished in exile, the Ottoman sultan tried to regain control over Syria, hoping that his recently reformed military forces could oust the rebellious Pasha of Egypt. The fighting went badly for the Ottoman army. Not only was its offensive repulsed, but the Egyptian counteroffensive pushed deep into Asia Minor. Muhammad Ali then demanded that the sultan grant him hereditary right to govern Egypt, Syria and Arabia. At that point, the British intervened to shore up Istanbul, primarily out of concern that a drastically weakened Ottoman Empire would come under Russian domination. London persuaded the European powers to support a diplomatic solution to the crisis. The 1840 Treaty of London confirmed Muhammad Ali as hereditary ruler of Egypt if he would withdraw from Syria and Arabia. When the Pasha balked, the British navy occupied Beirut and Acre, putting it in position to interfere with communications between Cairo and Damascus (under Egyptian rule since 1831). Recognizing that he could not defeat the British, Muhammad Ali accepted the Treaty of London and brought all his forces back to Egypt from Syria and Arabia. Without the Egyptian garrison to prop him up, Emir Khalid fell to a rival Saudi emir, Abdullah ibn Thunayan. Meanwhile, Emir Faisal managed to return to the scene. It is not clear whether he escaped or the Egyptians let him go. In any event, he assembled a coalition of settled and nomadic forces that he rode back to power in 1843.

In the second phase of Faisal's rule (1843–65), the second Saudi Emirate reached the height of its influence. He was keenly aware of the limits posed by the new political landscape. Muhammad Ali no longer occupied Hijaz, but the restored Ottoman administration was far more robust than the one his ancestors had defeated in the early 1800s. He also understood that British naval power stood behind the rulers of Oman and the Trucial sheikhdoms. Still, that left plenty of room in Arabia to dominate. The tricky part was figuring out exactly where the limits of British influence lay. Faisal tested those limits in Oman. It was not under formal British protection, but the Resident at Bushehr was committed to preserving the status quo. Furthermore, Oman's ports hosted scores of Indian traders possessing the status of British subjects. Any harm to them could trigger a harsh response. To complicate matters further, Abu Dhabi was firming up its claim to Buraimi. Consequently, for the Saudis to attempt a takeover there meant getting mixed up in local tribal rivalries, Abu Dhabi's and Oman's claims, and behind them, Britain's informal empire. Nevertheless, in 1845, Faisal sent a force to reoccupy Buraimi (during the Egyptian occupation of 1837–41, Buraimi's tribes had expelled a Saudi garrison set up by Emir Turki).

In the next 20 years, Buraimi was the object of political manoeuvring and military struggle in a three-way contest between the Saudis, Oman and Abu Dhabi. In 1852, Emir Faisal sent a large force to Buraimi in preparation for an ambitious campaign to depose Al Bu Said altogether. The British came to the rescue of their long-time ally by urging restraint. Emir Faisal was aware that the British could choke off his access to Gulf trade by blockading al-Hasa ports, so he settled for raising the amount of tribute. The British demonstrated that even though treaties limited their political and military commitments to sea and shore, they sufficed to influence inland political dynamics. They drove the point home forcefully in their 1866 bombardment of Saudi ports to make Riyadh cease its raids on the Omani coast (see above).

The second Saudi Emirate succumbed to the sort of dynastic strife that so frequently afflicted Persian Gulf sheikhdoms. Emir Faisal died in December 1865 and his designated successor, his son and deputy, Abdullah, took over. Because he ascended to power in the midst of the conflict with Britain over Oman, he sent an envoy to Bushehr to meet with the Resident and pledged not to harm British subjects in areas under London's protection: Oman, the Trucial sheikhdoms and Bahrain. Shortly afterward, Emir Abdullah's brother, Emir Saud, disputed his right to rule. Turning the tables on the Saudis now that they were immersed in dynastic conflict, Oman's Sayyid Azzan seized Buraimi.

In 1870, the rebellious Emir Saud expelled Abdullah from Riyadh, setting off a protracted civil war that sapped Saudi power to the point that their vassals, the Rashidis of Hail, were able to overthrow the Saudis and force them into exile in 1891. At the beginning of the civil war, Emir Abdullah went to Baghdad to seek Ottoman assistance. The Ottoman governor, Midhat Pasha, viewed the request as an opportunity to extend Istanbul's power into Arabia. An Ottoman force sailed down the Gulf and in 1871 seized al-Hasa, restoring the sultan's authority after a 200-year hiatus. Meanwhile, Wahhabi ulama raged against Emir Abdullah for violating a principle of Islamic law that prohibits seeking military assistance from infidels (in the Wahhabi view, the Ottomans were infidels for permitting idolatrous customs like visits to saints' tombs). Some ulama, however, considered Emir Saud to be in the wrong for rebelling against Emir Abdullah, whose standing as the legitimate heir Emir Faisal had clearly and publicly endorsed.

As the scholars argued over political theory, Riyadh changed hands several times before Saud died and Abdullah finally consolidated his position in 1876. During the fighting, the Rashidis of Hail extended their sphere of power at Riyadh's expense, leaving the Saudis in control of their capital and some nearby towns. In 1887, the sons of the late Emir Saud made a bid for power, taking Riyadh by force and throwing Emir Abdullah into prison. At that point, the Emir of Hail, Muhammad ibn Rashid, intervened. His powerful tribal army expelled the rebellious princes, released Emir Abdullah and transported him to Hail as an honoured 'guest'. A deputy of Ibn Rashid took over the duties of governing Riyadh. The last gasp of the second Saudi Emirate came in 1891, when Emir Faisal's youngest son, Abd al-Rahman, rallied tribal and settled forces to throw off Rashidi power, but Hail's superior forces crushed the allies at the Battle of Mulaida. The surviving Saudis abandoned Central Arabia to seek refuge in Kuwait.

The impact of the Saudi collapse on Central Arabia was not disruptive. The first Saudi Emirate was vanquished by an invading army in a seven-year war and the invaders sought to stamp out the Wahhabi mission. By contrast, the Rashidis had been reliable vassals to Riyadh, helping Al Saud consolidate their power over the northern reaches of Arabia. They expanded their power piecemeal, awaiting opportunities to encroach on Riyadh's authority. The Rashidis did not wage a long, destructive war. Instead, they stood aside while Saudi emirs fought themselves to exhaustion. Once they supplanted Al Saud, the Rashidis did not introduce a new order. They had embraced Wahhabism and they continued to support enforcement of Wahhabi norms. At the same time, they adopted a more relaxed attitude towards Muslims who diverged from Wahhabism, and in so doing they alarmed some of the more rigorous Wahhabi ulama. Overall, the Rashidi interlude in Central Arabia was tranquil.

The Saudi entourage in Kuwait included Emir Abd al-Rahman's young son, Abdulaziz, only 15 years old at the time of Al Rashid's final takeover of Riyadh. Towards the end of 1901, Abdulaziz departed Kuwait on a mission to regain the Saudi capital. In January 1902, he and his band of roughly sixty men surprised the Rashidi governor of Riyadh. After a brief skirmish, Abdulaziz was the master of Riyadh, setting in motion the rise of the third Saudi state. In the first few years, he consolidated his position in the settlements close by Riyadh, keeping a wary eye on the Rashidis and the Ottomans. Through astute tribal diplomacy and superb battlefield leadership, Abdulaziz managed to revive Saudi power and throw the Rashidis back towards Hail. In 1913, he won a major prize in an expedition to oust the Ottomans from al-Hasa.

At the time, Istanbul's military energies were concentrated on wars against an alliance of Balkan states that were seeking to expand at the sultan's expense. Abdulaziz was aware that he had to tread carefully in the Gulf to avoid antagonizing the British. For their part, the British wished to ensure that Abdulaziz maintained his enmity towards the Ottomans, who entered the First World War on the side of the Entente Powers against Britain and its allies. In 1915, the Saudi ruler signed a treaty with Britain whereby London recognized Abdulaziz as the ruler of Central Arabia and al-Hasa and supplied him with weapons and funds. In return, Abdulaziz pledged to the terms that Britain had with other rulers of the Gulf littoral: to have no contact with another foreign power and to refrain from aggression against rulers under British protection.

THE OTTOMAN EMPIRE

The nineteenth century was a period of institutional innovation and adjustment for the Ottoman Empire. Determined to reassert control over the provinces and defend against European

ends Mellet system

encroachment, Ottoman rulers and statesmen proclaimed new principles for governance based on plans to strengthen military forces, streamline administrative offices, unify law codes, and improve education. The common term used to describe the era of reform is *Tanzimat*, which normally refers to the period from the first general edict issued in 1839 to the political defeat of the bureaucrats driving reorganization in 1876. We can stretch the period of reform at both ends of the traditional dates. The stage for the Tanzimat era was set in 1826, when the sultan brutally eliminated the janissaries, the chief obstacle to thorough change. While the Tanzimat bureaucrats gave way to a resurgent autocrat in 1876, the technical and institutional momentum that they set in motion continued until the empire's demise in the First World War.

At the dawn of the nineteenth century, the Ottomans were in disarray. Saudi forces occupied the holy cities. Serbian rebels expelled imperial forces and obtained Austrian and Russian support to guarantee their independence. Warlords in the Balkans and Anatolia defied the sultan's authority. Starting in the early 1790s, Sultan Selim III had taken steps to strengthen imperial defence with an efficient new style military institution using European advisers, but vested interests at Istanbul opposed the reinvigoration of the sultan's authority. In May 1807, the imperial janissaries mutinied and overthrew Selim. The proponents of reform soon regained the initiative and installed Mahmud II on the Ottoman throne. Keenly aware of his uncle Selim III's fate, Sultan Mahmud II proceeded cautiously at first, but the erosion of Ottoman domains continued in the 1820s when the Greeks launched a war for independence. In that war, the janissaries proved ineffective. To deal with them once and for all, the sultan resolved to eliminate them by building a military and political alliance and a powerful new artillery corps. In June 1826, he provoked a janissary uprising that the artillery and other loyal forces quickly suppressed. Imperial forces followed up with assaults on janissary units in the provinces. The path was clear for the sultan to proceed with the reassertion of his power in Istanbul and of Istanbul's power over its territories.

In Baghdad, the Mamluk governor Daud Pasha presided over the disbanding of the janissaries and their incorporation into the sultan's new army. Unfortunately for Daud Pasha, Sultan Mahmud's vision of central control had no place for strong provincial figures. Daud Pasha refused to hand over Baghdad to an imperial appointee and shored up his defences to withstand Istanbul's attempt to remove him by force. The siege of Baghdad was a brief affair, cut short by the outbreak of plague that decimated Daud Pasha's forces. He wound up surrendering and retiring to Anatolia. Doing more to shore up central authority than installing Istanbul's choice for governor took some time. The 1830s were consumed by the confrontation with Muhammad Ali Pasha. Baghdad Governor Ali Rida Pasha managed to control the city, but for much of his 11 years in office, Arab tribes continued to dominate the countryside. His successor scored a success for centralizing power when his forces wrested Kerbala from the control of a set of unruly Shi'i gangs. But apart from imposing imperial representatives on Iraq's major towns, Ottoman rule in Iraq did not undergo major change until the 1870s.

In 1869, a new governor arrived in Baghdad. Midhat Pasha was no ordinary Ottoman bureaucrat. He already had successful tenures as governor in Balkan provinces, and in the future he would figure as a leader of the movement for constitutional government for the entire empire. During his energetic three-year leadership in Iraq, he put into practice the 1864 Provincial Reorganization Law. He presided over the introduction of uniform administrative bodies at province, district and sub-district levels, each possessing a council for consultation between imperial officials and local notables. He dealt with the powerful Muntafiq tribe by naming its sheikh the chief of a specially designated district in the tribe's historic domain. Major towns saw the formation of municipal councils to tackle matters like roads and hygiene. A recently drafted education law for the entire empire had its initial application with the opening of a handful of schools. Midhat also introduced the first newspaper to Iraq.

The reforming governor's long-term impact was to introduce novel institutions and mechanisms for government authorities to interact with their subjects. No longer filling only military, fiscal and symbolic religious roles, imperial officials sat on councils with local dignitaries to deliberate local affairs, presided over public works designed to boost prosperity, and set up schools to train future public servants and foster a common sense of imperial identity. Such functions and measures were part of a project to more firmly bind together state and society as well as integrate disparate communities. Those communities did not all respond in the same way. Sunni townsmen tended to latch onto advantages for education and representation on councils, in part because of religious affinity with the empire's rulers. Sunni merchants and ulama became part of the new provincial service stratum.

By contrast, Shi'i ulama and their flock both avoided and were not particularly sought to join councils and therefore stood aloof from Ottoman officialdom, alienated by bans on the Shi'i call to prayer that invokes Imam Ali and cursing the first three caliphs. The circumstances of Shi'is in Iraq sometimes caused strains in Ottoman relations with Qajar Iran. In general, the Ottomans tended to mistrust the loyalty of Shi'is. Discrimination against Shi'is and episodic desecration of their holy shrines evoked protests from Tehran. At a grassroots level, sectarian enmity sometimes erupted in attacks on Shi'is, prompting the Qajars to champion their rights, whether they were Qajar subjects on pilgrimage to the shrine cities or Ottoman Shi'is.

Religion proved less of an irritant in Ottoman–Qajar relations during the reign of Sultan Abdulhamid II (1876–1909). His espousal of Muslim unity to resist European aggression meant that he minimized historical differences with Iran. In addition, he promoted symbols of religious unity among Ottoman Muslims to shore up their allegiance to the sultan as the embodiment and guarantor of Islam's worldly standing. In Iraq, he paid for new embellishments at Ali's shrine and excavation of canals around Najaf. Nevertheless, popular feeling occasionally sabotaged imperial attempts to foster Muslim coexistence. For example, a scuffle between an Ottoman gendarme and the attendant of a prominent Shi'i cleric sparked an anti-Shi'i riot in Samarra in 1894. The Qajars intervened to seek restitution on behalf of fellow Shi'is for physical injuries and property damage.

Given Britain's view of its interests in the Gulf, it played a growing role in Iraq's affairs. The East India Company's dominant role in trade through Basra meant that merchants and sheikhs had incentives to form strong ties with Company representatives. The Company installed its first agent in Baghdad in 1798, as part of a strategy to block the spread of French influence. During the Tanzimat period, the British explored ways to modernize transportation and communications in Iraq, which remained an important channel for contacts between England and India. Survey teams explored the Euphrates with a view to introducing steamboats. British interests also ensured the laying down of the first telegraph connection between Istanbul and Baghdad in 1861, later extended through the Gulf to India. Steam power and the telegraph that made communication faster and cheaper had a multiplier effect on the institutional reforms Midhat Pasha initiated: more intensive engagement by political authorities was facilitated by easier communication with each other and the imperial centre. In the 1870s, the possibilities of expanding the reach of Ottoman power on the basis of a more solid framework opened a new chapter in the history of the Gulf.

In addition to introducing a range of reforms to Iraq, Midhat Pasha seized the opportunity presented by the Saudi civil war to extend Istanbul's authority into Arabia. He took Emir Abdullah's request for military support as a chance to recover the empire's position in al-Hasa, largely as a strategic measure to block the expansion of Britain's sphere of influence. In May–June 1871, Emir Abdullah returned to al-Hasa with the military backing of Istanbul. If he expected the Ottomans to depart after installing him in al-Hasa, he was to be disappointed. Instead, Midhat Pasha made him the governor of Najd and created a regular provincial administration for al-Hasa, with headquarters at Hofuf and district centres in Qatif and Mubarraz. The Ottoman recovery of al-Hasa impinged on Qatar as well. Sheikh Qasim Al Thani secured his recent split from Al Khalifah by taking the Ottoman side, agreeing to fly Ottoman flags at Qatar's main settlements and accepting Istanbul's appointment as district governor (*kaymakam*) under the governor of al-Hasa.

Midhat's campaign had projected Ottoman influence in the Gulf to its greatest extent in more than 200 years. As he surveyed the rich oases of al-Hasa, Midhat Pasha envisioned a prosperous district possessing some of Arabia's most valued date groves as well as lucrative pearl beds. He curried the support of al-Hasa's traders and cultivators by keeping taxes low and providing security against nomadic depredations. Ottoman governors after Midhat built schools according to the Tanzimat programme for a uniform imperial education system. The first decade of Ottoman rule was marked by calm and anticipation of economic growth if the desert tribes could be tamed. Unfortunately, Istanbul's chronic fiscal weakness meant that ambitious plans for telegraph lines, naval patrols and land reclamation were never implemented. The Ottoman Empire declared bankruptcy in 1875. In al-Hasa, that meant the only way to cover administrative costs was to raise taxes, a step that damaged relations with the local population, especially when tribal attacks on caravans again became frequent in the 1890s, making tradesmen and cultivators question what exactly their taxes paid for.

In response to the Saudi reconquest of Riyadh in 1902, the Ottomans decided to set up outposts in the heart of Central Arabia in order to shore up their vassals, the Rashidi emirs of Hail, who saw their authority in central and southern Najd rapidly crumble. When Istanbul sent troops to man garrisons in al-Qasim, the northern district of Najd, Abdulaziz ibn Saud announced that in order to avoid a confrontation he would not oppose the initiative. On the contrary, he expressed loyalty to the sultan, and in return, his father Abd al-Rahman, residing in Kuwait, was formally appointed the kaymakam of Riyadh. The Ottoman presence in al-Qasim, however, was very brief. Istanbul lacked funds to supply and pay troops at such remote outposts. They were too few to intervene in the simmering conflict between Rashidi and Saudi forces in the desert. In 1906, the Rashidi emir fell in battle. The Ottomans then pulled out their underfed troops, ceding Najd to Ibn Saud, who continued to profess loyalty to the sultan.

Back in Istanbul, a political earthquake jolted the empire in July 1908. Mutinous army units compelled the sultan to restore the constitution of 1876. The centre of power then shifted from the sultan to the cabinet, which became the object of control for rival political factions. Constitutional governance did not have a chance to ripen before the empire was beset by a series of military crises close to Istanbul. In just five years, a coalition of Balkan states, formerly Ottoman subjects, launched two expansionist wars and Italy invaded Libya. To meet the challenge of the Balkan Wars, Istanbul withdrew about 80 per cent of the troops posted to the al-Hasa garrisons. Ottoman officials and troops retreated to the towns as tribesmen dominated the desert, and townsmen grumbled about insecure conditions strangling trade.

With turmoil in Istanbul and war raging at its doorstep, the constitutional government was willing to relinquish much of the Ottoman claim to Arabia that Midhat Pasha had staked out. In May 1913, Istanbul and London agreed on a formal division of Arabia. The Ottomans gave up Bahrain and Qatar and recognized the autonomy of Kuwait. In return, the British recognized al-Hasa as Ottoman territory, but that became meaningless when Saudi forces seized its towns before the Anglo–Ottoman Agreement was even ratified. Ottoman troops were permitted to evacuate safely and Abdulaziz reaffirmed his loyalty to the sultan, excusing his action as a necessary measure to restore order to the region. In May 1914, Istanbul granted him official recognition as the governor of Najd and Hasa.

BAHRAIN AND QATAR

Al Khalifah's accession to the 1820 Treaty of General Peace committed its rulers to refrain from abetting piracy but it did not bar them from waging war nor did it protect them from external aggression. Due to Bahrain's rich pearl beds and command of navigation along the al-Hasa coast, it presented a tempting prize to regional powers, namely Oman, Saudi Arabia and Iran. Al Khalifah rejected Sayyid Said's demands for tribute and thwarted one attack after another until he gave up after a final attempt in 1828. Having fended off one threat, Bahrain's rulers confronted a new one when the Saudi ruler Emir Turki recovered al-Hasa in 1830. Al Khalifah submitted to his demand for tribute in exchange for his promise not to attack. Just a few years later, they turned the tables on the Saudis by mounting a naval blockade of al-Hasa ports.

Bahrain's rulers proved more adept at staving off external domination than composing their own affairs. Dynastic strife among Al Khalifah made Bahrain the scene of incessant intrigue and warfare. The roots of factional discord can be traced back to the clan's transfer from Zubara to Bahrain. At that time, the ruling sheikh, Ahmad ibn Khalifah, had two powerful sons, Sheikh Salman, who settled at Manama, and Sheikh Abdullah, who settled at Muharraq. The two branches of the ruling clan became known as Al Salman and Al Abdullah. When Sheikh Ahmad died in 1796 while on pilgrimage to Mecca, both sons claimed the right to rule and an uneasy partnership evolved. In 1835, Sheikh Abdullah emerged as sole ruler by virtue of outliving both Salman and Salman's son. Salman's grandson, Sheikh Muhammad ibn Khalifah, rallied other disgruntled Al Khalifah sheikhs and seized power in 1843. The feud between Al Salman and Al Abdullah continued for the next quarter century, fuelled by Saudi Arabia's Emir Faisal, who allowed the head of Al Abdullah, Sheikh Muhammad ibn Abdullah, to settle at Dammam, just across the bay from Bahrain. Emir Faisal wished to exact tribute if he could not rule Bahrain directly. In 1851, Sheikh Muhammad ibn Khalifah agreed to pay tribute, hoping that it would suffice to ward off a Saudi attack, but three years later, Emir Faisal mounted an invasion that was repulsed by Al Khalifah and their tribal allies.

At that point, the British decided to mediate the dispute. They persuaded Sheikh Muhammad ibn Khalifah to grant to his rival the revenues from his former estates on the island in exchange for renouncing his claim to rule. The agreement brought a few years of calm before the ruler broke the agreement by confiscating the disputed estates. The British were annoyed with Sheikh Muhammad for reneging on a deal they had brokered and also for mistreating Indian traders under British protection. Sheikh Muhammad resorted to diplomatic manoeuvres to pre-empt pressure from the British, exploiting occasional Iranian and Ottoman claims to sovereignty over Bahrain. In 1860, he offered his allegiance to the Qajars. Two months later, he switched allegiance to the Ottomans. Sheikh Muhammad may have supposed that he had obtained immunity from British action by taking shelter under the flags of Tehran and Istanbul. He imposed a blockade on the Saudi ports of al-Hasa, seized half-a-dozen merchant vessels, and even threatened Britain's native agent.

The Government of India dismissed the legality of either Ottoman or Iranian claims and proceeded to dispatch a squadron to confiscate two of the sheikh's warships. Seeing that neither the Ottomans nor the Qajars could defend him, Sheikh Muhammad signed the 1861 Friendly Convention drafted by the British obliging him to refrain from maritime violence and to respect British subjects residing and trading in his realm. In return for these concessions, he obtained British recognition of Bahrain's independence, negating Saudi claims in particular, and a guarantee of protection against attack. To secure Sheikh Muhammad's position, the British forcibly evicted Sheikh Muhammad ibn Abdullah from Dammam. Emir Faisal saw the odds stacked against him and he left Bahrain alone thereafter as long as he received his annual zakat payment in return for ensuring the security of Qatar.

By signing the Friendly Convention, Sheikh Muhammad ibn Khalifah bought himself time, but a collision with the British later in the decade resulted in his deposition. The occasion for his downfall was a rebellion in Qatar in 1867 that Sheikh Muhammad put down with assistance from Abu Dhabi's Sheikh Zayid ibn Khalifah. Even though the matter might have been regarded as a purely internal affair, the British considered it a violation of the 1861 Convention because Sheikh Muhammad transported troops by sea and plundered a number of ports. The British instructed Sheikhs Muhammad and Zayid to pay a fine and return stolen goods. Sheikh Muhammad rejected Britain's demands and fled to Qatar. The British Resident then installed his brother Sheikh Ali as the new ruler. But that was not the end of Bahrain's dynastic strife.

The final chapter of Al Khalifah's violent struggles was aptly complex. In 1869, Sheikh Muhammad ibn Khalifah joined forces with his old adversary Sheikh Muhammad ibn Abdullah for an invasion of Bahrain. Sheikh Muhammad ibn Abdullah's forces killed the man the British had installed, Sheikh Ali, and threw Sheikh Muhammad ibn Khalifah in jail. The British decided to intervene yet again, seizing the rebel sheikhs and transporting them to India, then installing Sheikh Ali's son Isa as the new ruler. The British also drafted a new treaty that obliged Sheikh Isa to surrender all of his warships, cede authority over foreign residents to Britain, and acknowledge the permanent separation of Qatar. In return, Sheikh Isa Al Salman obtained firm British backing that kept him in power until 1923. Foreign protection, however, was a mixed blessing, as Sheikh Isa found himself not only sheltered by but also beholden to British power. For instance, in 1904, retainers of his brother Sheikh Ali roughed up a German trader in one incident and some Persian Shi'i workers in a second. The British feared the incidents could give Germany and Iran opportunities to challenge their ability to ensure the security of foreign traders and residents, so they insisted that Sheikh Isa compel his brother to pay restitution. When he hesitated, the British Resident went to Bahrain accompanied by a well-armed fleet prepared to bombard the island. At that point, Sheikh Isa bowed to superior power at the cost of his reputation and independence.

Bahrain's record of dynastic strife and treaty relations with Britain resembled the Trucial sheikhdoms. In two fundamental respects, however, Bahrain has unique features that shaped its modern political experience. First, there is a sharp distinction between the Sunni dynasty and the mostly Shi'i population. The sectarian imprint on the archipelago's political hierarchy was accentuated by the immigration and settlement of Sunni tribes allied to Al Khalifah. Together they comprised a ruling stratum that subjugated the indigenous Shi'i Baharna concentrated in fishing villages and agricultural hamlets. The Baharnah kept aloof from feuds between the sheikhs; nevertheless, they suffered occasional Bedouin depredations and looting. The second unique feature is a corollary of the sectarian hierarchy, namely the economic domination exercised by Sunni sheikhs over Shi'i villagers labouring in date palm groves and vegetable gardens. The ruling sheikh distributed estates to fellow clansmen, who treated their domains as fiefdoms, collecting taxes from Shi'is who owned date trees, and rent in kind and services from Shi'is who worked on the sheikhs' private lands. Economic power was backed up by coercion since each sheikh had armed retainers to enforce his will. The ruling sheikh did not interfere in the affairs of subordinate clansmen's estates, so the Baharnah had no recourse when their sheikh levied extra taxes and drafted them to work on projects without compensation.

Another distinctive feature of the political economy of Al Khalifah rule was that the sheikhs rarely lived on their estates, preferring to reside in Muharraq. They left the management of their estates to stewards. While the ruling sheikh did not exercise direct influence on a daily basis, he had the power to grant and withdraw estates from fellow clansmen because the estates were not hereditary. Furthermore, the ruling sheikh exercised sole authority over the main towns, ports and trade. Finally, he alone dealt with external powers, namely, Britain. The blend of sectarian hierarchy and feudal land regime was quite different from conditions in the other sheikhdoms where the populations were more homogeneous and agriculture less significant in the economy. In the long run, Bahrain's unique configuration resulted in political dynamics more heavily marked by contestation and conflict.

One of the consequences of Al Khalifah's dynastic infighting was the weakening of their grasp on Qatar which was emerging as an independent sheikhdom. Between 1820 and 1860, the barren peninsula became a refuge for disaffected Al Khalifah sheikhs, dissident tribal segments as well as deposed Bani Yas sheikhs from Abu Dhabi. Furthermore, Qatar's Bedouin tribes resented efforts by Bahrain's rulers to assert their authority. Around 1850, a clan from one of Qatar's old fishing hamlets, Al Thani, relocated to Doha, on the eastern side of the peninsula, where its members were less vulnerable to pressure from Bahrain. In the wake of Al Khalifah's raid on Doha in 1867, the British Resident met with the leader of the rebels, Sheikh Muhammad ibn Thani, and convinced him to sign an agreement to refrain from maritime violence in return for British recognition as the ruler of Qatar.

After the Ottoman conquest of al-Hasa in 1871, Sheikh Muhammad agreed to fly the Ottoman flag and accepted the stationing of a small Ottoman garrison at Doha. He preferred to acknowledge Istanbul's distant authority to the proximate threat of renewed intervention by Al Khalifah. When Sheikh Muhammad died in 1876, his son Qasim succeeded him and accepted the Ottoman title of kaymakam. There remained a dispute with Al Khalifah over Zubara, raided by Sheikh Isa in 1872. The British warned him against making a forceful claim in order to avoid complications involving the Ottomans. Nonetheless, Sheikh Isa and later rulers maintained their claim to Zubara, which became a chronic sore point in relations with Qatar's Al Thani.

Sheikh Qasim's relations with Istanbul deteriorated in the 1880s. The Ottomans suspected him of having secret contacts with the British Resident and stoking unrest in al-Hasa while he believed Istanbul was backing dissident Al Thani sheikhs seeking to unseat him. In 1893, tensions erupted into crisis when the governor of Basra decided to visit Qatar to replenish troops at the Ottoman garrison in Doha and to conduct an investigation of Sheikh Qasim. He in turn believed that the governor's true purpose was to remove him, so he retreated to the desert where his Bedouin allies protected him. The Ottoman governor dispatched troops to fetch him but they soon found themselves under attack by a large tribal force. The expedition turned into a rout, with over 100 soldiers killed in retreat. To make matters worse for the Ottomans, rumours swirled that Britain was seeking to extend the trucial network to Qatar. Istanbul wished to avoid giving Sheikh Qasim the opportunity to invoke British protection, so it decided to leave him alone and make do with a nominal proclamation of loyalty. For his part, Sheikh Qasim remained at a desert settlement, leaving Doha and dealings with the small Ottoman garrison to his brother Sheikh Ahmad.

For the next two decades, Qatar remained a loosely held, distant Ottoman province. Its political status suddenly changed in July 1913 at the signing of the Anglo–Ottoman Convention that determined the empire's boundaries in the Gulf. According to the Convention, Istanbul gave up its claim to Qatar. At the same time, Britain denied that Bahrain had a right to resume the collection of tribute. In essence, Qatar was now an independent sheikhdom. That status was secured by the Anglo–Saudi Treaty of 1915 whereby Ibn Saud recognized British protection over Qatar, Bahrain, Kuwait and the Trucial sheikhdoms. The following year, Qatar's Sheikh Abdullah ibn Qasim (his father died in 1913) signed a treaty with the British, the last Arab Gulf ruler to do so. The treaty included provision for non-alienation of territory, renunciation of contacts with foreign powers except with British consent, and guarantees for the security of British subjects (Indian traders had been expelled in the 1890s because they were commercial rivals to Al Thani merchants). Sheikh Abdullah believed that the treaty also entitled him to British protection from attack, but London held to a different interpretation, claiming it was committed only to offering diplomatic support. Sheikh Abdullah failed to get assurances that Britain would safeguard Qatar's independence (he regarded Saudi Arabia as a threat notwithstanding its 1915 treaty with Britain) or support him against rival sheikhs. Hence, he got less than he thought he had bargained for and had to make do with titular authority while dissident members of Al Thani plotted and Bedouin tribes flouted his authority. On the other hand, he and his father had succeeded in breaking away from Bahrain and forging official ties with the Gulf's dominant power.

KUWAIT

Kuwait's Al Sabah sheikhs strove to maintain their independence and advance the port's role in regional trade. The rising sheikhdom's low customs duties made it attractive to merchants transporting goods from the Gulf to Baghdad and Aleppo. Unpredictable political conditions in Basra and Bushehr in the first half of the nineteenth century redirected some trade at the northern end of the Gulf to Kuwait, which enjoyed a degree of stability that was unusual on the Arab shore. Unlike their Utub cousins at Bahrain or the fractious clans of the Trucial Coast and Oman, Al Sabah were blessed by long reigns and smooth successions. Sheikh Abdullah ibn Sabah's reign from 1764 to 1815 was almost matched by his son Jabir's from 1815 to 1859. British visitors marvelled at Kuwait's security and prosperity. Its good fortune probably had a number of causes. The town's population was predominantly homogeneous in contrast to Bahrain's uneasy imposition of an exogenous Sunni stratum over the indigenous Shi'is. With domestic political stability a given, the primary political challenge to Kuwait's rulers was navigating the tricky currents generated by rivalry among the Ottomans, Saudis, Egyptians and British. Given Kuwait's small population, its rulers relied on deft diplomacy to keep larger powers at arm's length.

An illustration of Sheikh Jabir's adroitness was his support for an Ottoman expedition against the headquarters of the Bani Ka'b in 1837. In the 1790s, the tribe had founded a new town, Mohammerah (presently known as Khorramshahr), at the confluence of the Karun River with the Shatt al-Arab. It was developing into a commercial rival to both Basra and Kuwait, so when the governor of Baghdad requested support, Sheikh Jabir had the opportunity to crush a competitor and stay on the good side of the Ottomans, who appeared to be on the road to exercising effective power in the provinces. His part in the expedition was to blockade the Shatt al-Arab to prevent supplies reaching Mohammerah. Ottoman forces overwhelmed the town's defences and levelled it. Then Sheikh Jabir allowed the defeated Bani Ka'b sheikh to take up residence in Kuwait. The custom of granting asylum to fugitives, conniving dynasts and deposed rulers figured as a distinctive feature of Kuwait's position in the region.

Sheikh Jabir's ability to adjust to sudden political shifts was tested during the second Egyptian occupation of Arabia (1837–43). Claiming neutrality allowed Kuwait to serve as a conduit for communication between the British Resident and the Egyptian commander, Khurshid Pasha. He may have bent neutrality when he allowed food supplies for Egyptian troops in al-Hasa to pass through Kuwait, but in doing so he gave Khurshid Pasha no reason to attack even if he did not appreciate the sheikh's providing refuge to the defeated Saudi commander of al-Hasa. Flexibility was the hallmark of Sheikh Jabir's manoeuvring. He did not go so far in the direction of placating Khurshid Pasha as Bahrain's Sheikh Abdullah ibn Khalifah, who formally acknowledged Egyptian authority.

In later decades, the primary threat to Kuwait's independence came from the Ottoman Empire. Thirty years after initiating the Tanzimat reforms, Istanbul was tightening control over the provinces and pushing for the recovery of territories lost in the centuries of weakness. When Midhat Pasha organized the 1871 invasion of al-Hasa, he called on Kuwait's Sheikh Abdullah ibn Jabir (r. 1866–92) to supply fighters and logistical support. Kuwait served as the staging point for land and naval forces. Some 300 Kuwaiti ships transported Ottoman troops, with Sheikh Abdullah himself leading the fleet. In addition, a contingent of Kuwaiti cavalry under his brother (and future ruler) Sheikh Mubarak accompanied Ottoman land forces. After the campaign, Midhat recognized Sheikh Abdullah's contribution by appointing him kaymakam of Kuwait, implying its incorporation into the empire and setting off an uncomfortable phase of tenuous recognition of Ottoman authority when Istanbul defined Kuwait as a district of Basra province. Sheikh Abdullah participated in later expeditions in Qatar and southern Iran yet he resisted the posting of Ottoman officials. Istanbul was satisfied with proclamations of loyalty and occasional military support.

Al Sabah's good fortune in avoiding dynastic strife was ruptured on 8 May 1896 when Sheikh Mubarak orchestrated the killing of his brothers, Sheikh Muhammad, at the time the ruling member of Al Sabah, and Sheikh Jarrah. Historians have cited various reasons for the murders. Local observers emphasized Sheikh Mubarak's frustration with his brothers' control over the family's wealth and landholdings. Whatever the cause, Sheikh Mubarak was able to consolidate control and forced his nephews (sons of the murdered brothers) to flee to Basra, where they urged the Ottoman authorities to punish the perpetrator of their fathers' murder. For his part, Mubarak pledged his loyalty to Istanbul and sought confirmation of his succession as kaymakam of Kuwait. While provincial and imperial officials debated whether to remove him by force or recognize his fait accompli, Mubarak sent out feelers to the British Resident to see about entering the network of protected sheikhs.

Britain's initial reluctance gave way to keen interest because of changes in its officials in the region and alarm at a Russian initiative. At the end of 1898, one of the leading proponents of a forward imperial policy, Lord Curzon, became Viceroy of India. At the same time, London learned that a Russian count in Istanbul was seeking a railroad concession for a link from Syria to Kuwait. In the geopolitical scope of Anglo–Russian rivalry, the so-called Great Game, such a link might serve as the basis for rail lines to extend through Iran and Afghanistan to the borders of India, Britain's most valuable possession. In order to abort the Russian project, London authorized the Resident to sign a non-alienation bond with Sheikh Mubarak. The bond stipulated that he not cede territory to a foreign individual or entity without first obtaining British consent. It implied a British guarantee for Sheikh Mubarak's rule and Kuwait's independence, even though the agreement was kept secret. The motivation for firmly incorporating Kuwait into Britain's sphere of influence was the same that lay behind its exclusive treaty with Oman, blocking a European rival from gaining a foothold that could threaten its regional position.

The rationale for the non-alienation bond with Kuwait was expressed in a landmark speech to the House of Commons given by the Foreign Secretary, Lord Lansdowne, in May 1903. He referred to the Persian Gulf as a vital imperial interest, whereby the British government 'should regard the establishment of a naval base, or of a fortified port, in the Persian Gulf by any other Power as a very grave menace to British interests, and we should certainly resist it with all the means at our disposal'.[1] That sentiment was reiterated in the Gulf later that year, in November, when Lord Curzon, Viceroy of India, spoke at a formal ceremony attended by all the Trucial sheikhs. He declared,

> We were here before any other Power, in modern times, had shown its face in these waters. We found strife and we have created order. It was our commerce as well as your security that was threatened and called for protection. At every port along these coasts, the subjects of the King of England still reside and trade .... We saved you from extinction at the hands of your neighbours. We opened these seas to the ships of all nations, and enabled their flags to fly in peace. We have not seized or held your territory. We have not destroyed your independence but have preserved it ... The peace of these waters must still be maintained; your independence will continue to be upheld; and the influence of the British Government must remain supreme.[2]

In the next few years, Sheikh Mubarak's relations with Britain became more transparent. For example, when Lord Curzon toured the Gulf in 1903, he stopped at Kuwait, much to Istanbul's annoyance and as a signal to Russia, which had recently initiated naval patrols in the Gulf and established consular posts at Bandar Abbas, Bushehr and Mohammerah to support Russian merchant vessels. The following year, Mubarak signed a secret non-alienation agreement with the British that ceded rights to sites on the coast that were suitable for use as railway terminals. The agreement with Kuwait made it possible for London to forestall a German plan to extend the Berlin-to-Istanbul railway line to Baghdad. The sultan had approved a concession for the railway in 1899, and German engineers dispatched to the Gulf concluded that Kuwait was a more suitable terminal than Basra. This new agreement did not quite convert Kuwait into a British protectorate, but it met the purposes of both parties: Britain ensured that no European rival would be able to construct a railroad from Baghdad to the Gulf, and Mubarak deepened Britain's stake in Kuwait's *de facto* independence.

Once Sheikh Mubarak strengthened his political position, he shored up his fiscal resources. Kuwait's ruling sheikhs had counted on income from date palm groves south of Basra for a good portion of their revenue, but Mubarak's right to that property was contested by the sons of his murdered brothers. The Ottomans took a deliberate approach to determining the conflicting claims, so Mubarak augmented his revenues by centralizing control over customs duties. In so doing, he also increased his power *vis-à-vis* Kuwait's merchants. His political balancing act, making public declarations of loyalty to Istanbul and private professions of commitment to British interests, yielded stipends from both powers. Not all his initiatives met with success. In 1901, he joined with Saudi emirs and allied tribes in an attempt to wrest control over Najd from the Rashidis. The battle was a complete defeat for the allies and Sheikh Mubarak thereafter limited himself to preserving his power in Kuwait.

After Sheikh Mubarak died in 1915, his son Sheikh Jabir became the ruler but he died little more than a year later and his younger brother Sheikh Salim took over. The major development in his four-year reign was an attack by the Saudis. In October 1920, Saudi forces advanced into Kuwaiti territory and put the southern port of al-Jahra under siege. The British came to the rescue, sending a naval squadron and landing troops to back up their ally. Rather than take on the Western power, Emir Abdulaziz had his forces withdraw. Sheikh Mubarak's acquisition of British protection had paid off.

QAJAR IRAN

Iran recovered from decades of political fragmentation with the rise of the Qajar shahs. Because their roots lay in the north and they faced challenges from northern neighbours (the Russians and the Ottomans), early Qajar shahs paid little attention to the Gulf. They confirmed Arab chieftains along the coast as vassals responsible to the governor of Fars, who was content with occasional tribute payments and verbal affirmations of loyalty. In the first half of the nineteenth century, Iran came under strong European military and political pressure. Efforts to duplicate Ottoman programmes for self-strengthening fell short, primarily because Iran's administrative, military and fiscal institutions were in a weaker position *vis-à-vis* provincial warlords and tribal khans than were their Ottoman counterparts. Nevertheless, in the second half of the nineteenth century, the Qajar shahs and their advisers were able to chalk up modest achievements that enabled Tehran to take steps towards exercising central authority over its shore of the Gulf.

The impetus for Iran's first reform programme came from the 1826–8 war with Russia. Popular agitation in the north for the recovery of the territories Russia had acquired in 1813 led to a renewal of war in 1826. The outcome was an even worse defeat for Persia sealed by the 1828 Treaty of Turkmanchai which drew the boundary at the Aras River, the modern-day border between Iran and Azerbaijan. The treaty obliged the Qajars to pay a large indemnity, to lower the duty on Russian imports, to grant Russia the right to protect consular employees, and to confer extraterritorial status on Russian subjects. This was the first of a series of treaties of Capitulations that European powers imposed on Persia, opening the country to a rising tide of European manufactures in exchange for Persian raw materials and carpets. Hence, the major lasting effects of the Russo–Persian wars were twofold. First, Persia became integrated into an economic network dominated by Europe. Second, growing numbers of European consuls and traders triggered strong anti-Western feeling.

The Crown Prince, Abbas Mirza, was acutely aware of the need to strengthen defences against further encroachment. He took the first steps to create a modern army based on European models. A bureau was established to translate European scientific and military treatises, and an educational mission was dispatched to Europe to study military sciences and medicine. To finance these costly initiatives, Abbas Mirza raised tariffs and reduced expenditures, targeting the allowances of courtiers and

princes. The cost-cutting measures angered powerful circles at
the Qajar court; so when the reforming prince died in 1833, his
reform programme petered out.

Fifteen years later, a former adviser to Abbas Mirza reju-
venated the cause of reform. Mirza Muhammad Taqi Khan
Farahani, known as Amir Kabir, was the Qajar envoy to Istanbul
in the 1840s, the dawn of sustained institutional reform in
the Ottoman Empire. In 1848, Nasir al-Din Shah ascended the
Peacock Throne and appointed Amir Kabir his *vizier* or chief minister. In that position, Amir Kabir revived military reforms and
ordered the construction of factories for military equipment and
uniforms. Under his direction, the first secular school, known as
Dar al-Funun, opened in 1851, and Persia's first newspaper came
out. But just like his mentor, he ran into resistance because he
too resorted to raising tariffs and cutting court expenses. Amir
Kabir was dismissed from office in 1851.

Amir Kabir's efforts overlapped with the appearance of a major
eruption on the Persian religious and social landscape. The Babi
movement mounted a direct challenge to Islam, claiming to
represent a new revelation superseding the Qur'an. Its roots lay
in the mystical teachings of Twelver Shi'ism's Sheikhi school,
developed by Ahmad al-Ahsa'i (1754–1826), a charismatic figure from a village in Bahrain. He claimed to have dreams and
visions of the Imams instructing him in the esoteric meaning
of the Qur'an. As such, he incurred the enmity of Twelver Shi'i
clerics whose claim to authority rested on years of study, not
on intuitive insight into the Imams' knowledge. Nevertheless,
during his roving as a preacher in Iran and Iraq, the charismatic
sheikh drew a following among religious students and townsmen convinced that al-Ahsa'i was the 'Gate to the Imam'. The
Persian word for gate is *bab*. He designated a disciple, Kazim
Rashti, to be his successor. Rashti settled in Kerbala, where he
met a young trader from Shiraz named Sayyid Ali Muhammad
(1819–50) and drew him to the Sheikhi school. Upon Rashti's
death in 1844, Sayyid Ali, back in Shiraz, announced that he
was the new Bab. It so happened that in the Muslim lunar calendar, 1844 corresponded with the year 1260, the millennium
after the occultation of the Twelfth Imam. It was the perfect
moment to proclaim the arrival of a new divine dispensation.
Sayyid Ali soon departed from the Sheikhi doctrine of the Gate
to the Imam, first declaring that he was in fact the Imam himself, and later asserting that he was indeed a prophet bearing a
new divine revelation.

Sayyid Ali issued his teachings in the *Bayan*, or the
Clarification, a Persian language text that refers to him as the

Prophet of the Age and the source of God's will. The *Bayan* was to supplant the Qur'an; Persian was to replace Arabic as the holy language; Shiraz took Mecca's place as the centre of the religion; obedience to the Bab and his disciples, termed 'Letters of the Living', replaced obedience to Islamic law. In social terms, Sayyid Ali attacked the Shi'i clergy for corruption and called for a new social and political order of equality. He attracted a wide following among religious students, merchants, artisans, peasants and even government officials. The Shi'i clergy, however, harassed him and pressed the Qajar authorities to stop the spread of the heretical doctrine. In 1848, he was transported to a village in Azerbaijan to isolate him from his supporters. They, in turn, launched a revolt in northern Iran, taking over a shrine called Sheikh Tabarsi, which they turned into a fortress. Qajar forces laid siege to the Babi stronghold, and massacred hundreds of Babis when they overran it. Further uprisings broke out in 1850, leading the Qajars to allow the clergy to try Sayyid Ali and sentence him in July 1850 to death by firing squad. The movement then went underground and its leaders fled to Ottoman Iraq. In subsequent years, one of his disciples, Hussein Ali Nuri, known as Baha'ullah, proclaimed new revelations that resulted in schism and the formation of the Bahai religion.

The suppression of the Babis coincided with Tehran's first step towards asserting direct rule over the Gulf coast, taken in 1850 when the shah sent forces to remove Bushehr's Al Madhkur sheikhs from power. The next step in 1868 was to reabsorb Bandar Abbas; which had been leased to the sultan of Oman. Fiscal pressures on the chronically thin treasury prompted Nasir al-Din Shah to undertake provincial reorganization to increase revenues from customs duties. In 1887, he established the Gulf Ports District to administer Bushehr, Bandar Abbas and Lingah, which Iran seized from the Qasimi sheikhs in a military expedition that year. The immediate results were unimpressive, but revenues rose around 1900 with the appointment of Belgian experts to manage customs. A sign of the new regime's fiscal efficacy was the emigration of traders to Dubai.

In the second half of the nineteenth century new intellectual influences brought about cultural change. Amir Kabir's Dar al-Funun remained the only modern school for two decades, training cadres of bureaucrats and military officers. Starting in 1873, the Qajars established special schools for diplomacy, foreign language and agriculture. Liberal ideas began to penetrate from British India via Persian merchants with agencies in Bombay and Calcutta, from exiled intellectuals residing in Istanbul, and from migrant workers employed in the oilfields opening in Baku, the capital of Russian Azerbaijan. One exemplar of the new thinking was Malkom Khan (1833–1908), a proponent of systematic administrative and legal reform similar to the Tanzimat in the neighbouring Ottoman Empire. He briefly served the shah as ambassador to Britain. After conservative courtiers pressed for his dismissal, he launched a reformist publication in London (*Qanun*) that called for parliamentary government.

A second cultural strain was represented by Jamal al-Din Asadabadi al-Afghani (1839–97), the leading proponent of pan-Islamic resistance to European domination. Born and educated in Persia, Jamal al-Din is known for his peripatetic activism and efforts to energize Muslims in Afghanistan, India and Egypt. Rather than viewing liberal political reform as the key to gathering the power to ward off European imperialism, he emphasized the need for Muslims to close ranks and adopt modern technology and science. He passed through Persia a number of times in the late 1880s, stirring up anti-Western feeling and falling foul of the shah, who deported him to Turkey. Jamal al-Din took revenge by plotting the 1896 assassination of Nasir al-Din Shah.

Reformist ideas proved sterile in the last decades of the nineteenth century, but the shah did try out new ways to raise funds to pay for projects to modernize Persia's infrastructure. The boldest initiative in this area was the Reuter Concession of 1872. A British subject, Julius de Reuter, obtained exclusive rights to minerals (except gold, silver and gems), customs, a state bank, and construction of railways, telegraph lines, canals and irrigation works in return for paying the Qajar treasury a lump sum and a share of profits. A combination of Russian opposition and disgruntled courtiers resulted in the concession's cancellation, but it pointed the way to later deals that mortgaged assets to compensate for the dynasty's feeble fiscal capacity. Thus, Reuter later obtained mining and banking privileges; British agencies acquired contracts to develop telegraph lines and build roads; and Russian agencies developed ports on the Caspian Sea and operated telegraph lines in the north. In 1879, the Qajars turned to Russia to train a new palace guard, the Cossack Brigade. The advances in transportation and communications expanded the horizons of townsmen, who found it easier than ever to share information about prices and merchandise.

Progress towards physical unification was also felt in the political arena. In March 1890, the shah granted a British subject a monopoly for the distribution and export of tobacco, one of the country's major cash crops. As word spread and agents for the monopoly fanned across the country, tobacco merchants spearheaded protests, shutting down trade in Shiraz in April 1891. The strike spread to other towns in the next few months. In December, a religious edict circulated banning the handling and consumption of tobacco on grounds of ritual pollution by non-Muslim hands. The edict was associated with a leading Islamic scholar in Najaf. Demonstrations in Tehran against the concession and widespread observance of the boycott led the government to cancel the concession, at the price of a large indemnity.

At the dawn of the twentieth century, Persia was weak but stable in spite of the failure of Qajar shahs to undertake the kind of administrative reform that had transformed governance in the Ottoman Empire. Under the surface, however, currents of political dissent were swirling in Azerbaijan and Tehran. The Russian Social Democratic Party attracted Persian migrant workers in Baku. In 1904, they formed the Social Democratic Party of Iran to campaign for workers' rights, free speech and free education. In Tehran, intellectuals gathered in secret societies, known as *anjumans*, dedicated to constitutional government and social reform. The various trends for change crystallized in the Constitutional Revolution.

In 1905, the Persian economy was buffeted by bad harvests, high prices and disruption of trade with Russia, due to political turmoil in its northern neighbour arising from its defeat in war against Japan. To deflect popular unrest over rising prices, the authorities arrested and flogged two sugar merchants on 12 December. Fellow merchants responded by declaring a general strike. Over the next several months, members of the *anjumans* agitated for the convening of a constituent assembly. Muzaffar al-Din Shah resorted to arrests and violent suppression of demonstrations. In one instance, Cossack Brigadesmen killed more than 20 demonstrators. The mood of protest swept up religious students and clerical leaders in addition to merchants and guild leaders. Unable to calm the situation through repression, the shah relented in August 1906, declaring the formation of a constituent assembly. On 30 December 1906, Muzaffar al-Din Shah enacted the constitution (modelled on Belgium's 1831 constitution), just days before he died. His son and successor Muhammad Ali Shah resented the imposition of constitutional restrictions on royal authority and plotted to overturn them. In the meantime, the national assembly deliberated on a set of laws to more clearly define the allocation of authority to name the prime minister and cabinet members and approve the budget.

The constitutionalists were not a unified bloc. They included freethinking clerics, including secret Babis, and secular intellectuals. Muhammad Ali Shah wooed conservative clerics with popular followings to counter the pro-constitution crowds. He also rallied an assortment of large landowners and tribal chiefs to oppose the national assembly. In June 1908, he declared martial law, dissolved the assembly, and had its leading members arrested and executed. The constitutionalists, however, had strong support in Azerbaijan, where they seized control of Tabriz, forming a Provisional Government in defiance of Tehran. In early 1909, constitutionalist forces gained control of the Caspian Sea port of Rasht. Their military strength was reinforced by Bakhtiari tribesmen from the south under a chieftain whose regional rivals backed the shah. In July, constitutional forces from north and south converged on Tehran, seized the capital, and forced the shah to seek refuge in the Russian embassy. The triumphant constitutionalists then deposed Muhammad Ali Shah and enthroned his 12-year-old son Ahmad.

The second national assembly convened in November 1909. Like its predecessor, it was divided into factions. The Democrats favoured universal male suffrage, free education, equal rights for all citizens, the abolition of child labour and land reform. The Moderates focused on preserving private property and supporting the public role of religion, especially in law and education. The split between secular and religious factions paralysed the national assembly. At the same time, disorder spread in the provinces as southern tribes resented the power accumulated by the Bakhtiaris under the constitutional government. Tribal clashes alarmed the British, who decided to invade in October 1911, sending forces to restore order in Shiraz and Isfahan. Meanwhile, Russia was angry at the national assembly's American financial adviser, Morgan Shuster, whose measures to establish regular customs collection jeopardized the profits of Russian merchants. On 24 December 1911, Russian forces invaded the northern provinces and threatened to march on Tehran if the national assembly did not dissolve itself, ending Persia's experiment in representative government. Constitutionalists resisted the Russians, but eventually succumbed to superior forces.

Persia was now effectively partitioned between British troops in the south and Russian troops in the north. Belgian officials managed the country's customs posts. Britain and Russia's arrangement reflected an agreement reached in August 1907 to carve the country into spheres of influence, leaving a neutral zone in the centre. In so doing, Russia ensured its domination in the northern provinces and Britain safeguarded its interests in the Gulf. Nationalist groups managed to recuperate in 1914 and pressed for elections to the national assembly. The results reflected widespread resentment of Russian and British occupations. When the First World War broke out, deputies expressed support for Germany and the Ottoman Empire and formed a Committee of National Resistance. Russian forces chased them out of their headquarters in Qom and they found refuge in Kermanshah and support from Qashqai and Baluchi tribesmen, while the British organized a cluster of tribal forces into the South Persia Rifles. With funds and arms from the British, their tribal allies crushed the National Resistance by 1916.

Conditions in northern Persia were dramatically affected by the November 1917 Bolshevik Revolution. The communists overthrew the Russian czar, renounced the czar's imperialist treaties with Persia, and evacuated troops from the northern provinces. In their wake, regional political movements rose to power in Azerbaijan and Gilan. When the war in Europe ended, Britain held the dominant position in the country, supporting the central government in Tehran with subsidies and containing the northern constitutionalists in their provincial retreats. It appeared that the Qajar dynasty's only chance for survival was to seek British protection. London proposed a treaty in 1919 that would have provided financial support to Tehran as well as military and administrative advisers. If the national assembly had ratified the treaty, Persia would have rounded out Britain's informal empire in the Gulf.

OIL

In May 1908, British prospectors made the first large oil strike in the Middle East about one hundred miles north of the Gulf, in the rugged hills of western Iran. The path to the gusher at Masjid-i Sulaiman was anything but smooth: investors came close to bankruptcy and surveyors nearly gave up on finding oil. The significance of the find was not obvious at the time. The world oil market was about 50 years old, dating back to John D. Rockefeller's development of fields in western Pennsylvania. By the early 1900s, geologists and investors were combing the world for new fields, from the Dutch East Indies to the Gulf of Mexico. Persia's entry into the ranks of oil producers came about as a result of the Qajar dynasty's chronic fiscal deficits.

Unable to draw enough revenue from the country's poor, unruly population, royal advisers sold natural assets and rights to develop infrastructure as concessions to foreign companies. In May 1901, an English subject, William Knox D'Arcy, obtained a concession for the production and sale of oil in exchange for a lump sum cash payment and a share of annual net profits. The concession covered all of Persia, except for the provinces bordering Russia. D'Arcy's prospectors initially picked a site 300 miles north of the Gulf. They shipped equipment up the Tigris River from Basra to Baghdad, then overland on pack mules to a location just across the Ottoman–Persian border. In two years, they found only small quantities of oil, not enough to justify the cost of a pipeline. The project would most likely have ended in failure at that juncture but for a change in British strategic calculations.

First, London opposed Germany's effort to extend the Berlin to Baghdad railway to the Persian Gulf. A second compelling factor was the growing interest in finding a secure supply of oil for the British Royal Navy. The two major sources were under the control of foreign companies in lands that lay outside the British Empire's realm: the East Indies had large oil fields run by Royal Dutch/Shell and the United States had oil reserves owned by American firms led by Standard Oil. To acquire a secure supply, the Admiralty sought a private company to inject new funds into the D'Arcy concession. In 1905, it found the right match in Burmah Oil, a well financed Scottish-owned firm that had fairly modest prospects in South-east Asia.

Burmah Oil replenished D'Arcy's funds and his men set out to prospect further south. More than two years lapsed without success. In April 1908, corporate headquarters in Glasgow was ready to pull the plug on the drilling operation and sent word to Persia that it was not going to keep the project alive by throwing more money at more dry holes. While the letter was en route, the drillers hit an enormous gusher, ensuring the long-term commitment of London to the Gulf as the major source for oil. In April 1909, the venture was put on a firmer footing with the formation of the Anglo-Persian Oil Company (APOC).

The final step in placing Persian oil near the centre of British imperial policy turned on a push among admirals and high officials to convert the Royal Navy's fleet from coal to oil. The early 1900s saw a growing rivalry between Germany and Britain, including an arms race on the world's oceans. Proponents of switching to oil argued that it would make British warships faster and require fewer labourers to load and maintain fuel. If the Royal Navy were to implement the conversion, it was imperative to secure a reliable supply of oil. Although the concession area did not lie in a crown possession, the APOC's field of operations fell in the British Empire's sphere of influence and that was good enough for London. In May 1914, the British government bought a 51-per cent share of APOC, putting Persian Gulf security on a higher plane than ever before.

6 The Formation of Modern States, 1920–56

The First World War was a turning point in the history of the entire Middle East. The most important consequence of the war was the destruction of the Ottoman Empire. In the wider Muslim world, it represented one of the last independent powers confronting European imperialism. Before the war, the Ottomans had already lost their foothold in al-Hasa to the Saudis in 1913; and Kuwait's emir had entered a secret arrangement with the British to safeguard his autonomy. The empire's defeat and dismemberment at European hands fundamentally altered Muslims' political horizon from India to Egypt and removed the largest Muslim player in Arabian politics, changing the calculations of local parties as well as those of the British, now the unchallenged hegemon of the region.

Standard historical treatments of the war's aftermath emphasize the new political map of the Middle East after the British and the French divided the Ottoman Arab lands, and how the boundaries they drew planted the seeds for future internal instability (in Lebanon and Iraq) and international conflict (in Palestine). In the Gulf, blurry frontiers had been tolerable when the Ottomans and the British were the main powers but now that Britain had a League of Nations mandate for Iraq, it had to fix its borders, and that meant establishing clear boundaries with Saudi Arabia and Kuwait.

In other respects, the war did not have much impact in the Gulf. Britain reinforced its position as the dominant power, advising Arab sheikhs from Kuwait to Oman, intervening in Persian affairs at crucial junctures, and using its fleet to ensure the flow of trade. During the period between the two world wars, the Gulf economy underwent transformation, starting with the Great Depression, which threw pearling into a downward spiral exacerbated by Japan's development of less costly cultured pearls. According to some estimates, one-quarter of the male population along the Arabian shore worked in the pearl industry in one capacity or another. At the same time as the region's perennial treasure lost much of its value, a more valuable and easily accessible commodity for export, petroleum, was discovered. The region's emergence as a major fuel supplier for global industrial economies raised its profile in geostrategic affairs. By 1950, Britain obtained more than 80 per cent of its petroleum from the Gulf.

Less frequently noticed in standard historical accounts is the Gulf's place in the development of air routes, starting in the 1920s, when civil and military aviation assumed an important role in communications, commerce and strategic affairs. Air bases complemented naval installations as assets of imperial power. In 1929, Britain's Imperial Airways initiated a route from Basra to Karachi, touching down at airfields on the coast of Iran. The route shifted to the Arabian shore in 1932 as a result of Anglo–Iranian political tensions over the oil concession. Britain then bargained with Arab sheikhs for landing rights to replace the Iranian airfields. Saudi Arabia balked, but the British reached agreement with the sheikh of Sharjah.

The Second World War had four major consequences for the Gulf. First, although Great Britain was part of the victorious alliance, the costs of war in blood and treasure exhausted its capacity to sustain its empire. The dreary post-war years saw the Union Jack lowered in India and Palestine. Decolonization bolstered the ubiquitous mood of nationalist assertion in Asia and Africa. Challenges to British interests in Iran and Iraq during the early 1950s foreshadowed a period of waning prestige and influence. Second, nationalist assertion in Iran, Iraq and the Arab world at large reshaped politics in the smaller Gulf countries, where popular protest movements surfaced for the first time. Third, the rise of the United States in global affairs reverberated in the Gulf even if Washington remained the secondary Western power. And fourth, the Gulf's strategic position (air bases) and natural resources (oil) ensured that it became ensnared in the era's Cold War between communist and capitalist camps.

By the end of the period, Oman, Saudi Arabia and the Arab sheikhdoms were taking on the attributes of nations. The formation of national political arenas was not merely a matter of drawing boundaries. It was also a process subject to contestation between rulers and the population over the conduct of politics and power sharing. At the same time that sheikhly families were consolidating their positions, societies were undergoing structural changes that redefined the framework for politics. One facet of social change unfolded around the oilfields, where a new market for labour filled the gap left by the crash of the pearling sector and contributed to ending the Bedouins' nomadic way of life by offering them jobs as drivers and guards. The oil industry became the arena for the region's first labour move- ments as workers in the oilfields, transportation and construc- tion organized trade unions to strike and demonstrate for better working conditions.

A second facet of social change was the rapid growth of towns as rulers spent oil revenues on urban housing, roads, schools, medical clinics and amenities. Control over rising revenues turned into a focus of political struggle between sheikhs and merchants, who demanded a say in spending projects, and when sheikhs resisted, pushed for representation in municipal councils. Finally, the 1940s saw the emergence of a professional, educated middle class. Its members worked alongside Arab expatriate teachers and advisers, who imported the political agendas of Arab nationalists and the Muslim Brothers.

The formation of modern politics pitting rulers against citizens also divided citizens, leading to the emergence of sectarian political divisions between Sunni and Shi'i. Political contestation revolved around control over oil revenues, debate over its equitable division and nationalization of oil concessions. The dynamics of contestation included showdowns, bargaining and compromises. With the spread of literacy, print media and the radio, dissent found outlets both inside national political arenas and from exile. In response, rulers grasped for instruments, institutions and norms that allowed them to resist and co-opt demands for power sharing. These dynamics were complicated by the continuation of regional tensions inherited from the territorial and dynastic disputes of the previous century as well as the aspirations of rising regional powers (Egypt, Iran and Iraq) to influence the domestic politics of the smaller sheikhdoms.

IRAN

Qajar Persia entered the post-war era with a weak central government dependent on British arms and subsidies to bolster what little authority it exercised over the country. In a bid to place Anglo–Persian relations on firmer footing, the British proposed a treaty that would have turned Persia into a protectorate. Townsmen and tribesmen demonstrated against the treaty, so it was not ratified. The country's political fortunes took a drastic turn on 21 February 1921, when the commander of the only modern military unit seized power in a *coup d'état*. That commander, Reza Khan, had risen through the ranks of the Cossack Brigade. To give a legal face to the coup, Reza Khan allied with a well-known civilian politician Sayyid Zia al-Din, who became the Prime Minister. It was clear at the time, however, that Reza was the strongman in the government.

For the next quarter century, Reza Khan was a dominant figure, imposing his will to achieve independence from foreign interference, national unity and economic modernization. Unlike the emerging states along the Arabian shore, Persia's national boundaries had been fixed during the nineteenth century except for parts of the boundary with Iraq. The primary challenge confronting Reza was internal fragmentation. Within a few years, however, he defeated one provincial strongman and tribal chieftain after another, demonstrating the capacity of the armed forces that he supplied with modern equipment. He did stumble in 1925, when he briefly supported an initiative to turn Persia into a republic, following in the footsteps of neighbouring Turkey, but he backtracked in the face of vigorous protest from conservative clerics. At the end of the same year, Reza manoeuvred to have parliament depose the last Qajar shah and crown him Reza Shah, assuming the dynastic name of Pahlavi.

The revival of strong central authority in Tehran augured a new distribution of power in the Gulf. At the time of Reza Khan's coup, Khuzistan province, located at the northern end of the Gulf, was under the effective rule of Sheikh Khaz'al of Mohammerah, who thought that he had a British pledge to defend his autonomy against Tehran. But when Reza sent forces to occupy the province and depose the sheikh, British officials decided not to rescue their protégé. In fact, they were divided on how to regard Iran's revival. The Foreign Office viewed it favourably because a strong Iran would be better able to defend itself against Soviet expansion and guarantee the security of British-owned oil interests. By contrast, the India Office viewed Reza's ambitions as a threat to British hegemony in the Gulf. For instance, in 1927, Reza notified the British that he intended to redeem Iran's claim to Bahrain as part of its sovereign territory. The sheikhdom's independence was not threatened immediately due to its treaty with Great Britain, but the assertion certainly fostered unease at the court in Manama. The Political Resident disputed Iran's claim, observing that Bahrain had changed hands a number of times and that Iran had lost possession in 1783. A few years later, Reza Shah challenged the British navy's right to facilities on Qeshm and Hangam Islands near the Hormuz Strait. In 1934,

London agreed to withdraw and relocated to Bahrain, where oil had just been discovered. Iran established its own naval stations on the two islands the following year.

Reza Shah's core goals were to consolidate national unity and safeguard independence of foreign domination. Attaining them required an expansion of the central government's coercive and administration capacity. Consequently, he modernized and increased the size of the armed forces and the gendarmerie in order to quell unrest. One measure of his success at buttressing the state's coercive capacity was the forcible settlement of Iran's nomadic tribes in villages, effectively breaking the power of the tribal chieftains who had dominated the countryside for centuries. Villagers who had endured their depredations enjoyed more security but traded one form of domination for another, as rural lands came under the control of absentee landlords allied to the monarchy.

The early twentieth century was an era of firm belief in heavy industry as a measure of economic development. Therefore, Reza Shah presided over efforts to industrialize Iran under an umbrella of protective tariffs. The government established factories to manufacture primary products for construction such as cement and glass, as well as food-processing firms to supply the burgeoning urban population of civil servants and workers. Reza Shah took particular pride in a costly project to construct the Trans-Iranian Railway connecting the Gulf and the Caspian Sea. Unlike the major nineteenth century infrastructure projects in other parts of the Middle East (such as the Suez Canal), the railroad was wholly funded by Iran to signify independence from European capital. Nevertheless, Iran's most valuable resource, petroleum, remained under foreign control.

In 1931, the global economic depression caused a steep fall in royalty payments by the Anglo-Iranian Oil Company (AIOC), an importance source of revenue for Reza Shah's ambitious development programme. The next year he cancelled the oil concession and demanded a revision of the terms of concession, but the British firm resisted before agreeing to adjustments. The parties signed a new concession in 1933 that scaled back the size of the concession area, which meant that Iran could invite other foreign companies to explore for oil in areas formerly reserved to the British. The new concession also created a minimum annual payment and higher dividend rates. In return, Reza Shah extended the expiration date from 1963 to 1993.

He had greater success in his programme for Persian cultural unification. With roughly half the population distributed among various non-Persian groups – Kurdish, Turcoman, Arab, Lur and so on – forging a nation sharing a common culture was not a simple matter. The government took several measures to attain that goal: building and staffing schools that gave instruction exclusively in Persian; banning ethnic costume; and launching an academy to purge Persian of foreign words. Nation-building also required decisions about how to define the nation. Reza Shah envisioned a secular nation, embracing a modern outlook while conscious of historic roots in ancient dynasties. His disdain for the clergy and disregard for Islam set the stage for intermittent clashes with conservative religious opinion. Tensions between court and mosque mounted until they exploded in 1935, when he announced a policy to discourage women from wearing the face veil. Protestors at the shrine city of Mashhad were ruthlessly gunned down. Disgruntled Iranians could only resort to subterfuge to guard the honour of their womenfolk, transporting wives and mothers to public baths in wagons buried under bags of merchandise. Reza Shah carved away clerical authority in law and education, creating ministries to oversee both realms and thus place Islamic courts and schools under the supervision of bureaucrats trained in European ways.

It seems that Reza Shah's successes blinded him to geopolitical realities. In the 1930s, he cultivated economic ties with Germany. When war erupted in Europe in 1939, he declared Iran's neutrality, but British observers perceived a tilt towards the Axis powers. After the Soviet Union entered the war and became allied with Britain, the two powers invaded Iran in August 1941 to secure communications from the Gulf to the Iranian–Soviet border. Reza Shah's military forces that so effectively tamed rebellious strongmen and tribal khans proved no match for European armies. In a matter of weeks, British and Soviet troops crossed the country from opposite directions, converging on Tehran, where they forced the shah to abdicate and leave the country in the hands of his young son, Muhammad Reza Shah, while he departed for exile.

With Reza Shah's removal, long suppressed political forces and energies surfaced. Liberals, socialists and communists jostled with landlords and resurgent tribal khans for power as the elected parliament and cabinet exercised their constitutional prerogatives for the first time in a generation. When the war ended, Britain complied with its pledge to withdraw forces within six months, but the Soviet Union left its forces in the northern province of Azerbaijan, where they supported a socialist administration they had established. The United States and Britain vigorously protested while Iran's elected officials negotiated with Moscow. The Azerbaijan crisis was both an early contest

in the Cold War between capitalist and communist camps and
a replay of earlier historical episodes of Russian encroachment
on Iran. The crisis ended peacefully when the Soviets agreed
to withdraw forces in return for an oil concession. Given the
heightened nationalist mood after five years of renewed foreign
occupation, it is hardly surprising that Iran's parliament never
ratified the concession.

Indeed, the next few years saw sovereign control over oil
become the most significant and contentious issue in Iran. On
one side, nationalists led by veteran politician Muhammad
Musaddiq called for renegotiating the concession held by the
AIOC. On the other side, Muhammad Reza Shah seemed to
favour the status quo and certainly opposed handing control
over relations with the AIOC to parliament. A power struggle
between the court and parliament for control over the army paralleled the oil company controversy. Popular opinion favoured
the nationalists and Musaddiq, and in April 1951 the shah
appointed him Prime Minister. Within days, Musaddiq submitted to parliament a bill to nationalize the oil company, which
was promptly passed.

A major diplomatic crisis ensued, as the British government,
a majority shareholder in the AIOC, backed the oil company's demand to cancel nationalization. London organized
an international boycott of Iranian oil, the primary source of
government revenue. The United States under President Harry
Truman pursued diplomacy to resolve the impasse between
Iran and the AIOC, but to no avail. At the same time that Iran
confronted international pressure, its domestic political arena
was filled with tensions and confrontations. Musaddiq and the
Shah wrestled over control over the armed forces. Leftist parties tugged at the prime minister to advance progressive social
measures on behalf of workers. Religious conservatives, initially
drawn to Musaddiq's nationalist platform, became alarmed at
the prospects of rising secular forces and drifted from his coalition. How long Musaddiq could have balanced the competing
pressures from the court and parliament became moot when
the United States under President Dwight Eisenhower decided
early in 1953 to overthrow his government. The US Central
Intelligence Agency (CIA) plotted with General Fazlollah Zahedi,
a pro-Western officer, religious leaders and the shah to incite
street disturbances to demonstrate that the country was in danger of falling into the hands of communists. The plan went awry
on the first day and the shah fled to Italy, but the CIA impro-
vised an alternate plan that activated military units loyal to its
partner General Zahedi. On 19 August, the coup culminated in

a ten-hour battle outside Musaddiq's Tehran home that ended with his surrender.

Muhammad Reza Shah returned from Rome and instituted firm monarchical rule. The United States replaced Britain as the major foreign power influencing – or in the common Iranian view, manipulating – Iranian affairs. To stabilize the government, Washington approved immediate economic aid while Britain lifted the oil boycott. The United States and Britain then negotiated a new oil agreement with Tehran. In 1954, the British accepted nationalization of the AIOC in return for compensation. Under the agreement, a consortium of British and American companies was to divide operations with a newly formed National Iranian Oil Company (NIOC). The Iranian side would manage domestic distribution of petroleum and handle housing, education and health care for workers while the Anglo–American consortium operated the oilfields and refineries, purchased oil from NIOC, and sold it abroad, splitting the profits 50-50.

The overthrow of Musaddiq marked a turning point in Iran's national political development and international relations. For the next quarter century, Iran was a reliable backer of Western interests in the region and an asset in the Cold War. Thus, in February 1955, when Britain put together a Middle Eastern anti-communist coalition including Iraq and Turkey, the Shah joined the Baghdad Pact. Membership in the pro-Western military alliance was emblematic of both continuity and change since the First World War. On one hand, Iran found itself practically compelled to side with Western powers in geopolitical struggles, in spite of Reza Shah's and Musaddiq's efforts to chart a more independent, neutral course. On the other hand, the Baghdad Pact was a long way from the protectorate proposed in 1919 by British diplomats. That Western powers now sought Iran's participation rather than subjugation was a measure of the Pahlavi achievement in overcoming the country's condition under the Qajars as a weak, fragmented and poor country and in making strides towards becoming a strong, unified and prosperous nation.

IRAQ

In the aftermath of the war, Mesopotamia, the region's ancient cradle of civilization, became a new nation thanks to colonial map making. The three Ottoman provinces of Mosul, Baghdad and Basra shared the waters of the Tigris and Euphrates Rivers and a long history of political unity under a succession of empires. But the inhabitants did not share a common national identity as 'Iraqis' any more than did residents of other lands undergoing the transition from empire to nation. The ingredients making up Iraq included Shi'i Arabs in the south, Sunni Arabs in the west and centre, and Kurds in the north. Jews comprised a large portion of Baghdad's population; Christian villages and city quarters were dispersed in the centre and north.

Iraq's historical development under British tutelage unfolded in two main stages. From 1920 to 1932, Britain held a mandate from the League of Nations to establish national institutions in preparation for full independence. From 1932 to 1958, Iraq had an independent constitutional monarchy. Politics during that period was punctuated by military interventions in 1936 and 1941, British reoccupation during the Second World War, and intermittent tribal uprisings and urban popular protests. The monarchy came to a bloody end at the hands of mutinous officers in July 1958.

During the First World War, London planned to divide Mesopotamia with the French, turning the provinces of Baghdad and Basra into a sphere of direct influence and leaving the province of Mosul to its ally. After the war, British diplomats decided to hang onto Mosul because of the expectation that quantities of oil were present there. It took several years of diplomatic manoeuvring before Mosul's attachment to the rest of Mesopotamia was assured. For one thing, London and Paris had agreed in 1916 that Mosul would become part of a French sphere of indirect influence. Furthermore, the Turkish Republic claimed Mosul as part of its territory. The British dispensed with France's claim by promising a share in a new oil concession to replace the old one held by the Turkish Petroleum Company. The Iraqis sought a minority share (20 per cent) in the company, but British negotiators balked and held up the spectre of Turkish occupation if Baghdad did not accept their terms. In March 1925, the Turkish Petroleum Company (later renamed the Iraq Petroleum Company (IPC)) and the Iraqi government signed terms for a 75-year concession. Two years later, Turkey accepted Mosul's incorporation into Iraq and oil production commenced shortly afterward.

For all their diversity, Iraqis found themselves sharing outrage in April 1920, when the European powers decided to make Great Britain responsible for governing Iraq. In June, revolt broke out which shook off British control over much of the countryside for nearly a month. London then decided to install a son of Sharif Hussein of Mecca, Emir Faisal, as ruler of the country, turning it into a Hashemite monarchy under British tutelage. Faisal had cooperated with the British during the First World War in the Arab Revolt against Ottoman rule. Towards the end of the war, he led Arab forces into Damascus and set up a government, expecting to gain recognition as the ruler of independent Syria. French designs and Britain's decision to leave Syria's fate to Paris doomed that plan. French military forces invaded Syria in July 1920 and Faisal lost his short-lived kingdom. The decision to shift him to Iraq was taken in March 1921 at a meeting of British diplomats known as the Cairo Conference. Faisal moved to Baghdad with an entourage of military officers, Iraqi and Syrian veterans of the Arab Revolt known as the Sharifian officers.

The framework for governing Iraq emerged in stages. The first step took place in November 1922 with the signing of the Anglo–Iraqi Treaty that stipulated a strong advisory role for British officials. The next step was the drafting of a constitution, passed in 1924, that established a constitutional monarchy with an elected parliament, which became a stronghold for conservative tribal leaders. A particularly thorny problem was how to integrate the Kurds, who possess a distinctive culture and language. Moreover, shortly after the end of the First World War, the allies proposed the creation of an autonomous Kurdish region that would have included districts in Turkey and Iraq, but the allies backtracked in 1920. The British experimented with a separate Kurdish entity in northern Iraq, but ultimately decided to let Faisal incorporate the region. According to the 1924 constitution, the Kurds were allowed to use the Kurdish language for official business in their region.

In drawing Iraq's boundaries, British High Commissioner Percy Cox decided to constrict its Gulf shoreline to a band of about sixty miles. His imperious verdict restricted Iraq's capacity to develop port facilities. To make matters worse, the beneficiary of Cox's decision was Kuwait. The lack of clarity surrounding Kuwait's relationship to the Ottoman province of Basra made it plausible for Iraqis to maintain that Kuwait should be part of Iraq, not an independent country. Given the constructed character of modern nations in general, both in terms of their national identities and their international boundaries, the Iraqi claim to Kuwait was neither more nor less valid than that of similar claims.

Emir Faisal's primary concern was not the boundary dispute with Kuwait but consolidation of the monarchy. Apart from the Sharifian officers and urban Sunni Arab dignitaries, he found reliable partners in tribal sheikhs, who dominated the countryside, where three-quarters of the population lived. He curried favour with the sheikhs through two measures; first, by reaffirming their control over tribal lands, supporting a trend dating to the Ottoman land code of 1858 that gradually converted tribesmen into tenants working for large landowning sheikhs. Second, he augmented the sheikhs' power by recognizing the jurisdiction of tribal custom in rural areas. While this arrangement achieved its immediate goal of binding the rural leadership to the central government, it planted the seeds of instability by erecting a highly unequal social and economic order in the countryside that gave impetus to migration from village to city, where shanty towns sprang up in the 1940s and early 1950s.

While Faisal's primary goal was to consolidate the monarchy, Iraqi nationalists strove for independence. In 1930, Iraqi and British negotiators agreed on a draft treaty to pave the way for independence. According to the Anglo–Iraqi Treaty, the two countries would establish an alliance, Britain would continue to occupy the military bases it had set up, and London would support Iraq's admission to the League of Nations as an independent state, a standing it achieved in October 1932. Iraqi nationalists, however, felt that the treaty denied Iraq full independence. Consequently, relations with London remained a sensitive issue in Iraqi politics. Given the treaty's provisions for British control over air bases and reserving to British military advisers exclusive rights to train Iraqi forces, the army became a focal point for nationalist grievances.

Under the constitutional monarchy, Iraqi politics had multiple centres of gravity: the royal court and the cabinet in Baghdad; the Shi'i heartland south of Baghdad; the army; rural tribesmen and landowners; and the British embassy. With power diffused among various interests and freshly minted political institutions not yet capable of withstanding cross-cutting pressures emanating from so many directions, instability was inevitable. The strongest political force to emerge in the 1930s and 1940s was Arab nationalism, which appealed in particular to educated townsmen. Three issues became the focus of nationalist agitation. First, the Anglo–Iraqi Treaty of 1930 restricted Iraq's sovereignty in military and foreign affairs. Second, Jewish colonization of Palestine under British auspices stoked anger at London and suspicion of Iraq's large and ancient Jewish community. Third, the IPC moved slowly to develop oil production and export capacity, primarily because the Western consortium that owned it held oil rights in other parts of the world, so their interest in Iraq's oil was to keep the price high, not to maximize revenues for national development.

In addition to Arab nationalism, political movements for social and economic equality incubated among workers in traditional and modern sectors, such as the railroad and oilfields. In the scope of Gulf history, Iraq's current of leftist parties and organizations was precocious and influential. The first large-scale organized labour strike occurred in 1931. Workers protested at a tax increase imposed in the midst of the global depression. In the face of a widespread labour strike, the government rescinded the tax. It also kept a close eye on the labour – leftist alliance to contain its influence thereafter.

In 1933, King Faisal died and his son Ghazi became the new king. The young monarch exhibited sympathy for the Arab nationalists and resistance to British influence, not only in Iraq but also in the Middle East and the Gulf in general. For instance, King Ghazi raised the question of Kuwait's sovereignty and Iraq's claim to it. His ardent nationalist sentiment made him popular with army officers, who were growing restless over British refusal to supply heavy armaments. The officer corps was forming political factions mirroring splits among civilian political leaders. In October 1936, a group of officers seized power in the Arab world's first military *coup d'état*. The plot's strongman, General Bakr Sidqi, led a faction of officers and civilians that admired Kemalist Turkey's model of secular rule under a dominant personality. The Sidqi government's one lasting achievement was a border agreement with Iran to resolve the dispute over the Shatt al-Arab. That agreement formed part of a larger security arrangement among Iraq, Iran, Turkey and Afghanistan, the Saadabad Pact of July 1937. The next month, the Sidqi government ended as it began, in a military coup, as Arab nationalist officers assassinated him and restored civilian government.

When the Second World War broke out, Britain invoked its treaty right to use Iraqi air bases. Although it was entitled to do so, the move exacerbated nationalist resentment. The Iraqi cabinet was divided between pro-British and Arab nationalist politicians pulling the government in opposite directions on wartime matters, such as whether to sever ties with Italy. In April 1941, Arab nationalist colonels joined nationalist politicians to seize power in Iraq's second *coup d'état*. The colonels wanted to deny the British access to the air bases, in violation of the treaty, and to order all British troops out of the country. The British responded in May by sending forces from India through Basra and from Transjordan to reoccupy Iraq. They then installed a friendly cabinet that purged nationalist officers. As a short-term wartime measure, London's resort to armed force filled the immediate need to secure communications between the Gulf and the Mediterranean. Its impact on the long-term trajectory of Iraq's politics was to undermine the legitimacy of the monarchy and pro-British politicians like Prime Minister Nuri al-Said.

The post-war decolonization trend in Asia and Africa further tilted Iraq's political playing field in favour of nationalist forces. For one thing, the very *raison d'être* for the build-up of British power in the Gulf, securing imperial communications to India, ended in August 1947, when India and Pakistan gained independence. That did not mean, however, that Britain no longer had a stake in Gulf affairs. Treaty relations with the Arab sheikhdoms and access to oil offered compelling reasons for ongoing involvement. Popular sentiment, however, made it increasingly difficult for Iraq's political elite to maintain close relations with London. In 1947–8, nationalist feeling crystallized around two issues, one a purely Anglo–Iraqi matter, the other Palestine.

Baghdad's pro-British leadership renegotiated the 1930 Treaty to establish Iraqi control over the air bases in return for extending the treaty from 1957 to 1973. London and Baghdad were prepared to sign the treaty of Portsmouth in January 1948, but Iraqis were not in the mood to accept a British military presence any longer and massive protests erupted throughout the country. The scale of the protests, known in Iraqi history as The Leap (*al-Wathba*), compelled the government to renounce the treaty. At the same time, the struggle for Palestine was entering a decisive phase, with the United Nations voting in November 1947 in favour of dividing the land into Jewish and Arab states. When the British left Palestine in May 1948, Israel proclaimed its independence. Iraq sent forces to Transjordan to participate in the war. In Iraq itself, the establishment of Israel generated a popular backlash against the ancient Jewish community, large numbers of which departed in the next few years.

The government tried to regain its footing in the early 1950s with plans for economic development. In 1950, Iraqi negotiators reached agreement with IPC to increase royalty payments; two years later, the company agreed to another revision that established profit sharing on an equal basis. Oil revenues rose, bolstered by the development of oilfields in the south around Basra and the completion of a pipeline to transport oil from the northern fields around Kirkuk to Baniyas, a Syrian port on the Mediterranean. Unlike the smaller sheikhdoms that had very favourable ratios of oil income to population, Iraq's oil wealth could not make an immediate impact visible throughout the country. The government invested in basic infrastructure projects to prevent flooding and to maximize water utilization through new irrigation networks; the expansion of Basra's port to handle more volume, and the enlargement of Baghdad's airport. The authors of development from above hoped that advances would diminish the appeal of leftist parties and labour movements and prevent occurrences like the August 1952 strike by workers at the port of Basra for higher wages, improved housing and better working conditions.

In the mid-1950s, the constitutional monarchy's political foundation was eroding in the face of domestic and regional events. Bickering between the court and the cabinet undermined the government's coherence. Arab nationalism was gaining momentum, especially after the consolidation of Egypt's Free Officers government led by Gamal Abdul Nasser, whose speeches broadcast over 'The Voice of the Arabs' radio programme roused anti-imperialism throughout the region. The Iraqi government's decision in February 1955 to join the Baghdad Pact, a security alliance with Iran, Turkey, Pakistan and Great Britain, may have appeared to its authors as a positive step away from the 1930 Treaty to a more independent security relationship with the West. To its domestic critics and to Nasser, however, it looked like Britain is going out the front door by allowing the 1930 Treaty to lapse and re-entering through the back door. In the propaganda battle waged over the newly introduced medium of radio, Nasser's call for neutrality in the Cold War and a complete break with all forms of Western domination appealed to many Iraqis. Furthermore, the British did their Iraqi supporters no favour by participating in the ill-fated 1956 Suez War with Israel and France against Egypt. The government had to impose martial law for six months to cope with the wave of anti-British demonstrations that swept the country.

The next regional jolt came in February 1958, when Egypt and Syria fulfilled Arab nationalist dreams by declaring the formation of the United Arab Republic (UAR). In a bid to display its own inclination to pursue Arab unity, the Iraqi government formed a federation with the monarchy in Jordan. An invitation to the Kuwaitis to join fell flat: Kuwait was still a British protectorate and quite uncertain about long-term Iraqi intentions. Regional tensions escalated in spring 1958, with the outbreak of violence in Lebanon pitting pro-Western and Arab nationalist forces against each other. It appeared that pro-Nasser, Arab nationalist demonstrations might destabilize Jordan, and the Iraqi government ordered army units to head westward to bolster the neighbouring Hashemite monarchy. On their way through Baghdad on 14 July, a group of officers seized the opportunity to take over the capital, storm the palace, massacre the royal family, and proclaim the overthrow of the monarchy.

Over the course of 35 years, the constitutional monarchy had failed to develop enduring political institutions to ensure its survival in the stormy era of decolonization. On the other hand, under the mandate and as an independent nation, the monarchy laid down the framework of a modern state encompassing the three former Ottoman provinces, establishing a national army to defend the borders and pacify restless elements of the population, and developing a national bureaucracy to implement government policy throughout the country in education, industry, labour, health and finance. These were historical departures in the region's political culture that paralleled the course in neighbouring Iran.

SAUDI ARABIA

The end of Ottoman influence in Arabia simplified the geopolitical framework by leaving Great Britain as the uncontested external power. London used its sway to broker struggles among contenders for supremacy in the peninsula. Abdulaziz ibn Saud had consolidated control over much of Najd and al-Hasa during the war, while Sharif Hussein of Mecca proclaimed the independent Hashemite Kingdom of Hijaz. In Hail, the Rashidis, bereft of their Ottoman sponsors, hunkered down to defend their shrunken domain. Ibn Saud unleashed his fighters against the Rashidis and conquered Hail in 1921. He then used superior tribal diplomacy and military forces against Sharif Hussein. At the end of 1924, Saudi forces occupied Mecca. Sharif Hussein abdicated in favour of his son Ali, who retreated to Jeddah. Through a combination of military and economic pressures, Ibn Saud compelled Sharif Ali to surrender the 'bride of the sea' the following year.

The military forces that Ibn Saud commanded were a mix of levies from the towns of Najd, allied tribesmen and warriors known as the *Ikhwan* (the Brethren). This last element had first taken shape around 1912, when Ibn Saud sent Wahhabi preachers to proselytize Bedouin tribesmen who had settled in agricultural colonies. From the perspective of consolidating central authority, settling the Bedouin removed a perennial obstacle to state formation because their mobility and loyalty to tribal chiefs made them difficult, if not impossible, to control. Wahhabi clerics supported the project because they regarded the Bedouin as Muslims in name only. The former nomads proved eager pupils

Ibn Saud cannot control Bedu tribesmen

and embraced the Wahhabi view of others as polytheists against
whom waging jihad was a duty to bring into the fold of Islam.
Thus, when Ibn Saud commanded the Ikhwan to fight the
Rashidis or the Hashemites, they willingly mobilized. On the
other hand, when the Ikhwan waged jihad against 'polytheist'
tribesmen and villagers in Iraq and Transjordan, Ibn Saud found
himself in a quandary, for both governments were under British
mandate. He had to choose between the Ikhwan's doctrinal
purity and international order. The Ikhwan forced the issue after
the conquest of Hijaz with a series of raids on Iraqi border posts.
The British insisted that Ibn Saud rein in his zealous subjects. He
convened two conferences in Riyadh to find a way to mollify the
Ikhwan, but religious zeal on the part of rank and file tribesmen,
and political ambition on the part of tribal chiefs made it impossible to cut a deal. In March 1929, Ibn Saud inflicted a decisive
defeat on rebellious Ikhwan at Sibila in north-eastern Arabia.

In a larger sense, the battle marked the definitive triumph of
the centralizing impulse driving the expansion and consolidation
of the third Saudi state. Pacifying the desert was an essential step.
Ibn Saud rounded out his domains with conquests in Asir province in the south-west. In 1932, he proclaimed the Kingdom of
Saudi Arabia. Turning a patchwork of conquered territories, their
fractious tribesmen and diverse regions into a unified polity was
a project that would take decades to achieve. In Najd, the Saudi
heartland, Ibn Saud cultivated his authority through customary
means and relationships, forming alliances with tribal chieftains
through patronage and allocating them subsidies to distribute to
their own tribal followers. He used marriage with women from
various tribes to forge kinship links through offspring. To administer different parts of the country, he broke with the practice of
the first and second Saudi states which ruled through local notables. Instead, he designated members of Al Saud.

Managing Hijaz required a special set of arrangements for
three reasons. First, possession of the holy cities necessitated
sensitive diplomatic antennae for Ibn Saud to receive general
Muslim acceptance of his rule over them. Second, the religious scene in Mecca and Medina featured different Sunni legal
schools, a small Shi'i community, and devotees of Sufi orders.
Extending Wahhabi norms required some degree of tact. Third,
the late Ottoman and Hashemite years had seen the arrival of
newspapers, private and public schooling with a modern fla-
vour, and a taste of constitutional government. Rather than
hastily devise a uniform framework that would inevitably roil
Hijazis or Najdis, or both, the king decided to leave things alone,
allowing Hijaz to pursue an independent course in educational

development under the guidance of its town notables, while Najd remained the preserve of Wahhabi religious authority, tribal sheikhs and town leaders.

Saudi Arabia's seizure of al-Hasa in 1913 was a natural step in Ibn Saud's bid to revive his patrimony. The first Saudi emirate had ruled the fertile coastal region for two decades and it was part of the second Saudi emirate for around four decades. From Riyadh's perspective, control over al-Hasa had three advantages. First, its oases were a rich agricultural base; second, its ports offered outlets to Persian Gulf trade; third, its proximity to Najd gave it strategic significance. Before the 1930s, nobody imagined that beneath its sands lay vast lakes of petroleum, the single resource that would bring to the kingdom prosperity and global economic importance. The incorporation of al-Hasa presented a distinctive challenge because of its large Shi'i population. In Wahhabi eyes, the Shi'is are polytheists who must convert to Islam. After an initial exodus of religious leaders, al-Hasa's Shi'is adjusted to Saudi rule under the stern hand of provincial governor Emir Abdullah ibn Jiluwi. In the 1920s, official policy fluctuated between persecution and toleration, reflecting the waxing and waning of Ikhwan influence. With their final defeat, Ibn Jiluwi settled on a policy of implicit toleration as long as Shi'is were discreet about their religious celebrations.

In foreign relations, Ibn Saud relied on advisers from Egypt and Syria. Men like Fuad Hamza and Hafiz Wahba brought familiarity with modern statecraft and institutions to the royal entourage in addition to experience in the broader Arab world and in dealings with Western officials. The king's receptivity to ideas and customs from the outside world was something new in the history of Saudi rulers and stemmed from his years in exile in Kuwait, where he witnessed the flow of foreign visitors to Sheikh Mubarak. Ibn Saud acquired a keen appreciation of British power, and the record of his contacts with British envoys during the world war reflects that. Yet he was determined to avoid the dependency that circumscribed the Gulf sheikhs. During the war, he received subsidies from Britain and then saw them dry up at war's end. In the late 1920s, his meagre treasury depended on revenues from the annual pilgrimage to Mecca, hence his sensitivity to foreign Muslim opinion and his eagerness to gain recognition for the legitimacy of his rule over the holy cities. The onset of the global economic depression in 1929 led to a protracted decline in the flow of pilgrims and a corresponding fall in revenues from Mecca. Within a couple of years, Ibn Saud was in dire need of a new source of funds.

5. Exploring for Oil in Saudi Arabia.

In 1932, Western petroleum engineers struck oil in Bahrain, British and American prospectors believed Saudi Arabia's Eastern Province (as al-Hasa was renamed in 1950) was worth exploring. The question for Ibn Saud, then, was which foreign company would get the opportunity to prospect for oil. British firms were possible candidates. In 1927, he had signed the Treaty of Jeddah with London whereby Great Britain recognized Saudi Arabia's independence in exchange for Ibn Saud's pledge to maintain good relations with the Gulf sheikhdoms under British protection. But he did not want to become a British client and was therefore open to the option of signing a concession with American oil companies. In 1933, an American consortium obtained the oil concession, the terms of which included a sizable loan to bring relief to the king's depleted coffers. Five years later, the Americans struck oil, but the outbreak of the Second World War delayed large-scale production.

During the war, the United States emerged on the world stage as a leading power, a role it would play for the rest of the century. America's 'rise to globalism' is a complex tale in its own right. Its Persian Gulf sub-plot stems not only from a voracious appetite for oil but also from Washington's strategic outlook. In 1943, President Franklin D. Roosevelt approved extending lend – lease assistance to Riyadh, in recognition of its important role as an oil supplier. The next step arose from the expansive redefinition of US military needs, which depended on a worldwide network of naval and air bases to station troops and supplies.

In 1945, the Americans constructed a military air field near the Aramco installations at Dhahran in the Eastern Province.

The arrival of American oil engineers and aviators on Saudi soil had profound effects on the social, cultural, economic and political realms. The Wahhabi establishment had always insisted on keeping its domain pure of infidels; the Americans had no wish to mingle with their hosts; Al Saud wanted revenue from oil production, not social transformation. The upshot was the creation of special enclaves for oilfields and residential compounds. Wahhabi clerics were satisfied that infidel ways were isolated from Saudi society; American oilmen and their families lived on compounds where they did not have to abide by local norms and could enjoy the amenities and leisure pastimes of Western suburbia.

Not everybody involved in the industry was so fortunate. The Aramco oil company operated according to a hierarchy running, in descending order, from Americans, to Italians, to Arabs. Wahhabi clerics viewed segregation as morally necessary, and Americans regarded the ethnic hierarchy as natural,

6. Khobar Aramco Petrol Station.

but company discrimination fostered discontent in the ranks of Saudi workers. For one thing, inequality in pay was stark. For another, the Americans refused to allow Saudis onto Western compounds, and Saudi employees lived in all-male compounds because the company refused to allow their families to live with them. In 1945, labour protests erupted over pay and working conditions. The company made some concessions and in the early 1950s sent a handful of Saudi employees to Beirut and Cairo for business training to meet demands for promotion opportunities. American directors in Eastern Province, however, continued to suppose that Arab employees were not entitled to improved living conditions, leading to a new round of confrontation in 1953.

It is notable that labour leaders first tried to solve their grievances by legitimate means, which in this case meant submitting to the king a petition setting forth their request for better housing and higher wages. When Crown Prince Saud had the leaders thrown into gaol, 13,000 workers went on strike in October 1953. The work stoppage lasted for two weeks before it collapsed, and its leaders were fired, but their efforts were not in vain. Not long after Saud ascended to the throne in November 1953, he got Aramco to grant higher wages, better conditions in the camps, and access to education for the children of workers. Having ensured the pacification of Eastern Province workers, Riyadh's rulers could enjoy the rising tide of income from the export of oil.

The incorporation of al-Hasa revived Saudi rule along the Gulf coast from Kuwait to Qatar and Trucial sheikhdoms. It also raised the vexing question of how to draw precise international borders. The first issue to arise involved the zone where Saudi claims intersected with Iraq and Kuwait. In the absence of any obvious physical boundary and the overlapping domains of nomadic tribes, an international border was bound to have an arbitrary quality. The issue was resolved, or perhaps more precisely a British solution was imposed, in 1922 at the Uqair Conference, by its High Commissioner for Iraq, Sir Percy Cox. The British official unilaterally allocated to Iraq territory that Ibn Saud claimed for Najd; compensated Ibn Saud with around two-thirds of the territory that Al Sabah believed properly belonged to Kuwait; and, perhaps most fatefully, pushed Kuwait's Gulf shoreline northward, leaving Iraq with a very narrow band of beach front and sowing the seed for recidivist sentiment in Baghdad (see below on the Buraimi dispute between Saudi Arabia, Abu Dhabi and Oman).

When King Abdulaziz ibn Saud died in November 1953, he bequeathed to his sons a realm that remained a patchwork of

loosely integrated regions held together by *ad hoc* administrative practices, with a Najdi core of loyal townsmen and Wahhabi
clerics, and a reliable revenue stream from petroleum exports.
Ibn Saud ruled through personal relationships, in large measure through personal charisma, tribal diplomacy and, when he
deemed necessary, brute force. Putting Saudi rule on firmer institutional foundations was a task that he left to his successors.

Succession was not to prove a simple matter. Crown Prince
Saud had ascended the throne in accordance with his father's
intentions. Whether he could have ruled in a manner that
pre-empted a power struggle within the family is not clear. He
proved unable to curb the extravagant spending habits of Saudi
princes, which outstripped income from royalties on oil sales.
His response to the political challenge emerging from Arab
nationalist forces outside the kingdom struck his brother Faisal,
the new crown prince, as inadequate, and he soon emerged as
a rival to King Saud. Prince Faisal had ably served his father as
the governor of Hijaz and *de facto* foreign minister. The royal
family formed factions around the king and the crown prince.
Complicating the picture was the emergence of younger princes
leaning towards internal reform and the Arab nationalist trend
in regional politics. The so-called 'Free Princes' were led by Talal
ibn Abdulaziz. At times, they favoured Saud, when he promised
to pursue policies that would throw Saudi support behind the
Arab nationalist current; at other times, they sided with Faisal
for his inclination to introduce measures that would modernize the country's infrastructure and governance. The contest
between Saud and Faisal lasted nearly a decade before it ended
in Saud's deposition and Faisal's coronation.

BAHRAIN

In considering Bahrain's political development, it is essential to keep in mind its distinctive demographic composition.
Most of the population was sedentary, living off the sea (fishing, pearling, ship building, trade) and cultivation; only a very
small population was nomadic. The heterogeneous population
included the ruling Sunni clan, Al Khalifah, and allied settled
Sunni tribes; the Hawala, Sunni immigrants from the Iranian
shore; the Baharnah, the Arab Shi'i majority residing in small
villages and towns; and Persian Shi'is. Al Khalifah and the Sunni
population had dominated local affairs since the late 1700s, but

the years after the First World War saw the British assume a more intrusive role in Bahrain's affairs manifest in the clarification of the Political Agent's formal responsibilities and the creation of administrative bodies. As a result, the Shi'i majority became more assertive in protesting discrimination and claiming their rights.

In February 1919, the stage was set for post-war political developments when London issued the Bahrain Order-in-Council, a regulation that expanded the formal powers of Britain's Political Agent at the expense of the ruling sheikh. Its provisions included assigning jurisdiction over resident foreigners to the Political Agent. In July 1920, the British persuaded Sheikh Isa to establish a Manama Municipal Council to supervise public health and roads. The sheikh was to name four Bahraini members and the Political Agent was to name four resident foreigners.

Tensions between the sheikh and the British worsened in the wake of a Shi'i uprising 1922 that erupted in response to the mistreatment of a Shi'i villager by one of the Sheikh Isa's retainers. After shopkeepers shut down the bazaar in Manama, a delegation submitted a petition to Sheikh Isa seeking relief from arbitrary arrest, detention by members of Al Khalifah other than the ruler and forced labour. After winning concessions on these points, the Baharnah then pushed for the abolition of taxes imposed on Shi'is. The Shi'i protest invited meddling from Bahrain's neighbours. Ibn Saud supported Sunni tribesmen opposed to sharing the burden of taxation and he worried that al-Hasa's Shi'is might seek similar relief from taxation. In Iran, the plight of fellow Shi'is became a popular cause and a justification for asserting historic claims. The British decided that a reform programme for Bahrain offered the best prospect of calming the political situation. Towards that end, the Political Resident visited in May 1923 and announced Sheikh Isa's retirement, supposedly due to his advanced age, and the succession of his son Sheikh Hamad.

Bahrain's new ruler proceeded with reforms of fiscal and judicial procedures. He instituted a budget and reorganized the collection of customs duties, the primary source of taxes at the time. Addressing the perennial Shi'i complaint of arbitrary treatment at the hands of Al Khalifah, the sheikh abolished private courts and ordered the establishment of the Bahrain State Court. Members of Al Khalifah, dissatisfied with the curbs on their power, joined with Sunni tribesmen and merchants to resist the reforms. In June 1923, a party of tribesmen attacked a Shi'i village. Sheikh Hamad arrested and punished the chief of the tribe and fined its members for killing three villagers, marking the end of immunity to retribution for attacking Baharnah. To discourage future attacks, a police force was created the following year staffed by British-trained Baluchi recruits. The British also intensified their supervision of local affairs by appointing a full-time adviser to the sheikh and special advisers to oversee the police, budget and customs departments. Britain's protection of Bahrain from annexation and conquest was turning into a virtual protectorate with shrinking powers for the ruling sheikh.

In the early 1930s, the Great Depression and competition from Japanese cultured pearls devastated Bahrain. In five years, pearl sales lost half their value. Fortunately, a new field of employment opened up with the development of the oil industry. Bahrain was the first Gulf sheikhdom to sign an oil concession and begin producing oil. The origin of the concession for Bahraini oil went back to 1924, when a British firm made a deal with Sheikh Hamad to drill artesian wells. A year later, the sheikh agreed to an oil concession but British petroleum engineers regarded Bahrain as an unlikely site for a strike, so the concession passed along to an American firm, Standard Oil Company of California. In 1929, Standard Oil formed the Bahrain Petroleum Company (BAPCO) to operate the concession. In May 1932, drillers struck oil, triggering a rush of prospecting up and down the Gulf, from Kuwait to Oman. The first shipment was exported in June 1934; the next year, Al Khalifah received the first royalty payment. Production increased to eight million barrels per year by 1937, the same year construction of the first refinery was completed.

Petroleum production had pervasive effects. It provided new employment for pearl divers. Revenues made possible the expansion of education, medical and municipal services. Higher incomes stimulated trade and opened opportunities for merchants. Finally, by concentrating workers in a single industry, petroleum stimulated the appearance of a labour movement that brought together Sunni and Shi'i workers. The struggle between workers and the oil company in Bahrain was unique in the way it blended labour grievances with nationalist feeling. To develop the oilfields, BAPCO recruited workers from Iran, which already had a pool of skilled, experienced men familiar with the operations of the AIOC. By 1938, several hundred Iranians were employed by BAPCO. Bahraini authorities and British officials wanted to avoid increasing the Iranian presence because they felt it might buttress Tehran's claim over the country. When BAPCO started building its refinery, the British encouraged the company to hire skilled workers from India to diminish dependence on Iranian labour and deflate Iran's territorial ambition. Labour protests by Bahraini workers in November 1938 focused on preferential treatment for foreign workers, who outnumbered Bahrainis, received higher wages and had better housing. A delegation of Bahraini workers demanded improved wages and housing along with training courses to qualify them for skilled positions. The company offered partial satisfaction by agreeing to provide better housing.

In addition to labour unrest, Bahrain was the scene of a robust movement for political reform that followed counterparts in Kuwait and Dubai in 1938. The movement was propelled by a number of factors. Economic distress caused by the decline of pearling affected all strata whereas oil revenues chiefly benefited Al Khalifah and a small number of workers. Egyptian newspapers circulated articles criticizing the extent of foreign influence in Bahrain. Finally, Sheikh Hamad's health was failing and members of Al Khalifah began to manoeuvre for a succession struggle. (Hamad lived until 1942, when Salman succeeded him as the ruling sheikh.) In September, Sheikh Salman, the eldest son of Sheikh Hamad, joined with prominent merchants to call for reforms, in exchange for their support for his bid to be designated as crown prince. The merchants' list of demands included the creation of a legislative council, codification of the law and measures to reform the police. The legislative council would take over daily administration of the country, a change that would turn the ruling sheikh into a figurehead. The British Political Agent firmly supported Sheikh Hamad's refusal to yield on the legislative council. The outbreak of the oil workers' protest focused attention on their demands and the reform movement died down.

One reason for the subsequent calm was the appearance of new opportunities for Bahrain's distressed traders. Western companies came looking for local merchants to form business partnerships. One former pearling merchant who provisioned the British air base developed contacts with General Electric, and became the sole distributor of its products. The same merchant later obtained the rights to market General Motors vehicles. Other merchants entered lucrative contracts with Aramco and Western airline companies. In the decade following the Second World War, Manama blossomed as the hub for the import of commercial goods sought by the growing number of Westerners living in the region and of equipment for oil firms prospecting in the Lower Gulf.

Important developments in education occurred during the inter-war period. The earliest Western school had been founded by American missionaries in the 1890s. On a visit to England in 1919, one of Sheikh Isa's sons visited schools and upon returning to Bahrain he gained support from merchants to set up a school on the English model. Shi'is seeking admission for their children to the school were turned away, so they formed a committee to raise funds to build their own school with the blessings of Sheikh Hamad. The growing number of Sunni and Shi'i schools for boys and girls led the government to establish in 1929 an education department. Three years later, separate schools for Sunni and Shi'i pupils were abolished without incident. Oil revenue expanded state budgets starting in 1935, allowing for the construction of additional schools and expanding access to education. The British encouraged the creation of secondary schools in order to discourage families from sending children to Iraq, Lebanon and Egypt, where the British feared Bahrainis would become exposed to Arab nationalist sentiment and come home with anti-imperialist ideas. To staff the first secondary schools to open in 1939, teachers were recruited from Palestine and Egypt. As a by-product of the spread of education, school graduates and traders set up literary clubs to promote Arab and Persian culture. Parallel to the literary clubs, Shi'i Baharnah developed 'mourning associations' (*ma'tam*s), established in the early 1900s to organize celebrations of the Ashura holy day, into cultural clubs.

A new round of political unrest in the mid-1950s brought together previously disparate strands of activism surrounding liberal measures, labour rights and Arab nationalist demands. The backdrop to the unrest was a decline in foreign trade caused by regional developments. The embargo on Iran during the oil nationalization crisis curtailed trade with one of Bahrain's main partners. Saudi Arabia's development of a new port at Dammam diverted the kingdom's imports that used to pass through Bahrain. Within Bahrain, competition for choice jobs between South Asian and Bahraini workers simmered at BAPCO, and sectarian skirmishes erupted between Sunnis and Shi'is over seats on local councils. Arab nationalists, considering sectarian strife a distraction from anti-British activism, tried to unify Bahrainis in pursuit of liberal reforms. In October 1954, they formed a body called the Higher Executive Committee, demanding judicial reforms, a representative legislature and legal trade unions. But the customary obstacles to bringing all elements of Bahraini society into a single nationalist organization were embodied by the decision of the Hawala Sunni Arabs to form a separate group. The Higher Executive Committee petitioned and pressed for its programme. It eventually persuaded Sheikh Salman to issue legislation that allowed the formation of a labour federation, but he rejected the proposal for an elected legislative council because it would have struck a blow at the core of Al Khalifah's power. As enthusiasm in the region swelled for Arab nationalism, the Higher Executive Committee pressed ahead with its campaign for more labour rights, better education and health care and press freedom.

The popular mood was growing angrier in early 1956 as the region polarized over the escalating confrontation between Arab nationalists and the Western powers. When British Foreign Secretary John Selwyn Lloyd visited Bahrain in March, demonstrators pelted his motorcade. A few days later, the Higher Executive Committee called for a strike to protest at the killing of five demonstrators by police. Resentment at British domination and Al Khalifah's resistance to loosening the reins of power kept alive the mood of dissent for several months. When Britain joined with France and Israel in the Suez War against Egypt at the end of October, demonstrations swept the country and protestors torched foreign commercial properties. The government declared martial law to quell the unrest, arresting the leading figures in the Higher Executive Committee. The authorities also moved to isolate activists by co-opting merchants with new opportunities for selling goods to BAPCO. In 1957, the regime issued a new labour law that improved basic conditions for workers with limits on hours and granting sick leave, while placing firm restrictions on labour activism. These measures worked to bring about a few years of calm before labour issues resurfaced in the 1960s.

KUWAIT

Compared to Bahrain, Kuwait's internal affairs enjoyed a period of quiet development. For one thing, Al Sabah ruled a more homogenous population largely comprised of fellow Sunni Arabs than did their Utub tribal cousins in Manama. Kuwait's Shi'i minority was divided into four distinct communities: Persians, Hawala, Baharnah and immigrants from al-Hasa. The nomadic element in the population, a source of unrest for much of Arabia's history, numbered only around 10,000 out of a total population of 60,000 in 1918. Most Kuwaitis depended for livelihoods on the traditional coastal activities of pearling, fishing and trade. The development of the oil industry affected the relationship between Al Sabah sheikhs and merchants who made one notable attempt to gather a share of political power, but it did not trigger the kind of labour unrest that roiled Bahrain because most of the workers in Kuwait were expatriates, so the few protests were contained. The major source of concern came from external pressure. It was no longer the Ottoman Empire pressing on the sheikhdom but Saudi Arabia.

Tensions between Kuwait and Saudi Arabia arose for a number of reasons. First, Kuwait resented the British decision at the Uqair Conference to give a large chunk of its territory to Saudi Arabia. Second, Ikhwan tribesmen raided the sheikhdom as an extension of their jihad against neighbouring territories. Third, Abdulaziz ibn Saud frequently referred to the Najdi origin of many clans residing in Kuwait, suggesting that he harboured the intention of asserting a claim to the sheikhdom. And fourth, Ibn Saud wanted the Kuwaitis to establish border control to collect customs duties on his behalf. To get his way, he imposed a blockade but it was only selectively enforced because of the difficulty of patrolling all of the possible routes by land and sea that smugglers could use. Furthermore, Abdulaziz allowed shipments of food supplies to pass from Kuwait to Najd. Even so, the blockade caused dissatisfaction among Najdi tribesmen accustomed to trade with Kuwait and it inclined them in the later 1920s to join with rebellious elements of the Ikhwan. Left to its own devices, Kuwait would have had a hard time dealing with the Ikhwan, but British air and armoured car patrols proved effective at repelling their raids. It was the prospect of oil concessions in the Saudi–Kuwaiti neutral zone drawn by the British that brought about negotiations in the mid-1930s to end the blockade, but they did not reach formal agreement until 1943.

Kuwait's internal political development turned on efforts by merchants to gain a share in governance. A group of them viewed the death of Sheikh Salim in February 1921 as an occasion to make their voices heard on the question of choosing a successor, but the ruling clan closed ranks and chose Sheikh Ahmad al-Jabir as the new ruler. He then met with the leading merchants and promised to consult with them on important matters. In 1930, a group of merchants decided to form a municipal council, the first formal administrative and elective body in the sheikhdom. Its members were elected by fellow merchants to two-year terms. The council took responsibility for sanitation, roads and town planning. A second initiative by merchants in 1936 was to establish an education council.

Kuwait's precocious movement for political participation blossomed into a fully fledged confrontation between Al Sabah and reformist merchants in the 1938 Majles Movement. In addition to the formation of the education and municipal councils, the background to the 1938 reform movement included economic hardship and the question of control over oil. In 1934, Sheikh Ahmad signed an oil concession with British Petroleum and Gulf Oil, which operated as the Kuwait Oil Company. When drillers struck oil in 1938, the local economy was suffering the effects of Saudi Arabia's blockade, the decline of pearling and the global depression. To make matters worse, Al Sabah responded to the fall in customs revenues by raising taxes on local trade. The experience of running municipal and education councils emboldened the merchants to seek a share of royalty payments for Kuwait's oil, which was somewhat premature since the first exports did not ship out until 1946. Sheikh Ahmad was bent on keeping oil revenue under his control and decided to go on the offensive by dissolving the education council and interfering in elections to the municipal council. It was a bold move because until then the merchants and the ruling clan had not meddled in each other's affairs. Merchants circulated leaflets calling for deeper administrative reforms and the sheikh's abdication. In March, Sheikh Ahmad had a leader of the protest arrested and beaten, prompting several merchants to move to Iraq, a customary form of protest throughout the Gulf.

Such a move made sense for merchants who owned properties in southern Iraq, but at the same time it strengthened the Iraqi tendency to view Kuwait as its territory. Dissident merchants who remained in Kuwait petitioned for an elected legislative council or Majles. Under pressure from Iraq, which took up the reform cause, and facing splits within Al Sabah, Sheikh Ahmad let the merchants hold elections to the Majles, supported by Kuwait's first political party, the National Bloc. At first, the sheikh tried to cooperate with the Majles, but it alarmed him by issuing a charter that proclaimed its authority over the budget, security, justice, health and education. The Majles then turned to curbing Al Sabah's privileges in imposing taxes and mustering forced labour. When the Majles claimed control over oil revenues, Sheikh Ahmad proclaimed its dissolution on 17 December 1938.

Hoping to find a way to reconcile the pressures for political participation with sheikhly power, he endorsed new elections to an expanded Majles. But the men elected to the second Majles proved no more docile than the first. Sheikh Ahmad submitted a draft constitution but the Majles rejected it because it assigned more power to the executive than its members wished to see. In March 1939, the sheikh again dissolved the elected body. Dissident legislators took their protest to the streets. Sheikh Ahmad announced that the authorities had discovered a plot by members of the Majles movement to annex the country to Iraq and suppressed the movement by force.

The Majles Movement revealed significant cleavages in Kuwaiti society. The merchants seeking a share in power were all Sunnis from Utub clans and saw themselves as part of the ruling elite alongside Al Sabah. The Majles would ensure the perpetuation of their position at the top of the social hierarchy. They made no attempt to include Shi'is in their movement or in the Majles, handing Sheikh Ahmad the opportunity to cultivate Shi'i backing. Thus, when he dissolved the Majles, Shi'is openly backed him. The movement also aggravated rifts within Al Sabah that Sheikh Ahmad had tried to mend by distributing responsibility for administrative functions to fellow clansmen. By the late 1930s, the police, the treasury, courts and the port had become private fiefdoms run by members of Al Sabah. The reformers did gain an important ally from Al Sabah when the ruler's cousin Sheikh Abdullah al-Salim expressed his support, but the demands of the Majles led the sheikhs to close ranks against the merchants.

A new compact between sheikhs and merchants emerged after the Second World War. Its author was Sheikh Abdullah al-Salim, who became the ruler after Sheikh Ahmad died in 1950. His accession coincided with an increase in oil revenues that stemmed from two regional developments. First, Saudi Arabia negotiated a 50-50 profit sharing arrangement with Aramco in 1950. The Kuwait Oil Company accepted the same arrangement in November 1951. Second, Iran's nationalization of the AIOC in 1953 resulted in a worldwide boycott of Iranian oil. The removal of Britain's largest supplier of oil boosted demand for Kuwaiti production.

With abundant oil revenue, Sheikh Abdullah launched an ambitious programme to develop Kuwait's infrastructure. The government drew up a six-year plan which included projects to expand the number of schools, construct new port facilities, increase electric power generation and enlarge the water treatment facility to reduce Kuwait's dependence on supplies imported by boat from Shatt al-Arab. Responsibility for implementing the projects was turned over to five large British firms. The scale of the plans stimulated an influx of workers from the entire region, from Iraq to Oman, none of them needing visas. While expatriate workers laid down the first paved roads and erected water storage towers, they attracted resentment. Kuwait's traditional boat-building and pearling sectors were on the verge of extinction as the number of pearling vessels fell from 82 in 1948 to a dozen or so ten years later. Displaced workers did not welcome foreign competition although the scale of construction projects created so much demand for labour that both local and foreign workers were kept busy.

Kuwait's rush to physical transformation came at the cost of corruption and loose budget oversight. In spite of rising oil revenues, it faced a budget crisis in 1954. Sheikh Abdullah had to address both the budget squeeze and disgruntled merchants objecting to the dominant role assigned to British firms. He decided to pull the largest construction contracts from the British and turn them over to Kuwaiti merchants. He also pledged to keep Al Sabah out of business ventures so they could not use their political leverage to steal contracts from merchants. Soon traditional merchants were turning large profits by managing modern agencies in banking, air travel, oil tankers and cinemas. Sheikh Abdullah further mollified merchants by injecting oil revenues into the private sector with lucrative real estate deals whereby he purchased urban property from merchants at high prices and then resold lots at low prices.

Sheikh Abdullah presided over the formation of Kuwait's rentier bargain, the exchange of generous public services funded by oil wealth for citizens' loyalty to the ruler. His administration provided free education and medical care to ordinary Kuwaitis. The sheikhdom became the Gulf's leader in specialized medicine with the construction of several hospitals. Furthermore, the government expanded the range of jobs available only to Kuwaitis as the number of expatriate workers grew in medicine and education. The political effect was profound and lasting. For instance, during the years of Arab nationalist ferment that caused so much concern in Saudi Arabia and Bahrain, Kuwait saw limited activism, primarily among expatriate Arab workers from Iraq and Egypt. Only during the height of the Suez Crisis did Kuwaitis join with Egyptian, Lebanese and Palestinian workers in demonstrations to denounce the British and criticize the ruling clan for its pro-British posture.

One of the Kuwaitis to join the demonstrations became the leader of the sheikhdom's Arab nationalists for the next three decades. Ahmad al-Khatib came from humble social background. He studied medicine at the American University of Beirut, where he joined the Arab Nationalist Movement, a rival to the Baath Party. When Khatib returned to Kuwait, he became active in the National Culture Club, which called for creating representative bodies to give commoners a voice in political affairs and to curb the excessive powers and spending of Al Sabah. In August 1956, Khatib and other Arab nationalist Kuwaitis joined crowds demonstrating in support of Nasser's nationalization of the Suez

Canal. After the crisis, however, the protests subsided. The rentier bargain of sharing the fruits of oil revenues with the general population sufficed to win the loyalty of most Kuwaitis.

QATAR

Whereas Bahrain and Kuwait underwent significant political development in this period, Qatar took modest steps to start building administrative capacity, primarily at the behest of British advisers. From top to bottom, the population proved difficult for Sheikh Abdullah to tame. His own large and unruly Al Thani clan often defied his authority. When oil entered the picture, labour unrest assumed a unique form because of the persistence of slavery. Qatar's neighbours Bahrain and Saudi Arabia eyed the thinly populated peninsula for openings to seize territory. Ibn Saud was receptive to meeting with Sheikh Abdullah's ambitious, disgruntled brothers who wished to depose him. In order to keep Ibn Saud at arm's length, Sheikh Abdullah paid annual tribute to Riyadh. These destabilizing factors had the potential to undermine Qatar's independence were it not for the British protection obtained under the 1916 treaty.

The collapse of pearling hit Qatar harder than Bahrain, which had vibrant agricultural and commercial sectors. Apart from a small stream of regional trade and camel-breeding, Qatar's economy was wholly dependent on pearling. To make matters worse, in 1937 Bahrain imposed an embargo to press its claim to Zubara. Thousands of Qataris, as much as one-third of the population, migrated to Bahrain, al-Hasa and other parts of the Gulf in search of work. Sheikh Abdullah signed a concession with the AIOC in 1935, putting his own financial situation on firmer ground. Drillers struck oil in 1939, but the war delayed exports until 1946.

As oil revenues increased after the Second World War, Al Thani clansmen demanded higher allowances in the belief that the proceeds from oil were a joint possession rather than the share of the ruler alone. Sheikh Abdullah resisted their demands. When he got word that some of his kin were planning a violent takeover, he decided to abdicate and arranged for his son Ali to succeed him in August 1949. The British Political Agent came to Doha from Bahrain to oversee the succession. He promised to guarantee Sheikh Ali's rule in return for a pledge that he would implement articles in the Treaty of 1916 that Abdullah had neglected, including the abolition of slavery and the stationing of British advisers at Doha. The British sealed the succession with a display of naval might, stationing a warship offshore and landing a small detachment of forces to attend the ceremony. Oddly, the winner in the episode was the abdicating sheikh, who got to take most of the treasury and left little for Sheikh Ali. For the next few years, Qatar's ruler borrowed from merchants to cover state expenses.

Sheikh Ali's vulnerability to quarrelsome kinsmen led him to accept guidance from his British advisers. They urged him to take the first steps to lay down the building blocks of a modern administration. He established a budget office to keep track of revenues and expenditures and a police force to provide security in Doha and for the oil installations. A transportation infrastructure began to develop with the construction of an airstrip and a jetty. Basic public services were initiated with a clean water supply, schools and medical services.

Qatar did not witness a reform movement similar to those in Bahrain, Kuwait or Dubai (see below), but its oilfields did spawn the first demonstrations of organized labour, albeit with an unusual twist. In 1950, the oilfields employed former divers, expatriates, mainly from Oman's Dhufar region, and slaves, even after Sheikh Ali promised to abolish slavery in 1952. The oil company paid wages to slaves, who turned over most of their pay to their owners, who sent their men to work in the oil sector instead of the dying pearling sector where slaves had formerly worked as divers. Qatari workers resented the Dhufaris as interlopers, and in 1951 they went on strike to demand the expulsion of Dhufaris. The slave-holders, many from the ruling family, encouraged the labour unrest since higher wages and more jobs for Qataris would augment their profits from the sweat of their slaves. Sheikh Ali too benefitted from the unrest by getting the oil company to revise the concession terms in his favour in return for his pledge to quell the labour movement.

The problems in the oilfields merged with nationalist politics during the 1956 Suez Crisis. The sheikhdom's new schools hired Egyptians to teach Qatari pupils and they naturally spread the dominant political sentiment of the day, Arab nationalism. Soon, it spread among educated youth and merchants. In August 1956, during the international stand-off over Nasser's nationalization of the Suez Canal, an anti-British demonstration marched through Doha. The nationalists also sought the right to participate in political life. Much like the ruling families in Bahrain and Kuwait, Sheikh Ali and Al Thani closed ranks in the wake of the Suez Crisis. He expanded the police force to strengthen its ability to contain political and worker unrest.

While the sheikh was able to quiet the streets, he continued to face pressing demands from his clansmen for larger allowances as oil revenues rose.

THE TRUCIAL STATES

Politics in the Trucial States, also known as Trucial Oman, continued to consist of rivalries within ruling families, intermittent quarrels between neighbouring sheikhdoms, feuds among nomadic tribesmen in the desert hinterland, and managing relations with the British. These dynamics intersected with changing British interests to bring about secessions from Sharjah of Ra's al-Khaima and Kalba (an enclave on the Arabian Sea). Only in Dubai did merchants figure in politics as a significant force comparable to their counterparts in Kuwait and Bahrain. As for economic trends, the pearling bust brought hardship to the sheikhdoms but prospects improved when Western companies showed up to explore for oil. The concessions required definitive marking of boundaries to give the Western oilmen an exact idea of what territory they were entitled to survey. Rulers claimed as large an area as possible to maximize potential oil supplies, but doing so was bound to cause border disputes. Another development during this period that was important for bringing the Trucial States into closer contact with the outside world was the establishment of landing strips that incorporated the sheikhdoms into the world's network of air routes.

The sheikhdoms' internal politics exhibited two patterns. Dubai, Ajman and Umm al-Qaiwain were stable, while intrigue and strife plagued Abu Dhabi, Sharjah and Ra's al-Khaima. Dubai's Said ibn Maktum followed his cousin, who died of natural causes in 1912, and ruled until his death in 1958. As ruler of a diverse, cosmopolitan commercial port, Sheikh Said displayed a knack for bargaining that was characteristic of merchants. Ajman enjoyed a peaceful, uncontested succession when Sheikh Rashid followed his father Sheikh Humaid as ruler in 1928. Umm al-Qaiwain passed through a brief period of instability in the 1920s before Sheikh Ahmad ibn Rashid took power after having his cousin killed in 1929. By contrast, Abu Dhabi's Al Nahayyan entered a phase of instability marked by plots and murders. Sheikhs clashed over the distribution of allowances. Two ruling sheikhs were killed in plots orchestrated by their brothers. The situation settled down after Sheikh Shakhbut ibn

Sultan seized power in 1928. Sharjah's chronic strife resulted in Ra's al-Khaima's second secession, this time gaining official British recognition as a separate sheikhdom in 1921. Sharjah's dynastic quarrels ended with Sheikh Sultan ibn Saqr's accession in 1924.

In Abu Dhabi, Al Nahayyan's internal strife affected their ability to control their extensive domain. In the typical power struggle, members of the ruling clan made allies with tribal relatives in the desert who shared the fate of victorious and vanquished sheikhly allies. In the early 1920s, defeated tribal leaders went to Ibn Saud's governor of al-Hasa, Abdullah ibn Jiluwi, to seek his protection. Ibn Jiluwi then sent agents to collect the religious tax (*zakat*) from the protected tribes, thereby establishing a basis for territorial claims at Abu Dhabi's expense. Britain was in no position to dispatch land forces to guard its client against Riyadh's encroachment, but without the leaky umbrella of British protection, it is likely that Ibn Saud would have absorbed the Trucial States. At any event, Abu Dhabi's Sheikh Shakhbut was able to restore authority over the hinterland in the later 1920s and 1930s through astute tribal diplomacy and occasional resort to force.

During the inter-war period, the arrival of aviation marked the region's first advance in speed of transport since steam navigation. The new technology offered imperial officials the prospect of rapidly moving officials, soldiers and equipment vast distances. After the First World War, the British developed an air route connecting Egypt and India via Iraq and the Gulf. The first flight from Iraq to India at the end of 1918 hugged the Iranian shore. Limits on aviation technology meant that Britain's Royal Air Force needed landing fields at 200-mile intervals in order to refuel. Efforts to negotiate long-term landing rights at Iranian Gulf stopping points foundered on Reza Shah's nationalistic attitude, so the Arabian shore became the focus of aviation planners. Opposition in Dubai and Ra's al-Khaima then turned the British to Sharjah's Sheikh Sultan ibn Saqr, who needed the rent that the British offered and also viewed an air base as a potential stimulus to trade. After several months of talks, and some British pressure, he signed an agreement in July 1932 to set up an airport and a rest house for overnight stays. Britain then pressed for an emergency landing strip at Kalba on the Arabian Sea. The sheikh of Kalba agreed to landing rights in return for Britain recognizing his independence, in spite of London's official recognition of Sharjah's possession of Kalba in 1903, which was reaffirmed in 1932 in order to get Sheikh Sultan's agreement to the air base there. Promises fell by the wayside and Kalba became independent until 1952. Abu Dhabi became part of the air route in 1935 only after the British threatened to blockade pearling vessels, the sheikh's main source of income.

At the same time as London was leaning on the sheikhs for landing rights, oil companies were negotiating for rights to explore their domains. In 1922, the British obtained pledges from the sheikhs to obtain their approval before signing concessions with oil companies. The exclusive agreements followed the examples of similar arrangements struck with Kuwait in 1913 and Bahrain in 1914. The sheikhs watched Bahrain's development with keen interest when oil was struck there in 1932. Ra's al-Khaima led the way in inviting geological prospecting in 1935. In the next four years, IPC created subsidiary companies under the name of Petroleum Development Limited (PDL) that reached agreements with Dubai, Ra's al-Khaima, Sharjah and Abu Dhabi to explore and develop oil resources.

The acquisition of airstrips, landing rights and oil concessions ended Britain's customary hands-off position towards the desert hinterland. Pacification of the tribes and definition of borders became priorities for the sake of establishing secure conditions for geological surveys and transportation facilities. Petroleum Development Limited (PDL) wanted to make the annual subsidies paid to the sheikhs worthwhile and that meant sending survey teams to the interior where the sheikhs' authority was tenuous. The Bedouin tribes did not want to explicitly acknowledge the sovereignty of the sheikhs, so they frequently harassed survey teams. Moreover, the wealth that would accrue from oil discovered in the desert was destined for the coastal sheikhs, not the Bedouin tribesmen who saw no advantage to surrendering their autonomy. The arrival of petroleum geologists triggered conflict between the sheikhs of Abu Dhabi and Dubai over their inland border as they sought to maximize the chance of an oil strike in their respective realms. Armed conflict erupted in 1945 and the desert fighting between tribal allies of Abu Dhabi and Dubai lasted for three years before the British intervened to dictate the boundary. The need to pacify the desert resulted in a new British initiative, the formation in 1951 of the Trucial Oman Levies (renamed the Trucial Oman Scouts in 1956), the first Western-trained armed force in the sheikhdoms. British officers commanded Arab soldiers patrolling the desert and intervened in local disputes.

Dubai was the scene of Trucial Oman's first movement for political reform. The Majles Movement of 1938 stemmed from local forces and took the Kuwaiti Majles Movement as its model. As in Kuwait, economic pressures and dynastic rivalries were the underlying forces. The decline in the pearl trade hurt merchants' profits at the same time as Sheikh Said began receiving payments for the oil concession. For the first time, the sheikh's wealth outstripped that of the major merchants. In addition, his cousin Sheikh Mani' and local merchants resented Said's submitting to British pressure to manumit slaves, suppress trade in arms and allow an air base. It was a minor incident that precipitated the outbreak of protests: a clash between Sheikh Said's son and a cousin over the right to provide a local taxi service. After the sheikh's son attacked his cousin's vehicle, merchants and Maktum clansmen drafted a petition demanding a public accounting of the budget, a regular police force, abolition of the sheikh's monopolies on a variety of services and limits on the sheikh's spending. When Sheikh Said resisted, the protestors escalated their demands, calling for a representative council to oversee administrative and fiscal affairs. Neighbouring sheikhs got involved as well, some supporting Sheikh Said, others offering to arbitrate. The British dispatched an agent to resolve the dispute and in October 1938, the sheikh consented to the formation of a Majles.

The Dubai Majles established the first administrative institutions in Trucial Oman, schools and market inspectors. In early 1939, the Majles announced plans for improving roads and expanding the port. It also declared a cap on the Sheikh's annual allowance and claimed control over income from the airport and oil concession, raising the stakes to a classic struggle over power of the purse, with the council demanding a clear distinction between the sheikh's personal wealth and the public treasury. At this point, Sheikh Said held his ground. In the face of the assertive councillors, he summoned Bedouin allies to attack their stronghold in the Deira section of Dubai. The assault scattered the sheikh's opponents; some of them took refuge in Sharjah. Said then dissolved the Majles in March.

After the Second World War and India's independence in 1947, British administration of Gulf affairs shifted from the Government of India in Calcutta to the Foreign Office in London. Within Trucial Oman, Dubai's rapid development as a centre for oil company business resulted in the transfer of the British Political Agency from Sharjah, its location since 1829, to Dubai in 1954. In the post-war years, British officials focused on combating arms smuggling and a revival of the slave trade. Patrols by the Trucial Oman Levies helped reduce both kinds of illegal traffic. The post-war years also witnessed the first formal institution for consultation among the sheikhs. The Trucial States Council, in a sense the forerunner of the UAE, was formed in 1952. The British Political Agent chaired the body until 1965, when the sheikhs assumed the chairmanship on a rotating basis.

The Trucial States did not see the sort of labour unrest that spread in the rest of the Gulf states because no oil was struck until 1960, but Arab nationalist ideas incubated in Dubai's growing network of schools. Because of the small number of local residents with modern education, Dubai hired teachers from other Arab countries. In the early 1950s, Iraqi teachers gave lessons in anti-imperialist politics and organized protests against British domination. In 1953, merchants, staff from the customs office and a disgruntled Maktum sheikh established the Dubai National Front. At first, the Front called for curbing the influence of non-Arab merchants in the local economy and curtailing the powers of the ruler and the British. During the Suez Crisis, the home of the British agent and the vehicle of a British officer were targets of attack. The Dubai National Front also drew support from abroad from Nasser's Egypt and Saudi Arabia.

In the other sheikhdoms, Arab nationalism did not become a popular cause in the 1950s because the ranks of the educated were still small. On the other hand, a local appetite for education and modern medical facilities did arise. Former pearl divers who migrated for jobs in the oilfields of Bahrain and Qatar became familiar with public services and brought back the idea that the sheikhs should use oil revenues for the benefit of ordinary folk. The Trucial States trailed the rest of the Gulf in economic and social development but they were on the same path, thanks to historical patterns of mobility and endowment with the same resources, pearls and oil.

OMAN

Oman entered the post-war period divided between the coastal sultanate based at Muscat and the tribal interior, where the Ibadi imamate remained a compelling political ideal. Sultan Taimur was barely able to defend the ports against powerful tribes, which briefly occupied Muscat and other towns. The political crisis had damaging effects on the economy of the coast as trade between the two regions plummeted. Furthermore, the stagnation of trade struck a huge blow to Taimur's revenues. He turned to Arab and Indian merchants for loans, but by 1918, he was having difficulty paying them back. The British offered to liquidate his debt with a single, consolidated loan if he agreed to accept

British advisers to manage the government. The sultan took the loan along with the conditions that the British attached to it. They installed advisers to manage the treasury and customs and established a new military force.

The stalemate with the Ibadi imamate dissolved after the assassination of Imam al-Kharusi and the election of Sheikh Muhammad al-Khalili, who proved receptive to negotiations mediated by the British Political Agent. In the September 1920 Agreement of Sib, representatives of Taimur and the imam deposited separate letters with the British. Taimur pledged to limit taxes on internal trade, to guarantee the personal security of Omani tribesmen in coastal towns, to extradite criminals back to their home region when requested, and to refrain from interfering in the interior. For their part, the tribes pledged to refrain from attacks on the coastal region, to respect the security of persons and merchandise passing through their lands, and to extradite criminals. The Agreement of Sib inaugurated a prolonged truce, during which the coast and the interior followed separate lines of development.

The impetus for introducing formal institutions of government at Muscat came from the British, who were keen to see the sultanate acquire the capacity to provide security and to set up a stable fiscal regime. Sultan Taimur went along with British advice to form a council of ministers but did not give it substantial powers. He was, moreover, not particularly interested in governing and he wound up delegating authority for everyday matters to Omani and British advisers. In fact, he yearned to be relieved of the responsibilities of rule, but the British prevented him from abdicating until his son Said was old enough to replace him. In 1929, Said took charge of daily administration. Three years later, Sultan Taimur abdicated and Said ascended the throne. He focused on the sultanate's shaky finances by appointing foreign experts, British and Indian accountants, to introduce regular record keeping. He also placed the customs office, the main source of revenue, in the hands of British and Indian staff. In 1937, Sultan Said instituted municipal government for Muscat, responsible for public health and sanitation.

Apart from basic functions, Sultan Said adopted a cautious approach towards developing public facilities, in large measure out of fiscal prudence because the treasury had been insolvent when he succeeded his father. The financial outlook improved with Oman's integration into Britain's network of civilian and military airstrips, with the payment of an annual subsidy for those rights. In 1937, he issued a concession to PDL. To turn that concession into a significant source of wealth, however, Sultan Said would have to assert his authority over the interior, which geologists believed might hold oil deposits.

According to the Agreement of Sib, inner Oman lay beyond the sultan's reach. Muhammad ibn Abd Allah al-Khalili was the titular Ibadi imam with his seat at Nizwa, but effective power rested in the hands of tribal leaders. Imam Muhammad appointed men to collect taxes and mediate disputes over access to grazing land and water but he took no steps to augment his power with formal fiscal and military bodies, in part because he owed his position to tribal leaders opposed to building up centralized authority. His passivity provided an opening for Sultan Said to gradually absorb inner Oman through tribal diplomacy. He built alliances with tribal leaders by paying subsidies, resolved tribal disputes, and dispatched American missionaries to offer medical treatment. The sultan also co-opted Ibadi clerics by appointing them to religious courts in coastal towns. To buttress his military power, he purchased arms from the British.

The 1937 oil concession altered the dynamics of Oman's tribal politics, relations between the coast and the interior, and relations between Oman and Saudi Arabia. Tribal leaders had effectively enforced the imam's prohibition against allowing foreigners to enter his realm but the prospect of oil deposits proved so tempting that they granted exceptions for geological surveyors. PDL considered the Buraimi oasis, a region containing ten villages, a promising area, but it was unclear if its concession area included the region because of conflicting claims put forth by Oman, Abu Dhabi and Saudi Arabia. Sultan Said maintained a tenuous claim by courting Buraimi's tribal sheikhs. In 1949, Riyadh declared that Buraimi belonged to Saudi Arabia and three years later sent a military force to occupy one of its villages (see below for details).

When Imam Muhammad died in 1954, his successor Imam Ghalib ibn Ali al-Hinai turned to the Saudis for backing against the sultan's encroachments, but several of Buraimi's sheikhs, hostile to the Saudis, opposed the imam's move and declared their allegiance to Sultan Said. London's decision to expel the Saudis from Buraimi in October 1955 dovetailed with Sultan Said's ambition to bring the interior under his authority. He launched an expedition to seize the main towns of inner Oman. Imam Ghalib accepted defeat but his brother Talib fled to Saudi territory, where he prepared a counter-attack to restore the imamate. In the meantime, Sultan Said marked the reunification of Oman with a triumphant tour of the interior towns. He reconciled local leaders by confirming their standing. Saudi Arabia, however, refused to relinquish its claim to Buraimi, and in the later 1950s it backed forces bent on restoring the imamate. Clearly, political ambition overshadowed religious principle in the light of doctrinal enmity between Wahhabi and Ibadi ulama.

Sultan Said's defeat of Imam Ghalib was a turning point in Oman's history. It signified coastal Muscat's conquest of the interior, a feat made possible by Al Bu Said's alliance with Britain dating back to the nineteenth century. In other words, Muscat's integration with the Western imperialist order supplied the economic, military and political resources for it to become the centre of power in Oman, ending the perennial balance of forces between coast and interior. Sultan Said then manoeuvred to establish his personal supremacy over his own clan – ending a long stretch of assassination, secession and civil war – and over all tribes and regions. His success owed mainly to assistance and resources from outside forces such as the British, Indian traders and Baluchi fighters.

DRAWING NATIONAL BORDERS

The tangle of national claims to land, islands and coastal waters is part of modern history around the world. In Europe, millions of lives were lost in wars in the course of drawing, revising and redrawing national borders. In the Gulf, tensions more than bloody conflict have been the norm. The passage from loose sovereignty to tightly packaged modern states was muddled by the Western notion that a ruler's domain was determined by the allegiance of settled folk and nomadic tribes, expressed by payment of tribute or the religious tax, *zakat*. But the customary mobility of Gulf peoples made it impossible to draw tidy borders on the basis of putative allegiance. For example, in the nineteenth century, Manasir tribesmen depended on a variety of economic activities – date farming, fishing, pearling and tending livestock – that required extensive migration in south-east Arabia from al-Hasa and Qatar to the foothills of Oman's Hajar Range. Manasir tribal sections were dispersed over territories under the nominal authority of two or three different sheikhs. Furthermore, a tribe's allegiance was conditional, revocable by rebellion or migration. Therefore, to say that a tribe was loyal to a particular sheikh on a permanent basis was seldom true. Nevertheless, the modern political system of international relations rests on the concept of firmly established borders. In addition, the terms of oil concessions included hazy definitions of sovereign territory that required clarification. Given the novelty of such clarity in the Gulf, boundary disputes were inevitable.

One of the longest running territorial disputes centres on a handful of barren islands in the southern part of the Gulf. Abu Musa, Greater Tunb and Lesser Tunb lie between the UAE and Iran, both of which assert historical claims to the islands. In the early 1700s, the Qasimi sheikhs of Ra's al-Khaima conquered the three islands and the nearby Iranian port of Lingah. In the 1770s, Karim Khan Zand imposed his authority on the Qasimi sheikh of Lingah, but after his death, the Qasimis regained complete control and maintained it for the next hundred years. In the late 1800s, the Qajar shah forced the Qasimi sheikh of Lingah to pay tribute and acknowledge the shah as the ruler. The Qasimi sheikh ruled the three islands (Abu Musa and the Tunbs), so Qajars regarded them as part of their realm too. Matters became more complicated when the Qajars expelled Lingah's Qasimi sheikh in 1887. Sharjah's Qasimi sheikh then appointed an agent to Abu Musa while Ra's al-Khaima's other Qasimi sheikh held the Tunbs.

In the late 1920s, Reza Shah's government paid closer attention to the islands because smugglers were using the Tunbs as a base for moving contraband. Beginning in 1930, Iran tried to obtain a lease from Ra's al-Khaima for the Greater Tunb, but the Qasimi sheikh feared that once an Iranian presence was established, it would be difficult to dislodge. British officials got tied up in knots in trying to decide the disposition of the islands. The Government of India and the Political Resident followed their inclination against yielding advantage to Iran. They formulated a complex argument that defined the Qasimi sheikhs of Lingah as vassals of both the Qajars on the mainland and the Arabian Qasimis on the islands. The Foreign Office in London preferred to smooth over secondary matters with Tehran and adopted the more consistent view that the Qasimis governed both the coast and the islands on behalf of the Qajars, therefore Iran's claim to the islands was valid. The Government of India prevailed in British discussions and the Iranians let the matter drop without formally renouncing their claim. When British protection for the Trucial States ended in 1971, Iran occupied the islands and they have been a sore point in Arab–Iranian relations ever since, with each side reading history in a way that supports its claim.

As already noted, oil concessions forced the issue of determining land borders. The desert domain of Bedouin tribes became the object of conflicting territorial claims since nobody knew where oil might be found, and Western geologists needed to know where exactly their companies' concessions allowed them to travel to conduct surveys. Deciding the boundaries largely turned out to be a function of the power of the contenders for territory. In the 1920s, for instance, Abu Dhabi was weak because of bloody succession struggles while Saudi Arabia was resurgent, with Ibn Saud firmly in control of al-Hasa. Hence, for a number of years, some tribes in Dhafra and Buraimi paid zakat to Ibn Saud's governor in al-Hasa. In the 1930s, Sheikh Shakhbut revived Abu Dhabi's authority over Buraimi and Dhafra, diminishing the strength of Saudi claims. Such fluctuations in power were characteristic of the region. There were no fixed tribal loyalties and no fixed territorial lines.

The Aramco concession with Ibn Saud in 1933 prompted American government officials to seek clarification from Britain regarding the border between Saudi Arabia and Abu Dhabi to allow the American company to know the exact extent of its concession. London referred the Americans to the Blue Line established in a series of Anglo–Ottoman conventions in 1913–14, which drew the border in a favourable manner for Abu Dhabi by allocating to it the land around a pocket of the Gulf called Khor al-Udaid, located at the south-east foot of the Qatar peninsula. The Blue Line also assigned a stretch of land at Qatar's south-west foot to Doha, which granted a concession to a British firm in 1935. That year, the Saudis proposed a different course for their borders with Qatar and Abu Dhabi, known as the Red Line, which claimed both areas for Riyadh as well as a substantial portion of the Empty Quarter. The British invited Saudi representatives to London for talks to resolve the dispute, but failed to close the gap then and in subsequent contacts in 1937. Matters rested there for 12 years.

In spring 1949, American surveyors accompanied by Saudi guards explored for oil in the vicinity of the Saudi border with Qatar and Abu Dhabi. Sheikh Shakhbut notified the British that the Saudis had crossed into his territory. When the British conveyed his complaint to the Saudis, they contended that the survey party was in the domain of tribes loyal to Riyadh. At a meeting in Riyadh to discuss the issue in October 1949, the Saudi government announced a more expansive claim because of speculation that south-east Arabia might contain oil deposits. The Saudis claimed both Buraimi and the Liwa oasis, the ancestral homeland of Abu Dhabi's ruling Bani Yas tribe. If Riyadh were successful, it would annex roughly 80 per cent of Abu Dhabi's territory.

Settling the matter was complicated by Buraimi's location at the juncture of Saudi, Omani and Abu Dhabi domains. Since the late 1700s, the collection of ten villages in the oasis had come under the rule of one or the other. In the 1920s, the Saudi governor of al-Hasa, Ibn Jiluwi, sent tax collectors to the oasis, reviving the historic Saudi claim and setting up a collision with Abu Dhabi and Oman. Riyadh announced a formal claim in 1949, and dispatched forces to occupy one of the villages to cement that claim in August 1952. The British responded by deploying the Trucial Oman Levies to the area and issuing a diplomatic protest. The Buraimi dispute also strained Anglo–American relations because American oil companies, anticipating the presence of more petroleum reserves in that quarter of Arabia, supported the Saudi claim, while London supported the positions of Abu Dhabi and Oman that denied Saudi sovereignty.

In July 1954, Anglo–Saudi negotiators agreed on a procedure to resolve the dispute by submitting it to the United Nations for arbitration, but the proceedings quickly collapsed in October 1955 amid mutual accusations of bad faith. Britain then forcibly expelled the Saudis and unilaterally declared what it regarded as the official boundary between Saudi Arabia, Qatar, Abu Dhabi and Oman. Ultimately, Abu Dhabi and Oman divided the villages spread across the oasis, leaving Riyadh empty-handed. But the Saudis did not let the matter rest there. They supported a candidate for the Ibadi mamate to keep their hand in the area. Furthermore, the Buraimi dispute turned into an Arab nationalist cause when Egyptian President Gamal Abdul Nasser supported the Saudi position as part of his campaign against Western colonial domination.

THE EARLY EFFECTS OF OIL
ON THE GULF STATES

Even in its initial phase, the petroleum industry had profound effects on the Gulf. First, oilfields replaced pearl beds as sources of livelihood. During the years of exploration, Western companies hired tribesmen for seasonal work as guards and drivers without disrupting traditional activities such as harvesting dates, grazing herds and fishing. Second, oil revenues tilted the balance of power and wealth in favour of the ruling sheikhs at the expense of the merchants. Before oil, rulers had to curry favour with merchants for loans whenever they were strapped for funds. Rulers used control over the oil revenues to dispense economic favours to merchants in the forms of construction contracts and licenses for operating franchises of Western firms. Oil also gave rulers the means to alter the relationship between government and nomadic tribesmen. While it was British military power that pacified the coast, the propensity of tribesmen to rebel ended when governments acquired the means to turn them into clients of the state with salaried positions. Third, oil had the indirect effect of stimulating demands for power-sharing arrangements in Bahrain, Kuwait and Dubai. In each case, the reform movement stemmed from a coalition of merchants feeling their influence wane and cadet branches of sheikhly families jealous of the ruling sheikhs' monopoly on revenues from oil concessions. Fourth, oilfields were incubators of a modern working class. In Saudi Arabia, Bahrain and Qatar, workers demanded better working conditions and pressed for higher wages. The rise of labour activism provided one of the foundations for the spread of Arab nationalism, which became the dominant political idea of the 1960s.

7 The Gulf in the Era of Arab Nationalism, 1956–71

The era of British domination in the Gulf formally ended in 1971. That year, Bahrain, Qatar and the Trucial States became independent. Kuwait had gained its independence ten years earlier. The ebb of the British Empire was an important chapter in the larger story of decolonization, as European powers relinquished control over vast portions of Asia and Africa. Decolonization sometimes meant a smooth, peaceful transition from European to national sovereignty, as in Kuwait and the Gulf states. Other times it entailed a prolonged political struggle between nationalists and the colonial power, as in India. In the Gulf, decolonization involved not only bilateral negotiations between Britain and individual countries; it also had bearing on relations among local states and their relations with the rest of the Arab world.

Decolonization unfolded during the peak years of the Cold War. In the context of global competition between the capitalist and communist camps, former colonies were viewed as allies, sources of raw materials and sites of military bases. Great Britain and the United States did not always agree on the right policy to achieve their common aim. Nevertheless, they formed a solid phalanx opposed to the growth of local communist movements and Soviet inroads. As conservative monarchies, Iran and Saudi Arabia had no hesitation about siding with the capitalist camp. Iran's Muhammad Reza Shah harshly suppressed the communist Tudeh Party in the mid-1950s and was on the alert to prevent its revival. Saudi Arabia's rulers and Wahhabi religious establishment regarded communism as a form of atheism, to be barred from the kingdom and combated in the region. Iraq had a robust communist movement that emerged in the 1930s and grew in influence during the late 1950s and early 1960s. The republican regimes that succeeded each other between 1958 and 1968 shared deep mistrust of the Western powers as heirs to the colonial legacy, but they also regarded the communists as dangerous rivals in the local struggle for power. Consequently, Baghdad tended to follow a neutral path in the Cold War at the same time as its anti-colonial posture disposed its leaders to be critical of avowedly pro-Western governments in Riyadh and Tehran. Of the smaller countries, Kuwait became independent in these years, and the prospect of forceful annexation by Iraq left its rulers little option but a pro-Western policy as a safeguard. At the lower end of the Gulf, Oman remained firmly in the Western camp, from habit and in response to the outbreak of a Marxist insurgency in the late 1960s.

As colonial powers came to terms with the inevitability of granting independence, they tried to protect their interests through treaties that allowed them to retain military bases and economic privileges in return for expedited transition to full independence. Nationalists resented such special treaty provisions as measures that compromised sovereignty, if not political bad faith. From the perspective of former colonial powers, new military arrangements were necessary to preserve local stability. The Anglo–Iraqi Treaty of 1930, however, contributed to destabilizing political life in Iraq. In the context of the Cold War, they represented strategic assets against Soviet expansion. Nationalist leaders, however, did not appreciate being treated as pawns in a global chess match. They viewed pro-Western treaties as new tactics in the old game of colonial domination.

ARAB NATIONALISM

In the Arab world of the late 1950s and early 1960s, Egyptian President Gamal Abdul Nasser emerged as the dominant leader. He came to power in the July 1952 revolution that overthrew Egypt's monarchy, a dynasty founded by Muhammad Ali Pasha in 1840. One of his early successes was negotiating a treaty with Britain that stipulated complete withdrawal of its military forces from the Suez Canal zone. Less than two years after that diplomatic success, in July 1956, he nationalized the Suez Canal, causing a crisis that exploded into war at the end of October. Britain colluded with France and Israel to humble and if possible overthrow Nasser through a joint invasion on Egypt and occupation of the Suez Canal zone. After all, had not Iran's Prime Minister Musaddiq been forced from office just three years earlier for having the audacity to nationalize the Anglo-Iranian Oil Company? The plot was an utter failure for two reasons. First, Nasser's domestic political standing was far sturdier than Musaddiq's, and the spectre of former colonial powers cooperating with Israel ensured a strong nationalist backlash in support of the Egyptian leader, not just in the Nile Valley but throughout the Arab world. Second, the dynamics of the Cold War were quite different in the two instances. In 1953, the United States was alarmed at the prospect of a communist takeover in Iran and took the lead in the plot to overthrow Musaddiq. In 1956, Washington regarded Nasser as a nuisance to Western interests, but did not anticipate that Egypt would fall into the communist orbit, unless Western pressure pushed it into Soviet arms. The stark difference between London's and Washington's judgment of how to cope with Nasser was revealed when United States President Dwight Eisenhower publicly condemned the aggression by Britain, France and Israel against Egypt. Washington and Moscow pressed for a ceasefire and evacuation from Egyptian soil. Britain's economic dependence on the United States meant it had to comply, signalling her definitive fall into the ranks of second-tier powers.

The obverse of Britain's decline was Nasser's rise to regional influence under the banner of Arab nationalism. For the next decade, Nasser was the dominant force in Arab politics, enjoying enthusiastic support not only from Egyptians but from Arabs, especially the rising generation of educated youth, from North Africa to the Gulf. He was far less popular with fellow Arab rulers, who did not appreciate his claim that Egypt was the natural leader of the Arab world, and that as Egypt's leader, he had the right to influence, if not meddle in, the politics of other Arab states.

Nasser was not the only contender for the right to speak in the name of Arab nationalism. The Baath Party, founded in Syria during the early 1940s, considered itself a more genuine expression of the impulse to Arab unity. By the mid-1950s, the party had established branches in Lebanon, Jordan and Iraq. Its leaders appreciated Nasser's popularity but regarded him as shallow and in need of their intellectual tutelage. The Baath Party's Syrian founders thought they gained the opportunity to take Nasser under their wings when Egypt and Syria declared their unification in the UAR in February 1958. The romance soon soured as Nasser outmanoeuvred the Syrians and turned the moment of Arab unity into an instrument for advancing Cairo's regional agenda. The Syrian Baathists were thoroughly defeated and many departed for exile, disgusted with Nasser's failure to appreciate their wisdom and talents. The result was an enduring a rift between Nasser and the Baath Party.

The Arab nationalist split was a central theme in Iraqi politics during this period. It damaged Nasser's standing in Arab regional affairs as Baathists competed with Nasserists for the same constituency: educated, urban and young folk. Notwithstanding divisions among Arab nationalists, they challenged conservative Gulf leaders, regarded as tools of Western neocolonial domination. Saudi Arabia confronted the Arab nationalist challenge at home, as it took root among military officers and young princes. King Faisal purged military and royal ranks of nationalists and took on Nasser in a proxy war in Yemen. He also developed a counter-ideology emphasizing Islamic solidarity to endow Saudi national interests with religious legitimacy. In the smaller Gulf states, Arab nationalism resonated with the growing Arab expatriate labour force imported to construct and manage transportation, communications, technical, education and medical fields. It had less appeal to Gulf Arabs for four main reasons. First, Arab unity could serve as a pretext for their annexation by larger neighbours like Iraq or Saudi Arabia. Second, Arab solidarity could undermine the special privileges enjoyed by nationals and denied to expatriate Arab workers. Third, most Gulf Arabs remained more attached to local and tribal affiliations than to a larger sense of belonging to the Arab world. Not until the 1970s did many Gulf Arabs have direct contact with non-peninsular Arabs. Fourth, anti-colonial feeling was weaker in the Gulf. The rulers did not love the British, but they understood they owed their rule and independence to them. Moreover, the Western presence in the Gulf was far lighter than in the central Arab lands. Consequently, there was less of a foreign target for nationalists to attack. Certainly, the oil companies were Western owned, but in this period, they showed willingness to renegotiate concessions on more favourable terms for the Gulf states. To the extent that a feeling of Arab solidarity did spread in the Gulf, it tended to find expression as sympathy and support for the Palestinian cause.

Arab nationalism crested in 1958 with the Egyptian–Syrian unity experiment. The failure to attract other governments to join the union and the UAR's 1961 dissolution was the beginning of Arab nationalism's decline. It suffered a major blow from the June 1967 war. In just six days, Israeli forces devastated the armies of Egypt, Jordan and Syria, and conquered Sinai, Gaza, the West Bank and the Golan Heights. Nasser and the Syrian Baath (which seized power in Damascus in 1963 through a military *coup d'état*) were shown to be paper tigers. By the time Nasser died of a heart attack in September 1970, his influence had dwindled abroad and at home, where Israeli occupation of the Sinai peninsula contributed to chronic economic woes. He did not live to see the final days of the British Empire in the Gulf, which ended in an orderly withdrawal of forces and transition to independence.

OIL

One sphere where Western influence maintained its advantage for much of the period was the oil industry. For decades, the Western companies calibrated the level of production to maintain stable supplies and prices in the global market, leaving host countries with no influence over the price and production level of their most valuable resource. In pursuit of leverage against the oil companies, five oil-producing countries – Venezuela, Saudi Arabia, Iran, Iraq and Kuwait – formed the Organization of Petroleum Exporting Countries (OPEC) in September 1960. The immediate impetus for its formation came from the August 1960 decision by the oil companies to lower prices in order to cut tax payments to the host governments. OPEC remained a weak player in the oil trade as long as global production levels were high enough to allow the major oil companies to respond to local falls in production by raising it somewhere else. Thus, when Arab oil producers scaled back production during the June 1967 war, the companies boosted output in other countries. A few years later, the balance of power in the oil sector shifted in OPEC's favour.

In 1970, domestic oil production in the United States reached its peak and steadily declined in subsequent years. The oil companies responded by increasing imports to meet growing demand, but falling domestic output meant that they had lost the extra capacity necessary to blunt the impact of production cuts by other oil-producing countries. Coincidentally, in 1969, Arab nationalist officers in Libya seized power in a military *coup d'état*. The following year, Libya's new leader, Muammar Qaddafi, threatened to shut down the oilfields if Western companies did not agree to his demand for a larger share of profits, pushing it from 50 to 55 per cent. The radical nationalist's success inspired the conservative shah of Iran to press for a similar deal. The piecemeal movement for revising the terms of the oil business turned into an organized endeavour in February 1971, when representatives of the major oil companies met in Tehran with officials from all the Gulf oil states. The talks resulted in higher prices and a larger share of profits for all of the producers. In less than a year, the balance of power in the global oil industry tilted from the major oil companies to the producing countries. When the United States devalued the dollar in August 1971, the oil producers were in a position to raise prices to make up the difference. Producers profited nicely: Iran and Saudi Arabia doubled their annual sales between 1969 and 1971. At the time, those figures were impressive, although they would be dwarfed just two years later.

IRAN

Muhammad Reza Shah reconsolidated royal authority after the Musaddiq crisis. Repression of independent political forces was thorough and fierce. The leaders of the Tudeh Party were arrested and many of them were executed. The leaders of the National Front faced frequent harassment. Musaddiq was put on trial at the end of 1953 and sentenced to jail for three years and then subjected to house arrest for the remainder of his life (he died in 1967). In 1957, the government established a new agency called SAVAK, the National Security and Information Organization. SAVAK was divided into departments specializing in internal security, foreign intelligence and counter-intelligence. It acquired a fearsome reputation that intimidated Iranians but over time its notoriety for torturing political prisoners inspired hatred towards the monarchy.

The United States viewed Iran as an asset in the Cold War, a view that meshed with the shah's anti-communist outlook. During the Eisenhower Administration (1953–60), American technicians and advisers came to Iran to administer economic development programmes. Washington appreciated Muhammad Reza Shah's support for the Baghdad Pact and his endorsement of the 1957 Eisenhower Doctrine, a statement declaring the commitment of the United States to oppose communist subversion of friendly governments. Washington rewarded Iran's pro-Western stance with one billion dollars in economic and military aid between 1954 and 1960, largely to expand the size and capacity of the armed forces and intelligence agencies.

Unconditional support from Washington was not forthcoming from President John Kennedy's administration (1961–3). After taking office, he had his advisers review patterns of political stability around the world with an eye to determining the conditions that made countries ripe for communist subversion. They concluded that poverty, inequality and underdevelopment gave openings to leftist propaganda to destabilize pro-Western governments. The way to pre-empt subversion, then, was to initiate fundamental reforms to raise living standards, especially in rural areas. The shah accepted Washington's advice and installed a progressive cabinet that included a veteran proponent of land reform as minister of agriculture, Hasan Arsanjani. In 1962, the cabinet approved Arsanjani's plan for a wide-ranging land reform programme.

Breaking up vast rural estates and distributing parcels to poor villagers would, in theory, have several salutary effects. First, it would boost rural incomes and expand the internal market for national products. Second, agronomists would work with new small landowners to introduce modern techniques to boost agricultural production. Third, it would weaken large landlords whose grip on peasants gave them an independent power base. Fourth, the shah expected to reap a wave of popularity for his benevolence. Redistribution of large estates got under way in a few provinces and it indeed undermined the large landlords and benefitted poor peasants. But before the reforms were implemented across much of the country, the shah dismissed the popular minister and curtailed land redistribution.

In January 1963, Muhammad Reza Shah initiated a set of economic and social reforms in a programme he dubbed 'the White Revolution', as opposed to a 'Red' or communist revolution. Its measures included further land redistribution, nationalization of the forests, the sale of state factories, a profit-sharing plan for workers, a rural literacy campaign and women's suffrage. The White Revolution demonstrated the shah's commitment to improving conditions for Iran's rural and urban poor and it garnered Washington's support. Nevertheless, a few months after its promulgation, riots broke out, inspired by a 61-year-old dissident cleric, Ruhollah Khomeini. In Qom, the main centre of Shi'i seminaries, Khomeini denounced the White Revolution and other facets of the shah's rule: women's suffrage, Western cultural influence and selling oil to Israel. When at the beginning of June authorities arrested Khomeini, demonstrations and riots broke out in Qom, Tehran and other cities. Security forces suppressed the protests with brutal force, killing at least several hundred demonstrators. Khomeini was released from prison in August, but continued to agitate against the government. In October 1964, the shah pushed through a treaty with the United States that provided legal immunity to military personnel. Khomeini harshly condemned the treaty

(Status of Forces Agreement), sparking protests once more. He was again arrested and this time expelled from the country. He settled in Najaf, Iraq, where he became a teacher at one of the Shi'i seminaries.

In the early 1960s, National Front leaders tried to reorganize, but tensions surfaced between a secular liberal wing and a religious wing led by clerics and lay Islamists. The latter left to form the Liberation Movement of Iran (it was to play a significant role in the first two years of the Islamic Republic). By the late 1960s, political opposition was deeply fragmented. The Tudeh Party had split into three factions with followings among university students, and workers in the oilfields and large industrial factories. The religious estate was divided between clergy primarily concerned with moral reform in the face of growing alcohol and drug use, moderates advocating political reform through legal means, and militants like Khomeini adamantly opposed to the shah.

Muhammad Reza Shah had an ambitious vision for the country's future as a wealthy, industrial power. His formula for economic development included rising oil income, educated citizens and state-guided economic plans. He built on the foundation of infrastructure that his father laid down in the 1930s, improving transportation and communications. The state directed investment into industries to increase production of iron ore, steel, cement, textiles and petrochemicals. New factories manufactured consumer goods such as automobiles, televisions and radios. Industrialization required a larger number of wage workers whose political quiescence he ensured with subsidies on basic consumer goods and utilities and high wages.

By 1970, Iran's political stability and economic development appeared to be a success story. The shah had survived challenges from the liberal stream represented by Musaddiq and the religious stream voiced by Khomeini. He had built a formidably well equipped military, expanded access to education, and advanced the country's industrial sector. He felt entitled to stage a lavish festival to demonstrate Iran's arrival as a world power. The occasion was the 2,500-year anniversary of the founding of the Achaemenid Empire. The shah envisioned the Pahlavi dynasty as a worthy heir to the first great Persian Empire. To mark the occasion, he invited leaders from around the world to a massive celebration at Persepolis in October 1971, spending $200 million on a party for 3,000 guests, most of them from abroad. Few Iranians shared the celebratory mood. Famine gripped two of Iran's southern provinces. Security forces patrolled the hills around Persepolis in helicopters to guard against leftist guerrillas. From his exile in Iraq, Khomeini condemned the celebration as a waste of money when many Iranians were suffering the effects of famine.

The shah was confident that he could afford to ignore his critics. In addition to evident internal stability, he enjoyed close relations with the United States. He allowed American intelligence to maintain stations along the Soviet border to spy on communications and he was unusual among non-Western leaders in supporting the American war in Vietnam. He was even more unusual among Muslim leaders in maintaining extensive covert relations with Israel, selling it oil and offering military and intelligence cooperation. Compared to its Gulf neighbours, Iran appeared to have weathered the era of post-colonial nationalism and was poised for a long stretch of prosperity and stability.

IRAQ

By contrast, Iraq passed through a stormy stretch of instability starting with the July 1958 military overthrow of the Hashemite monarchy. It was the first of four coups in ten years, as politicized officer factions intrigued, purged, and fell from power in succession. The monarchy had failed to consolidate durable institutions, a shortcoming particularly conspicuous in the sphere of representative bodies. Consequently, each new military regime began with the formation of a new executive body to direct national government and issue decrees. On the ideological level, the dominant currents were Arab nationalism, divided between Baathist and Nasserist currents, and communism, as the old regime's liberal parties were eclipsed in the climate of violence and street crowds.

Each military regime had to contend with the same menu of issues: Iraq's place in the regional order, particularly *vis-à-vis* Nasser; Iraq's alignment in the Cold War; the state's role in economic development; and the relationship between the central government and the Kurdish region. The difficulties of coping with the Kurdish issue and maintaining power in such a challenging domestic climate so preoccupied successive Iraqi regimes that they paid little attention to the rest of the Gulf. Moreover, the balance of military power in the Gulf still lay overwhelmingly on Britain's side, enabling London to easily deflect Baghdad the one time that it did threaten a smaller neighbour.

The officers who seized power in July 1958 had two political goals: to abolish the monarchy and to pull Iraq out of the colonial orbit once and for all. The first was achieved in short order with the murder of the royal family in the first days of the revolution. Before turning to the second goal, the revolutionary regime had to resolve internal tensions. The two major personalities were Abd al-Karim Qasim and Abd al-Salam Arif. They had opposing views on whether Iraq should join the Egyptian–Syrian union, with Arif leaning strongly in favour and Qasim preferring to maintain Iraqi independence because he wished to avoid subordination to Nasser, which joining the UAR would have entailed. The deadlock was broken in November, when Qasim had Arif arrested, put on trial for treason, and thrown into prison. At that point, the Baathists and Nasserists rallied the full spectrum of Arab nationalists to challenge Qasim. He turned to the Iraqi Communist Party for backing. Arab nationalist army officers planned a military revolt in Mosul in March 1959 but Qasim foiled the plot. Communist demonstrators went on a rampage and massacred nationalists and wealthy Mosul families. Qasim tightened his grip on power and purged the army of Arab nationalists, driving the Baath Party underground. On 7 October 1959, a Baathist cell attempted to assassinate Qasim as he was riding through the streets of Baghdad. One of the gunmen in the failed plot was a 22-year-old Baathist named Saddam Hussein, who fled to Egypt.

In the wake of the abortive Mosul revolt, the Iraqi Communist Party gained influence as Qasim looked to Moscow for support. The Soviet Union took advantage of the opening in the Middle East. In short order, the Soviets granted a large loan for Iraq to pursue industrial development, dispatched experts to assist with technical projects, initiated academic and cultural exchanges, and provided military assistance with arms and war planes. While Qasim was not a communist and did not pursue communist programmes in the economy, Moscow was satisfied with the new turn in relations and encouraged the Iraqi Communist Party to support him.

The Qasim regime's warm relations with the Soviet Union signalled Iraq's move out of the region's pro-Western camp. On 24 March 1959, Iraq officially withdrew from the Baghdad Pact. But complete escape from Western domination was not so simple because the Iraq Petroleum Company (IPC) still controlled the country's oil production. Qasim tussled with the IPC over three main issues. First, he wanted to increase Iraq's share of company ownership. Second, he wanted to see Iraq take a larger share in company profits. Third, he wanted the IPC to relinquish rights to areas of the concession that were being left unused.

The IPC's parent companies opposed any revision of terms because they would then have come under pressure to revise concessions with other Gulf producers. Qasim became frustrated with the stalemate in negotiations and on 11 December 1961 he promulgated Public Law (PL) 80.

The new law seized almost the entire concession area except for the zone around Kirkuk where the company was extracting oil. The law also established the Iraqi National Oil Company (INOC) to develop oil in the rest of the country. In the short term, PL 80 had little tangible effect. The IPC cut back production and its parent companies compensated by raising production in other countries. As a political move, however, issuing the law foreshadowed the assertion of sovereignty over a resource that in 1961 provided nearly half the government revenue and roughly 90 per cent of foreign exchange.

In the spirit of the period's anti-colonial politics, the Qasim regime initiated economic measures intended to ease pressures on the country's poor. East Baghdad, a section with some of the country's worst slums, saw a new housing development dubbed Revolution City (renamed Saddam City in the 1980s, and then Sadr City in 2003). The government tried to carry through significant agrarian reform with a bill in September 1958. Its objective was to equalize rural landholdings by imposing a ceiling on the size of estates and redistributing land to the rural poor. Because the government lacked administrative capacity in rural areas to deliver credit, seeds and marketing – functions previously performed by large landlords – the measure caused disruption and a decline in agricultural production. The gap between purpose and outcome led the government to create a ministry of planning to direct and implement programmes in industry, education, health and housing. In the social arena, Qasim advanced women's rights with revisions to family law that restricted a man's right to more than one wife and to unconditional divorce, raised the minimum marriage age to 18, and gave women equal inheritance rights.

Iraq's relations with Gulf neighbours were rocky under Qasim. His withdrawal from the Baghdad Pact and pursuit of ties with Moscow alienated the pro-Western shah of Iran. In November 1959, the shah announced that Iran wanted to renegotiate terms of navigation on the Shatt al-Arab established in the 1937 Saadabad Agreement that had conceded control over shipping to Iraq. Qasim retaliated by announcing the nullification of the agreement altogether and then claiming the Iranian province of Khuzistan, which he referred to as 'Arabistan' since a large number of its inhabitants were Arab. In 1961, Iraq formally designated the Gulf as the Persian Gulf for the first time.

That same year, Kuwait became independent in June. One month later, Qasim announced that Kuwait was part of Iraq. He argued that Kuwait had formed part of the province of Basra in the Ottoman period, and that since Iraq was the successor state to the Ottoman Empire, its territory should include former Ottoman lands. Kuwait solicited British military protection to deter the Iraqis. The Arab League sided with Kuwait in the dispute and dispatched troops in September, making it possible for the British to withdraw their forces. Qasim was in no position to force the issue because the bulk of his military forces were bogged down in fruitless combat in the northern Kurdish region, where autonomist militias put up stiff resistance to the Iraqi armed forces.

On 8 February 1963, Arab nationalist officers mounted a *coup d'état* and Abd al-Karim Qasim was killed resisting them. A coalition of Baathist and Nasserist army officers established a National Command of the Revolutionary Council as a collective executive head of the government. The new regime quickly distanced itself from Qasim, renouncing the claim to Kuwait and subjecting the Iraqi Communist Party to a brutal crackdown. Internal tensions undermined the Arab nationalist government. Baath Party officers expelled the Nasserists. But the Baath itself was deeply torn between (1) radical purists who wished to exclude other Arab nationalists from governing and to pursue a sweeping socialist agenda on one hand and (2) moderates willing to cooperate with other Arab nationalists and inclined to a more gradual approach to economic and social change on the other. Infighting was so severe that armed clashes broke out between rival cliques in the armed forces. To mediate the intra-Baath conflict, leaders of the Syrian Baath Party were invited to Baghdad in November 1963. Iraqis witnessed the odd spectre of Syrians settling their political disputes. That peculiar form of Arab unity, having outsiders from a neighbouring Arab country determine national political affairs, grated on Iraqi nationalist feeling. On 18 November, a group of Nasserist and moderate Baathist officers led by Abd al-Salam Arif seized power, marking yet another swing in the country's political direction.

Arif moved Iraq closer to Nasser, adopting Egyptian-style Arab socialism with a series of nationalization measures affecting banks, insurance, major industries and foreign trade. In foreign relations, Arif revived military ties to Moscow, which rewarded Iraq with an atomic reactor, giving birth to what would become Iraq's controversial nuclear programme. Even though Iraq was

closer to Egypt than before, Nasserist officers made a bid
for power in September 1965 but military forces loyal to Arif
defeated them. He then took steps to eliminate the role of army
officers in politics by appointing civilian politicians to cabinet
posts. Arif also planned to back away from socialist policies and
to attract more private and foreign investment in the economy.
Whether he would have continued on a path towards civilian
rule is impossible to tell because he was killed in a helicopter
crash on 13 April 1966. Government leaders chose his brother
Abd al-Rahman Arif to succeed him.

The third new government in three years faced a worsening
situation in the Kurdish regions, where the movement for
autonomy received arms from Iran. By summer 1965, Kurdish
militiamen controlled the countryside and increased military
pressure on army units dispersed among the main towns. To
put an end to the fighting, Baghdad and the Kurds worked out
in June 1966 a blueprint for an autonomy agreement. Arab
nationalist officers were furious at what they viewed as a compromise of Iraq's national unity. The Arif government delayed
implementation of the agreement, so Kurds became restive as
well. The government's reputation took another blow from the
Arab defeat in the June 1967 war. Iraqi forces played a very minor
part on the Jordanian front, but the humiliating loss damaged
the regime's credibility.

The Arif regime took significant steps in extending sovereign control over oil. PL97 of August 1967 barred IPC from
participating in a promising oilfield located along the border
with Kuwait and assigned the field's development to INOC.
To tighten central authority over oil production, PL123 placed
INOC directly under the president. INOC then made a deal with
the French state oil company that allowed it to explore for and
market Iraqi oil. The Iraqi company also entered an agreement
with Moscow for Soviet technicians to assist with the development of oil resources. At the end of 1967, IPC still dominated
the production and sale of Iraqi oil from the Kirkuk fields, but
the company's monopoly was over.

During the Arif years, the Iraqi Baath Party absorbed the
lessons of its failure to hold on to power. The internal power
struggle between factions emphasizing Arab unity or socialism
was resolved in favour of the former. By contrast, the socialist
faction prevailed in the party's Syrian branch. The split poisoned
relations between the Iraqi and Syrian branches of the Baath
Party, which wound up in control of their respective countries
by 1968, setting the stage for decades of mutual enmity. The
victorious wing in Iraq patiently prepared for an opportunity to

return to power. It formed a party militia, developed intelligence cells, and infiltrated professional and student organizations. The Baath could not easily depose the Arif government without allies in the critical military commands situated in Baghdad. In early 1968, disaffected army officers reached out to the Baath to plot Arif's removal. On 17 July 1968, the conspirators moved against Arif, who relinquished power without a struggle and left the country.

The Baathist leaders moved to consolidate their grip on power. The head of the party, Ahmad Hasan al-Bakr, became President and Commander of the armed forces. Cabinet posts went to members of the party and its close allies. There would be no more reaching out to Nasserists. On the contrary, the regime put leaders of rival groups on trial for conspiring with the United States, Israel and Iran. Most of the defendants received prison sentences; others were executed for treason. In November 1969, the regime announced the establishment of the Revolutionary Command Council (RCC) as the ruling body. Then in July 1970, it promulgated an interim constitution that concentrated power in the RCC and turned Iraq into a one-party state. The RCC presided over the budget, the military, the courts and legislation. Parallel to the rigorous construction of new mechanisms for exercising power the Baathists took steps to prevent further military coups with a series of purges against army officers in the government and party leadership. President Ahmad al-Bakr relied on a small circle of fellow tribesmen from Tikrit. The vice-chairman of the RCC, and hence the second most powerful figure in the regime, was his cousin, Saddam Hussein.

At the same time as the Baathists were solidifying power, they confronted two challenges that would vex the regime for many years. Iran tested Baghdad's resolve over navigation rights on the Shatt al-Arab when the shah renounced the 1937 Saadabad Treaty on 19 April 1969. Iraq retaliated by expelling some Iranians. Tehran then renewed military aid to the Kurds. With open backing from Iran, the Kurds resumed their struggle for autonomy. The Baathists were still preoccupied with internal consolidation and decided to accommodate Kurdish demands for autonomy, language rights and a Kurdish vice-president. The agreement provided for a four-year transition period to implement the accord, giving the regime much needed breathing space. In the long term, however, the Kurds' willingness to obtain support from Iran engendered deep mistrust and resentment in Baathist circles.

The Baathist regime also regarded the Shi'i Da'wa Party as a threat. The party's roots go back to the 1950s, when Najaf's religious leadership was alarmed by a number of developments, including the spread of secular trends and Western morality in Iraqi cities and towns; the Iraqi Communist Party's success at recruiting Shi'is uprooted from the countryside; and the Qasim regime's Personal Status Code that unified Sunni and Shi'i legal rules. Clerics in Najaf regarded the reform as an encroachment on one of the few areas of influence left to religious institutions. Furthermore, Qasim's land reform measures weakened the religious institution's backers among large landowners. The primary intellectual inspiration for the Da'wa Party was Muhammad Baqir al-Sadr, a member of a prominent clerical family. He considered it necessary to reformulate religious authority and religious ideas to address contemporary political and social issues. His first major work of 1958, *Our Philosophy*, used Islamic terms and concepts to frame a critique of Marxism, which was proving attractive to Shi'i youth at the time. His later writings of the 1960s and 1970s extended his anti-Marxist polemic and formulated the foundation for a modern economy based on Islamic law. He also published an essay on Islamic banking. Sadr's intellectual force and vision gained him audiences among Sunni Islamists as well as his natural Shi'i constituency. Within Iraq, the increasingly Sunni complexion of Arab nationalist regimes and the suppression of the Communist Party made the Da'wa Party attractive to educated, urban Shi'is.

When the Baath Party regained power in July 1968, it was Iraq's fourth coup in ten years. Based on the party's dismal performance in 1963 and the country's persistent instability, few would have predicted that the regime would remain in power for 35 years. Nevertheless, by the time the Baathists consolidated power in 1970, the region was entering a new phase. The passing of Nasser diminished Egypt's influence as a model and as a partner for unity experiment. With a stable government, oil and an educated population, Baathist Iraq was in a position to assert a more prominent role in the Arab world.

SAUDI ARABIA

The Arab nationalist era posed daunting challenges to Saudi Arabia's leadership. While Al Saud ruled the largest country in Arabia, the realm was beset by vulnerabilities. Long uninhabited borders were a challenge to control and defend. Two northern neighbours, Jordan and Iraq, were under Hashemite rulers whose ancestral home in Hijaz Abdulaziz ibn Saud had conquered in the 1920s. In the south-east, boundaries with Oman, the Trucial States and Qatar were disputed. Iran's pro-Western shah aspired to a dominant role in the Gulf. Anglo-French collusion with Israel in the Suez war embarrassed pro-Western monarchies like Saudi Arabia's. The kingdom's primary asset, petroleum, was proving a destabilizing force, as oil workers agitating for better conditions and pay introduced modern political dissent. Moreover, the kingdom lacked administrative mechanisms to turn oil into development projects. Formulating an effective and coherent posture in regional relations was particularly difficult, with the ruling family split into three factions: King Saud and his sons; Crown Prince Faisal and some brothers; and a set of young princes who wanted to modernize the administration and take steps in the direction of a constitutional monarchy.

The royal political drama began at the death of King Abdulaziz in 1953 and lasted until Faisal forced Saud's abdication in 1964. The details of the power struggle were specific to Saudi Arabia, but the dynamics were common to Gulf hereditary monarchies for two reasons. First, according to custom, leadership resided with the ruling family as a whole, not with a single individual and his immediate descendants. Second, it followed that there was no rule for succession from father to son. Power frequently passed to a ruler's brother, uncle, or cousin. In the particular case of Al Saud, the last smooth succession had taken place in the early 1800s.

King Saud's chief defect was his failure to manage the budget even as oil income expanded in the mid-1950s. His extravagant spending set the pace for other princes to treat oil income as a private asset rather than a public resource to fund national development. In the sphere of foreign relations, Saud continued to regard the Hashemite monarchies on his northern border as adversaries. When he first ascended the throne, he supported Nasser, whose anti-colonial outlook made him view the Hashemites as British agents. Nasser took the Saudi side in the dispute over Buraimi because it provided an opportunity to undermine Britain's position in the Gulf.

King Saud's attitude towards Nasser changed in 1956. That year the Eastern Province was the scene of labour unrest, calls for liberal political reforms and Arab nationalist demonstrations over the Suez Crisis. The king worried that enthusiasm for Nasser might compromise royal authority. In 1957, he visited the United States, where he voiced his support for the Eisenhower doctrine. Washington rewarded him by providing economic and military assistance; Saud reciprocated by renewing the lease for Americans to use the air base at Dhahran for another five years. The proclamation of the UAR in February 1958 boosted Nasser's popularity to new heights. At that point, Crown Prince Faisal rallied leading princes to demand that Saud hand over the reins of government, making Faisal prime minister and commander-in-chief.

Faisal brought order to the budget. He curbed spending on royal palaces and other luxuries, devalued the currency and improved the balance of payments. He did nothing, however, to meet the demands of the young princes for fundamental political reform. Saud courted their leader, Prince Talal, with hints that he would enact basic reforms if the young princes backed him against Faisal. Saud also rallied tribal and religious leaders who had previously benefitted from his patronage and resented Faisal's cost-cutting measures. In December 1960, the anti-Faisal coalition was able to thwart his policies and he ceded power to Saud, who installed Prince Talal and other liberal princes to the cabinet. Even more startling, he appointed a majority of commoners to the cabinet. The king's coalition, however, proved more effective at prying the reins out of Faisal's hands than at governing. It soon fractured over the question of adopting a constitution. Senior princes were alarmed at the prospect of constitutional government, which could mark the beginning of the end of royal prerogatives and wealth. Saud was not keen on constitutional limits either. In September 1961, the king removed Talal from the cabinet. Two months later, Saud entered hospital and then left for medical treatment in the United States, where he spent most of the next year. In his absence, Faisal took over running the government. Once it became clear that Faisal would obstruct steps towards a constitutional monarchy, Prince Talal left the country. In Beirut, Lebanon, he declared the formation of an exile bloc called the Free Princes. Riyadh pressed the Lebanese authorities to make Talal unwelcome, so he then moved to Cairo, where he spent the remainder of Faisal's reign.

A new threat to the Saudi monarchy suddenly appeared on its southern frontier in September 1962 when Nasserist army officers in North Yemen seized power and deposed the hereditary ruler. For the next six years, North Yemen's civil war pitting royalist forces against a republican regime tore the country apart. Nasser quickly dispatched Egyptian troops to shore up the republican officers, but Yemen's rugged terrain and experienced tribal warriors proved insurmountable. Riyadh armed and funded the royalist side but did not commit its own military forces because they were too few and too unreliable: a number of Saudi pilots on flights to deliver supplies to royalists defected to Cairo. In 1963, Egyptian war planes carried out attacks along the Saudi border, causing alarm in Riyadh. The Saudis then invited the Americans back to Dhahran air base and the United States bolstered air defences along the border, sending its own war planes to patrol the border as a warning to the Egyptians.

It was in this atmosphere of regional crisis that Crown Prince Faisal issued a Ten-Point Programme in November 1962. The Programme pledged to improve living conditions by expanding access to education, health care and social security. It also committed the government to expanding infrastructure: building roads, developing water resources for cultivators and pastoralists, founding industrial enterprises and establishing banks. The abolition of slavery satisfied foreign critics and annoyed traditionalists at home. The Programme mentioned the formation of a consultative council and a basic law along the lines of a constitution, but those were not implemented until decades later.

The longer King Saud remained outside the country because of his fragile health, the firmer became Faisal's grip on power. In November 1964, Faisal took the final step to have the Wahhabi religious leaders confirm Saud's removal from the throne and his own accession. Faisal's triumph marked the arrival of an alliance of princes that has lasted to the present day. Two of King Faisal's half-brothers – Fahd and Sultan – occupied powerful posts in defence and security, while a third – Salman – managed the politically sensitive region of Riyadh. In March 1965, Faisal named another half-brother, Khalid ibn Abdulaziz, the Crown Prince; while Prince Abdullah became head of the National Guard. Saud's sons and Talal's bloc of liberal princes were marginalized. Faisal prevailed in the drawn-out succession struggle more than ten years after the passing of Abdulaziz.

With power firmly in his hands, King Faisal moved forward with plans to strengthen the government's administrative capacity and to develop a modern economy, both sorely needed. In spite of rising oil revenues, the lot of most Saudis had not improved, and for many it had worsened. Government income had grown from around $50 million in 1948 to $330 million in 1960, but Riyadh lacked a national development strategy. Moreover, when Saud was king, he skimmed up to one-fifth of the budget for his personal and political purposes. Modest projects resulted in the construction of some schools, clinics and hospitals but did not reverse the trend for the average Saudi whose lot was becoming worse under the impact of exposure to global trade and new technology. Nomads formerly earned fees for transporting goods on pack animals but motorized transport replaced them. Oil paid for food imports, which was essential during drought years but at other times undermined the market for cultivators' and pastoralists' products. The court and the rich merchants were developing an appetite for imported Western products, and that drove down demand for local artisan goods. The second half of the 1960s, however, saw the first steps to spread the bounty of oil to ordinary Saudis.

In the 1960s, the government established the General Organization of Petroleum and Minerals (Petromin) to represent the kingdom in dealings with Western oil companies. Petromin negotiated concessions for exploration and production with a number of smaller companies as a way to break Aramco's monopoly. Devising productive ways to spend revenue became the task of the Central Planning Organization, founded in 1965. The kingdom's first generation of Western-educated technocrats invested in raising electricity production, laying down a transportation network, building schools and expanding medical services. In addition, King Faisal's cabinet produced legislation to address the need for clear banking regulations to promote private investment and rules on land tenure to encourage agricultural improvement. The cabinet also issued a new labour law forbidding trade union activity in order to prevent a repetition of the 1950s unrest. In the early 1960s, Saudis still comprised the vast majority of workers, probably 90 per cent (statistics for the period are largely guesswork). Implementation of development projects in the early 1970s triggered a flood of immigration that brought the ratio of expatriate labour in the workforce to approximately 30 per cent.

Among the various development projects, introducing a modern education system was the most sensitive. Ever since the founding of the first Saudi state in the eighteenth century, Wahhabi ulama exercised full control over education and made Wahhabi religious texts the focus of learning. The annexation of Hijaz in the 1920s absorbed a network of modern private schools that blended religious instruction with secular subjects. Wahhabi ulama opposed the inclusion of science and foreign languages in the curriculum, but King Abdulaziz overruled them. In the late 1950s, King Saud created a ministry of education and increased its budget to build and staff schools. Until that time, girls were excluded, but Crown Prince Faisal's wife Princess Iffat pushed for opening schools to girls, and in 1960, Faisal endorsed the creation of separate schools for girls. In order to persuade the religious establishment that the innovation would not corrupt the morals of young girls, Faisal put the schools under a separate agency administered by the leading Wahhabi cleric, Sheikh Muhammad ibn Ibrahim Al al-Sheikh.

Faisal's willingness to tinker with conservative ways encountered violent resistance when he introduced television to the
kingdom in 1965. Two years earlier, religious leaders had objected
to a female radio broadcaster. Faisal's position on television had
nothing to do with religion and everything to do with politics.
Egyptian President Nasser used radio and television to rally support in the Arab world for his policies and to undermine his rivals.
Faisal saw the media as important weapons in Riyadh's battle
with Cairo. To defuse opposition rooted in religious principles,
he promised television programming would promote religious
observance and that censorship would prevent airing of cor-
rupting subjects, such as romantic relationships. Those measures
did not satisfy conservatives. Angry protestors tried to storm the
television station in Riyadh but were blocked by the police. In
the course of the stand-off, a grandson of King Abdulaziz, Prince
Khalid ibn Musaid, was shot dead. In spite of that incident, the
king prevailed and televisions became common in Saudi homes.

While Faisal contended with religious resistance to cultural
innovation, he turned to religion as an instrument of foreign
policy in the Arab Cold War. In general terms, this political conflict pitted republican nationalist regimes in Egypt, Syria and
Iraq against hereditary monarchies in Jordan, Saudi Arabia and
the Gulf. Fundamental differences separated the two camps.
The republican regimes wished to eliminate all vestiges of colonial influence and to pursue a neutral course in the global Cold
War. The monarchies felt threatened by the populist appeal of
Arab nationalism and depended on Western powers to secure
them against subversion. Political dynamics were complicated
by tensions within each camp. Thus, Syria and Iraq's relations
with Egypt blew hot and cold. Saudi Arabia and Jordan contended with their legacy of warfare and enmity from earlier
decades.

The closest the Arab Cold War came to turning into real
warfare was in North Yemen's civil war. By 1967, Cairo had
escalated its military commitment to 60,000 troops while
the Saudis continued to fund and equip royalist forces. The
conflict turned into a stalemate that sapped Egypt's military and economic resources. It seemed destined to drag on
indefinitely until the June 1967 war struck a huge blow to
Egypt. A few months after losing the Sinai Peninsula to Israeli
forces, Nasser agreed to withdraw his troops from Yemen in
exchange for Faisal's promise to provide funds to Egypt as a
front-line state in the confrontation with Israel. The thaw
in relations between Riyadh and Cairo was the beginning of
the end of the Arab Cold War. The radical nationalist threat

revived, however, with the return of the Baath Party to power in Baghdad, which became the new headquarters for Saudi dissidents.

King Faisal developed an 'Islamic' foreign policy to deflect Arab nationalism's domestic appeal and to construct a coalition of conservative governments opposed to socialist and secularist currents. Islamic solidarity seemed a natural principle for the home of the two holy places. Faisal invited Muslim leaders to an Islamic conference which established the Muslim World League for the promotion of religious observance and Muslims' interests. In the Gulf, Faisal and the shah of Iran were aware of their mutual interest in combating radical political influences. The shah endorsed Faisal's proposal for an Islamic summit in 1966. Jordan's King Hussein was the only Arab leader to attend the summit. It was a significant moment in the warming of Hashemite–Saudi relations, prompted by the rising influence of radical nationalism. Faisal's Islamic foreign policy underwent further development after the June 1967 war in which Israel captured East Jerusalem, site of a holy shrine, the Noble Sanctuary, the Dome of the Rock and al-Aqsa Mosque. Faisal made recovery of East Jerusalem a pan-Islamic issue at the Rabat summit convened in September 1969.

It is worth recalling that Saudi Arabia was still a poor country in the 1960s, with physical and economic transformation some years in the future. With more resources than ever before, but not close to the scale attained after the 1973 oil price revolution, the rulers took the first steps to creating formal government institutions and modern infrastructure. They navigated a tricky and drawn-out succession struggle, whose impact on dynastic stability could not be taken lightly in view of the second Saudi emirate's collapse as a result of internal strife. And they survived the tumultuous years of Arab nationalist ferment. The next decade would see unprecedented opportunities to develop the country and project Riyadh's influence on the Muslim world.

KUWAIT

When Kuwait became independent on 19 June 1961 with the end of the British Protectorate, Emir Abdullah supported the formation of a constitutional government for two reasons. First, it would unify Kuwaitis behind Al Sabah in the face of

Iraqi claims. Second, it had roots in Kuwait's experiment with a representative council, which Abdullah had supported, in 1938. Kuwait's constitution, drafted by an elected constituent assembly, took nineteenth-century European constitutional monarchies as its model. It confirmed Al Sabah's position as hereditary rulers and guaranteed citizens' rights to assembly and a free press. Under the constitution, the emir possesses executive authority while he shares legislative authority with an elected national assembly, comprised of 50 elected members and as many as 15 cabinet members. The emir appoints the prime minister (by custom until 2003, the crown prince), and the prime minister then chooses members of the cabinet. Since the emir controls appointments to the cabinet, he has a reliable bloc of votes that usually combines with a loyalist minority to dominate proceedings. Parliamentary deputies have the right to question ministers and call for their resignation, but only the emir has the authority to dismiss the prime minister. The constitution also gives the emir the power to dissolve parliament but he must then hold elections within 60 days. On two occasions, in 1976 and in 1986, emirs violated the constitution by suspending parliament indefinitely. Apart from presiding over the making of the Arab Gulf's first constitutional government, Sheikh Abdullah changed his title from sheikh to emir and designated his brother Sabah as his heir.

The emir signed the constitution on 11 November 1962, and elections to the national assembly were held in January 1963. Winning candidates included the Arab nationalist Ahmad al-Khatib and several other Nasserists, organized in the National Bloc. The limits of Arab nationalism's reach became clear when Khatib called for extending citizens' privileges to Arab expatriates. It was a very unpopular position among Kuwaitis. In order to dilute the strength of the Arab nationalist deputies, the government turned to the Bedouins. They had been passed over in the first set of laws defining Kuwaiti citizenship. Now the government not only granted them citizenship, but also provided free housing to Bedouins wishing to settle in towns as well as jobs in the army and the police. In return, the newly enfranchised Bedouins voted for pro-government national assembly candidates.

In the mid-1960s, legislation solidified a social order that divided Kuwait into three estates: the ruling family, commoners and expatriates. Al Sabah stood at the top of the social hierarchy. The ruler came from their ranks; they occupied the most powerful positions in the government; and the sheikhs enjoyed special allowances. Commoners possessed privileges by comparison to expatriates. The legal framework for citizenship evolved through a series of decrees starting in 1948, when nationality was restricted to those whose ancestors were residents as of 1898. That criterion was relaxed in 1959 to include descendants of residents present in Kuwait as of 1920. The following year, a Civil Service law reserved high-ranking positions to Kuwaiti citizens. Also in 1960, legislation mandated majority Kuwaiti ownership of business enterprises and excluded expatriates completely from the financial sector. Similar legislation in the other Gulf emirates later replicated the three-estate model. By endowing exclusive privileges on citizens, the model generates solidarity between citizens and rulers against expatriates, whose growing presence up and down the Gulf coast seemed to threaten the local population.

By 1965, expatriates outnumbered citizens even though reductions in infant mortality spurred fast population growth for Kuwaitis: their numbers rose from around 220,000 in 1965 to 550,000 in 1980. But development projects and jobs requiring technical skills caused a faster growth in expatriate numbers, rising from half the population to 60 per cent over the same period. The pitfalls of depending on foreign labour would materialize in later years, but in its first decade of independence, Kuwait's constitutional experiment and rentier bargain provided solid foundations for domestic calm and prosperity, making it a symbol of forward-thinking leadership and stability in the rest of the Gulf.

BAHRAIN

Bahrain recovered its political equilibrium after the labour and Arab nationalist unrest of the mid-1950s. It helped that Al Khalifah handled the matter of succession in smooth fashion when Sheikh Salman died in December 1961. He had designated his son Isa heir in 1948. The ruling sheikhs faced a complex political landscape of historical communities divided between Sunni and Shi'i as well as modern social groups that included merchants, industrial workers and salaried professionals. The prominent role of these groups reflected the early development of Bahrain's oil industry, administrative bodies and educational institutions. Strong nationalist sentiment fed on unease at the large number of South Asian workers, the American oil company and the official British role.

The complexity of Bahrain's social and communal profile spawned popular nationalist organizations, which in turn spurred the rulers to devise elaborate means to shield their power. First, in response to labour and nationalist protests in the mid-1950s, the authorities strengthened security forces, tapping the British Empire's reservoir of trained manpower for recruits from Iraq, Jordan and Yemen. Al Khalifah also bolstered armed units of Sunni tribesmen whose loyalty was assured with land allotments and sheikhly patronage. Another strategy to lower the political temperature was the drafting of labour laws setting a 40-hour working week and stipulating sick leave and vacation. The laws did not provide for the right to form labour unions. Rather, a labour advisory council, headed by an Al Khalifah sheikh, was formed to arbitrate disputes. Finally, the government drew a clear line between the sheikhs' and the merchants' respective spheres, essentially leaving governance to Al Khalifah and turning lucrative monopolies and agencies for foreign trade over to merchants, who had recovered from the collapse of pearling by making Bahrain a centre for re-exporting goods from the West to Saudi Arabia, Iran and the less developed sheikhdoms of the lower Gulf. By requiring foreign companies to work through Bahraini merchants, the framework for privileged citizenship elaborated in Kuwait emerged in Bahrain too. In the sphere of government, the sheikhs formed an administrative council to oversee public affairs. The council gradually created specialized bureaux dedicated to transportation, customs, agriculture and the like.

The new political structures and favourable economic conditions gave Bahrain a respite from turmoil. The tide of Nasserism certainly touched the archipelago, but did not penetrate deeply enough to foster instability. The next round of unrest erupted in March 1965, when the Bahrain Petroleum Company (BAPCO) announced lay-offs and workers went on strike. They called for the dismissal of foreign workers to preserve jobs for Bahraini nationals, revived demands for the right to form trade unions and for the end of the state of emergency in place since 1956, and pressed the ruler to grant political liberties for speech, press and assembly. The authorities had the leaders arrested and sentenced to prison terms and exile. In April, the government passed a set of security laws that authorized the sheikh to declare emergency rule and detain individuals suspected of disturbing public order, ratifying powers he already exercised. The government also enacted rules to regulate the press. Notwithstanding the new instruments devised for repression, labour unrest and political protest occasionally broke the surface calm of daily life in the late 1960s.

QATAR

Power struggles between rival factions of Al Thani remained the focus of politics in Qatar. When Sheikh Abdullah abdicated to his son Ali in 1949, he had promised that the next succession would elevate a member of the Hamad branch to ruler. The senior member of that branch was Sheikh Khalifah. To build his power base, he championed workers' rights and Arab nationalism. As minister of education, Sheikh Khalifah recruited expatriate Arab teachers to staff Qatar's schools. Khalifah's efforts, however, did not assure his position. In 1957, Sheikh Ali named his son Sheikh Ahmad heir apparent, with the backing of the British Political Agent.

Dynastic intrigue was highly sensitive to Qatar's oil revenues, which dropped due to global economic conditions in 1959–60. Reductions in allowances to Al Thani sheikhs naturally followed but left Sheikh Ali vulnerable to complaints because his own extravagant spending showed no sign of letting up. A handful of forward-thinking sheikhs also thought that Ali should channel funds to public development projects as in Kuwait. In October 1960, one of Sheikh Khalifah's brothers attempted to assassinate Sheikh Ali. Happy to get away with his life, Sheikh Ali decided to step down in favour of his son Sheikh Ahmad. He in turn named Sheikh Khalifah as his heir and reallocated oil revenues to pacify the sheikhs and declared his intention to increase spending on public projects.

Sheikh Ahmad also placated fellow Qataris with legislation that drew formal boundaries between citizens and expatriates. A 1961 nationality law set the date of residence for acquiring citizenship at 1930. In 1963, the government issued a law prohibiting foreigners from buying real estate and stipulating majority Qatari ownership of businesses. At the same time, Sheikh Ahmad fortified the position of Al Thani by granting members preferential access to land for real estate development in addition to their allowances and domination of leading positions in the government and nascent administration.

Qatar's Arab nationalist crisis took place in April 1963, when the Baathist regimes in Syria and Iraq were negotiating with Nasser to revive Arab unity. A coalition of Qatari workers, low-ranking Al Thani sheikhs and disaffected notables formed the National Unity Front. The Front called for a general strike that lasted for three weeks. Its platform combined demands for improving workers' rights, more social services and an elective municipal council. The government responded with a combination of concessions and repression. It agreed to demands for preferential hiring for citizens in the oil and public sectors as well as the formation of a representative municipal council. At the same time, the government arrested several dozen leaders of the National Unity Front. With the end of the strike in early May, political tensions subsided.

Sheikh Ahmad's appetite for politics was diminished in the wake of the crisis and he spent more time on extended vacations abroad. In his absence, Sheikh Khalifah encroached on his authority. When the British declared their intention to withdraw from the Gulf, the two leaders split on whether Qatar should join a federation with other sheikhdoms (see below). Sheikh Ahmad favoured adhering to a federation while Sheikh Khalifah wanted to see Qatar become independent. Sheikh Khalifah's view prevailed and Qatar became independent in September 1971 while Sheikh Ahmad was out of the country. A few months later, on 22 February 1972, Sheikh Khalifah deposed him and took over as ruler. At the moment of Qatar's emergence as an independent country, it had undergone little development of political institutions compared to the other Gulf states.

THE TRUCIAL STATES

Political dynamics in the Trucial States during the Arab nationalist era were a mix of traditional sheikhly rivalries, Bedouin feuds and nationalist agitation. The British did what they could to cement sheikhly authority by urging the sheikhs to push ahead with administrative and infrastructure development. Following British advice, the Trucial States Council adopted an organized approach through a five-year plan for 1956–61 that laid the foundation for public services in education and medicine. In order to put state-led planning on a firmer basis, the Trucial States established a Development Office in 1965. From its headquarters in Dubai, the Development Office oversaw experiments in agricultural production, expansion of technical schools and road construction. British veterans of colonial postings to India and Africa staffed the Office.

To pay for various projects, a Trucial States Development Fund was set up with donations from Abu Dhabi (the sole oil exporter at that time), Qatar and Bahrain. Dubai's Sheikh Rashid was particularly eager to improve infrastructure to expand trade. One challenge to that goal was the silting of Dubai's creek, a physical

7. Dubai Creek.

obstacle to ships loading and unloading cargo. To address that challenge, the sheikh approved a costly plan to dredge the creek to increase capacity for the size and number of commercial vessels. By contrast, Sharjah's ruler did not want to work through the British agent on financing and contracting for dredging its creek, and consequently its trade stagnated and numbers of merchants moved to Dubai. Other projects in Dubai included a new water system, a road to Ra's al-Khaima and a deep port. When Shaikh Zayid seized power in Abu Dhabi in 1966, he made a very large donation to the Development Fund, setting a precedent for the oil-rich sheikhdom to lead the way in financing infrastructure projects. Before these initiatives, travel between Ra's al-Khaima and Abu Dhabi was either by pack animal or by sea. By 1970, the Trucial States had a nascent network of roads.

In terms of internal politics, the main event during the period was the deposition of Abu Dhabi's Sheikh Shakhbut in 1966. Leading members of Al Nahayyan were disgruntled over his parsimonious handling of growing oil revenues. With a population of about 20,000 in 1962, Abu Dhabi's public services amounted to little more than a single school and one paved road. It did not have a hospital. As people saw the pace of change in Dubai, they became frustrated with Shakhbut's refusal to spend on education and medical services, and families began moving to Dubai, Qatar and Saudi Arabia.

The British also were losing patience with the conservative leader, especially over his opposition to efforts to coordinate development projects with the other Trucial States. Starting in the early 1960s, Shakhbut's brother Sheikh Zayid expressed his discontent to the British, who were aware of the improvements he introduced to Buraimi, where he was the ruling sheikh's deputy. He improved irrigation, established a school and supported an American missionary project to build a hospital. During a holiday visit to England in 1966, Sheikh Zayid met with the British Resident to discuss the ruling family's views. The British agreed that oil revenues should be spent on developing administrative institutions and to advance the welfare of the population.

Back in Abu Dhabi, the British Resident informed Sheikh Shakhbut that his clansmen wished him to abdicate. He bowed to the inevitable, ceding power to Sheikh Zayid and leaving the country for a few years before retiring to Buraimi. Sheikh Zayid consolidated his power base by appointing trusted relatives to key posts, including his son Sheikh Khalifah, who became the deputy ruler in Buraimi.

Abu Dhabi's oil production and revenues were growing in the late 1960s. To oversee development projects, Zayid established a Council of Planning in 1968. Soon, Abu Dhabi was brimming with projects to develop the commercial district, transportation infrastructure for land, air and sea, and a modern sewage system. The amount of oil wealth coming in meant the ruler was able to abolish all taxes. Instead of extracting surplus wealth, Sheikh Zayid distributed it through land grants and free housing for the poor.

In Dubai, Sheikh Said ibn Maktum's 45-year reign ended upon his death in 1958. His son Rashid continued along a path to make Dubai a centre for finance and commerce. During the 1938 reform movement, Rashid supported his father's insistence on sheikhly prerogative, but his aspirations for economic growth required cooperation with merchants. Thus, he presided over the creation of a council of merchants that would serve as a consultative body for the drafting of development plans. The new body did not exercise any authority over the sheikh's purse. To prevent a recurrence of Arab nationalist agitation along the lines of the Dubai National Front, Sheikh Rashid cooperated with the British on a programme to strengthen police, security forces and courts. He also took a tough line against expatriate nationalists, going so far as to deport teachers suspected of spreading Arab nationalist views.

In the Qasimi sheikhdoms of Sharjah and Ra's al-Khaima, Nasserism found a foothold with the ruling sheikhs. Sheikh Saqr ibn Sultan came to power in Sharjah in 1951 by seizing it from his father. In the early 1950s, he voiced support for Nasser to the annoyance of the British and the other sheikhs. In 1964, Sheikh Saqr agreed to open a branch of the Arab League, which the British viewed as little more than an agent of Nasser. They feared that anti-Western nationalism might spread through an Arab League office in the Trucial States, so they plotted with a dissident member of the Qasimi tribe, Sheikh Khalid ibn Muhammad, and in 1965 deposed Sheikh Saqr. Ra's al-Khaima's Sheikh Saqr ibn Muhammad also leaned towards Nasser and the Arab nationalists but was more cautious than his fellow Qasimi ruler in Sharjah. He had inoculated himself against plotting after seizing power from his uncle in 1948 by paying him and his uncle's son a pension. He did, however, maintain a fiercely independent posture towards the British and other Trucial sheikhs that made him a difficult partner in forging a common position when London decided it was time to leave the region.

In the early 1960s, the Political Resident William Luce foresaw the need for the sheikhdoms to combine if they were to avoid absorption by a neighbouring power in the event of Britain's withdrawal from the Gulf. London feared an even worse prospect were the Lower Gulf to enter Nasser's sphere of influence through the Arab League: Nasser tempted the Trucial sheikhs with offers of economic aid if they would cut ties to the British. Avoiding such an outcome was an impetus for Britain's proposal that the sheikhdoms form a federation. Unresolved territorial claims between the sheikhs on one side and Saudi Arabia and Iran on the other inclined them to consider cooperative arrangements. In June 1965, the nine sheikhs of Bahrain, Qatar and the Trucial States met in Dubai to discuss common interests. When London announced in February 1966 that it would pull out of Aden within two years, the case for Gulf cooperation grew more urgent, but few expected that the British would soon also withdraw from there.

London's announcement in January 1968 of its intention to withdraw naval forces from the Gulf by the end of 1971 came as a jolt. Government officials had only recently reiterated that they had no such plans or intentions. What changed was that the Labour Party underwent a complete ideological conversion into an anti-colonial party and chronic budget problems worsened after currency devaluation in November 1967. The Conservative Party opposed the new policy and vowed to fight it. Meanwhile, Muhammad Reza Shah greased the skids by declaring that Iran would not force Bahrain to return to Iranian control, bringing sighs of relief to Manama. On the other hand, he said that Iran's claim to Abu Musa and the Tunbs stood. By the time the Conservative Party defeated Labour in national elections in June 1970, the political momentum in the Gulf was irreversible: Iran, Saudi Arabia and Kuwait all opposed any postponement of withdrawal.

British diplomats tried to pave the way for combining the nine Gulf sheikhdoms into a single federation. Saudi Arabia conditioned its support for a federation on resolving to its satisfaction the border dispute with Abu Dhabi; Iran placed similar conditions regarding the three Gulf islands. Sharjah reached agreement with Iran on a compromise over Abu Musa: Iranian troops would take over one half of the island; both countries would maintain their claims to the island; any oil would be divided; and Iran promised to pay a subsidy. By contrast, Ra's al-Khaima's Sheikh Saqr refused to budge from the Tunbs.

Negotiations for combining the sheikhdoms into a federation stumbled from the outset. First of all, none of the sheikhs wished to dilute his power. Second, their respective resources and populations were highly diverse: Bahrain was by far the most populous; Abu Dhabi had the clear potential to become the wealthiest; the northern sheikhdoms were doomed to be poor cousins. Sheikh Zayid proposed a solution by combining the five northern sheikhdoms – Ra's al-Khaima, Sharjah, Fujaira, Ajman and Umm al-Qaiwain – into their own United Arab Coastal Emirates, but the proud Qasimi sheikhs rejected the notion of their being on the same level as the other three. Meanwhile, historical tensions between Bahrain and Qatar over Zubara precluded their working together. Bahrain was the first to declare that it would not join the federation, opting for independence on 14 August 1971. Qatar followed two weeks later. At that late stage, the rulers of Abu Dhabi and Dubai sensed that the remaining sheikhdoms were unprepared for independence under a federal umbrella, so they offered to pay the costs of keeping British military forces in the area. London was not open to the last minute suggestion but did put forward a provisional federal constitution. On 25 November, the UAE was officially formed from six sheikhdoms, with Ra's al-Khaima's Sheikh Saqr holding out because he wanted to avoid coming under the domination of Abu Dhabi and Dubai. He hoped that oil companies might find substantial reserves or that the United States might lease a naval base: either possibility could give him the means to stand apart from the federation.

Five days after the British terminated their protection agreement, Iran seized the Tunb Islands from Ra's al-Khaima and Sheikh Saqr returned to talks about adhering to the federation as long as his emirate had equal footing with the other Qasimi member, Sharjah. With that assurance, Ra's al-Khaima became the seventh member of the UAE on 10 February 1972. The hastily conceived framework for the Arab world's first experiment in federation meant that the UAE would have to navigate rough waters in order keep all members together, but the prospect of future Iranian or Saudi territorial encroachment was enough incentive for the sheikhs to begin independence under one flag.

OMAN

In 1956, Oman had just undergone reunification through the sultan's conquest of the interior at the end of the previous year. Imam Ghalib admitted military defeat and abdicated, but his brother Talib had fled to Saudi Arabia to continue the fight. Riyadh nursed a grudge against Sultan Said and his British backers over the Buraimi oasis dispute. Nasser made the restoration of the Ibadi imamate an Arab nationalist cause because of his enmity towards Britain in the wake of Suez. What had been a political dispute between the coastal sultanate and the interior coalition of tribal and imamate forces thereby turned into a confrontation between rival regional blocs.

In June 1957, Talib appeared in the interior at the head of the Oman Revolutionary Movement to rally tribesmen against the sultan's forces. Sultan Said appealed to London to intervene with land and air power to thwart the campaign for a restoration of the imamate. The Royal Air Force base at Sharjah supported the Trucial Oman Scouts in expelling Talib's forces from the main towns and driving them into the higher reaches of the Jabal Akhdar range. Sultan Said then approached the British for additional military assistance to put out the last embers of rebellion. The British agreed to train a new military body called the Sultan's Armed Forces in exchange for renewal of Royal Air Force basing rights at al-Masira Island. In January 1959, the combination of British air power and the Sultan's Armed Forces captured Jabal Akhdar and the rebel leaders fled to Saudi Arabia and Iraq. The Oman Revolutionary Movement then broadcast anti-government propaganda with the backing of Egypt, Syria and Saudi Arabia, all three pursuing anti-British agendas. The Arab governments brought the issue of restoring the imamate to the United Nations, and the General Assembly appointed commissions to study the case. Their reports basically found in favour of the sultan as the legitimate ruler; nevertheless, the Arab nationalists and the Saudis kept the issue alive in UN forums until Oman became a member in 1971.

When it came to developing the country's infrastructure and governing institutions, Sultan Said moved cautiously. His first years on the throne in the early 1930s made him careful to avoid deficits and determined to implement only those projects he could afford rather than resort to loans. Nevertheless, he did begin to modernize the instruments of government. Rebellion was a major driving force behind developments in the sultanate's governing capacity. With British guidance, he authorized the creation of three regiments that evolved into the Sultan's Armed Forces. The flaring of the Dhufar rebellion spurred the formation of a small air force and navy. The 1958 agreement with Britain to build up military forces also stipulated a subsidy to finance a Development Department. In its first ten years, the department took modest steps to pave roads, set up medical services and train schoolteachers. The possibilities for development expanded with the onset of oil production in 1968.

Even though the British subsidy lapsed at the time, the government drew up plans to improve port facilities, create an Omani currency, build a school for girls and construct a hospital. In spite of the modest scale of institutional expansion, Sultan Said was able to project his authority over the country more effectively as time passed. The suppression of the Oman Revolutionary Movement spelled the decline of independent tribal power in the hinterland more than the eclipse of the imamate's religious authority. The sultan's agents, largely chosen from his extended family, assumed greater authority, paving the way for centralization of power.

As the imamate's cause was slowly dying in the corridors of the UN, a new challenge to the sultanate flared at the other end of the country. Dhufar was Oman's western province, weakly integrated with the rest of the country. Sultan Said preferred the climate at its capital Salalah and spent more of his time there from the late 1930s onward. In 1958, he settled there permanently to ill effect: His high-handed treatment of Dhufaris sparked a separatist movement in the early 1960s. A number of small organizations came together in June 1965 to form the Dhufar Liberation Front to fight for independence. Once again, Arab nationalist governments came to the aid of a separatist movement against the pro-British monarchy. The Dhufar movement took a leftist turn, spurred by the radical mood fermenting in Arab nationalist circles and by the emergence of the socialist People's Democratic Republic of Yemen just across the border. The more radical elements in the Dhufar Liberation Front gained control of the movement. In September 1968, they announced the formation of the Popular Front for the Liberation of the Occupied Arabian Gulf. The avowedly Marxists organization enjoyed backing from the Soviet Union and China as well as South Yemen and Iraq. An influx of funds and arms boosted the rebellion's forces and enabled it to gain control over the province's rough mountainous interior by 1970. Rebel successes encouraged dissidents in northern Oman to launch the National Democratic Front for the Liberation of Oman and the Arabian Gulf (NDFLOAG). It did little more than carry out a handful of small attacks in June 1970, but the spread of radical violence forced the hand of plotters against the sultan seeking to replace him with his son Qabus.

In the late 1960s, British advisers were becoming concerned about Sultan Said's capacity to keep Oman in the Western orbit. With Britain planning its withdrawal from the region by the end of 1971, the rebellion in Dhufar and the emergence of a radical regime in Aden, the prospects for Oman's stability under Said were doubtful. His son Qabus had studied in England and since returning home resided in Salalah, but the sultan refused to assign him any role in government, a decision that may have prompted Qabus to plot a coup. He slowly put together a team of conspirators among officials in Dhufar and Muscat – family members, British advisers and oil company officials – all of the major players in the country's political and economic management. An attack by NDFLOAG on one of interior Oman's towns in June 1970 underscored the urgency of the situation. On 23 July, Qabus staged the coup to remove his father from the throne and sent him out of the country to London, where he died three years later.

Sultan Qabus moved quickly on political and military fronts to pacify the country. The son of a Dhufari woman, he deftly divided the opposition with an offer to pardon rebels who agreed to surrender. He declared his firm commitment to establishing modern government. He also pledged to devote resources to developing education and health services in Dhufar. The offer succeeded in placating rebels fighting for regional rights, leaving the ideological revolutionaries to carry on the fight in smaller numbers. Sultan Qabus also built up the armed forces fighting on his side by increasing defence expenditures. The government counteroffensive began in 1971 as Qabus moved to stream-line the government's civilian institutions, converting *ad hoc* offices managed by expatriate advisers into ministries headed by Omanis. The youngest ruler in the Gulf was off to a fast start in putting a historically fractious region in order.

8 Affluence, Revolution and War, 1971–91

Britain's withdrawal from the Gulf was bound to have disruptive effects, particularly for the small sheikhdoms that had lost the guarantor of their sovereignty for the past 150 years. The new major external power, the United States, may have replaced the British in a general sense, but its approach to the region was coloured by a different historical experience. Its ideological and political rivalry with the Soviet Union had recent origins in the aftermath of the Second World War, but in the long historical perspective, it marked a continuation of the Great Game geopolitical contest between Russia and Britain. The second factor that made the Gulf a matter of interest for Washington, access to oil supplies, enhanced its desire for the stability of friendly governments.

The Gulf states received Britain's withdrawal with a mixture of eagerness and apprehension for the opportunities and challenges it promised. Bahrain, Qatar and the UAE were now fully independent nations. Securing their independence hinged not only on the implicit backing of the United States but also on consolidating stable political orders in the face of habits of dynastic strife and threats from powerful neighbours. Iran, Iraq and Saudi Arabia had viewed the British presence as a hindrance to their full exercise of regional leadership and aspirations to dominate and perhaps even annex their smaller neighbours. Iran had never completely abandoned its claim to Bahrain, nor had Iraq been reconciled with Kuwait's independence. Saudi Arabia had a long-running boundary dispute with Abu Dhabi. Furthermore, the three larger countries were rivals, and differences in fundamental ideology exacerbated the perhaps inevitable mistrust among them. Muhammad Reza Shah believed that history and size made it natural and right that his country should be recognized as the leading power in the Gulf. Saudi Arabia shared the shah's pro-western outlook and his assertion that dynastic monarchy is a perfectly legitimate form of government, but Riyadh was wary of Iran's ambition and unwilling to accept the idea that it was necessarily the regional leader. Iraq's revolutionary Baathist government was at odds with both neighbours for what it saw as their accommodation to Western imperialist domination and perpetuation of an illegitimate and archaic form of government.

The United States viewed the Gulf through the lens of its policy of containment towards the Soviet Union and supporting friendly governments. Washington's strategy for pursuing its goals was shaped by the impact of the Vietnam War on American public opinion, which opposed further military adventures. The upshot was the application of the Nixon Doctrine, an approach to safeguarding United States interests that eschewed direct intervention in favour of strengthening local allies. In the Gulf, this meant bolstering the military capacities of Iran and Saudi Arabia as the 'twin pillars' of Washington's position.

When the British withdrew, Washington did not increase its naval presence: its Middle East Force established in 1948 to transport oil from Gulf producers to the US Navy remained steady at three to four vessels. The only immediate change was to establish terms with Bahrain for the US Navy to replace the British fleet at the port of Jufair. The October 1973 Arab–Israeli war and the oil crisis alerted American policymakers to Washington's lack of military capacity to intervene. In response, the US Navy enlarged its base on the Indian Ocean island of Diego Garcia as a transport, storage and logistics facility. Washington's reluctance to replicate Britain's network of military bases was the reason it turned down offers from Oman to use its air base on al-Masira Island. The Nixon Doctrine's preference for depending on proxy powers was facilitated by high oil prices, which during the 1970s funded more than $35 billion in arms purchases by Iran and Saudi Arabia.

Three developments in 1979 forced the United States to abandon the 'twin pillars' approach. First, a popular revolution swept away Iran's pro-Western Iranian monarchy. Second, Saudi Arabia's stability was rocked by simultaneous uprisings in Mecca and the Eastern Province. Third, the Soviet Union invaded Afghanistan, bringing Moscow's military forces within a couple of hundred miles of the Gulf. Washington's response was announced in President Jimmy Carter's January 1980 State of the Union address, when he echoed Lord Lansdowne's 1903 declaration, stating that the United States would use all means to prevent the Gulf from coming under the domination of a hostile power. The problem for Washington was that it lacked the tools to enforce the Carter Doctrine. The Pentagon established a Rapid Deployment Joint Task Force to fill the gap. In addition, the United States took up Oman's offer to use the air base on al-Masira Island.

The British withdrawal from the Gulf coincided with a transition in the geopolitics of the Arab world when Arab nationalism began to fade. Egypt's President Nasser died in September 1970. His successor, Anwar al-Sadat, was initially preoccupied with internal consolidation. He indicated that he wanted to mend relations with conservative regimes, auguring the end of Egypt's campaign to undermine Arab dynasts. Two months after Nasser died, a less doctrinaire wing of Syria's Baathist regime seized power. The new head of state in Damascus, Hafiz al-Asad, duplicated Sadat's bid to improve relations with conservative leaders. With Egypt and Syria heading in a conservative direction, that left the Iraqi Baath as the major Arab country at the head of radical forces, including South Yemen's People's Democratic Republic and an assortment of socialist and Arab nationalist political movements. The new political alignment spelled the end of the Arab Cold War. The Gulf dynasties had survived the revolutionary challenge. The influx of oil wealth would give them increased leverage over the larger but oil-deprived countries.

THE OIL REVOLUTION

After the departure of the British, the next major development affecting the entire region was the sudden, staggering increase in the price of oil. In just a few months from late 1973 to early 1974, the price of a barrel of oil quadrupled. The oil producing countries acquired far more wealth than ever anticipated. In Iran and Iraq, the effects were diluted by large populations and mature infrastructures. Tehran and Baghdad used the bonanza to bulk up their armed forces. Oil's most dramatic impact was felt in countries with small populations. There, the flood of oil revenue made possible expansion and acceleration of national development projects. Their ambitious scale far exceeded the technical and manpower capacities of Saudi Arabia and the sheikhdoms. Consequently, tens of thousands of expatriate workers were hired to work as schoolteachers, medical doctors and nurses, and engineers, while hundreds of thousands filled jobs in construction and unskilled labour. Saudi Arabia alone saw its expatriate workforce grow from 500,000 to 1.5 million between 1975 and 1980. By the late 1970s, nationals in the smaller sheikhdoms were fractional minorities of the workforce. While the littoral had always been home to a shifting cosmopolitan population, by the early 1980s the indigenous element was submerged by a tide of Asian and Arab guest workers.

A shift in the balance of power in the global oil industry was clearly under way by the early 1970s when two trends in the global economy converged to multiply oil revenues. First, global demand for oil gave producing countries leverage over the major companies. Second, nationalist political demands led to the takeover of oil production by host governments. Together, these trends set the stage for the sudden rise in oil prices and enormous windfall revenues. Nationalization, participation and profit-sharing deals were symptoms of growing leverage in the hands of oil-producing countries. Iraq's decision to nationalize the foreign consortium in June 1972 was a turning point in transferring control over the industry from Western companies to producers. The pro-Western Gulf states did not nationalize the foreign companies but bargained for participation, which amounted to an incremental approach to taking full control. Saudi Arabia led the way with an agreement to take 25 per cent control; Qatar and the UAE obtained similar deals.

Meanwhile, the largest oil consumer, the United States, experienced intermittent shortages in late 1972 and early 1973 because of quotas on imports established in 1959 to protect domestic producers. The US government lifted the quotas in April 1973, increasing the country's dependence on foreign sources. After seven decades of Western control over Middle Eastern oil, the centre of gravity had tipped in favour of countries with oil in the ground. The steps to raise shares of profits, then prices, then control seemed momentous at the time, but their full ramifications only became apparent in October 1973 when oil politics intersected with the Arab–Israeli conflict.

In Cairo and Damascus, the new leaders adopted a more pragmatic spirit that made it possible to repair Egyptian–Syrian relations that had been frayed ever since the failure of their union experiment in 1961. In spring 1973, Anwar al-Sadat and Hafiz al-Asad agreed that Israel's occupation of their lands, Egyptian Sinai and Syrian Golan Heights, appeared likely to continue indefinitely, so they decided to combine forces for a joint attack to recover those territories. The mood of pragmatism extended to Egyptian–Saudi relations. Sadat informed King Faisal of the impending war and secured a pledge that Saudi Arabia would use its sway in oil markets to support the Arab cause. On 6 October

8. The Conquest of Scarcity: Kuwait's Water Towers.

1973, Egyptian and Syrian forces launched simultaneous massive assaults on Israeli defences on the East Bank of the Suez Canal and in the Golan Heights. In the first two days of fighting, the Arab allies achieved significant advances and compelled Israel to retreat. The Israeli military quickly mounted a counter-attack that drove back the Syrians while the Egyptians adopted a static defensive posture.

At the same time that war was raging in the Middle East, the Organization of the Petroleum Exporting Countries (OPEC) was holding a meeting in Vienna with representatives of the major oil companies. Saudi Arabia's oil minister demanded a 100-per cent price increase. The companies flatly rejected that. Arab members of OPEC then convened in Kuwait and on 16 October declared a 70-per cent price increase. Meanwhile, the United States decided to grant an Israeli request for an emergency airlift of military supplies. The Saudis had warned Washington months before the war that they would cut oil production if the United States backed Israel in a new outbreak of fighting. Thus, on 17 October, Arab members of OPEC declared a 5-per cent cutback in production. Three days later, Saudi Arabia imposed an embargo on shipments to the United States; Kuwait and the UAE followed suit. Tensions abated after Israel, Egypt and Syria accepted a ceasefire on 25 October, but the push by OPEC price hawks for increases continued. The coordination among Arab OPEC members during the war concealed a fundamental divide in OPEC between price moderates and price hawks. Iran, Iraq and Libya pushed for higher prices while Saudi Arabia led moderates seeking lower increases. At a momentous OPEC meeting in Tehran on 22–3 December, the shah of Iran prevailed and the price per barrel reached nearly $12: the price had quadrupled in one year.

Quite suddenly, the Gulf was awash in oil revenues of such magnitude that governments commanded the means to accelerate national development plans beyond any previously conceived scale. It is instructive to list some of the increases in annual oil sales from 1972 to 1974. Saudi Arabia's oil revenues rose from $2.7 to $22.6 billion; Iran's grew from $2.4 billion to nearly $18 billion; Kuwait's went from $1.4 billion to $6.5 billion; Iraq's ballooned from $600 million to $5.7 billion. Higher prices were the major reason for larger revenues. In addition, in 1974–5, the oil producers obtained larger ownership shares from the Western companies. In September 1974, Abu Dhabi raised its share from 25 to 65 per cent. Bahrain followed with a 60-per cent participation agreement in November; six months later, it announced it would obtain 100 per cent ownership. In December 1975, Kuwait announced an agreement with Gulf and British Petroleum for the government to assume full ownership in exchange for guaranteed supplies to the companies. Qatar trailed the pack, but took a 40-per cent share in September 1976. The torrent of revenues gave governments the means to devise vast plans for infrastructure development and urban construction. Massive investments boosted electricity generation, paved roads and port facilities. In a few years, the landscape of the Persian Gulf was fundamentally altered. Saudi Arabia invested in petrochemical factories located in new industrial cities at Jubail on the Gulf coast and Yanbu along the Red Sea. From Kuwait to Oman, governments turned oil into a burgeoning petrochemical sector and factories for producing cement, aluminium and steel.

The strains of October frayed relations between Riyadh and Washington: Arabs were furious with the United States for its unqualified support for Israel; Americans were filled with anger at the 'rich oil sheikhs' for disrupting oil supplies and creating shortages that forced motorists to wait for hours to fill up their cars. Saudi Arabia embargoed exports to the United States until March 1974, when Washington pledged to mediate a disengagement accord between Syria and Israel. Both the Saudis and the Americans wanted to return to the amicable spirit that had marked relations for decades. In June, they agreed on terms for increasing trade and military cooperation. The Saudis used some of the windfall oil profits to go on a shopping spree for US military hardware. In 1975, US military sales to Riyadh totalled $2 billion. Oil revenues fuelled an even larger set of arms deals between Washington and Tehran, who signed an agreement in March 1975 to purchase $15 billion in military equipment in five years.

The effects of oil on Gulf politics and societies were profound and enduring. A new term, the rentier state, was coined to describe the distinctive traits of countries like the Gulf states.[1] Whereas the wealth of most countries arises from productive activity – be it in agriculture, manufacturing or trade – a rentier state generates wealth by virtue of possessing a natural resource that is produced and sold with minimal productive activity by a small number of workers. In the case of the Arab Gulf states, Western oil companies provided the technical means and global distribution networks to sell oil. Because the oil companies had obtained the right to produce and sell oil from rulers, the rulers directly received royalty payments on oil sales. National economies and politics now pivoted around the distribution of oil revenues so immense that they could assure a high standard of living for citizens for years on end. Budget officials did not fret over taxing citizens but over funnelling oil wealth to them. Citizenship, in turn, became an economic asset, a claim to a share of national wealth. The rentier state is an ideal type, not an empirical category, but it is a useful concept for understanding a class of countries sharing the trait of small population and large oil revenues. Yet it is important to keep in mind that the population to revenue ratio is variable. For example, Qatar and the UAE closely approximate the rentier paradigm in a pure form. Saudi Arabia has by far the largest amount of oil but it also has a large population, so it cannot sustain high living standards on rent alone but must spur productive activities.

Allowing for variation among rentier states, they share three common features. First, they provide economic necessities for their citizens: housing, health, education, social security and jobs. In so doing, they obviate the common foundation of modern politics, the contest for allocating scare resources. Second, they can afford to hire foreign labour for tasks that citizens lack either the qualifications or desire to assume. The proportion of foreign labour varies from over 90 per cent in the UAE to about 50 per cent in Saudi Arabia, but there is a common denominator in all the Gulf states, namely a preponderance of foreign labour in the private sector and of nationals in the public sector. Third, once a government has extended an array of benefits to its citizens, it becomes hazardous to reduce or withdraw them when revenues decline (due to either low prices or dwindling reserves). In the 1970s and 1980s, the Arab Gulf states dealt with the exuberance of sudden wealth and then the disappointment of austerity.

In the long term, the social effects of oil wealth were profound. To illustrate with the case of education, revenues paid for a vast expansion of national school systems that resulted in much higher literacy rates. Oman was the most dramatic success story, raising literacy from 5 per cent in 1970 to 75 per cent by 1990. Saudi Arabia's literacy rate in 1960 was under 10 per cent and hit nearly 70 per cent by 1990. Bahrain and Kuwait had older education systems dating to the 1930s. With their head start, they hit close to 100 per cent literacy by 1990.

OMAN

The British withdrawal came at a delicate moment for Oman. Sultan Qabus had taken power in July 1970 and the Dhufar struggle for independence threatened the sultanate's territorial integrity. The sultan's preoccupation in the first five years of his reign was to suppress the uprising, a feat he achieved with assistance from Britain and regional allies. His strategy to defeat the rebellion required replacing complete dependence on a single power with broad diplomatic engagement, thereby ending Oman's diplomatic isolation, which dated to the Exclusive Treaty of 1892. Oman joined international organizations (the Arab League and the United Nations) and established official diplomatic relations with Arab and Western governments. Sultan Qabus also benefitted from the rising flow of oil revenue, which he spent on development projects in Dhufar to gain the loyalty of its population. He also upgraded the instruments of governance by building up institutions and forging political alliances with various elements of Oman's diverse society. By the time he celebrated the end of two decades of rule in 1990, he had succeeded at consolidating central authority to a degree unprecedented in Oman's history. The imamate and the tribes were reduced to vestiges of heritage, a possession of the newly forged Omani nation.

In 1970, the Dhufar rebels controlled the mountains and strategic points along the coast, leaving the sultan with little more than Salalah and its environs. The rebels also possessed sanctuaries in the People's Democratic Republic of South Yemen and enjoyed firm support from Iraq, China and the Soviet Union. For his part, Sultan Qabus had the backing of Great Britain and Jordan. In October 1970, government forces launched offensives coordinated with British air power. The Sultan's Armed Forces began to turn the tide in 1971. Their effectiveness spurred Dhufari and Northern Omani rebels to merge in the Popular Front for the Liberation of Oman and the Arabian Gulf (PFLOAG), but they were unable to stem steady advances by the government. External support for Oman grew when Iran dispatched military forces to join the fight. Oman's civil war expanded into a proxy war in Arab and Great Power politics, with British advisers, air power and arms reinforcing Iranian and Omani ground troops against guerrillas armed and funded by Marxist Yemen and Moscow.

Apart from applying increased military pressure on the rebels, Sultan Qabus needed a political strategy to erode popular Dhufari support for secession. To that end, he initiated plans to introduce medical services, schools and water facilities to the region. In addition, he offered amnesty to rebels who laid down their arms. Steady military pressure and the lure of development projects diminished the ranks of the insurgents and allowed the sultan's forces to gradually consolidate control over Dhufar's mountainous hinterland. In 1974, the PFLOAG suffered defections and reconstituted itself as the Popular Front for the Liberation of Oman. The rump force was unable to stall the methodical advance of Omani and Iranian troops. By the end of 1975, their rout was complete and the remaining fighters crossed the border into South Yemen. They continued to launch raids across the border until they petered out altogether in 1985.

Defeating the Dhufar rebellion was an important step towards cementing Oman's territorial cohesion. There remained the daunting tasks of crafting institutions of governance to establish Muscat as the locus of political power and knitting together a population with a deep-rooted tendency to resist central authority. It was a tall order to turn Ibadis and Sunnis, Hinawi and Ghafiri tribesmen, coastal merchants and interior cultivators into a national community of Omanis. Initially, Sultan Qabus proceeded through trial and error to replace British advisers with Omanis. Shortly after seizing power, he invited his uncle Tariq ibn Taimur to return from exile (he had lived in Germany and Lebanon) to become prime minister. Other expatriates joined Tariq to form a cabinet of Omanis. Tariq wished to move the country in the direction of constitutional monarchy by placing oil revenues, the budget and defence under the control of the cabinet. The sultan, however, insisted on keeping control over oil income and retaining British advisers for defence and budget. Tariq resigned his post in December 1971 and the sultan assumed the offices of prime minister, foreign affairs, defence and finance. Three months later, the sultan appointed an Interim Planning Council, comprised largely of educated Omani expatriates. British defence advisers remained in place until the early 1980s, when Qabus installed Omanis in such sensitive defence and intelligence positions as chief of staff of the Sultan's Armed Forces, head of the air force, and adviser for domestic and foreign intelligence.

Unlike the Gulf sheikhdoms that allocated powerful government position to members of ruling clans, Oman's political system concentrated power in the sultan. The ruling dynasty is divided between the close relatives of Sultan Qabus who are descendants of Sultan Said – known as Al Said – and the extended clan – known as al-Busaidi. The Al Said dominate the core of the government and the al-Busaidis serve in lesser cabinet positions and local offices. In order to promote national unity, Qabus broadened his government's political foundations by incorporating diverse segments of the population through appointment to high positions and distribution of lower-level jobs.

The merchants of Muscat and Matrah were allowed to manage domestic and foreign trade. The sultan traded access to oil revenues for political support by steering commercial agencies and government contracts their way. The ministry of interior absorbed the tribal nobility with subsidies, gifts and appointments to posts as intermediaries between Muscat and fellow tribesmen. Baluchis and tribesmen of the interior became conspicuous in the security forces. Former Dhufar rebels were co-opted, as in the case of Yusuf ibn Alawi, who became minister of state for foreign affairs, and a second ex-rebel became minister of information. Many Dhufaris found employment in the ministry of oil and gas. As for Oman's historical divide between Ibadi and Sunni Muslims, official publications mute those distinctions. The sultan incorporated Ibadis into the state by recruiting them to serve as muftis and ministers of justice and religious affairs. The sultan's tactic of distributing jobs to win acquiescence, if not loyalty, from the diverse population unified the country in an unprecedented fashion.

Sultan Qabus's strategy of co-opting the country's diverse communities through appointment to state offices required a reliable and sizable stream of revenues for the government. Even though Oman's oil reserves are modest compared to the major producers, they are sufficient for economic development on the rentier model, amounting to more than 70 per cent of government revenue in the late twentieth century. Sultan Qabus came to power at the same time that Gulf states were inching towards fuller participation in the petroleum business. In 1974, Oman twice raised its share in Petroleum Development (Oman), first to 25 per cent and then to 60 per cent. Higher revenues enabled the government to extend transportation and communications networks with roads and telephone lines. Clinics and hospitals reduced infant mortality and extended life expectancy. A national education system for boys and girls raised literacy rates and paved the way for the establishment of Sultan Qabus University in 1986. The impact of national development was uneven, with coastal areas showing greater improvement than the interior regions.

To meet the demand for skilled labour, Sultan Qabus drew on the extensive Omani Diaspora that had taken shape at different historical stages, first during the formation of the nineteenth-century Indian Ocean empire and then in the mid-twentieth century with emigration to work in Kuwait and Bahrain's oilfields. Descendants of Omanis who settled along the coast of East Africa and in Zanzibar in the nineteenth century had assimilated to Swahili culture. The 1964 revolution in Zanzibar resulted in the expulsion of the 'Swahili' Omanis, many of whom resettled in Kuwait, Dubai and Egypt. By the late 1960s, the expatriate Omani population of around 50,000, Arab and Dhufari, concentrated in Kuwait, Bahrain, Qatar and Saudi Arabia, filled jobs for unskilled labour, police and construction projects. Under Sultan Qabus, the government encouraged expatriates to return by offering them citizenship, a privilege unattainable in host sheikhdoms. In short order, educated Omanis returned to participate in national development. Even so, the national workforce was too small to meet the demands of the expanding list of projects, compelling Oman to attract foreign workers. In 1970, expatriate labour comprised just 10 per cent of the workforce. It rose to two-thirds by 1980, and it continued to rise, leading the government to begin a push for 'Omanisation', that is, reducing reliance on foreign workers. Oman confronted the same hurdles to achieving that goal as would other Gulf states: expatriate workers accept lower wages than Omanis and they enjoy a reputation for a more vigorous work ethic than their Omani counterparts.

With respect to foreign policy, Sultan Qabus tended to balance regional and great powers, preferring to maintain ties with all neighbours, even at times of regional tension. Thus, Oman was one of just two Arab countries not to sever relations with Egypt when it signed a peace treaty with Israel; it retained relations with Iran after the revolution deposed the shah, who had assisted in quelling the Dhufar rebellion; it kept lines open to both Iran and Iraq during their eight-year war; and it preserved relations with Saddam Hussein's government after it invaded Kuwait, even though it allowed the United States and Britain to use military bases during the 1991 war against Iraq. In 1981, Oman joined the Gulf Cooperation Council (see below). With regard to the Western powers, Sultan Qabus oversaw the departure of British forces in 1977, and later signed military cooperation agreements with the United Kingdom (1985) and the United States (1996).

THE UNITED ARAB EMIRATES

Oman's difficulties in coping with a secessionist movement and external meddling in Dhufar were indicative of the fragility of Gulf states no longer sheltered by Britain's protection. The newly formed UAE confronted less drastic but similar challenges. Iran quickly occupied and annexed three disputed islands, and the adherence of Ra's al-Khaima to the federation was briefly in doubt. More enduring questions included whether the federation had any substance or was a polite fiction providing nominal unity to virtually independent emirates. The historical pattern for disgruntled tribal segments to emigrate did not bode well for federal unity. The brake on centrifugal tendencies was Abu Dhabi's accumulation of oil wealth that gave its ruler the means to bind the emirates together.

The provisional constitution established a loose federation, preserving a high degree of autonomy for each emirate. The highest body is the Supreme Council of Rulers (SCR), formerly the Trucial States Council, comprised of each emirate's hereditary sheikh. The Council elects a president to a five-year term, but the custom has been to recognize Abu Dhabi's sheikh as the president due to its preponderant wealth. A second body, the Council of Ministers, handles matters at the federal level and reports to the Federal National Council, which has 40 seats allocated among the emirates: Abu Dhabi and Dubai each have eight seats; Ra's al-Khaima and Sharjah each have six seats; Umm al-Qaiwain, Ajman and Fujaira have four seats each. The distribution of seats reflected the emirates' relative wealth, not their populations, as both Ra's al-Khaima and Sharjah have more nationals than either Abu Dhabi or Dubai. The Federal National Council advises the Council of Ministers, which has the authority to initiate policies that are then raised to the SCR. Under the constitution, each emirate is responsible for its own budget, public works and economic development while the federal authority deals with foreign relations, defence and immigration. In practice, the emirates tended to resist subjugation to federal authority. For example, the Trucial Oman Scouts became the Union Defence Force, but each emirate developed its own militia. Common currency and postal services were established, as well as a national flag. On the crucial matter of oil, each emirate exercised complete control over its resources. In addition, each emirate has its own informal council (*majlis*) for citizens to express concerns to the rulers. Finally, British advisers continued to play substantial roles in military and judicial affairs.

The UAE faced its first internal crisis in its second month of existence. Sharjah's Sheikh Khalid ibn Muhammad had seized power in 1965 from his cousin Sheikh Saqr ibn Sultan and sent the deposed ruler to live in exile. In January 1972, Sheikh Saqr infiltrated the ruler's palace with an armed band and seized several dozen hostages. Dubai's militia surrounded the palace and negotiated Sheikh Saqr's surrender after a 16-hour siege. Upon entering the palace, Dubai's forces found that Sheikh Khalid had been killed. Sheikh Saqr was imprisoned while the SCR deliberated on a replacement, settling on Sheikh Sultan ibn Muhammad, the first ruler to have an advanced Western education. Sheikh Saqr was then sent off into his exile. In its fundamental aspect as an instance of strife within a ruling clan, the episode was typical. For the first time, however, it was not the British who stepped in to resolve the conflict but the freshly minted UAE government. In 1987, Sheikh Sultan again benefited from SCR's desire for stability. His brother Abdulaziz accused him of bungling economic policy and announced his abdication, but the Council of Rulers forced him to restore Sheikh Sultan in return for the positions of deputy ruler and crown prince. That arrangement only lasted until 1990 when Sheikh Sultan dismissed Abdulaziz.

The crisis in Sharjah was not a harbinger of instability because rising oil revenues alleviated endemic tensions within ruling clans that historically plagued them as a result of the poverty of the sheikhdoms. Earnings from oil exports, distributed by Abu Dhabi to the less well-endowed emirates, provided enough revenue for allowances and positions in the armed forces, government bodies and oil companies to satisfy members of the ruling lineages and end the historical pattern of political contestation within them.

Politics largely operated at the level of rivalry among the leading emirates. Given the small number of educated Emiratis and the absence of a local working class population, the sort of contestation between rulers and citizens that arose in Kuwait and

Bahrain was absent. The most enduring issue has been the struggle between proponents of strengthening federal authority and defenders of emirate autonomy. Abu Dhabi consistently backed the first position, arguing that all emirates would benefit from a higher level of coordination. Dubai, however, preferred to maximize emirate autonomy in order to preserve the emir's local prerogatives and to prevent domination by oil-rich Abu Dhabi.

In 1976, Abu Dhabi's Sheikh Zayid and federalist members of the Federal National Council moved to revise the provisional constitution and make it permanent. The effort stumbled on Article 23, which reserves to emirates full control over their oil and gas resources. The proposed revision would have reduced emirates' share to one-quarter of income. Dubai led opposition to the change, even threatening secession, while Sheikh Zayid threatened to resign as president of the SCR if he did not get his way. In the end, a compromise formula in Dubai's favour resolved the crisis: its sheikh agreed to augment his contribution to the federal budget and the movement for a permanent constitution was shelved. Two years later, Dubai joined with Ra's al-Khaima and Umm al-Qaiwain to thwart a proposal by Abu Dhabi to centralize command of military forces. In another illustration of weak federalism, Ra's al-Khaima asserted independence in foreign policy in the late 1970s when it offered the Soviet Union naval base rights if it would support the emirate's secession.

The glue holding the emirates together was Abu Dhabi's vast oil reserves. In the early 1970s, Sheikh Zayid renegotiated the terms of oil concessions to acquire a 60-per cent share for the Abu Dhabi National Oil Company, which collaborated with Western oil companies to explore for new oil and gas fields, both onshore and in the Gulf's shallow waters. With abundant wealth, Abu Dhabi and Dubai followed the development path laid down by the northern Gulf states in the 1950s and 1960s. Physical development of the emirates proceeded at a fast pace. In 1965, Abu Dhabi had no paved roads; by the 1980s, it had a new skyline and busy commercial thoroughfares. Massive investments in roads, ports and communications transformed their landscapes; more widely available and advanced medical services extended life expectancy and reduced infant mortality; an expanding education system reduced illiteracy rates for boys and girls. Also like the northern Gulf states, the UAE granted nationals free land, loans and exclusive agencies to represent foreign companies. As Emiratis abandoned desert tents for city dwellings, the social and cultural character of their society underwent a basic transformation that replicated the dynamics of sedentarization in the rest of Arabia. Given the economic preponderance of Abu Dhabi and Dubai, the effects of development were skewed as they far outstripped the northern emirates in economic growth and drew on them for unskilled labour.

Like the upper Gulf states, the UAE lacked a population of skilled manpower and turned to expatriate labour for construction and maintenance of new transportation, communications, health and education projects. In 1968, expatriate labour accounted for under 40 per cent of the workforce; in 2000, that figure surpassed 90 per cent, and the total resident population was comprised of only 30 per cent or so Emirati nationals. A second distinctive facet of the population is the preponderance of men in the expatriate workforce, leading to a public space dominated by Indian and Pakistani men. Efforts to get nationals into the workforce have made progress in a few sectors such as banking and the law courts, but in the private sector, employers prefer expatriates who settle for lower wages and have a reputation for high qualifications.

In a notable departure from the conventional rentier model, Dubai's Sheikh Rashid ibn Maktum (r. 1958–90) expanded his political autonomy by pursuing a strategy to diversify sources of wealth, partly in response to revisions of the constitution that strengthened the federal government dominated by Abu Dhabi. Given Abu Dhabi's massive oilfields and Dubai's modest stores, the latter strove for diversification of its economy on the basis of its position as a centre for commerce – a Dubai trademark ever since the arrival of traders from Lingah in the early 1900s – complemented by financial services and tourism. The strategy relied on promoting tourism, attracting foreign direct investment, and developing the emirate into a regional transportation hub. With new infrastructure, low-cost expatriate labour and business friendly regulations, Dubai advanced down a path independent of oil. By the late 1970s, its non-oil income was over 90 per cent of total income. In the early 1980s, Dubai conceived the idea of creating a 'free zone', an area immune from laws requiring local participation in private ventures. Jebel Ali became the first such free zone to open in 1985. It appeared that Sheikh Rashid had discovered a formula for prosperity without oils or pearls.

BAHRAIN AND QATAR

In Bahrain's first years of independence, Al Khalifah confronted pressure to share power with representative bodies. Emir Isa ibn Salman bowed to demands for constitutional government and approved a December 1972 election for a constituent assembly. Even though women's organizations agitated for the right to vote, the franchise was restricted to men. The constituent assembly's 22 elected members, including Arab nationalists, joined with eight appointed members to work on a basic charter. On 2 June 1973, the assembly ratified a document that took Kuwait's constitution as its model. Bahrain's constitution established the principle of hereditary succession and concentrated authority for defence and foreign relations in the hands of the emir, who also had the power to appoint the prime minister and the cabinet. Legislative authority was divided between the emir and an elected national assembly, whose deputies had the right to question cabinet ministers and to subject them to no-confidence votes.

The national assembly (NA) elected on 7 December 1973 held a diverse group of labour activists, Arab nationalists and religious conservatives willing to challenge government policies. Emir Isa appointed members of Al Khalifah to leading positions in the cabinet, including prime minister, defence minister and foreign minister. The emir's alliance with wealthy merchants was reflected in their domination of the government administrative bodies, the chamber of commerce and municipal councils. The NA's Arab nationalist bloc included members of the National Liberation Front of Bahrain, one Baathist and one Marxist. They called for giving women the vote, terminating basing rights for the US Navy and nationalization of the oil company. In 1974, the government and the NA battled over a proposal to allow the Ministry of Interior to detain for up to three years individuals suspected of subversion. Frustrated with the impasse, the emir dissolved the NA on 26 August 1975, passed the security law, and carried out a number of arrests. Bahrain's short-lived experiment in representative government suffered from deep social cleavage between the ruling dynasty and the majority Shi'i population on one hand and the demands of Arab nationalists and leftists on the other.

Whereas Oman, Qatar and the UAE enjoyed rising revenues in this period, Bahrain's oil production peaked in the early 1970s, making it difficult to depend on the rentier bargain to pre-empt political restlessness. By the early 1980s, oil's share in gross domestic product fell from three-quarters to around one-fifth. The prospect of falling oil revenues motivated the government to seek new fields of economic activity. In March 1976 it reinforced Bahrain's position as a financial centre by increasing the number of licences for offshore banks. The government also got the United States to agree to pay a much higher annual amount for the use of the Jufair naval base. Finally, a new project was initiated to construct a causeway between Bahrain and Saudi Arabia, known as the King Fahd Causeway (completed in 1986), to expand trade and tourism with its neighbour.

Just five months after Qatar gained its independence, on 22 February 1972, Sheikh Khalifah ibn Hamad seized power from his cousin Sheikh Ahmad. The ruling clan was dissatisfied with Sheikh Ahmad, who frequently took long vacations outside the country. By contrast, Sheikh Khalifah, who had been awaiting his turn to rule since 1949, exhibited keen interest in public affairs. His coup had the support of both Al Thani and the Saudi government. Two months after coming to power, the new ruler issued a provisional constitution. The document established Al Thani as the hereditary rulers of Qatar and vested executive authority in the ruling sheikh. It provided for a Council of Ministers to draft laws for the sheikh to enact or refer to the council for revision. The constitution included an article that provided for the creation of an elected council, but it remained a dead letter. Instead, Sheikh Khalifah activated an Advisory Council that had been proposed in 1964 but never convened. He appointed the council's 20 members (enlarged to 30 in 1975) from among the country's tribal leaders and important merchants. While the sheikh and his cabinet, almost entirely fellow members of Al Thani, held the reins of power, the Advisory Council did offer suggestions on draft laws issued by the cabinet.

Sheikh Khalifah also took steps to redistribute Qatar's rising oil and gas revenues by reducing allowances for Al Thani sheikhs and increasing benefits for ordinary citizens. The 1970s saw impressive expansion in education and health care, and university graduates were guaranteed jobs in the public sector. Sheikh Khalifah paid for these programmes by following the example of Gulf states that nationalized British-owned oil companies, turning the local firm into the Qatar Petroleum Company.

KUWAIT

Kuwait was the scene of political tensions between the elected national assembly and the hereditary Al Sabah rulers in the early 1970s. While controversy centred on oil policy and foreign relations, the underlying problem was an unresolved question of how far the national assembly could encroach on the emirs' presumptions of dominance. In 1976, Emir Sabah decided that

Arab nationalist members of the assembly had pushed too far, so he decided to dissolve it and rule by decree.

Given the central role for oil in the economy, parliamentary deputies considered it natural that they should have a say on government policy. In 1974, they called for nationalization of the Kuwait Oil Company to be achieved in stages by the end of the decade. Aware of the country's dependence on a finite resource, they urged the Company to cut daily production levels, and the Company complied. When it came to attempts to penetrate the secret records of the government body responsible for administering surplus oil wealth, the Kuwait Investment Organization, the national assembly came up short.

Regional political issues also spurred assertiveness on the part of elected representatives. After the October 1973 war, Kuwait joined with Saudi Arabia in paying an annual subsidy to Syria as a sign of Arab solidarity. But Arab nationalist sentiment turned sharply against Syria when it intervened in the Lebanese civil war in spring 1976 because it attacked the Palestinian–Arab nationalist side in that conflict. It so happened that Palestinians comprised the largest expatriate Arab community in Kuwait, so both expatriate Arabs and sympathetic Kuwaitis demanded the government suspend payments to Damascus. The Arab nationalist mood swelled to the point that a group of deputies proposed allowing long-time Arab residents to become Kuwaiti citizens. The government was unwilling to cede foreign policy to the Arab nationalist bloc, nor was it interested in extending citizenship to Arab residents.

Adding to Al Sabah irritation was the growing frequency with which deputies accused cabinet ministers of corruption. In August 1976, Emir Sabah dissolved the national assembly, suspended the article in the constitution requiring elections within two months, and suspended three opposition newspapers. After he died on 31 December 1977, his successor Emir Jabir promised to hold elections, but he dragged his feet for another three years, putting Kuwait in the same political situation as Bahrain: stalled experiments in democracy.

SAUDI ARABIA

On the eve of the oil price revolution, Saudi society was changing at a gradual pace. It is difficult to gauge the degree of change because population figures are elusive before the mid-1970s. Estimates for the total population range from four to six million with an additional 500,000 to 800,000 foreign workers. The inaccuracy of statistics is evident from figures for the kingdom's nomads, which range from 15 to 50 per cent of the total population. Part of the difficulty in counting nomads was that many shifted between the desert and casual labour in the cities. While motor transport had supplanted their transport function, their herds of sheep and goats made up half of the country's meat supply. In any event, the demographic trend for nomads was downward, as Saudi rulers continued settlement projects initiated during the reign of King Abdulaziz. In the 1950s and 1960s, the government developed wells to irrigate farmland and built schools and health clinics at settlements in the hope that nomads would take up agriculture. The pastoral economy was suffering from drought and overgrazing, so a steady stream of nomads showed up at such settlements and moved to cities or filled posts in the National Guard.

The onset of Saudi Arabia's oil rush occurred in the midst of the kingdom's first initiative to manage economic and social development through central planning. The Central Planning Organization (after 1975, the Ministry of Planning) issued its first five-year plan for 1970–5 according to which officials envisioned spending $9 billion on defence, transportation, education and water and power. By the end of 1974, the windfall from higher oil prices tripled the government's budget, leading to a far more ambitious $142 billion five-year plan for 1975–80 to upgrade infrastructure, alleviate housing shortages in the main cities, and expand the communications network. Implementing projects hinged on vast expansion of the two main ports, Jeddah and Dammam, to import equipment and goods and the construction of a national road network. The need to train a workforce capable of filling jobs in a modern economy meant doubling the number of students enrolled in primary and secondary schools.

Planners aspired to diversify the economy through the development of petroleum-related industries, a goal that required Saudis qualified to work in technical fields. To help meet that goal, the government undertook the construction of an engineering and science university (King Faisal University) near the oilfields in Dhahran. The Saudis also invested in improved facilities for the annual pilgrimage. The number of pilgrims grew from 400,000 in 1970 to more than 900,000 in 1974. The logistics of moving such massive numbers required expanding

Jeddah's airport and putting up hostels and hotels there and in the holy cities.

The early years of the oil rush were characterized by disorganization and inefficiency, as nothing so grand had been tried before in the region. Bureaucratic procedures for clearing cargoes were not designed for the quantities that began to arrive in 1975. By the end of the year, 200 merchant ships were anchored off the ports of Jeddah and Dammam, with waits of two to four months. Reorganization of the Ports Authority in late 1976 helped clear the backlog.

The influx of foreign workers also took place in haphazard fashion until planners organized recruitment through bulk contracts to accomplish specific projects, such as a sewer system for Jeddah. The demand for labour seemed insatiable. By the end of 1978, the number of expatriates exceeded the total number of Saudi nationals in the workforce by 1.3 million to one million. So much money chasing so many workers and goods in a compressed time frame fuelled inflation for two years (as in Iran), reaching around 50 per cent in 1975 and 1976 before easing.

On balance, the challenges and problems officials and ordinary people confronted might have been avoided if the government had set less ambitious targets, but given the low level of basic national development, the pressures for reaching high were irresistible. Moreover, by the end of the second plan in 1980, the kingdom had notched up impressive gains in education, health and infrastructure.

The political cost of choosing to integrate modern ways came home in brutal fashion on 12 March 1975 when King Faisal was shot dead by a nephew at a reception at the royal palace. The gunman, Faisal ibn Musaid, was avenging the death of his brother Khalid, one of the protestors killed in a demonstration against the opening of the Riyadh television station in 1965. Khalid ibn Abdulaziz became the next Saudi king, and unlike the struggle for succession at King Abdulaziz's death, this time the royal family showed no sign of behind-the-scenes quarrels. Instead, Prince Fahd was named the new heir to the throne. He soon emerged as the primary decision maker, in part due to King Khalid's health problems. Fahd became the next king when Khalid died of a heart attack in June 1982, and Prince Abdullah became the next Crown Prince. Exactly how decisions about succession were made remained a matter known only to the family's most powerful members, but two smooth transitions in less than a decade indicated their success at achieving consensus for the sake of stability.

IRAQ

The consolidation of the Baath Party regime in Baghdad was the start of a new phase of continuity if not stability in Iraq. In the wake of Britain's withdrawal from the Gulf, Iraq was in a position to assert regional leadership if it could put its domestic house in order. President Ahmad Hasan al-Bakr and Saddam Hussein methodically removed potential rivals from the regime, taking special care to purge the officer corps to forestall the sort of military coup that had overthrown governments four times since 1958. As veterans of conspiratorial politics, they exercised caution in filling sensitive positions with men they felt they could trust. In large part, that meant men from their home town of Takrit, in the heart of the Sunni north, and members of their extended clan in particular.

The formal structures of the regime took shape in a new interim constitution. Promulgated in 1970, the document established the Revolutionary Command Council (RCC) as the supreme executive and legislative authority. The constitution restricted positions on the RCC to Baath Party members. In effect, this meant that all state functions came under the authority of the Baath Party. Besides controlling the RCC and major cabinet positions, the party's cells permeated all levels of society: schools, workplaces, neighbourhoods, and syndicates for peasants, workers and professionals. The upshot was a more effective regime of control and surveillance over the population than had been achieved by previous Iraqi governments.

The Baathist government's power was augmented by the explosion of oil prices thanks to the nationalization of the Iraqi Petroleum Company (IPC) in 1972. That measure stemmed from accumulating grievances over the IPC's resistance to the Iraqi government's desire to maintain a high level of production. The influx of oil revenues in the mid-to-late 1970s enabled the government to expand access to free education and health care in the name of socialism. Oil wealth also funded greater investment in heavy industrial projects to turn Iraq into a producer of steel, petrochemicals and textiles. In rural areas, the government encouraged the formation of cooperatives that funnelled state-subsidized seed, fertilizer and machinery to cultivators.

In the name of progress, the regime also amended personal status laws in 1978 in favour of women's rights in marriage, divorce and custody of minors. Girls' school attendance notably increased under the Baath, and public sector jobs opened to women. These economic and social measures reinforced tendencies inherited from previous republican regimes in reshaping Iraqi society. Perhaps the most notable shift since the end of the monarchy was the growing weight of the urban population, doubling from around 35 per cent in the late 1950s to 70 per cent in 1980. Rural–urban migration was the chief cause of that change, with the lion's share of migrants heading for Baghdad, Mosul and Basra. Moreover, the profile of urban Iraqis assumed a more educated form as graduates of secondary schools and universities filled the growing number of positions in technical industries, professions and the civil service.

Notwithstanding gains in standards of living, the Baathists grappled with Iraq's perennial sources of political tension. Fighting between government troops and Kurdish forces supported by Iran resulted in Baghdad's offering concessions. The March 1970 compromise provided for Kurdish autonomy, establishing Kurdish as an official language along with Arabic in the Kurdish provinces, and political representation in the national government. The details were to be negotiated in the course of a four-year transitional period. The government seized the transitional period as an opportunity to temporize. Arabs were encouraged to settle in the Kurdish region. Government agents tried to assassinate Kurdish leaders. As the four-year deadline approached, Baghdad offered a narrow definition of autonomy, sparking a new round of fighting. This time, the Kurds had the backing not only of Iran but the United States and Israel, who viewed the Baathist regime as a threat.

The latest episode in the Kurds' struggle for autonomy ended abruptly. Iran's Muhammad Reza Shah and the Iraqi government signed the Algiers Agreement on 6 March 1975. In exchange for withdrawing military assistance to the Kurds, the Shah obtained Iraqi recognition of the 1913–14 Constantinople Protocol defining the international boundary. In so doing, Baghdad accepted Iran's position that the border along the Shatt al-Arab followed the waterway's channel rather than placing it entirely in Iraqi possession. The Baathists also agreed to end support for the Dhufar rebellion in Oman, to abandon claims to the largely Arab province of Khuzistan, and to cease challenging Iran's possession of the UAE islands Abu Musa and the Tunbs. In essence, Baghdad surrendered a number of foreign policy positions in return for a free hand to deal with the Kurds. Army forces soon occupied the entire Kurdish region, driving guerrilla fighters into Iran. Baghdad followed up with a variety of measures to pacify the

Kurdish region. Spending on infrastructure improved transportation, education and health services. Inclusion of Kurds
in a regional legislative council was cosmetic, given the RCC's
control over the council, like all other political institutions.
Baghdad also turned to demographic measures by transferring
Arabs from southern Iraq to Kurdish regions, deporting Kurds
to the south, and levelling dozens of villages along the Iranian
border. The combination of military defeat and political measures threw the Kurdish political factions into disarray, reducing their ability to oppose the government.

The integration of Iraq's Shi'is into the Baathist political order
was less vexing than the Kurdish case. While Sunnis from the
north-west dominated the republican regimes starting with Abd
al-Karim Qasim, Shi'is took advantage of opportunities to enter
the professions by pursuing education. Furthermore, Shi'is were
not excluded from political office and military careers although
their presence was smaller than in the general population. Many
conservative Shi'is followed Grand Ayatollah Abu al-Qasim
al-Kho'i in refraining from political activity. Others backed the
underground Da'wa Party led by the cleric Muhammad Baqir
al-Sadr.

When it came to foreign policy, the Iraqi Baathists were less
dogmatic about Arab unity than party ideology would suggest.
Their pragmatic approach to foreign relations stemmed from
an instrumental attitude towards Arab solidarity. If it strengthened the regime's domestic base, Arab causes were embraced;
but if it threatened the regime's power, Arab causes were
expendable. For instance, Iraq strenuously objected to Iran's
occupation of the UAE's Abu Musa and Tunb islands at the end
of 1971, and severed diplomatic relations with Tehran. But as
we have seen, Baghdad dropped its objection in exchange for
Iran's ending support for Iraqi Kurdish insurgents. Sentiments
of Arab brotherhood did not stand in the way of briefly occupying a Kuwaiti border post in 1973 to press Al Sabah to allow
Iraq to lease two islands for better access to the Gulf.

The most conspicuous hole in Arab solidarity showed up
in relations between Iraq and Syria, both ruled by Baath Party
factions. Their enmity went back to Baath Party feuds of the
1960s and the expulsion from Syria of the party's founders.
Far from finding ground for cooperation in party doctrine,
Damascus and Baghdad hatched plots against each other and
took opposite sides on various regional issues. Another illustration of ideology's secondary relevance was Iraq's relations
with the Gulf states after the Algiers Agreement of 1975. Saudi
Arabia, Oman and Jordan all upgraded relations with Baghdad,

especially after Egypt broke Arab ranks to pursue a separate peace agreement with Israel in 1979. The alignment of hereditary monarchies with a nominally revolutionary republic was inconceivable in the heyday of the Arab Cold War.

Beyond the Arab world, the Baathist regime demonstrated flexibility in relations with the superpowers. Nationalizing the IPC disrupted relations with Western governments, so Baghdad tacked in the direction of the Soviet Union for economic, technical and military support. In 1972, they signed a treaty of friendship to formalize their ties. Moscow gained a foothold in a major Arab country as well as occasional access to Iraq's Gulf port for its warships. Baghdad balanced the deepening of ties to the Soviet Union with commercial deals with Western companies. The oil price increases gave Iraq unprecedented funds to spend on development projects, and Western companies proved willing to forgive oil nationalization in pursuit of lucrative contracts to implement those projects. Hence, the later 1970s saw a large increase in trade with Europe and Japan.

IRAN

Muhammad Reza Shah welcomed the British departure as an opportunity to flex Iran's muscles. While he dropped Iran's claim to Bahrain, he seized the Tunb Islands from Ra's al-Khaima, setting off a dispute that tapped Arab nationalist resentment of 'the Persians'. The shah was ready to play the role of a regional proxy for the United States in the framework of the Nixon Doctrine. Both Tehran and Washington viewed the Dhufar rebellion in Oman as communist meddling demanding a forceful response that allowed the shah to demonstrate Iran's military prowess.

The shah's expansive vision for Iran transcended the Gulf. He believed that his country possessed the natural and human resources to join the ranks of the world's major powers, and the leap in oil prices seemed to offer the means to make that possible. In the decade from 1964 to 1974, oil revenue was $13 billion. Revenue from oil exports grew from $5 billion in 1972–3 to $20 billion in 1975–6. The shah spent billions of dollars on the newest and most expensive military hardware from the United States. The Nixon administration encouraged Iran's weapons purchases as a way to recycle petroleum dollars to US arms companies. In addition to military power, the shah wanted to make Iran an industrial power by pouring hundreds of millions of dollars into projects like steel and petrochemicals. Iran soon had factories turning out consumer goods such as cars and televisions.

The shah's vision of a powerful, modern Iran had no place for democracy, which he considered an alien Western concept that could never take root in his country. Instead, he made the monarchy the pillar of national politics and culture. To underscore the centrality of monarchy, the shah abandoned the Islamic calendar and ordered the adoption of a royal calendar that started at the founding of the Achaemenid Empire. In 1975, he established an official political party, *Rastakhiz* (Resurgence), which promoted loyalty to the Pahlavi dynasty. Party members charged with disseminating the royalist vision managed the Ministry of Information (which had the authority to censor publications), the Ministry of Art and Culture and national television and radio stations.

Rastakhiz Party propaganda bolstered Muhammad Reza Shah's efforts to curtail the influence of Iran's Shi'i clergy by hailing him as the country's true spiritual leader and castigating clerical opponents as 'black' (for the colour of their turbans) reactionaries and as obstacles to national progress. The shah rewrote the Islamic rules for marriage. He changed the minimum age for marriage from 15 to 18 for girls and from 18 to 20 for boys. New legislation restricted men's rights to divorce and to polygamous marriage. When clerics and students in the seminary city of Qom protested, the authorities conscripted 250 students into the army. From his exile in Iraq, Ayatollah Ruhollah Khomeini called on Iranians to boycott the Rastakhiz, which he described as an instrument to destroy Islam and an agent of American imperialism. The government retaliated by placing Khomeini's clerical colleagues under arrest.

While the shah promoted his royalist agenda, Ayatollah Khomeini was giving lectures to Shi'i students at Najaf setting forth a theory of Islamic government. The core of Khomeini's political theory involves a reinterpretation of the traditional Islamic legal principle of guardianship. According to that principle, minors and widows must have a guardian, ordinarily a male relative. In the absence of a surviving male relative, a religious scholar with knowledge of the law, a jurist, assumes guardianship. In Khomeini's theory, the community of believers is in analogous situation to that of a minor because the guardian of the community's interests is the Hidden Imam. During the occultation of the Imam, the community must have a qualified guardian, and that would be a jurist, in this instance, one not only possessing legal expertise but also political judgment.

Khomeini expanded the traditional concept of guardianship of the jurist (*velayat-e faqih*) from a private relationship between a religious scholar and a child or widow to an institution for political authority. Believers are to choose a jurist to interpret and enforce Islamic law through the government. As long as Khomeini was an exiled malcontent, few Iranians outside his immediate circle knew about his innovative political doctrine.

Religious opposition to the monarchy was not limited to Khomeini. Educated youth found the eclectic teachings of Ali Shariati a compelling blend of Shi'ism, Third World anti-colonialism and socialism. In the early 1960s, Shariati studied in Paris, where he assimilated ideas current among radical students. The writings of Algerian and Cuban revolutionaries were particularly influential. Shariati became convinced of religion's central role in preserving cultural authenticity against Western cultural penetration. According to Shariati, Islam is a revolutionary ideology committed to resisting oppression and striving to bring about a just social order. The Shi'i imams were heroes in the struggle against tyranny in all forms, from Umayyad caliphs to multinational companies and imperialism. Shariati's radical cultural nationalism included a critique of Marxism for its materialist assumptions. Marxist regimes were guilty of excessive bureaucratic power, overlooking the vital role of nationalism in the struggle against imperialism and neglecting Islam as an essential element of Iranian nationalism.

Shariati's critical outlook did not spare Iran's Shi'i clerics. He considered them guilty of promoting what he called 'Safavid' Shi'ism, a conservative, fossilized form of religion that focused on matters of ritual purity. He reinterpreted key symbols of Shi'ism like Kerbala and Hussein's martyrdom to underscore Muslims' duty to rebel against tyranny. Barred from teaching at Tehran University, Shariati gave lectures at a meeting hall in Tehran in the late 1960s and early 1970s. His followers recorded his lectures and distributed cassette tapes to high-school and religious students. The authorities arrested him in 1972 and put him in prison. After his release in 1975, he was kept under house arrest. In May 1977, he was allowed to go to London, where he died of a heart attack soon after his arrival.

Khomeini and Shariati expressed different strains of religious opposition to the Pahlavi monarchy but they did not create political movements actively resisting the government. That role fell to guerrilla groups that resorted to armed struggle against the regime in the 1970s. The two largest were the Fedayan and the Mojahedin. The first was a splinter organization that formed in the late 1960s after the suppression of legal political opposition.

Its members espoused spontaneous violence against the regime and its foreign supporters in the name of Marxist revolution. The Fedayan assassinated government officials and bombed American and British embassies and the offices of multinational corporations. The Mojahedin grew out of the religious wing of the National Front and included young people attracted to Ali Shariati's radical interpretation of Islam. Its members assassinated a US military adviser and the Tehran chief of police; they also carried out bombings of the Tehran electricity plant, British Petroleum, Shell and the Israeli national airline.

From Muhammad Reza Shah's perspective, none of his opponents posed a genuine threat. Khomeini was in exile; Shariati was under surveillance; the guerrilla organizations were hounded by the ubiquitous and ruthless secret police of the National Security and Information Organization (SAVAK). The shah commanded a well-equipped army that fought effectively against Dhufar's leftist guerrillas. High oil prices provided the means to co-opt industrial workers with good wages. Finally, he had solid support from the United States. The shah was supremely confident of his popularity and the wisdom of his policies in spite of clear evidence that many Iranians were vexed by economic and cultural conditions. In the mid-1970s, the economy passed through a volatile period of acute inflation due to the influx of oil revenue, then a recession due to retrenchment. Rural Iranians migrated to cities seeking jobs in factories and on construction sites, but lacking the means to afford expensive urban housing, they gathered in squatter settlements on the outskirts of Tehran and other major cities. The spread of Western leisure habits and dress caused unease among traditional Iranians. Other Middle Eastern countries were passing through similar economic and social strains, but the political effects were contained. Iran turned out to be different.

Most accounts of the Iranian Revolution of 1978–9 start with the shah's decision in 1977 to ease restrictions on political expression. Explanations for that move vary. Some cite a wish to placate the new American president, Jimmy Carter, who promised during his election campaign to make human rights a consideration in foreign policy. Others maintain that the shah viewed limited dissent at a time of economic hardship as natural and harmless as long as dissent was non-violent. Yet others cite the shah's desire to secure his son's succession by demonstrating a lenient attitude towards moderate criticism. In the later months of 1977, professional associations tested the relaxation of control with demonstrations and protests, putting the shah on notice that educated opinion was dissatisfied with his policies. Nobody expected that Iran was about to pass through one of the most remarkable events of the twentieth century: a mass revolution that overthrew a wealthy and well-armed regime to install a regime dominated by clergy.

Matters took a violent turn in January 1978 when a government newspaper published an article condemning Ayatollah Khomeini as a British spy. His supporters in Qom rallied religious students and shopkeepers to protest his defamation. On 8–9 January, crowds of demonstrators clashed with security forces, which killed several protestors. Because it is an Iranian custom to hold a gathering on the fortieth day after someone has died, 40 days later, on 18 February, crowds assembled in several cities to mourn the Qom martyrs. Some of the mourning ceremonies turned into occasions to vent anger at the government. In Tabriz, demonstrators attacked the headquarters of the Rastakhiz Party and symbols of Western culture such as cinemas and liquor stores. Security forces again were called to quell the rioting, and yet again clashes resulted in bloodshed and deaths. The 40-day cycle of mourning and protest continued from March to early May.

Different political forces propelled the protests advancing various agendas. Moderate figures in the National Front and in its religious offshoot, the Liberation Movement of Iran, sought restoration of constitutional government under which the shah would become a mere figurehead. Religious youth inspired by Ali Shariati's teachings adopted an uncompromising militant stance for replacing the Pahlavis with an Islamic regime. Marxists and socialists of various stripes threw their weight behind the demonstrations. Khomeini voiced opposition to the shah but did not openly call for his replacement by clerical rule, preferring to emphasize common grievances rather than divisive agendas. The shah tried to stem the tide of protest with spending cuts to reduce the rate of inflation, curbs on the Rastakhiz Party and the appointment of a new cabinet to implement liberal reforms. But the breadth of the protest movement increased over the summer months.

Most historians consider the monarchy's point of no return to be 7–8 September 1978. One-and-a-half million demonstrators filled the streets of Tehran and the first cries for an Islamic Republic were heard. The government had just declared martial law but protesters gathered at a central city square where troops gunned down more than two hundred of them, sparking national outrage at the massacre. Oil workers at the refinery in Tehran went on strike, inspiring widespread worker unrest and crippling the economy. In early October, the Iraqi regime responded to the Iranian government's request that it expel Ayatollah Khomeini, in the hope that his removal would hinder the organizing efforts of his supporters. Khomeini relocated to the outskirts of Paris, where Western reporters would have access to him. His entourage included media handlers able to shape the ayatollah's message to make it more acceptable to Western audiences. On 16 October, the fortieth day after the 8 September massacre, strikes shut down banks, schools, shops, oil installations and even government ministries. Protesters called for Khomeini's return and measures against the SAVAK, a target for popular ire because of its complicity in repression and torture.

In his final months in power, the shah vacillated between declaring military rule and granting amnesty to political prisoners. His inability to take decisive action stemmed from a number of factors. First, he hoped to transfer power to his son and did not want to close the door on potential allies in the moderate opposition who could pave the way for his succession. Second, his foreign sponsor, the United States, did not give clear guidance on whether he should launch a bloody crackdown or compromise with moderates. Third, his judgment may have been clouded by poor health: he was suffering from terminal cancer, although few outside his closest confidants knew that was so. Perhaps most critically, the shah did not have a political base to rally on his behalf. His policies had alienated all segments of society: cultural policies offended the pious; economic policies hurt all but a few hundred cronies; political closure pushed moderates into the arms of radicals. Furthermore, he had incapacitated high-ranking advisers and generals by sowing mistrust among them. That tactic worked to head off potential coups but it also made it impossible for the political and military elite to act as a coherent body to command the government's different branches to deal with the crisis.

In December, the regime began to crumble. High officials transferred assets abroad and fled the country; soldiers deserted their units and joined the ranks of demonstrators. Meanwhile, the scale of popular participation swelled and spread throughout the country. Two million protestors jammed Tehran's streets on 10–11 December chanting slogans for Islamic government. On 16 January 1979, the Shah bowed to the irresistible tide of history and left the country. The caretaker government that he had appointed had no legitimacy as Iran descended into anarchy. Then on 1 February 1979, Ayatollah Khomeini arrived on an Air France jet. Three million people thronged Tehran's streets to celebrate his return from exile. Days later he appointed a veteran leader of the Liberation Movement of Iran, Mehdi Bazargan, to head a provisional government. In the provinces, clergy, religious students and merchants formed revolutionary committees to take over basic functions of police and justice, often in *ad hoc* and brutal fashion. The caretaker government collapsed on 11 February when radical guerrilla groups attacked garrisons of the Imperial Guard and overran the main army garrison in Tehran. A little more than a year after the Qom protests, the Pahlavi monarchy collapsed in the face of the first popular revolution in the modern Middle East before the Arab Spring of 2011. It would take three years for a ruthless power struggle among revolutionary forces to settle the question of what sort of government would replace the Pahlavis.

The contenders for power included the Liberation Movement of Iran's corps of lay Islamists. Its leader Mehdi Bazargan stood at the head of the official government and seemed well positioned to advance the Liberation Movement's programme for blending religious and democratic principles. Secular and religious guerrilla organizations pressed for a radical social and economic agenda as well as severing ties with the West, especially the United States. Meanwhile, Bazargan's authority was undermined by a parallel shadow government under the firm control of clergy loyal to Khomeini. They operated revolutionary courts imposing harsh penalties and commanded a militia of revolutionary guards. In addition to a power struggle at the centre, Kurds, Arabs and Turcomen in the provinces made a strong push for autonomy. To cope with forces threatening to fragment the country, Bazargan bolstered the government by inviting Khomeini's disciples Ali Akbar Rafsanjani and Ali Khamenei into the cabinet. Both men would remain at the centre of the political stage long after Bazargan's interim leadership.

For the United States, the Shah's overthrow was a huge blow. His pro-Western government had filled a gap in regional security following Britain's departure. Washington feared that the Soviet Union would exploit the chaotic situation to bolster its influence in the Gulf. Therefore, the Carter administration kept open lines of communication with the revolutionary government. In November 1979, Bazargan met with American officials in Algeria. Radical leftists and religious activists construed the meeting as a prelude to American intervention to restore the shah, in a repetition of the 1953 coup against Musaddiq. On 4 November, a group of students stormed the US embassy and took the captured American staff hostage. The humiliated Bazargan was forced to step down.

As confrontation between the United States and Iran unfolded over the hostages, Khomeini's faction tightened its grip on power.

A referendum approved a draft constitution that made the jurist the supreme figure in the political system. National elections under the new constitution were held in January 1980, installing Abdhasan Bani-Sadr, a lay Islamist and confidant of Khomeini, as president, and electing a parliament (*majles*) dominated by clerics organized in the Islamic Republican Party (IRP). The government then launched a cultural revolution to purge universities, law courts and government offices, targeting Westernized men and women who refused to conform to the Islamic dress code. Thousands of teachers, civil servants and army officers were dismissed. Islamic government had to *look* Islamic, not Western.

EXPORTING REVOLUTION

For the activist clergy, Iran's revolution was not a purely domestic affair. In a manner similar to other revolutions in history, intense enthusiasm for the prospect of an ideal new order fuelled efforts to export radical change. The logical pathways for Iranian revolutionary fervour were the networks of patronage and student–teacher relationships that connected Iran's clerics to Shi'is in the Gulf, Iraq and Lebanon. Their propaganda was a blend of Khomeini's doctrine of Islamic government and Shariati's vision of Shi'ism as a religion of social justice and opposition to tyranny.

In the 1960s and 1970s, Iraq's shrine cities were the hubs of two separate Shi'i networks that radiated throughout the Gulf. Students seeking religious training travelled to Najaf and Kerbala, where they mixed with Iraqis, Iranians, Lebanese and Gulf nationals. In Najaf, Gulf Shi'is frequently came into contact with members of Iraq's Da'wa Party and returned home to spread its agenda of combating secular nationalism. That is how a branch of the party came to be set up in Bahrain. Because political parties were banned there, Da'wa sympathizers founded a religious club instead, the Islamic Enlightenment Society, in 1972. From its ranks came the emirate's leading Shi'i activists for the next 30 years. Kuwait's Shi'is did not have a tradition of pursuing religious learning, so few young men studied in Najaf. Rather, wealthy Shi'i merchants invited its clerics to provide religious guidance. When the Baath Party regime cracked down on the Da'wa Party in the early 1970s, its activists found refuge in Kuwait's Shi'i community. Political pressure caused a Da'wa Party leader, Mahdi al-Hakim, to move to Dubai in 1971. The emirate's small Shi'i population was made up of descendants of Persian and Bahraini merchant immigrants. Like Kuwait, it lacked a local tradition of learning and relied on clerics from Iraq. Al-Hakim spent nearly a decade there, concentrating on raising funds from Dubai's Shi'i community to develop religious institutions. By the end of the 1970s, the combination of political repression in Iraq and hospitable Shi'i communities in the Gulf spread a network of Da'wa sympathizers in the region.

The second Shi'i network is named for Muhammad Shirazi, a Kerbala cleric descended from a family of Iranian religious scholars that settled in Iraq. When Ayatollah Khomeini lived in Najaf, he came into contact with Shirazi, known for endorsing the notion that religious scholars ought to assume political leadership. Given the convergence of his views with Khomeini's, it was natural that Shirazi publicly welcomed the exiled cleric upon his arrival in Iraq. His followers, known as Shiraziyyin, gravitated to a political movement that his nephew, Muhammad Taqi al-Mudarrisi, founded in the late 1960s. Before the movement assumed definite shape, persecution by the Baathist government chased Shirazi and his associates out of the country. They landed in Lebanon, Syria and the Gulf states.

During the 1970s, Muhammad Shirazi resided in Kuwait where wealthy merchants supported his efforts to set up religious institutions, including a new Shi'i seminary that drew pupils from Iraq, Bahrain and Saudi Arabia. Besides purely religious instruction, Muhammad Taqi al-Mudarrisi gave political lessons inspired by Sunni activists like Egypt's Hasan al-Banna and Sayyid Qutb, and Pakistan's Abu'l Ala Mawdudi. It is noteworthy that the Shirazi tendency did not endorse opposition to Al Sabah, who had a long history of comfortable relations with Shi'i merchants. The Shirazis also established a base in Bahrain through the scion of a wealthy Shi'i family on good terms with Al Khalifah. The Bahraini branch of the Shirazis, the Association of Islamic Guidance, avoided sectarian issues and concentrated instead on combating moral corruption.

Another notable Shirazi activist is Hasan al-Saffar, a Saudi Shi'i from al-Qatif who studied in Najaf and Qom. He met Shirazi and Mudarrisi in Kuwait in 1974. When he returned home, he recruited Saudi Shi'is to study at the Shirazi seminary in Kuwait. He also spent five years in Muscat among its Shi'i merchants, descendants of Bahraini immigrants. Al-Mudarrisi's brother Hadi introduced the Shirazi movement to Sharjah, which has an old population of Shi'is known as Lawatis, descendants of immigrants from Sind. Hadi al-Mudarrisi met and gained favour with the emir, who granted him Emirati citizenship.

By the late 1970s, the Gulf's Shi'i population was connected through a dense web of activist networks. They were not a destabilizing factor in the region because they did not have a revolutionary ideology. Rather, they focused on serving Shi'i communities' religious needs. To the extent that they had a political aspect, it concentrated on combating Western cultural influences. Nevertheless, they offered the Iranian Revolution's propagandists ready-made avenues for spreading their calls for radical change. Revolutionary messages played on grievances and discontent with Sunni domination. In 1978–9, the Gulf's Shi'is demonstrated in solidarity with Iran and demanded better treatment from the governments of Kuwait, Bahrain and Saudi Arabia.

In order to coordinate the revolutionary project abroad, Iran formed the Islamic Revolutionary Council. Under its auspices, Iraqi Shi'i dissidents established the Supreme Council for Islamic Revolution in Iraq, or SCIRI. It later became a leading political force in Iraq after the overthrow of Saddam Hussein in 2003. The Islamic Revolutionary Council's clients included the Islamic Front for the Liberation of Bahrain and the Islamic Revolution Movement of the Arabian peninsula. Underground cells of militants formed in Kuwait. In Lebanon, Iranian envoys helped Shi'is form a militia, the Party of God, or Hizballah, to fight invading Israeli forces in June 1982. One of the most significant manifestations of Shi'i discontent exploded in Saudi Arabia at the very same time that the dynasty was threatened by a militant band of puritans in Mecca.

After the shock of the King Faisal's assassination wore off, it seemed as though the kingdom would continue on the same path of headlong development that Faisal had charted during his reign. Nevertheless, the rapid pace of change may have been a force behind the most serious challenge to Al Saud since the defeat of the Ikhwan in 1929. The royals had incorporated the Wahhabi establishment into the modern state by letting it manage the religious law courts, girls' schools, public morality and censorship. In return, the clerics endorsed Saudi rule, as they had for more than two centuries. But not all pious Saudis accepted the validity of that bargain. At the same time that Saudi technocrats were dominating national news coverage of development schemes, disgruntled young religious students were faulting Al Saud for allowing Westerners into the kingdom. From their ranks came Juhaiman al-Utaibi, a descendant of Ikhwan tribesmen. In Medina, he became active in religious circles that viewed the growing adoption of Western ways as a violation of Arabia's Islamic purity and blamed the rulers for failing to rule according to Islamic law. On 20 November 1979, the last day of the year's pilgrimage, Juahiman led a band of militants to seize the Holy Sanctuary of Mecca. Then he called on Muslims to overthrow the dynasty, declaring it had forfeited legitimacy when King Abdulaziz betrayed the Ikhwan, cancelled jihad against infidels, and allied himself with the Christians, that is to say, Great Britain. The present rulers, according to Juhaiman, were guilty of allying with the infidels and allowing them to exploit the kingdom's resources. Furthermore, Juhaiman accused Wahhabi clerics of meekly acquiescing to the dynasty for the sake of enjoying honours and riches. The government's initial effort to regain the Holy Mosque was repulsed in a hail of bullets. It took two weeks of bloody fighting before security forces were able to put down the revolt at the cost of 300 dead. Juhaiman was taken alive, tried, and executed along with 60 followers.

At the same time as the crisis in Mecca shook the country, Shi'is in the Eastern Province erupted in violent protests. The spark for their uprising was the revolution in Iran but the long background was a history of discrimination arising from the Wahhabi doctrine's view of Shi'is as infidels who must abandon their beliefs and practices. On top of religious grievances, Shi'i towns and villages suffered neglect instead of benefitting from the oil wealth that came from the region where they comprise about one-third of the population. The region's major cities – Dhahran, Dammam and Khobar – burgeoned as centres of the Saudi oil industry and petrochemical complexes while nearby Shi'i villages and towns lacked basic amenities such as clean drinking water and modern sewage systems. Grandiose agricultural development projects had failed to reverse environmental deterioration as sand dunes overran oases, and high concentrations of saline water ruined irrigation works. The Islamic Republic viewed Saudi Shi'is as natural allies in the campaign to spread revolution against unjust rulers and incited them to rise up against the monarchy. Saudi Shi'is, inspired by the Shirazi network established by Sheikh Hasan al-Saffar, set up the Organization for the Islamic Revolution, which called on fellow Shi'is to combine religious assertion with anti-government demonstrations.

On 26 November, while the government was in the midst of quelling Juhaiman's revolt in Mecca, Shi'is in eastern towns violated the prohibition against public celebration of their holy day of Ashura, the commemoration of Imam Hussein's martyrdom. Two days later, marchers chanting anti-government slogans clashed with security forces which fired on the crowd and killed a protestor. Violent protests continued for a few days before petering out. Some two dozen protestors were killed in the uprising. A second round of demonstrations erupted in February 1980 on the first anniversary of the Iranian Revolution. Shi'i protestors carrying posters of Ayatollah Khomeini clashed with security forces. The authorities imprisoned dissident leaders and promised the government would address grievances arising from neglect of Shi'i towns and villages. The blend of force and concessions proved effective at pacifying the region.

1979 also was a fateful year for Iraq. In the early months, the Iranian Revolution threatened to ignite Kurdish and Shi'i unrest. Tehran lost firm control over its own Kurdish provinces, and exiled Iraqi Kurdish insurgents crossed the border to revive their armed struggle. Islamic ideologues in Tehran sought to export revolution to Iraq, calling on its Shi'is to rise up to over-throw the secular Baathist regime and install a religious repub-lic. At this precarious juncture, Saddam Hussein took control in Baghdad. For some years he had been gradually encroaching on the powers of President Ahmad Hasan al-Bakr, whose declining health had diminished his leadership. On 16 July 1979, Saddam arranged for his senior partner to resign. He then assumed the reins of power as president, chairman of the RCC and head of the Baath Party. He moved quickly to purge the RCC and the Baath of men whose loyalty he did not trust and staged show trials for several dozen high-ranking officials on charges of plot-ting a coup against him. Death sentences were quickly imple-mented. It is not altogether clear that there was such a plot, but the public confessions and executions put would-be plotters on notice they would be playing a high stakes game.

Relations between Iraq and Iran deteriorated in late 1979 and early 1980. The fall of Mehdi Bazargan's provisional government removed a brake on the faction seeking to export the revolu-tion. In Iraq, pro-Iranian figures became bolder in expressing opposition to the Baathist government. The regime placed the popular Shi'i cleric and Da'wa Party leader Muhammad Baqir al-Sadr under house arrest in June 1979 to prevent him from going to visit Ayatollah Khomeini in Iran. Then, in April 1980, Shi'i militants carried out a series of assassination attempts and bombings against high-ranking officials. The regime struck back by expelling over 30,000 Shi'is to Iran. It also ordered the arrest and execution of Muhammad Baqir al-Sadr and his sister, Bint al-Huda, a prominent activist. It was the first time the Baath had put a major religious leader to death, suggesting the degree of alarm among authorities.

In September 1980, Iran and Iraq edged closer to war when a series of border skirmishes broke out. Saddam Hussein raised the political stakes by renouncing the 1975 Algiers Agreement on 17 September and claiming the entire Shatt al-Arab waterway for Iraq. Five days later, Iraqi forces invaded Iran. Saddam expected Iran's political chaos would render its military unable to defend the country. He supposed that his forces could cause the collapse of the Islamic Republic in retaliation for its urging Iraqi Shi'is to revolt. Baghdad's more modest declared war aims were to force Iran to recognize Iraq's claim to Shatt al-Arab and to evacuate the UAE islands the shah had occupied in 1971. By the end of October, Iraqi forces occupied a swathe of Iranian territory up to 25 miles deep, including Khorramshahr but falling short of Abadan, the centre of oil production. The logistical challenges of mounting and sustaining a deeper invasion exceeded Iraq's military capacities. Nevertheless, Saddam hoped that disarray in Tehran and recent purges of Iranian officer ranks to weed out vestiges of Pahlavi loyalists would compel Iran to agree to his terms. He miscalculated. Instead, Iran took advantage of the pause in major combat to prepare a counteroffensive.

In January 1981, Iranian forces began a methodical assault on Iraqi positions. Iran's army fought with surprising effectiveness, forcing the Iraqis to end their siege of Abadan in September. In May 1982, Iraq pulled its forces out of Khorramshahr; by the end of June, Iraqi forces had withdrawn from Iranian territory. Baghdad announced its willingness to call an end to the war, but now Iran declared it sought the removal of Saddam Hussein and the replacement of the Baathist regime by an Islamic Republic. While the Iraqis were still fighting to hold onto Iranian terri-tory, Israeli war planes destroyed Iraq's Osirak nuclear research plant on 7 June 1981. It was not clear whether the Iraqis were close to having a nuclear weapon. The timing of the raid on the eve of Israeli elections suggested that Prime Minister Menahem Begin was attuned to domestic political considerations as well as national security.

REPERCUSSIONS OF REVOLUTION AND WAR

Both the Iranian Revolution and the Iran–Iraq war triggered fluctuations in oil prices, which had stabilized in 1975. In real dollar terms, prices fell in the next three years as new oilfields in Alaska, the North Sea and Mexico bolstered global supplies. In the autumn of 1978, however, prices spiked once again due to the impact of turmoil in Iran. When workers in the oilfields around Abadan went on strike, Iranian production fell from 5.5 million to 2.4 million barrels per day. Saudi Arabia partially filled the gap by raising its output from 8 to 10 million barrels per day. At the end of December, Iran's oil workers completely shut down production and expatriate employees of the Western company managing production evacuated the country. Just as the revolution was reaching its climax in early 1979, Saudi Arabia cut back production, perhaps because of the technical challenge of sustaining higher output. The Islamic Republic got the oilfields back into production, but output remained well below pre-revolution levels, putting upward pressure on prices.

Towards the end of 1979, three regional events jolted world oil markets. First, the takeover of the American embassy in Iran caused a hostile confrontation between Washington and Tehran. Second, Juhaiman's revolt seemed to put the Saudi monarchy in jeopardy. Third, Soviet military forces entered Afghanistan at the end of December in an effort to stabilize that country's communist government. With the fate of Saudi Arabia in question, Iran in upheaval, and Soviet forces thrusting southward in the direction of the Arabian Sea, oil prices spiralled, hitting $30 per barrel in June 1980.

At the outset of the Iran–Iraq war, the belligerents targeted each other's oil facilities, driving the price to $40 per barrel. Saudi Arabia responded by raising production to compensate for declines in Iranian and Iraqi exports and prices eased to the $30 per barrel range. Pressure on oil supplies mounted when Iran blocked Iraq's port on the Gulf, Umm al-Qasr. Baghdad responded by constructing pipelines through Turkey, Jordan and Saudi Arabia as alternate outlets for the oil exports it needed to finance the war. Iraq struck back at Iranian oil facilities, directing heavy attacks on Kharg Island, a storage and offloading site. Although global oil markets reacted to the eruption of war with alarm, the spike in prices was brief. Saudi Arabia's production increase compensated for reductions in Iraqi and Iranian exports. Moreover, high prices stimulated production increases in areas outside the Gulf. Even the communist Soviet Union sought to profit from conditions favourable to sellers by joining the ranks of oil exporters. The combination of expanded supplies, and slackening demand pushed prices below $30 per barrel in 1983. Saudi Arabia cut its output in an effort to keep prices from falling, but Riyadh decided in late 1985 to reverse course and hike production once again. In part, the decision was calculated to retaliate against Iran for its hostile propaganda slamming Riyadh's close relations with the United States. Raising production would lower oil prices and reduce Iran's revenues. In part, the decision was related to the refusal of other OPEC members to comply with production quotas. Kuwait, for instance, consistently exceeded its quota in order to maximize revenues and thereby cover the costs of generous welfare benefits for its citizens. The effect of overproduction was to drive prices under $15 per barrel. Governments now had to realign their budgets and plans in light of the lowest revenues since 1973. From 1981 to 1985, Saudi Arabia's oil earnings fell more than 70 per cent. With prices hovering between $15 and $20 per barrel, Gulf states drew down the huge sums of foreign reserves dating to the mid-1970s and faced an era of austerity.

The political fallout from the Iranian Revolution and the Iran–Iraq war was more difficult to contain than their effects on oil markets. Quite simply, the Iranian Revolution threatened the political survival of the Gulf states. Saudi Arabia, Bahrain and Kuwait had to deal with hostile propaganda from the Islamic Republic and efforts to turn their Shi'i populations into agents of subversion. One of the ayatollahs infamously declared that if Bahrain did not embrace Tehran's model of an Islamic Republic, then Iran would annex the island nation, a threat that echoed earlier Iranian claims to Bahrain. The Gulf states also feared that the Soviet invasion of Afghanistan would stir communist forces in the region, namely the People's Democratic Republic of Yemen and Ethiopia, across the Red Sea from Saudi Arabia. In response to the more threatening climate, Gulf rulers increased mutual consultations in 1980. Their discussions led to a foreign ministers' conference in February 1981 at which the governments of Saudi Arabia, Kuwait, Bahrain, Qatar, UAE and Oman decide to create a collective security body. In May, they formally established the Gulf Cooperation Council, with headquarters in Riyadh. The Council's charter stipulated that its members would develop a collective approach to economic matters, trade, education and culture, but in fact, the focus was on security. But the coordination of military strategy and armed forces collided with diverse approaches to foreign relations as well as historical rivalries and disputes. Nevertheless, the member states did plan and execute joint military exercises and created a multinational force.

Bahrain was the Gulf state most vulnerable to Iranian revolutionary propaganda. First, its Shi'i majority felt disenfranchised and excluded from its rightful share of oil revenues. Second, Iranian rulers since the Safavids had claimed Bahrain as sovereign territory. Third, Bahrain's warm relationship with the United States made it a reactionary regime that the revolution wanted to sweep away. The leader of pro-Iranian Shi'is in Bahrain was the Shirazi cleric, Hadi al-Mudarrisi, who had close support from a Bahraini cleric, Sadiq al-Ruhani. In summer 1978, Khomeini named him his deputy. In August 1979, Mudarrisi instigated two anti-government demonstrations. In the larger one, he managed to raise a modest crowd of about five hundred demonstrators. The police broke up the protest, arrested about twenty leaders, and deported Mudarrisi and Ruhani to Iran. In Tehran, they contributed to the Voice of the Islamic Revolution radio station broadcasts urging Shi'is to rebel against oppressive rulers. They also set up the Islamic Front for the Liberation of Bahrain. On 13 December 1981, Bahrain security forces uncovered a plot by agents of the Islamic Front to seize power and install an Islamic Republic under Mudarrisi. The trial ended in the execution of the conspirators.

In Kuwait, Tehran's agent for spreading revolution was Ayatollah Khomeini's brother-in-law Abbas Muhri. He and his followers used Shi'i mosques to deliver sermons in support of Khomeini. In September 1979, the Kuwaiti authorities arrested him and deported him along with his family. Two months later, Shi'i protests in Saudi Arabia inspired Kuwaiti Shi'is to march on the US embassy, but security forces intervened to shield the embassy against a possible replay of the takeover in Tehran.

After the outbreak of the Iran–Iraq war, Kuwait's support for Iraq made it the target of a series of terrorist operations by pro-Iranian cells. The first major attack took place on 12 December 1983, when terrorists bombed the embassies of the United States and France and the international airport. The attack on the US embassy, carried out two months after the massive truck bombing of the US Marines barracks in Beirut, killed four people. Kuwaiti security forces rounded up 25 suspects, of whom only three were Kuwaitis. Most of the detainees were Iraqi members of the Da'wa Party headquartered in Tehran; three were Lebanese Shi'is. One year later, on 6 December 1984, Da'wa Party operatives hijacked a civilian Kuwaiti airliner to Tehran and demanded the release of their imprisoned comrades. On 25 May 1985, Emir Jabir was the target of an assassination attempt by a suicide bomber who managed to crash his motorcade but only inflicted minor injuries on his target. Two months later, terrorists struck a number of seaside cafes and killed 11 people.

As Shi'i unrest and Iranian subversion fostered deep anxiety in Kuwait, local Sunni Islamists gained influence. In the 1970s, Emir Jabir had developed a tacit political alliance with them to counter the Arab nationalists, whom he regarded as overly assertive on matters like oil policy. To signal his commitment to religious principles, he appointed an Islamist to a cabinet position. He also backed the call for solidarity with Afghans fighting the Soviet occupation. As Islamist influence grew, cultural mores became more conservative and religious activists spoke out against co-education at the university and women appearing with their hair uncovered.

In 1981, Emir Jabir decided to restore parliamentary government in a bid to buttress popular support for the government at a time of severe regional unrest. A new election law designed to tilt the political arena in favour of loyalists increased the number of election districts from 10 to 25. The February 1981 election produced the desired outcome: Arab nationalists did poorly; candidates from so-called tribal districts, areas with high concentrations of former Bedouins, did well; and Islamists made their debut in the national assembly. The largest Islamist organization was the Social Reform Society, basically the Kuwaiti branch of the Muslim Brothers. They used positions in government ministries to advance their agenda of injecting religion into public affairs. The Ministry of Education presented the opportunity to revise curricula and the Ministry of Information banned books and put television under tight regulation. Apart from acting on the ideology of the Muslim Brothers, it is striking that many Kuwaiti Islamists have humble social backgrounds, including former Bedouins, suggesting that the rise of this trend signifies a broadening of the scope of participation in national politics.

In August 1982, Kuwait was rocked by a financial crisis of purely local making, the collapse of its unofficial stock exchange known as Suq al-Manakh. The influx of capital generated by high oil prices in the late 1970s far exceeded the government's capacity to spend it. Consequently, Kuwait faced the unusual problem of having to find profitable investments for its surplus cash reserves. The official body responsible for safeguarding the public interest in preserving the national windfall was the Kuwait Investment Authority, which handled huge sums primarily by investing in Western companies. The country was also awash with abundant private capital. Individual investors with a bent for speculation funnelled huge sums into Suq al-Manakh, a completely unregulated exchange that was the scene of extensive fraud. In the enthusiasm characteristic of financial 'bubbles', ordinary Kuwaitis invested life savings in companies that sometimes existed only on paper. Traders bought shares with post-dated cheques, which were, in fact, legal, but if there was a rush on liquidating shares, the holders of such cheques found they were not redeemable. Such a rush took place in August, precipitating a huge speculative bust that cost investors nearly $100 billion. The collapse wiped out the personal savings of thousands of Kuwaitis. Criminal investigations into fraudulent dealings led to some convictions but government bailouts for well-connected speculators sparked popular outrage that poisoned public trust in the government for years.

The 1985 election returned a pro-government majority, but relations between the national assembly and the rulers deteriorated. The lingering economic effects of the Suq al-Manakh crash and suspicions about favouritism in resolving its financial effects fed a more assertive attitude among deputies. Iranian subversion and military advances against Iraq aggravated the rulers' unease. Iranian troops achieved a military breakthrough in February 1986 when they seized the Faw peninsula, practically on Kuwait's doorstep. In June, explosions shook a large oil installation. Economic conditions worsened when the price of oil fell to its lowest point in more than a decade. But many Kuwaitis did not believe that their woes stemmed from conditions beyond the government's control. Rumours about corruption and mismanagement at the Central Bank and several ministries prompted the parliament to investigate the government's handling of the economy. The investigation leaned hard on the minister of petroleum and forced the resignation of the minister of justice, both members of Al Sabah. On 3 July 1986, Emir Jabir dissolved the national assembly because, he declared, it was having a divisive effect on the nation at a moment of crisis. But opposition leaders suspected the government wanted to cover up malfeasance at the Central Bank. The emir appointed a cabinet to govern in the absence of the elected assembly, effectively freezing political life indefinitely.

In the UAE, the regional crises led to a more ambitious plan for centralizing federation affairs. Members of the Federal National Council and the Council of Ministers voted for unifying military forces and concentrating internal security functions in federal bodies. They also decided to expand the Federal National Council's legislative authority. But even in the face of the revolution in Iran, disarray among Arab governments over Egypt's peace treaty with Israel, and alarm at the Soviet Union's invasion of Afghanistan, Dubai and Ra's al-Khaima dragged their feet to resist what they viewed as a power grab by Abu Dhabi. Kuwaiti mediation broke the stalemate with a deal that established the emir of Dubai as prime minister in exchange for Abu Dhabi's pledge to share its oil revenues.

In foreign policy, the individual emirates continued go their own way in spite of a declared official position of neutrality. Abu

Dhabi, Ajman and Fujaira leaned in Iraq's favour while Dubai, Sharjah and Umm al-Qaiwain sided with Iran due to strong commercial ties and Dubai's large population of descendants from Persian immigrants. Iran's political isolation in the region benefited Dubai, which handled one-third of Iran's imports by the end of the war in 1988. The robust transit trade, however, did not compensate for the low oil prices of the late 1980s. Governments were forced to cut expenditures and Dubai led the way in placing more emphasis on the private sector and foreign investment for economic growth.

At the level of individual emirates, autonomy resulted in costly duplication of investment. For instance, the UAE has three airlines. Resistance to centralizing decision making meant the neglect of projects to integrate the emirates. In 1990, there were still no paved roads or public transportation systems connecting the emirates. Only in the mid-1990s did a paved road connect Dubai to Abu Dhabi. Furthermore, the Central Bank had no authority over emirate-level banks. The absence of a regulatory framework caused bank scandals. The most notorious instance was the failure of the Bank of Commerce and Credit International (BCCI) in 1991 that implicated Abu Dhabi's ruling family, cost about half a billion dollars, and uncovered black market, money laundering, criminal and terrorist operations. Finally, the constitution's Article 23 stipulated autonomy in oil and gas policies, so Dubai was free to opt out of joining OPEC, leaving Abu Dhabi, which joined in 1967, solely responsible for UAE violations of production quotas.

Oman's experience during the era of revolution and war was calmer than in other Gulf states. Sultan Qabus used patronage and military repression to realize a higher degree of stability and unity than ever before. This is not to say Oman did not feel any effects from the Iranian Revolution. In 1974, the Shirazi activist Hasan al-Saffar settled in Muscat, where he opened libraries and taught religious courses to receptive members of Oman's Shi'i minority. He left the country in 1979, but authorities kept close watch on his followers on suspicion of engaging in subversive activities. In 1981 and in 1987, the authorities arrested and jailed members of Saffar's Shi'i circle but Oman was spared the demonstrations and violence that rocked Saudi Arabia, Bahrain and Kuwait.

In summer 1982, the Iran-Iraq war entered a new phase of Iranian campaigns to invade Iraq. Iran staged offensives on the southern front directed at conquering Basra and on the northern front in Kurdish areas. Iraq responded with air and missile attacks on Iranian cities and oil facilities. Iran retaliated with attacks on oil tankers bound for and departing from ports in Kuwait and Saudi Arabia. Iraqi forces targeted tankers bound for Iran. Tehran struck back against tankers belonging to Iraqi allies like Kuwait and Saudi Arabia. As the war dragged on, the Arab Gulf states viewed Iraq as the barrier standing in the way of Iran's revolutionary aspirations and Saudi Arabia and Kuwait contributed billions of dollars to Iraq's war effort. As for the United States, even though it adopted an official position of neutrality, it quietly provided military intelligence to Baghdad. In November 1984, Washington restored diplomatic relations with Iraq and extended economic and technological aid. While Iraq enjoyed broad international support, the Islamic Republic was relatively isolated. Its chief regional ally was Syria, which was always ready to exploit Iraqi vulnerabilities and severed the oil pipeline from Iraq to the Mediterranean port of Baniyas. Iran also found Kurdish fighters in northern Iraq willing to cooperate. By 1985, they dominated rural areas in the Kurdish region of Iraq. Tehran also recruited dissident Iraqi Shi'is to its cause. Exiled clerics living in Iran formed SCIRI, which developed a military wing, the Badr Brigade that sometimes fought alongside Iranian forces.

In the later phases of the war, a stalemate developed along the military front as Iraq succeeded at withstanding Iran's massive assaults staged by poorly trained and armed recruits. Escalating violence in the Gulf threatened the flow of oil and brought about increased intervention by Western powers led by the United States. Washington had responded to the outbreak of hostilities by dispatching two aircraft carriers to the Arabian Sea, where they patrolled the approaches to the Strait of Hormuz. Although dozens of tankers were hit in 1984 and 1985, the United States and other major powers kept their navies out of the Gulf. The impetus for introducing warships into the Gulf came from a Kuwaiti request in November 1986 that Washington 're-flag' oil tankers, that is, to give military protection to commercial vessels in order to deter Iranian attacks. At first Washington balked, but when the Kuwaitis approached Moscow with the same request, Washington agreed in order to prevent the Soviets, already entrenched in Afghanistan, from increasing their strategic advantage in the region. The re-flagging operation commenced in March 1987. Soon, Soviet and Western European warships were participating as well. In spite of an accidental Iraqi strike on an American vessel, the USS *Stark*, that killed 37 crewmen on 17 May 1987, American commanders focused on suppressing Iranian naval forces, especially mine-laying ships. In October 1987, the United States struck Iranian oil facilities to retaliate for an Iranian missile attack on re-flagged tankers headed to Kuwait.

International pressure for ending the war led the United Nations Security Council to adopt Resolution 598 in July 1987. The resolution called for a ceasefire, withdrawal of forces, and the formation of a commission to investigate the question of who started the war. Iraq announced its willingness to comply but Iran said that it wanted the question of responsibility for the war to be established before it would implement the other provisions. More importantly, Ayatollah Khomeini was not ready to abandon his goal of driving Saddam Hussein from power. In the first months of 1988, Iraqi air attacks on Tehran eroded domestic support for continuing the war. Then in April, Baghdad achieved a breakthrough when its forces regained the Faw peninsula and followed with advances on the central and northern fronts. A conspicuous element in the Iraqi offensives was the use of chemical weapons. The United States also kept up pressure on Iranian ships and oil platforms. Iran's political and military leaders were coming to the realization that they could not sustain the war indefinitely. On 3 July, an American vessel, the USS *Vincennes*, mistook an Iranian civilian airliner for a military aircraft and shot it down, killing all 290 passengers aboard. It was apparently the final blow to the Islamic Republic's shrinking morale. Two weeks later, Ayatollah Khomeini announced he would accept a ceasefire, likening it to drinking a cup of poison. United Nations mediators arranged for the fighting to end on 20 August 1988.

The war's impact on the belligerents was devastating. Around 250,000 Iranians and 100,000 Iraqis perished. Baghdad borrowed around $80 billion to pay for the war. Saddam's gamble had put tremendous strains on manpower and resources that derailed Iraq from the impressive development path it followed in the 1970s. The destruction of oil facilities and industrial plants in the south was particularly severe. The drain on manpower to confront Iran's mass infantry attacks drove Iraq to rely on expatriate labour, mostly from Egypt and several Asian countries. At war's end, these workers were repatriated to alleviate pressure for jobs for demobilized troops. The most traumatic effects of the war were felt in the Kurdish region. In March 1987, Saddam sent his cousin Ali Hasan al-Majid to preside over a brutal campaign to uproot the Kurdish insurgency. Al-Majid would become known as 'Chemical Ali' for using chemical weapons against Kurdish fighters and civilians, most notoriously against the town of Halabja, where some 5000 townsmen were massacred in a single attack in March 1988. The assault on the Kurdish region, known as the *Anfal* (Spoils of War) Campaign, continued after Iran agreed to a ceasefire in July 1988. Without having to worry about Iranian military intervention, Chemical Ali launched a ferocious scorched earth assault that killed up to 100,000 Kurds to put an end to the insurgency.

The Islamic Republic emerged from the war deeply wounded but intact. In fact, the war had the paradoxical effect of strengthening the clerical regime. When Iraq invaded, the clerics had put the cultural revolution against 'un-Islamic' elements on hold because many Iranians blamed them for weakening the army by purging professional military officers. To regain the initiative, the IRP formed a Supreme Defence Council that would oversee the conduct of the war. It also enlarged the Revolutionary Guards to fight alongside the professional army. In contrast to the IRP's effective steps to bolster its position, President Bani-Sadr failed to shape his supporters into a coherent bloc. In June 1981 Khomeini gave the Majles the green light to depose him as president. Shortly after, Bani-Sadr fled the country. The one remaining political force standing in the way of clerical rule was the Mojahedin. In 1981–2, its members waged a campaign of bombings and assassinations to decapitate the IRP. In June 1981, a bombing of party headquarters killed its leader, government ministers and two dozen members of parliament. Later that year, another bomb attack killed the president and prime minister. The clerical government countered with a wave of arrests and summary executions of Mojahedin, killing as many as 10,000. In the midst of the bloody struggle for power, Iranians went to the polls to elect a president. The winner, Ali Khameni, would later succeed Ayatollah Khomeini as Supreme Leader in 1989.

By the time the Islamic Republic held its second round of elections for the Majles in 1984, all opposition had been crushed. The IRP, which dominated the elected body, was not a monolith. One bloc, arguing that the revolution should act according to Islamic principles rooted in justice and vindicating the rights of the oppressed, favoured land reform measures that would have redistributed rural fields from large landowners to poor peasants and legislation supporting the rights of industrial workers. Opponents of redistributive measures cited Islamic texts that upheld private property rights. The majority in the Majles passed measures conceived to help peasants and workers only to see those measures rejected by a body called the Council of Guardians, a group of clerics whose role is to review legislation for consistency with Islamic law, as interpreted by its members. The contest over economic reform was a signal that elected representatives would not have the final say in the Islamic Republic. Instead, officials and agencies appointed by Ayatollah Khomeini and his circle exercised ultimate power.

Khomeini's circle, however, was not of one mind either although disagreements were seldom aired in public. Factional rivalry between clerics, however, surfaced as a result of tensions over secret dealings with the United States. On one side, Majles Speaker Ali Akbar Rafsanjani backed a complex bargain with Washington in order to obtain American spare weapons parts that were needed in the war against Iraq. Even though the administration of President Ronald Reagan condemned Iran as a terrorist state and maintained economic sanctions on the Islamic Republic, members of his National Security Council devised a scheme to sell arms to Iran in exchange for the release of American hostages kidnapped by pro-Iranian Lebanese Shi'i militants. The scheme had two additional elements that required secrecy. First, the Americans planned to send the proceeds of arms sales to anti-communist forces in Nicaragua, in violation of legislation passed by the US Congress. Second, the Americans used Israeli arms dealers to provide the spare parts Iran was seeking. Obviously, the last thing Rafsanjani wanted was the disclosure of any dealings with Israel or the United States, the Little Satan and the Great Satan in the language of the Islamic revolution.

The Iran-Contra Affair became an embarrassing scandal for all the involved parties in November 1986 when Sayyid Mehdi Hashemi, the head of an organization for exporting the revolution, disclosed it to a Lebanese newspaper. In the United States, Congress formed a special committee to investigate the affair. In Iran, it resulted in a shake-up in clerical ranks. The whistle-blower, Mehdi Hashemi, was related to Khomeini's handpicked successor, Ayatollah Hussein Ali Montazeri, but even he could not shield Hashemi from Khomeini's wrath for revealing the Islamic Republic's hypocritical dealings with Israel and the United States. In June 1987, Khomeini established a special body, the Special Court for Clerics, to try Hashemi. He was found guilty and executed for counter-revolutionary activities in September. The fallout from the affair continued as Montazeri began to criticize the concentration of political power in clerical hands. On 28 March 1989, Khomeini abruptly ousted him as his successor and indicated that President Ali Khamenei would take his place.

When Ayatollah Ruhollah Khomeini died on 3 June 1989, the Assembly of Experts dutifully followed his instruction that

President Ali Khamenei succeed as the supreme religious leader, even though his clerical peers considered his religious learning deficient in terms of Khomeini's political theory of the learned jurist. That detail did not matter as much after the revision of the constitution undertaken in 1988 at Khomeini's behest. The revised constitution made political expertise the primary criterion for selecting the supreme leader and placed less emphasis on religious knowledge. The constitutional revisions also enumerated the supreme religious leader's powers over the army, security forces, intelligence bodies, the judiciary, the Council of Guardians and state-owned radio and television. Equipped with formidable institutional authority, the Islamic Republic's new supreme leader assumed the reins of power from its charismatic founder.

Saudi Arabia responded to the uprisings of November 1979 with new initiatives in the domestic and international spheres. The rulers had to counter Juhaiman's criticisms of royal corruption and the spread of immorality as well as Iran's accusations of betraying Islam by allying with the United States. To bolster their credentials as guardians of Islamic propriety, they approved more vigilant patrols by the religious police to ensure that businesses closed during prayer time and they increased budgets for religious universities to expand their staffs and enrolments. In 1986, King Fahd adopted the title 'Custodian of the Two Holy Mosques' to underscore the monarchy's religious character. Revolutionary Iran, however, used the annual pilgrimage to stage demonstrations condemning pro-Western Muslim governments. In 1987, clashes between Iranian pilgrims and Saudi security forces resulted in more than 400 deaths. The end of the Iran–Iraq war in 1988 and Ayatollah Khomeini's death in 1989 eased tensions between the Gulf rivals for a time.

The Iran–Iraq war cast a cloud over the region at the same time that low oil prices forced the Saudis to trim ambitious economic development plans. The cost of a barrel of oil fell from $27 in 1985 to around $14 in 1986. Annual earnings in the latter year amounted to barely 12 per cent of the record mark achieved in 1981. Government planners responded by cutting the budget for basic infrastructure while sustaining defence spending at high levels in the face of the threat posed by Iran. Drawing on foreign reserves to cover budget deficits in the late 1980s, the government allocated funds to expand roads, ports, electricity and desalinating water. Another area of growth was education, as more families enrolled girls in public schools, increasingly staffed by Saudi teachers trained in the previous 20 years.

Expectations by planners that educated Saudis would begin to replace expatriate workers, however, were not fulfilled. For one thing, the quality of science and technical education was deficient. Furthermore, Saudi business owners preferred employing foreign workers: they were considered more qualified, they worked for lower wages than would Saudis, and they were easier to fire. Educated young Saudis found employment in government offices and public sector companies: the pay was better, the hours and working conditions were easier, and they had job security. The preferences of Saudi employers and job seekers meant that the proportion of expatriate workers in the labour force continued to rise. In 1980, they represented half of the total, and by 1990 they accounted for two-thirds.

The general climate of economic austerity during the 1980s fuelled a new wave of political discontent. Per capita income plummeted at the same time as the government imposed charges on previously free public utilities. Disgruntled Saudis grumbled about corruption, extravagant allowances for members of the royal family, and incompetent management of the nation's wealth; but on the surface, the kingdom was calm and dissent was contained.

In foreign affairs, the Soviet invasion of Afghanistan presented the Saudi rulers the opportunity to demonstrate solidarity with fellow Muslims in order to refute critics who condemned their alliance with the United States at the expense of Palestinians. Riyadh lent diplomatic, humanitarian and financial support to Afghan factions, collectively known as the *mujahedin*, resisting the Soviet-backed regime in Kabul. Saudi intelligence cooperated with the US Central Intelligence Agency and Pakistan's military intelligence in channelling arms, equipment and funds to Afghan fighters. Private Saudi charities supported the Afghan jihad by tapping the kingdom's dense network of mosques and religious institutions. Idealistic youths flocked to the mujahedin's headquarters in Peshawar, Pakistan, to take up arms against the infidel Soviets. Newspaper and television coverage of the jihad underscored the kingdom's solidarity with Afghan fighters. When Moscow decided to withdraw its forces in 1988, Saudi citizens and officials celebrated the victory for faithful Muslim fighters. Nobody anticipated that Saudi veterans of the Afghan jihad would ever direct their religious zeal against the monarchy, but Iraq's invasion of Kuwait in August 1990 and Riyadh's response to it transformed the kingdom's political landscape.

THE KUWAIT CRISIS

To understand the crisis over Kuwait, it is necessary to take stock of Saddam Hussein's position after the Iran–Iraq war. He felt threatened by disgruntled officers who blamed him for the strategic blunder of invading Iran. Moreover, economic recovery was hampered by two factors beyond his control. First, low global demand kept oil prices low. Second, he owed billions of dollars to Kuwait and Saudi Arabia. Those two countries could have helped Iraq by forgiving its debt and accepting quotas on oil production to shore up prices. On both counts, Kuwait refused to cooperate. Rather than accept a slow, painful path to economic recovery that might weaken his political position, Saddam decided to invade Kuwait on 2 August 1990. Barely two years after finding its way out of an eight-year war, Iraq was at the centre of a new international crisis.

Saddam apparently expected to use Kuwait as a bargaining chip for concessions on oil production and wartime debt. Instead, he confronted a unified international coalition that insisted he withdraw his forces without conditions. A new factor in global politics may have played a role in Saddam's miscalculation. The Soviet Union was coming unravelled and its leader, Mikhail Gorbachev, and US President George H.W. Bush agreed to wind down the Cold War in a way that did not gratuitously humiliate Moscow. A consequence of the shift in superpower relations was Moscow's unwillingness to defy the United States on a matter such as Iraq's occupation of Kuwait. Saddam may also not have expected Saudi Arabia to invite US military forces to defend the kingdom. To signal his determination to hold fast, at the end of August Saddam announced the formal annexation of Kuwait to Iraq. The United Nations Security Council passed a resolution in November setting a deadline of 15 January 1991 for Iraq to completely withdraw from Kuwait. The resolution authorized the use of force to compel Iraq's compliance. By the end of 1990, the United States and coalition forces were poised to expel the Iraqis from Kuwait. Several last-minute diplomatic efforts to resolve the stand-off failed.

On 16 January 1991, the day after the Security Council deadline had passed, the United States and allied air forces launched a massive aerial offensive against Iraqi military positions and infrastructure. The assault lasted for six weeks before the ground campaign began on 24 February. In just four days of fighting, coalition troops forced the Iraqis to retreat in a rout. Before departing, the Iraqis devastated Kuwait, demolishing buildings, looting property, and setting oilfields on fire. A ceasefire took hold on 28 February.

The next development in Iraq was the eruption of anti-government uprisings in the heavily Shi'i south and the Kurdish north. The United States had called on Iraqis to overthrow Saddam even though President Bush had decided to refrain from direct intervention on behalf of the rebels. The regime was prepared for the uprisings as it had withheld its elite Republic Guard units from the conflict with the United States. In mid-March, a government counteroffensive in the south quelled the Shi'i rebellion. Thousands were killed and fled across the borders to Iran and Saudi Arabia. In the north, Kurdish rebels overran the major towns before facing a government counter-attack. Nearly two million Kurds fled the fighting, with thousands pouring into Iran and Turkey. The United Nations Security Council passed Resolution 688 to establish a safe zone for Kurds north of the 36th parallel beyond which Iraqi aircraft were not allowed. The so-called 'no-fly zone' created a safe haven for Kurds, who set about forming autonomous institutions sheltered by the new security guarantee.

The ill-fated adventure in Kuwait had dire consequences for Iraqi civilians. The United Nations resolution governing the ceasefire included conditions designed to keep Saddam from threatening his neighbours. One of those conditions was that Iraq had to accept UN inspectors to ensure that Baghdad removed its capacity to produce weapons of mass destruction (nuclear, biological and chemical weapons). Iraq was also obliged to renounce claims to Kuwait, pay reparations, and account for the fate of missing Kuwaitis. Saddam resisted full compliance, which in his view would have meant the surrender of Iraqi sovereignty. As a result, Iraq found itself at odds with the United Nations for the next decade, under economic sanctions that brought about shortages of food and medicine. The aftermath of the brief struggle for Kuwait proved far worse than that which followed the much longer war with Iran.

Iraq's August 1990 invasion of Kuwait generated a new phase of political contestation in Saudi Arabia. In the weeks before the invasion, Saudi officials and diplomats had tried to reduce tensions between its neighbours. A last-minute meeting in Jeddah on 1 August between Kuwaiti and Iraqi officials was nothing but deception by Baghdad. As Saddam's forces overran Kuwait, thousands of expatriate workers fled the country while citizens found refuge in Saudi Arabia, where Al Sabah formed a government in exile.

Saudi leaders had to decide whether Saddam Hussein was bent on invading the kingdom. The Bush administration sent political and military officials to Riyadh to persuade the Saudis that they had to open their country to a massive Western military intervention to deter the Iraqi leader. King Fahd agreed with the Americans but needed the approval of the Wahhabi establishment to admit foreign armies onto Saudi soil. The leading clerics delivered a ruling (*fatwa*) that endorsed the government decision as it was a necessity, skirting the fundamental question in Islamic law of whether a Muslim ruler may seek the assistance of infidels against another Muslim ruler. But not all Saudis accepted the ruling. Religious dissidents condemned the government for admitting infidel troops as a betrayal of its commitment to uphold Islamic principles. As far as the ruling family was concerned, Iraq posed a more urgent threat than domestic unrest.

Foreign military forces poured into the kingdom, at first to shore up its defences and eventually to prepare for the January–February 1991 war to expel Iraq from Kuwait. Riyadh was keen to rally as many Arab allies as possible to avoid the appearance of participating in a purely Western-inspired attack on a fellow Arab country. Egypt, Morocco and Syria contributed both political and military support. Yemen refused to go along and expressed its preference for Arab mediation to resolve the crisis. The Saudi government retaliated by expelling some 700,000 Yemeni workers. During the six-week air war, Iraqi troops seized a Saudi border town, al-Khafji, on 29 January. A counter-attack by Saudi and Qatari land forces with coalition air support, however, regained the town, repulsing the single Iraqi thrust into Saudi territory. Baghdad fired surface-to-surface SCUD missiles at Saudi targets, but the United States had anticipated the tactic and set up Patriot anti-missile systems to defend Saudi cities. While international forces succeeded at liberating Kuwait, Saddam Hussein's survival in power meant that Saudi Arabia still had a dangerous neighbour. Deterring him seemed to require a long-term American military presence in the kingdom, a presence that generated intense political controversy. 'Expel the Crusaders' became the slogan for a new generation of Saudi dissidents.

The Iraqi invasion interrupted a robust movement in Kuwait for the restoration of democracy, suspended since 1986. The regional situation had calmed with the end of the Iran–Iraq war, and events in Eastern Europe surrounding the collapse of communism inspired a wave of enthusiasm for democracy around the world. In July 1989, Kuwaiti activists launched a petition to support the revival of constitutional government. After obtaining several thousand signatures, the leaders went to present the petition to Emir Jabir, but he refused to meet with them. The opposition tried to mobilize public support at *diwaniyyas*, a local tradition of salons held at private homes. The government sent the police and National Guard to prevent people from attending and to break them up.

Emir Jabir refused to restore the national assembly, but he needed to take action to defuse the restless mood. In April 1990, he proposed the establishment of a National Council that would consist of 50 elected members and 25 appointed members who were to revise the constitutional powers of the national assembly, presumably to render it toothless. Opposition leaders rejected the initiative, but nearly two-thirds of the electorate voted to approve it in a special election that June. Two months later, the contest between democracy activists and the government was suspended by the Iraqi invasion.

During the seven-month occupation, about one in three Kuwaiti nationals lived in exile. Opposition leaders blamed the government for provoking Baghdad by exceeding Kuwait's OPEC oil production quota and for not alerting citizens to the danger posed by the Iraqi military build-up in the weeks before the invasion. The rulers and ministers gathered in the Saudi town of Taif, where they formed a government in exile. The Bush administration and its Western allies pressed the Kuwaiti leaders for a commitment to restore democracy after liberation. In October, the Crown Prince met with opposition leaders in Jeddah, where they agreed to a constitutional restoration under Al Sabah rule. Meanwhile, Kuwaitis who did not flee the country adapted to life under occupation. Efforts to wage armed resistance were crushed as thousands of Kuwaitis were arrested and sent to prisons in Iraq. Daily life became a matter of survival. The network of neighbourhood cooperative shops met everyday needs for food and basic supplies. The Iraqis allowed Kuwaiti utility workers to manage water and electricity functions, but phone communications to the outside world were severed. The arrival of liberation forces at the end of February 1991 ended the nightmare of occupation, permitted the restoration of Al Sabah rule, and restarted the tug of war between rulers and activists.

The paradox of the decades following Britain's departure is the stability of ostensibly fragile new states and the instability of what appeared to be sturdier states. The emirates and sheikhdoms developed political arrangements that proved capable of withstanding the boom–bust cycle of oil-based economies. In Iran, the shah failed to construct viable political institutions and the monarchy collapsed in the face of a popular revolutionary movement. In Saudi Arabia, a culture gap opened between religious conservatives and a stratum of technocrats and professionals willing to adopt Western ways. The monarchy decided to cope with political instability by reinforcing religious institutions, a tactic that later proved counterproductive. In Iraq, the Baathists whittled down their own political base through a succession of purges, creating a concentration of power that relied on harsh repression and co-optation. In addition to the internal stresses that threatened stability, Iraq's Saddam Hussein twice gambled on invading neighbours to assert supremacy in Gulf affairs. Both times, he miscalculated and wound up squandering lives and treasure on quixotic objectives. The broad picture 20 years after the end of Pax Britannica exhibited continuity in terms of a single foreign power, now the United States, wielding the greater influence and providing security to the Persian Gulf states. The United States and its allies deflected but did not suppress challenges to the status quo from revolutionary Iran and bellicose Iraq. In the early 1990s, the longevity of the new dispensation remained uncertain.

9 Years of Deepening American Intervention

The recent history of the Gulf is marked by governments holding fast in the face of political demands from their citizens, continued dependence on oil revenues for economic prosperity, and heightened intervention by the United States. For a brief moment in 2003, following the American overthrow of Saddam Hussein, it seemed that Washington might be able to impose its will through applying raw military power. The complete breakdown of order in Iraq and the outbreak of a savage insurgency called to mind Machiavelli's centuries-old warning, 'It should be considered that nothing is more difficult to handle, more doubtful of success, nor more dangerous to manage, than to put oneself at the head of introducing new orders.'[1] The United States soon abandoned the dream of birthing democracy in the Middle East to settle for guarding the old order of authoritarian regimes against domestic threats and Iranian expansionism. In 2011, with the exception of Iraq's Baathist regime, the line-up of Gulf states and rulers was roughly the same as 20 years earlier. This is not to say that the region was stagnant. Internal political dynamics showed notable variation, from the reform movements and terrorist campaign in Saudi Arabia to showdowns between democracy activists and rulers in Kuwait and Bahrain. At the level of society and culture, schooling and access to global electronic media broadened the spectrum of pastimes, manners, leisure habits and aspirations for national and religious communities.

THE UNITED STATES

The crisis and war over Kuwait resulted in a massive increase in US military forces stationed in the Gulf. They were destined to stay indefinitely because Saddam Hussein survived the war and anti-government uprisings, so he still loomed as a threat to the Gulf Cooperation Council states. Consequently, their leaders dropped their reluctance to host American forces, calculating that the risk of internal political turmoil was lower than doing without Washington's protection. To keep Saddam on the defensive, the United States and the United Kingdom conducted air patrols over southern Iraq from bases in Kuwait, Saudi Arabia, Bahrain, Qatar and the UAE. US Navy ships based at Bahrain enforced economic sanctions on Iraq. The Bahraini government approved a request to expand the naval base, which hosted over one thousand American military personnel by 2000. The Americans also reached an agreement with Qatar in 1992 for the establishment of a large army base to store equipment and supplies. A few years later, Qatar granted the Americans the right to develop al-Udaid air base, which became the regional headquarters for Central Command. American naval vessels also use Dubai's port at Jebel Ali. As time passed, the high profile of US military forces created problems for the Saudi government. Their stationing in Saudi Arabia was designed to shield the kingdom against Iraq, but it had the unintended effect of stoking dissent, as reformers called for the government to strengthen its capacity to defend the nation on its own rather than depend on foreign forces; religious militants viewed their presence as a military occupation that required armed struggle in the name of jihad against the Americans and the dynasty. In June 1996, anti-American terrorists bombed the main residence for US military personnel in Dhahran. At that point, the Americans transferred their operations to a more remote and secure air base in the desert south of Riyadh (Prince Sultan Air Base).

The massive American military presence in the Gulf was directed not only at Iraq but at Iran as well. That became perfectly clear in March 1993 when the Clinton administration declared a policy of 'dual containment' towards Iraq and Iran. The justification for adopting a hostile posture towards Iran was that it opposed American objectives in the Middle East, namely ensuring stability in the Gulf and advancing Arab–Israeli peace talks by supporting Hamas and Hizballah. American bases dotting the Arab shore and economic sanctions did the job of keeping the Islamic Republic on the defensive. As long as the Gulf's two largest countries were ruled by regimes at odds with Washington, the region would remain one of the most militarized on earth. The overthrow of Saddam Hussein removed the rationale for US forces to stay in Saudi Arabia and they withdrew from their bases by the end of 2003, only to build up an even larger network of military installations in Iraq. Washington shifted from dual containment to scrambling to hold Iraq together and blocking Iranian efforts to profit from Saddam Hussein's removal.

IRAQ

The war and uprisings of 1991 nearly destroyed the Baathist regime. Weeks of intensive aerial bombardment demolished the country's infrastructure but the regime survived for another decade in the face of international sanctions that prevented economic reconstruction. To a certain extent, the sanctions were part of the United States' strategy to deny Saddam Hussein the resources for reviving Iraqi military power and, if possible, to force his removal from power. The 1990s became a test of wills and wile between Washington and Baghdad, with international consensus on punitive sanctions wavering as time passed. By the time that George W. Bush became president in 2001, Saddam's efforts to escape diplomatic and economic isolation had succeeded. It seemed as though he might hang on to power indefinitely. Then, the 11 September 2001 terrorist attacks in the United States gave rise to an aggressive political mood and a strategic outlook that had little patience for international opinion or domestic debate. Less than two years later, American and British forces smashed Saddam's regime and embarked on an ambitious endeavour to remake Iraq into a liberal democracy.

On 3 April 1991, the United Nations (UN) adopted Resolution 687 which defined the terms for ending sanctions imposed on Iraq the previous August. The resolution called on Baghdad to recognize Kuwait's sovereignty and to pay war reparations. It also required Iraq to grant the inspectors of the UN Special Commission on Disarmament (UNSCOM) access to sites for the production of biological, chemical and nuclear weapons. In November 1994, Iraq declared its recognition of Kuwait, but throughout the decade it dragged its feet on cooperating with UNSCOM inspectors. US military pressure and occasional aerial and missile strikes proved effective at prying open Iraq's weapons of mass destruction programme, revealing stockpiles of biological and chemical weapons and facilities for developing nuclear weapons. On the other hand, economic sanctions failed to loosen Saddam Hussein's grip on power; instead, their punitive effects fell hard on ordinary Iraqis, who suffered the highest levels of malnutrition and infant mortality in half a century.

International sympathy for the plight of Iraqis created pressure for easing sanctions. In addition, Baghdad dangled trade and construction contracts before France and Russia in exchange for their support to allow the resumption of oil exports. In April 1995, the UN adopted Resolution 986 whereby Iraq would use revenues from oil sales to purchase food and other humanitarian supplies. Saddam bristled at the strings attached to the Resolution, namely that a portion of oil revenues would be set aside to pay reparations to Kuwait, channel funds to the Kurdish regional government, and offset expenses of the UNSCOM mission. He refused to accept those conditions until he finally relented in November 1996. Initially, the UN set a ceiling on oil revenues at $2 billion every six months. That amount increased as time passed, reaching $8.3 billion in 1999. The Iraqis grew bolder in denying UNSCOM inspectors access to suspected sites. In December 1998, the United States and the United Kingdom launched a punishing four-day aerial assault on military targets and suspected weapons development sites, but the Iraqis would not bend and UNSCOM's mission came to an end.

Saddam's objective throughout his confrontation with the United States was to hold on to power. Economic sanctions diminished the resources at hand to co-opt Iraqis with the generous welfare benefits that had secured acquiescence, if not loyalty, for many years. In the 1990s, Saddam tried a new political strategy of rejuvenating tribal authority. Ever since the 1958 revolution, Iraqi tribal leaders had seen the foundations of their power eroded by urbanization and the extension of central authority to the countryside, including the abolition of tribal courts that had been set up under the British Mandate. Saddam now sought support from tribal leaders to broaden the foundations of his regime. He allowed them to form armed retinues, which became autonomous rural tribal militias; and he granted them authority to settle disputes within their respective tribes and with other tribes.

Iraqi opposition to the Baathist government took two forms during the 1990s: religious Shi'i activists inside the country and political groups in exile. Saddam kept the former under close surveillance, subjecting them to harassment, house arrest and assassination. Exile groups formed the Iraqi National Congress (INC) at a meeting in Vienna in June 1992. Led by Ahmad Chalabi, the INC was comprised of secular nationalists, leftists, religious activists and the Kurdish factions. A second exile opposition party, the Iraqi National Accord, led by Ayad al-Allawi, attracted mostly former Baathists. Neither the exiles nor the religious Shi'as were capable of mounting an effective challenge to Saddam in spite of his isolation.

The one free political space in Iraq was the Kurdish districts, where the establishment of the no-fly zone in 1991 led to the emergence of an autonomous regional government. The two major Kurdish parties, the Kurdish Democratic Party (KDP) and the Patriotic Union of Kurdistan, both of which fielded guerrilla fighters known as *peshmerga*s, gained control. The KDP dominated in the north-western areas of Kurdistan and the Patriotic Union of Kurdistan (PUK) in the south-eastern areas. In May 1992, they organized elections to a provincial assembly, but democratic procedures failed to curtail the intense rivalry that had developed in previous decades. Disputes over the distribution of revenues and control of territory erupted into armed clashes in December 1993. The United States attempted to mediate the parties' differences, but intermittent skirmishes became a regular part of politics in the Kurdish zone. The enmity was so deep that in August 1996, the KDP requested military assistance from Baghdad. Saddam gladly obliged and sent forces to the north for the first time in five years. The incursion also targeted the INC, which had gained the backing of the United States. The KDP's brief alliance with the Baathist regime resulted in the smashing of the INC's base inside the country. In spite of the crisis for Kurdish civilians caused by Baghdad's military thrust, the leaders continued their feud until the United States mediated the Washington Agreement (September 1998) which divided matters of revenue and turf. Against the background of partisan conflict, the Kurds were forming a self-governing enclave. They set up schools with Kurdish-language curriculum and enjoyed the freedom to nurture cultural institutions unfettered by the dictates of Arab nationalist authorities.

A decade after the imposition of sanctions, it appeared Saddam's regime might emerge from economic isolation, notwithstanding the desire of American leaders to be rid of it. Then Al Qaeda's September 2001 attacks transformed the political climate in the United States and the outlook of President George W. Bush. Before 11 September, the Bush administration regarded Iraq through the lens of Gulf security as a regional power to be contained; after 11 September, it saw Iraq as an imminent threat to national security. The White House feared that Iraq may have resumed a nuclear weapons programme after the UNSCOM mission shut down in 1998. If Saddam developed a nuclear device, he might find a way to transfer it to Al Qaeda to carry out a catastrophic terrorist attack on the United States. The prospect of a terrorist wave hitting the United States gained credibility in the wake of a series of anthrax poisonings in October 2001. Iraq's experimentation with anthrax as a biological weapon had been verified in the 1990s. Even though Baghdad did not turn out to be the source for anthrax poisonings, the spectre of Saddam conspiring with Osama bin Laden prompted a shift in American policy.

In his January 2002 State of Union speech, President Bush described Iraq as part of an 'axis of evil', along with Iran and North Korea, so-called rogue states that pursued weapons of mass destruction and sponsored terrorism. In the next few months, Bush administration officials accused Saddam's regime of complicity in the 11 September attacks and of operating a clandestine programme to manufacture weapons of mass destruction. In September 2002, the Bush Doctrine was formally articulated in a document on the National Security Strategy of the United States, which asserted that if Washington deemed it necessary, it would launch a pre-emptive war in order to prevent a possible nuclear attack carried out by terrorists. The next month, the US Congress passed a resolution endorsing the use of force against Iraq.

Saddam responded to American military pressure by agreeing to allow UN weapons inspectors back into the country in November 2002. The UN Monitoring, Verification and Inspection Commission (UNMOVIC) had been established three years earlier under Security Council Resolution 1284. In December, Baghdad provided UNMOVIC documents related to its weapons programmes, and the following month the head of the UN mission announced that there was no clear evidence of ongoing programmes. Nevertheless, the United States was building up for war. While the UN did not issue a new Security Council Resolution authorizing force, Washington persuaded Britain, Spain, Italy and other European countries to participate in an invasion of Iraq. Kuwait turned much of its northern territory into staging ground for American forces, while the other Arab Gulf states allowed the US access to naval and air bases. A final American ultimatum calling for Saddam to step down from power and leave the country set the stage for war. On 19 March 2003, the United States and its allies invaded. The depleted Iraqi armed forces were no match for the Western armies. American generals feared that Iraq would use chemical weapons, as it had against Iran in the 1980s, but it turned out that the Iraqis had not resumed production after all: Saddam was bluffing. He wanted Iran and Iraqi Shi'as, whom he regarded as the most serious threats to his regime, to believe that he still possessed those weapons. The invading forces encountered stiff resistance at a few points, but the advance was rapid and Baghdad fell on 9 April. Saddam fled the city and his regime crumbled. As a matter of eliminating the Baathist regime, the invasion was a success, legitimized by UN Security Council Resolution 1483 on 22 May ending sanctions on Iraq. The post-Saddam period, however, would turn into a nightmare for Iraqis and occupiers alike.

The Bush administration expected that the Iraqi government would continue to function without the Baathist leadership. There was no appreciation of the extent to which the Iraqi government was held together through a dense network of personal ties of loyalty converging on Saddam Hussein, whose removal caused the government to disintegrate. Reshaping Iraq's authoritarian political system with its underlying norms into a democracy with elections, political parties and the rule of law would require years of painstaking negotiation amidst insurgency and sectarian warfare. To the extent that the United States had a plan, it expected to turn over power to a newly formed democratic Iraqi government and pull out its forces by the end of 2003.

Nothing went according to plan. As soon as the Baathist government fell, anarchy broke out. The American military command had not foreseen the need to deploy large numbers of troops to keep order. In April and May, looters plundered unguarded public buildings, gutting hospitals and schools, ministries and factories. Priceless national treasures dating to ancient Mesopotamian civilization were stolen from museums. Massive quantities of weapons and ammunition were plundered from unprotected arsenals, later to resurface in the hands of insurgents and death squads. The breakdown of order compounded the wartime damage to basic services – water, electricity and sanitation. Living conditions for Iraqis deteriorated and remained in shambles for years. The rapid emergence of a deadly insurgency took the White House by surprise. In December 2003, American forces captured Saddam Hussein hiding at a remote farm, but it made no difference to the insurgency, which gathered momentum in the following months.

Against a backdrop of chaos, the initial American attempt to guide Iraq on the path to sovereignty foundered. Washington sent a retired general to head the Office of Reconstruction and Humanitarian Assistance, which was supposed to preside over the return to normal life. That approach lasted less than a month. The United States changed course, sending Ambassador L. Paul Bremer to head a Coalition Provisional Authority with a mandate to set up a sovereign Iraqi government by June 2004. He created an Iraqi Governing Council, comprised of politicians from the various sectarian groups.

While the Americans groped for a way forward, dormant Iraqi political forces sprang to life. The Shi'i Da'wa Party and the

Sunni Muslim Brotherhood resurfaced after decades of furtive underground existence. A second Shi'i party, the Supreme Council for Islamic Revolution in Iraq (SCIRI), transferred headquarters from Iran, whose clerical leaders had presided over its founding in the early 1980s. In addition, a new home-grown Shi'i force led by Muqtada al-Sadr emerged. His father had been a prominent figure in Shi'i clerical circles until he was killed by the Baathist government in 1999. Muqtada lacked his father's scholarly stature, but he proved adept at mobilizing his network, which was deeply entrenched in Baghdad's densely packed, mostly Shi'i quarter, which now became known as Sadr City. His militia, the Mahdi Army, became a fierce weapon in the nascent sectarian war with the Sunni Muslims in addition to attacking American troops in Baghdad and British forces in Basra.

Ayatollah Ali al-Sistani represented traditionalist clerics who believed politics should be left to politicians while religious experts should offer advice and guidance. American officials preferred dealing with familiar exile activists such as Ahmad Chalabi of the INC and Ayad al-Allawi of the Iraqi National Accord. The Baath Party was the one political force the Americans would not countenance. In fact, not long after arriving in Baghdad, Ambassador Bremer ordered a ban on any Baathist above a certain grade of membership from working for the government. He also announced the dissolution of the Iraqi Army and of all security organs. At one stroke, Bremer created a sullen mass of 300,000 men, many of them professional army officers, lacking jobs and nursing resentment towards the occupying power. It was a sure recipe for boosting the anti-American insurgency brewing throughout the country. Given the largely Sunni complexion of the Baath Party, Iraqi Sunnis viewed its banishment as an attack on their community and a signal that the Americans intended to hand power to the country's Shi'as and Kurds.

Attacks on American troops escalated in June and July 2004. Commanders in Iraq acknowledged they were now engaged in guerrilla warfare even if officials in Washington imagined the violence represented the death throes of Saddam's regime and would shortly subside. In August, a truck bomb destroyed the headquarters of the UN mission in Baghdad, killing the head of the mission, veteran Brazilian diplomat Sergio Vieira de Mello and about sixteen others. American efforts to combat the insurgency were frustrated by its splintered character, reflected in local bands possessing an endless supply of weapons, thanks to the American failure to guard military stores and arsenals in spring 2003. Former army officers, unemployed

Baathist officials and religious militants of various stripes were no less effective for lacking a unified national leadership. Arab volunteers from other countries infiltrated Iraq, some of them enlisting with Al Qaeda in Mesopotamia, led by the Jordanian Abu Mus'ab al-Zarqawi. He made his mark by sending suicide bombers against American positions and slaughtering Shi'as, who, according to his extreme religious outlook, were infidels deserving death. Sectarian violence escalated as Muqtada al-Sadr's Mahdi Army and the SCIRI's Badr Brigade carried out revenge killings against Sunnis.

Inside the safety of the Green Zone, a vast walled compound of government buildings, American officials and the Iraqi Governing Council agreed on steps to form an interim government that would draft a constitution that Iraqis would then either approve or reject in a national referendum. On 28 June 2004, Bremer handed authority to the interim government headed by Ayad al-Allawi, formally re-establishing Iraqi sovereignty under the shadow of foreign occupation. Allawi's primary task was to prepare for elections to a transitional national assembly. Most Sunnis considered the entire political process a sham and boycotted the January 2005 balloting, leaving the field to the Shi'i and Kurdish parties. The main Shi'i parties, Da'wa and SCIRI, ran as the United Iraqi Alliance and took almost half the seats. The Kurdish parties took the second largest share of seats. In April, Da'wa Party leader Ibrahim al-Ja'fari became prime minister, heading a cabinet whose ministers took the opportunity to purge the civil service and fill it with loyalists. In October, a draft constitution was submitted to a national referendum. Among its contentious points was a provision pushed by the Kurdish parties that would allow the combination of provinces into regional governments. Sunni Arabs opposed the provision on the grounds that it could lead to Iraq's partition or, if the southern provinces combined into a single majority Shi'i region, to Iranian domination. Notwithstanding Sunni reservations, the constitution passed, and Iraqis prepared for yet another election in December 2005 to vote for a national assembly under the new constitution. This time Sunnis did participate, reckoning they would have more say in shaping the re-born Iraqi nation inside legal institutions than through rejectionism. Weeks before the election, an Iraqi court found Saddam Hussein guilty of ordering mass killings of Iraqi Shi'as in 1982. The former leader's conviction coincided with jostling among politicians for cabinet portfolios. It took five months for the national assembly to produce a coalition government led by Nuri al-Maliki of the Da'wa Party. Maliki's coalition, formed in

May 2006, included representatives from SCIRI, the Iraqi Accord Front (a Sunni religious party) and Allawi's secular Iraqi National List. Three years after the fall of Saddam, Iraq finally had a constitutional, elected government. Outside the Green Zone, the lot of ordinary Iraqis was one of misery and fear.

On 22 February 2006, an enormous explosion destroyed a Shi'i shrine in Samarra. There followed a huge escalation of sectarian violence, as Shi'i militias retaliated against Sunnis and their mosques. Cities with mixed populations – Baghdad, Kirkuk and Basra – underwent terrible spells of killings perpetrated by sectarian death squads, resulting in segregation of Sunni and Shi'i by flight and death. The number of internal refugees reached 2 million, almost matching the number of Iraqi refugees living outside the country. Large swathes of the mostly Sunni north-west provinces, especially Anbar, were under the control of insurgent groups. American forces were entwined in an Iraqi civil war that appeared to have no end. Against a backdrop of hellish violence, the Iraqi government scheduled Saddam Hussein's execution for 30 December 2006. Amateur videotape of the event showed partisans of Muqtada al-Sadr taunting the former ruler as they prepared him for the gallows. Three-and-a-half years after his fall from power, his punishment gratified survivors of his reign of terror but it did nothing to stem the carnage raging from Basra to Mosul.

In the United States, the November 2006 elections dealt a blow to President Bush by giving Democrats a majority in the House of Representatives and the Senate. Even with the political current turning against him, Bush ignored calls to pull out American forces. Instead, he appointed a new commander, General David Petraeus, to preside over an escalation of the war effort with 30,000 additional troops. The escalation, known as the surge, was intended to reduce violence to the point that Iraq's elected leadership could re-establish authority over the country. General Petraeus used the build-up to implement a counter-insurgency strategy that he had devised based on protecting civilians and thereby winning their support for the government. The strategy required deploying troops to urban neighbourhoods and villages rather than concentrating them in strongholds isolated from the population. The timing for his strategy was propitious.

In the second half of 2006, a growing number of Sunni tribal sheikhs in Anbar decided to fight Al Qaeda in Mesopotamia, which had taken over a number of towns and cities, where it used brutal measures to enforce its puritanical notions of religious rectitude. The shift in the political alignment of Anbar's sheikhs became known as the Awakening, or *sahwa*. American commanders suddenly found Iraqi Sunnis fighting with them against Al Qaeda rather than with Al Qaeda against them. At first, suicide and car bombings increased, but in the second half of 2007, violence began to subside, abetted in part by the results of earlier sectarian cleansing in cities that rearranged residential patterns along segregated lines as Sunnis and Shi'as retreated to the safe confines of co-religionists. Furthermore, after a bloody clash in Kerbala between the Mahdi Army and a rival Shi'i militia, Muqtada al-Sadr decided to keep his forces on the sidelines, a move that de-escalated communal strife. As the violence diminished, Prime Minister Maliki's government negotiated a Status of Forces Agreement with Washington, agreeing in November 2008 that the Americans would completely withdraw combat forces in three years.

Newly elected American President Barack Obama promised shortly after taking office to implement that agreement, starting with a reduction of American forces to 50,000 by August 2010. How Iraq would fare once a large American military presence was absent was the question nobody could answer. The result of Iraq's March 2010 parliamentary election did nothing to clarify the situation as Prime Minister Maliki's State of Law slate won two fewer seats (89) than Ayyad al-Allawi's Iraqi National Movement (91), a coalition of secular groups that received strong support from Sunnis. Given the need to build a majority of 163 deputies, it was a tall order to put together a coalition government, and the party leaders did not reach agreement until December. In the interim, insurgents exploited the mood of uncertainty by escalating attacks on government forces and terrorist bombings of civilians. Whether Iraqis had already passed through the worst phase of violence or were merely enjoying a pause while rival forces prepared for a new round of civil war when the Americans leave at the end of 2011 remained an open question.

IRAN

In the 1980s, Iran's revolutionary political forces defeated domestic and foreign enemies. They out-manoeuvred moderates in Mehdi Barzargan's Liberation Movement and crushed rival radicals like the Mojahedin and the Communists. On the battle-front, they thwarted Saddam Hussein's aggressive designs.

While Khomeini did not succeed in defeating the Baathist regime and ousting Saddam, and the last years of the war ravaged Iran's economy, the revolution was preserved. With the struggle for survival accomplished, latent tensions among revolutionary political forces became manifest. The first decade of the Islamic Republic was consumed with internal consolidation and foreign confrontation. In its second decade, internal political tensions were expressed in two kinds of rivalry, one between government institutions and a second between pragmatic leaders seeking to dilute revolutionary zeal and ideologues devoted to fanning the revolutionary flame.

President Ali Akbar Hashemi Rafsanjani made economic recovery from the ravages of war his priority. When he began his first term in 1989, Iran suffered from high inflation, shortages and the strains of demobilization. Iraqi attacks had damaged the oil refinery at Abadan and export facilities along the Gulf coast. To address these problems, Rafsanjani appointed a cabinet dominated by technocrats. His experts drafted the Islamic Republic's first five-year plan for the economy, one that emphasized privatizing industry, trade and agriculture in addition to encouraging foreign investment. In the early 1990s, the economy grew, stimulated by higher oil prices. Rafsanjani also boosted government resources by obtaining a loan from the International Monetary Fund in exchange for pledging to curtail subsidies, reform the currency and privatize some industries.

Advancing structural economic reform was hampered by Iran's troubled relations with Western governments and by entrenched domestic interests that benefited from the status quo. Iran needed Western investment and technical assistance to rejuvenate the petroleum sector which had suffered damage and neglect during the years of revolution and war. Rafsanjani welcomed bids by American companies for contracts to purchase oil and lend expertise to raise production, but powerful factions in Tehran and Washington bent on demonizing the other side undermined the resumption of commercial relations. Lingering American anger over the hostage affair, Iranian support for groups hostile to Washington's sponsorship of Israeli–Palestinian peace talks and suspicion of official Iranian complicity in assassinating dissidents in European cities and in bombings of Jewish targets in Argentina strengthened the American faction that wanted to isolate rather than engage with Iran. Commercial detente between Tehran and Washington ended abruptly in 1995 when Congress imposed sanctions. Comparable dynamics bedevilled the revival of trade with

Germany and Great Britain, although Iran did develop robust commerce with France and Russia.

The second obstacle to structural reform was a combination of powerful domestic interests controlling foundations and public sector companies. The foundations, in Persian, *bonyads*, were vast enterprises that the government confiscated from the monarchy in 1979. The Pahlavi Foundation alone owned thousands of properties and businesses. Rather than selling the foundations' assets, the Islamic Republic preserved them for the benefit of government officials, clerical families and well-connected merchants who made enormous fortunes from the foundations. In the early 1990s, they accounted for roughly 40 per cent of the economy. Supporters of the foundations in clerical institutions and the Majles blocked most efforts at privatization. Another domestic factor that hampered structural reform stemmed from Rafsanjani's attempt to channel the energies of the radical Islamic Revolutionary Guard Corps and the Basij militias into economic enterprises, giving them shares in defence industries and construction companies. That initiative failed to temper their politics and it augmented the hold of public agencies on the economy. By the end of Rafsanjani's second term in 1997, he had little to show for his technocratic approach to economic policy.

As for foreign policy, Rafsanjani muted strident calls for exporting revolution and argued that the Islamic Republic could foster change in Muslim countries by serving as an example of fidelity to religious principles. Impulses to export revolution, however, did not abate. A powerful faction of clerics and activists believed it essential to preserve the Islamic Republic's original spirit of sweeping away corrupt rulers. The regional crisis over Iraq's invasion of Kuwait highlighted this division in the Iranian leadership. Rafsanjani's faction supported the UN resolution demanding Iraqi withdrawal, whereas hardliners condemned Western military intervention. To some extent, though, Rafsanjani succeeded in moderating foreign policy. Thus, after Iraq's ouster from Kuwait, Iran and Saudi Arabia renewed official ties and exchanged high-level visits. Other Gulf Cooperation Council states followed with a delegation to Iran in 1992.

Rafsanjani's bid to reintegrate Iran into the regional political order extended to Egypt, long condemned by the Islamic Republic for its 1979 peace treaty with Israel. His gestures towards Washington did not enjoy as much success. When he helped secure the release of two American hostages held by pro-Iranian groups in Lebanon, hardliners in Tehran issued incendiary declarations of hostility towards the United States.

Rafsanjani signalled interest in having Iran attend the October 1991 Madrid Conference for Arab–Israeli peace negotiations, but the Americans took the August 1991 assassination of former Iranian Prime Minister Shapour Bakhtiar in Paris to mean that the Islamic Republic was still an outlaw nation. Rafsanjani fared no better when Bill Clinton became American President in 1993. Just a few months after his inauguration, his administration announced a new policy of 'dual containment' towards the Gulf, directed against Iran as well as Iraq. Washington could not decide whether Rafsanjani was playing a double game, organizing bombings of Jewish targets in Argentina and killing dissidents in Europe while seeking a bilateral thaw, or incapable of curbing hard-line elements in the government. Rafsanjani continued to court American oil companies until President Clinton issued an executive order against investing in Iran's oil industry.

As the end of Rafsanjani's second term approached, he tried to pass a constitutional amendment that would allow him to run for a third term, but Supreme Leader Ali Khamenei rebuffed him, hoping that one of his clients, Majles Speaker Abdullah Natiq-Nuri, would become the next president. At the same time, Khamenei kept Rafsanjani in a strong leadership position by moving him over to head the Expediency Council, a body that was created in the late 1980s to resolve legislative stalemates between the elected Majles and the appointed Council of Guardians. The pressures building for reform, however, elevated Muhammed Khatami to the presidency with nearly 70 per cent of the vote. The result was astonishing and the political movement that Khatami led became known for the Persian calendar date of the election, 2 Khordad (23 May 1997). Khatami was Minister of Islamic Culture and Guidance in Rafsanjani's first term. In that post, he had encouraged a cultural opening by lifting restrictions on the press and loosening censorship of films and music. Khatami's platform included delegating real authority to elected bodies – the Majles along with municipal and provincial councils – fostering a liberal political atmosphere and establishing the rule of law. Students and educated youth, women and radicals-turned-reformers harboured high hopes, whereas the clerical bodies, the judiciary and hardliners in the Revolutionary Guards were determined to thwart him.

Each time Khatami tried to pass laws that expanded political participation or constrained appointed clerical bodies, the Council of Guardians stood in his way, using its constitutional power of review to void one bill after another on the grounds they were 'un-Islamic'. On the other hand, in the early months of his presidency, newspapers and magazines proliferated, professional

associations sprouted, and non-governmental associations dealing with the environment, youth and women multiplied. In
response, the judiciary, the security organizations and the Special
Clergy Courts launched a ruthless campaign against liberal
measures. Khatami's minister of Islamic culture and guidance
encouraged a flourishing periodical press but the judiciary issued
closure orders against one newspaper after another, shutting
down more than 100 periodicals in five years. Reformist clerics
were hauled before the Special Clergy Court for inquisitions. In
November 1998, a number of prominent activists and writers for
the reform cause were murdered. In response, Khatami insisted
on upholding the rule of law and investigating the murders. The
probe led to arrests of officials in the Ministry of Intelligence.
Political tensions heightened in summer 1999 when university
students protested the closure of yet another reformist newspaper. In response, hundreds of vigilantes raided Tehran University,
beating up hundreds of students.

The first election contest between President Khatami and the
hardliners took place in the February 2000 vote for the Majles.
The president's backers organized the Islamic Participation
Front to recruit candidates and to campaign for them. The
Front's slate took nearly 70 per cent of the vote. The following month, however, its main organizer was shot and seriously
wounded. Meanwhile, the Council of Guardians disqualified
a number of victors in the recent election and the crackdown
on the press continued. The judiciary harassed and arrested
members of the Majles. Khatami appeared powerless to counter
the multi-pronged onslaught by government bodies managed
by unelected clerics beholden only to the Supreme Leader Ali
Khamenei. Even though he easily won re-election to a second
term in June 2001, support for the 'smiling cleric' melted away
as followers concluded he was either unable or unwilling to
advance his liberal agenda. The first sign of disaffection came in
a very low turnout by voters for 2003 municipal elections, opening the way for Iran's conservatives to begin their comeback.

President Khatami enjoyed modest success in foreign policy,
improving ties to the Gulf Cooperation Council, Egypt and
the European Union (EU). He announced a major shift in the
Islamic Republic's position towards the Palestinian–Israeli peace
talks, declaring that Iran would accept terms that Palestinian
negotiators reached with Israel. In 2000, he declared an initiative for a Dialogue between Civilizations. In that framework,
he proposed a series of cultural exchanges with the United
States. The Clinton administration saw Khatami's initiative as
a promising signal that a major source of tensions in the Gulf

could be resolved, but hardliners in Tehran again issued strident declarations that sabotaged the prospect for rapprochement.

When President George W. Bush took office in January 2001, the outlook for relations with Iran was to continue Clinton's policy of dual containment. An opening for improved ties followed the 11 September attacks on the United States and Washington's decision to overthrow the Taliban. Tehran had considered attacking Afghanistan three years earlier when Taliban fighters killed eight Iranian diplomats in the course of seizing a northern Afghan city. Relations between Kabul and Tehran remained tense because the Taliban's narrow Sunni doctrine held Shi'as in disdain as heretics. Consequently, Iran cooperated with the American campaign to overthrow the Taliban in October 2001 and attended the international talks at Bonn to establish a new Afghan government led by Hamid Karzai. But as always, hardliners in Tehran helped sabotage any rapprochement with the Great Satan: the Revolutionary Guards gave refuge to Al Qaeda members fleeing Afghanistan. In January 2002, President Bush labelled Iran a member of the 'axis of evil' in his State of the Union address, marking the ascent of hardliners in Washington. Despite President Khatami's endeavours to ease tensions, the voices of hardliners opposed to Israeli–Palestinian peace talks and American regional influence made the stronger impression on American ears.

The Bush administration's proclamations that the United States sought regime change in Iran, that is, the overthrow of the Islamic Republic, added weight to the feeling in Tehran that it needed to advance its nuclear programme. Muhammed Reza Shah had initiated a nuclear programme in the 1970s with technical assistance from the United States, France and Germany. The revolution interrupted the programme for about a decade before fear of Iraqi weapons of mass destruction prompted the resumption of efforts to develop nuclear technology with assistance from Pakistani scientists. In 1995, Russia agreed to complete work on two nuclear reactors at the Gulf port of Bushehr that the Germans had begun when the shah was in power.

The United States and Iran entered a new phase of confrontation following disclosure by an Iranian opposition group in August 2002 that Iran was operating a secret programme to enrich uranium, a vital step towards developing a nuclear weapon. The EU took the lead in talks with the Iranian government, which agreed in November 2003 to suspend uranium enrichment and to cooperate with International Atomic Energy Agency inspectors. At the end of Khatami's second term, the question surrounding Iran's nuclear programme was whether it was solely for increasing energy production or whether it also had a military purpose. Tehran maintained that it intended peaceful uses only, but intentions are hard to pin down and easy to change. Iranian proponents of developing nuclear power could observe that Saddam Hussein's failure to acquire nuclear arms left him vulnerable to American invasion whereas North Korea, the other 'axis of evil' member, did acquire them and effectively deterred military action by the United States.

The onslaught from the judiciary, the Council of Guardians and the Supreme Leader sapped morale from the 2 Khordad Movement during Khatami's second term. At the same time, the mayor of Tehran, Mahmud Ahmadinejad, was building a political movement rooted in populism and declarations of fidelity to the original spirit of the revolution. During the war against Iraq, Ahmadinejad had served with the Revolutionary Guard, which became a bastion of the country's hardliners. In the 1990s, he was provincial governor in a northern province before winning the Tehran mayoral race in May 2003. His speeches blended calls for social justice, expressions of firm belief in the imminent return of the Twelfth Imam, and exhortations to honour the memory of the martyrs of the revolution and the war. His rough-hewn manner contrasted sharply with the polished sophistication of Khatami and Rafsanjani. While critics derided him as an ignorant peasant, he made a virtue of his persona as the underdog, a simple, hardworking pious man taking on the arrogant and corrupt establishment. He also benefited from strong support from the Basij and the Islamic Revolutionary Guard. Former president Rafsanjani got the largest share of votes in the first stage, multi-candidate election but not a majority, so he had to face Ahmadinejad, who finished second, in a run-off. Much to the surprise of Iranian and foreign political observers, the lesser known mayor of Tehran scored a big victory, making him the first president since Abolhasan Bani-Sadr to come from outside the ranks of the clergy.

Ahmadinejad had no use for either Rafsanjani's pragmatism to remedy the country's economic ills by deploying experts and technocrats to privatize the *bonyad*s or for Khatami's vision of a post-revolutionary liberalization of politics and culture. The Council of Guardians was relieved to see the last of Khatami and threw its support behind the new president. In tune with that body's impulses, Ahmadinejad clamped down on the press and the burgeoning internet blogosphere. He initiated a new round of purges at universities to prevent professors from contaminating young minds with Western ideas. In the foreign arena, he alarmed Western leaders with remarks calling for

Israel's destruction and declaring the Holocaust a historical fiction. But there was more to the president than slogans and culture war against the reformers. Many Iranians welcomed his calls for social justice and using oil revenues to alleviate the burdens of poverty for millions of his countrymen. Ahmadinejad frequently visited Iran's neglected small towns and villages, issuing development grants and loans as displays of his compassion for the poor. While he condemned corruption as a cause of social inequality, he used his office to dispense patronage to his own backers, namely the Basij and the Revolutionary Guards, whose heroic sacrifices and martyrs he constantly celebrated in speeches. He awarded construction contracts to companies operated by the two military–industrial organizations.

Ahmadinejad's pugnacious speeches on foreign affairs and vocal support for Iran's nuclear programme signalled a resumption of hostility towards the United States. In February 2006, Iran ended its suspension of uranium enrichment. Washington responded by pressing the UN Security Council to impose economic sanctions if Iran refused to suspend its activities. Ahmadinejad defied the Western powers and boasted that Iran was accelerating its enrichment programme. In July, the UN issued a resolution calling on Iran to cease enrichment or face sanctions. Tehran refused to comply and in December the Security Council approved Resolution 1737, which placed sanctions on Iranian individuals and groups involved in the nuclear programme. The EU continued its diplomatic efforts to resolve the dispute, holding out promises of economic aid for cooperation and the threat of sanctions otherwise, but Russian opposition to a new round of punitive sanctions in the UN Security Council hampered the European negotiators.

The Western powers looked forward to Iran's June 2009 presidential election as a possible way out of the impasse if a moderate candidate defeated Ahmadinejad. Reformist leaders felt they had a good chance to regain the office. Four years of populist policies had not improved living conditions for the poorest Iranians; high-profile corruption campaigns had done little more than make enemies among well-connected clerics and merchants; and the president's provocative public declarations about the Holocaust and Israel left many Iranians uneasy at the prospect of returning to the international isolation of the 1980s. Two candidates, both veteran politicians in the Islamic Republic, ran for president under the banner of reform. Mir-Hussein Musavi was Prime Minister during the war against Iraq, and Mehdi Karrubi was Speaker of the Majles during the early 1990s and early 2000s. They drew broad support from the 2 Khordad Movement's constituency of students, youth and women as well as from Rafsanjani's pragmatist faction.

To signal the Musavi campaign's fidelity to Islam, it adopted the colour green, said by tradition to be the Prophet Muhammad's favourite colour. During and after the campaign, supporters of reform donned green clothing, scarves and headbands. As a result, the term 'Green Revolution' was adopted to refer to the political movement for reform. Popular enthusiasm for the Green Revolution and efforts by the Basij and Revolutionary Guards to rally Ahmadinejad's supporters resulted in a very large turnout. It was expected that tallying the vote would take several days, but the president's men at the Ministry of Interior announced a convincing victory for the incumbent just two days after the election. Ali Khamenei rushed to confirm the result without awaiting the formality of notification by the Council of Guardians. Huge crowds protested the outcome and accused the government of stealing the election. In the following weeks, demonstrators came out to condemn both Ahmadinejad and Khamenei. The government sent the Basij militia into the streets to attack protestors. In the first few weeks of turmoil, around two hundred demonstrators were killed. Musavi, Karrubi and their supporters wilted under the onslaught of vigilante attacks and arrests. By the end of 2009, Khamenei, Ahmadinejad and their clerical allies were firmly in control of the country.

The election result dismayed leaders in the West, who were hoping that a new leadership would be receptive to limits on Iran's nuclear programme. American President Barack Obama strove to forge a united international position on the issue in coordination with the UN Security Council and the EU. In May 2010, the UN's International Atomic Energy Agency reported that Iran's nuclear reactors had made strides towards producing the fuel necessary to yield two bombs. The Security Council then approved new economic sanctions against Iran while the United States and the EU announced separate, harsher sanctions. The Iranian government's response was to reiterate the peaceful nature of the programme and its sovereign right to nuclear power, a point it underscored in August when the plant in Bushehr began to generate electricity.

Neighbouring countries are nervous about the prospect of a nuclear weapon in the hands of Mahmud Ahmadinejad, who has repeatedly affirmed his belief that the advent of the Hidden Imam, a messianic event, is imminent. The confrontation over Iran's nuclear programme predated the current Iranian president and cannot be detached from political and ideological contests between Tehran and rival powers in the region. Although the

1978–9 Revolution transformed Iran from a secular monarchy into a religious republic, it did not affect the deep-rooted sentiment of national grandeur that considers it natural for Iran to be the great power of the Gulf by virtue of size, population, culture and history. Since the end of Khatami's term in 2005, the Islamic Republic has positioned itself as an opponent to the regional status quo. It offers firm support for Hizballah in Lebanon and Hamas in Palestine; its leaders make strident threats against Israel; in Iraq it bolsters Shi'i parties and projects influence through religious tourism and reconstruction assistance.

The leaders of Arab Gulf states, Egypt and Jordan share the view that Tehran poses a threat to stability. The stakes in the confrontation are similar to what they were during the Arab Cold War when Egypt's President Nasser challenged monarchies and pro-Western governments. In the end, Nasser was defeated on battlefields in Yemen and Sinai. If the confrontation between Iran and the United States escalates to open warfare, the fallout for the Gulf and the rest of the Middle East is unfathomable but few expect it to be contained.

SAUDI ARABIA

The Saudi government's decision to invite foreign forces in August 1990 triggered a wave of political turmoil that lasted for several years. A culture conflict between liberals and religious conservatives had already been simmering in the 1980s. Spokesmen for the religious conservatives became known as 'the sheikhs of the awakening', or *sahwa* sheikhs. The two most prominent sahwa sheikhs were Safar al-Hawali and Salman al-Awda, professors at religious universities in Mecca and Riyadh, respectively. They noted that even though the government had spent billions of dollars on arms in the 1980s, its defences were still incapable of warding off the Iraqi threat. In condemning the government for allowing hundreds of thousands of Western troops into the Islamic heartland, Hawali and Awda cited the Islamic principle against seeking military assistance from infidels, the same principle that Wahhabi ulama blamed Emir Abdullah ibn Faisal for violating when he invited Ottoman forces to intervene in his struggle against rival emirs a century earlier.

The government faced criticism from liberal activists as well. In December 1990, a group of merchants, professors and technocrats submitted a petition to King Fahd calling for the establishment of measures to ensure government accountability to citizens. The liberals proposed a list of institutional reforms: the creation of a consultative council to draft laws and supervise government bodies; the revival of municipal councils; the establishment of professional associations; broadening the scope of expression in the media; allowing women to participate in public affairs; and placing limits on religious authorities, especially the Committee for Commanding Virtue and Forbidding Vice (the religious police). In response to the liberal petition, a group of ulama and sahwa sheikhs published a Letter of Demands to King Fahd. In addition to supporting the idea of a consultative council, the Letter called for broadening the scope of Islamic law in public life by reviewing statutes with a view to repealing any that were not in accord with Islamic law and by appointing ulama and graduates of religious universities to monitor government offices. King Fahd angrily rejected the Letter's suggestion that he was lax in upholding Islam and the authorities arrested some of the signers and barred others from preaching.

On the other hand, King Fahd did respond to calls for reform by issuing the Basic Law of Government in March 1992. The Basic Law affirmed the country's form of government as a hereditary monarchy under Al Saud and the government's role in upholding Islam and protecting the Holy Places. The Basic Law stated that citizens have a duty to obey the government and that the government ensures the welfare of citizens by providing jobs, education and health care. The Basic Law seemed to satisfy both liberal and religious demands for the establishment of a Consultative Council to advise the government on matters of public interest. In October 1993, King Fahd appointed the council's 60 members, mostly from the ranks of Saudis with degrees from the kingdom's secular and Western universities.

The sahwa sheikhs, however, were not satisfied with the Basic Law, which ignored most of the items in the Letter of Demand. In September 1992, they sent a Memorandum of Advice to the head of the official Wahhabi religious estate, Sheikh Abdulaziz ibn Baz. This document called for building up a strong national military to eliminate the need to depend on Western powers. In foreign affairs, it protested the country's alignment with the United States as a betrayal of Islamic solidarity with the Palestinians. In the domestic arena, it urged the government to use oil wealth to ensure the welfare of citizens and their access to education and health care. It also called for enforcing the prohibition in Islamic law against usury by barring banks from charging interest. Sheikh Ibn Baz denounced the Memorandum for violating the taboo against public criticism of legitimate rulers. The impasse between the authorities and the sahwa sheikhs ended with a crackdown on the dissidents. By the end of 1994, over one hundred activists were in prison, including Awda and Hawali.

Religious dissidents then turned to violence. On 13 November 1995 militants exploded a truck bomb outside a building housing the US training mission for the Saudi National Guard in Riyadh. Five Americans and two Indians perished in the explosion. A Saudi investigation led to the arrest of four Saudi nationals, three of whom had fought in the Afghan jihad during the 1980s. It turned out that they had plotted the bombing to avenge the execution of a comrade a few months earlier. A Saudi court condemned the four men to death and they were executed in May 1996. The next month, a massive truck bomb in eastern Saudi Arabia destroyed the Khobar Towers, a residential complex for American military personnel. The attack killed 19 Americans and wounded 400 Saudis, Americans and others. This time the perpetrators were apparently Saudi Shi'i extremists and agents of Iranian intelligence. In the wake of the two bombings, Saudi authorities rounded up more than 3,000 activists. Many of them underwent torture in prison. Rather than taming the militants, physical abuse intensified their radicalism and convinced them that government officials represented as much of an enemy as did the United States. In 1999, the government shifted and adopted more lenient tactics to deal with religious dissidents. It abolished torture and granted amnesty to many detainees. The two sahwa leaders, Sheikhs Hawali and Awda, gained their freedom in June 1999.

After the suppression of the dissident movement inside the kingdom, opposition activists gathered in exile. One branch of the opposition made its headquarters in London. The Committee for the Defence of Legitimate Rights was formed in Saudi Arabia in May 1994 and then moved to the United Kingdom to escape the crackdown. Neither of its two leading spokesmen came from the ranks of the ulama: Muhammad al-Masari was a professor of physics and Saad al-Faqih was a medical doctor. Using fax machines and the internet, they escalated their attacks on the royal family, accusing it of corruption, failing to implement Islamic law, and persecuting sincere religious leaders like the sahwa sheikhs. In March 1996, Masari and Faqih split, with the latter forming a new organization, the Movement for Islamic Reform in Arabia. Their anti-government messages reached like-minded dissidents in the kingdom, but failed to instigate public protests.

A second branch of the opposition materialized in Sudan under Osama bin Laden. His father, Muhammed bin Laden, had immigrated to Saudi Arabia from Yemen in the early 1930s, when King Abdulaziz was consolidating control over Hijaz. Muhammed bin Laden grew enormously wealthy by securing bids for construction contracts and road-building projects. By the time Osama bin Laden was born in 1957, his father's enterprises had expanded to encompass real estate and manufacturing. When he enrolled to study business administration at King Abdulaziz University in Jeddah, it appeared that he would join the family business. But before completing his studies, he decided to travel to Afghanistan to support the jihad against the Soviet Union and Kabul's communist government. He spent four years in Peshawar assisting volunteers for the jihad and using his family connections to raise funds for the cause. In 1988, he established an organization for keeping track of volunteers and funds. He named the organization *al-qa'ida*, or 'the base'. When the Soviets decided to withdraw their forces from Afghanistan, he returned to Saudi Arabia, as did hundreds of other Saudi volunteers.

In August 1990, Bin Laden met with Saudi leaders to propose that he form a volunteer fighting force to deter Saddam Hussein from attacking Saudi Arabia, but the leaders thought the Americans would prove more effective. In the post-war period, Bin Laden supported the sahwa sheikhs' criticisms of dependence on Washington and insufficient commitment to Islamic principles. He left the country during the crackdown on dissidents, relocating to Sudan, where an Islamic regime had come to power in 1989. With a secure base in Khartoum, Bin Laden cultivated contacts with religious militants in Egypt, Bosnia and Yemen.

In 1996, Washington and Riyadh pressed the Sudanese government to expel Bin Laden, whereupon he relocated to Afghanistan. Shortly after arriving there, in August 1996, he issued a declaration of jihad against the United States on the grounds that American forces were not in Saudi Arabia as defenders but as military occupiers. Two years later, Al Qaeda carried out its first major attack on American targets, detonating massive truck bombs to destroy the American embassies in Nairobi, Kenya and Dar es Salaam, Tanzania. The United States retaliated with missile strikes against an Al Qaeda training camp in Afghanistan and a pharmaceutical company in Khartoum that Washington suspected of manufacturing materials to use in chemical weapons. Al Qaeda next struck in October 2000 by detonating explosives on a small craft next to an American navy destroyer, the USS *Cole*, anchored in Yemen's Aden harbour.

The 1998 and 2000 attacks grew out of Bin Laden's decision to wage jihad against the United States, which he deemed 'the far enemy', instead of targeting Muslim regimes he considered illegitimate, 'the near enemy'. Washington was frustrated that it could not deter or destroy Al Qaeda, but neither attack provoked an urgent sense among Americans that their country should go to war against Bin Laden. The 11 September 2001 attacks on the United States changed that. That morning, 19 Al Qaeda operatives (including 15 Saudis) hijacked four civilian airliners and crashed two of them into New York City's World Trade Center, bringing down the Twin Towers. They flew a third airplane into the Pentagon, the heart of US military power. The fourth airplane may have been intended to strike the White House or the Capitol Building, but passengers heroically struggled with the hijackers and the plane went down in a field in western Pennsylvania.

Altogether, Al Qaeda's attack killed nearly 3,000 people. President Bush announced that the Taliban must hand over Bin Laden and his associates or face the wrath of the United States. The Taliban refused to deliver Bin Laden. On 7 October 2001 American forces invaded Afghanistan and teamed up with the Taliban's Afghan enemies, the Northern Alliance, to overthrow the Taliban regime. Bin Laden and Al Qaeda escaped the Americans and relocated to the Pakistan side of the border, taking refuge in the rugged terrain with Pashtun tribesmen who paid only nominal allegiance to the Pakistani authorities.

In Saudi Arabia (and in the Muslim world in general), few people believed that Al Qaeda had carried out the 11 September attacks. Instead, they credited rumours that either the American Central Intelligence Agency (CIA) or the Israeli Mossad was the true perpetrator and that the attacks were intended to provide justification for the United States to invade Afghanistan and perhaps other Muslim countries such as Iraq and Iran. When the United States attacked the Taliban, hundreds of young Saudis made their way to Afghanistan, imagining a replay of the jihad against the Soviet Union. Anti-American feeling inside the kingdom, already robust due to the stationing of US military forces since 1990, resulted in a number of attacks on Westerners in the autumn of 2001. Even though Saddam Hussein remained in power and could conceivably threaten Saudi Arabia in the future, the American military shield had a destabilizing impact because so many Saudis regarded it as an abomination.

With the overthrow of the Taliban, Saudi volunteers returned home, some of them determined to attack Western targets to expel American military forces. The Saudi authorities tried to keep track of militant cells, and security forces uncovered weapons stores in Riyadh, arrested suspected militants, and got into a number of shoot-outs with militants who refused to surrender. The showdown between militants and the government unfolded against the backdrop of the United States' invasion of Iraq in March 2003. At the end of April, Washington announced that with Saddam's fall, it no longer needed to keep troops in Saudi Arabia. By early September, 7000 American military personnel had left the kingdom. By that time, however, Al Qaeda had already initiated a terrorist campaign against Westerners residing in Saudi Arabia and the government itself.

The first attack came on 12 May 2003. Al Qaeda in the Arabian Peninsula (AQAP), the local branch of Bin Laden's organization, carried out three suicide bombings on Western compounds in Riyadh that killed 26 people. That attack was the beginning of a bloody four-year struggle between the Saudi government and AQAP. Any shred of public sympathy for the militants dissipated after its second operation on 8 November 2003, when suicide truck bombers struck a Riyadh compound that housed Arab and Muslim expatriates, killing 17 people. Terrorists then took aim at Saudi security officials. On 21 April 2004, they detonated a car bomb in front of a Riyadh police station. Attacks on Western targets the next month struck a business office in the Red Sea town of Yanbu and a Khobar residential compound. In December, AQAP attempted to attack the United States consulate in Jeddah but the guards thwarted it. Gunmen also assassinated Western civilians outside their homes, places of work and on city streets. Gradually, the security forces gained the upper hand as they raided safe houses and wiped out militant cells in gun battles, including one outside a hideout in al-Qasim province that lasted for three days in April 2005. AQAP managed to carry out an attack on the huge refinery at Abqaiq in February 2006, but it was ineffective because the car bomb detonated at a gate to the facility. A year later, gunmen murdered four French tourists near the Mada'in Saleh ruins in the north-west.

The security forces eventually prevailed, but the government recognized the need to reform religious institutions and moderate religious discourse to combat extremism. A few months before the May 2003 attack in Riyadh, Saudi liberals had presented Crown Prince Abdullah (King Fahd was incapacitated by a stroke in 1995) with a set of proposals to amend the 1992 Basic Law by separating executive, legislative and judicial powers. The liberal petition also called for elections to national and provincial legislative councils and freedom of speech. The royals were not receptive to such deep changes in the political system, but they did accept the need for expanding the bounds of public discourse.

The government's approach to airing different views took the form of National Dialogues, a series of meetings to discuss urgent issues such as education reform, women's rights and terrorism. The first meeting in June 2003 acknowledged the presence of Muslims apart from Wahhabis by including Shi'as, Sufis and sahwa sheikhs. At the second session in December, discussion turned to religious violence, economic strains and schools. The third National Dialogue held in June 2004 addressed questions surrounding the status of women, such as working outside the home and the legal requirement for permission from a male guardian to pursue an education or obtain medical care. Modest progress on opening the political system followed the National Dialogues. The government held three rounds of municipal council elections in February–April 2005. In general, religious candidates supported by the official establishment and sahwa sheikhs prevailed over liberal candidates. Women were denied the vote in municipal elections, but they were allowed to run for seats on the Jeddah Chamber of Commerce and took two of the 12 seats.

Saudi Arabia's political difficulties during this period owed something to the economic malaise that had settled on the kingdom during the mid-1980s when oil prices, a barometer of prosperity or austerity, fell. In the early phase of the Kuwait crisis, exports from Kuwait and Iraq were cut off, reducing the world's supply of oil by around 5 million barrels per day and causing prices to spike from $18 to $40 per barrel. Washington urged Saudi Arabia and the UAE to boost production and calm markets to stabilize prices, so the overall impact of the crisis on revenues was modest. Any windfall profits were spent when Saudi Arabia assumed the lion's share of paying the cost of the war against Iraq, an estimated $55–$65 billion. For most of the 1990s, the price of oil hovered in the $15 to $20 per barrel range. Then the Asian financial crisis of 1997–8 drove down demand even further, and prices plummeted to around $12 per barrel. The Saudis responded by negotiating with Tehran, seizing the opportunity presented by President Khatami's expressions of good will. The two major oil producers agreed on lower production quotas in order to stabilize prices, which recovered in 1999 to their mid-decade level.

Saudi economic planners adjusted to lower oil revenues with smaller budgets. They ensured that the capital city received sufficient funds to expand water, sewage and electricity for its growing population, but Jeddah was less fortunate. By the end of the decade, its population growth and physical expansion outstripped basic infrastructure, causing severe water and sewage problems. Ordinary Saudis throughout the country faced higher rates for water, electricity and gasoline when the government cut subsidies in 1995 in order to meet requirements for accession to the recently founded World Trade Organization. Planners did increase allocations for education, partly because the government aspired to reduce dependence on foreign workers. The number of Saudis enrolled in schools and universities grew; and more Saudi teachers rather than Arab expatriates filled new positions. The impact on employment patterns, however, did not meet expectations. The number of Saudis graduating from vocational institutes and pursuing technical fields in universities remained stagnant. By contrast, the religious universities increased their enrolments, but they did not prepare graduates for careers in fields requiring scientific and engineering expertise. Moreover, Saudi employers continued to prefer foreign workers because they accepted lower salaries, worked longer hours and were more easily dismissed.

In the late 1990s, low oil prices constrained the government's ability to deal with rising poverty and high unemployment. Rapid population growth put strains on budgets for social welfare programmes and services. It was clear that oil revenues could no longer provide the means for addressing the kingdom's economic difficulties, so planners shifted strategy to rely on the private sector for growth. The political context was favourable for boosting the private sector as Crown Prince Abdullah had strong ties to chambers of commerce. The new approach benefited from rising oil prices, which doubled from $25 per barrel in 2002 to $50 per barrel in 2005, in large measure due to rapid growth in the economies of India and China. Saudi Arabia enjoyed the highest oil revenues in many years, but spent them more cautiously than during the first oil boom of the 1970s. Planners hoped that private companies would hire more Saudis, and the ratio of Saudis in the workforce rose from 37 per cent in 1999 to 43 per cent in 2004. They also hoped that pouring funds into technical and scientific education would produce a generation of young Saudis qualified for the competitive private sector and reduce unemployment.

On 1 August 2005, King Fahd died and Crown Prince Abdullah succeeded him, with Prince Sultan becoming the crown prince. King Abdullah favoured a programme of gradual reform in order to combat extremism and cope with structural economic problems. The security forces had put an end to AQAP terrorist attacks by the end of 2007 and continued to uncover and disband militant cells. The king encouraged proponents of women's rights by appointing a woman to be deputy minister of education, approving legal changes to allow women to work without approval from a male guardian, and establishing the first co-educational higher education institution, King Abdullah University of Science and Technology, itself a token of the king's awareness of the need for increasing the number of young Saudis qualified to work in a modern economy. Reform from above seemed designed to improve security and economic conditions for ordinary Saudis without impinging on the absolute right of the dynasty to rule. The public's patience with pledges to deliver jobs and to keep pace with the requirements of maintaining infrastructure in fast-growing cities is being tested. On the other hand, deep mistrust between religious and liberal critics of the monarchy makes it difficult for activists and would-be activists to form a common front to exert pressure on the rulers.

KUWAIT

In the months after liberation, thick smoke from hundreds of burning oil wells that retreating Iraqi forces set on fire blackened the skies over Kuwait. It took an international effort led by American firefighters specializing in oilfield fires eight months to extinguish them, making it possible to resume the oil exports vital to reconstruction. Against the backdrop of slow economic recovery, Kuwait resumed its place in the Gulf as having the most free political life, marked by competitive elections between clearly defined political tendencies, a free press and robust discussion of public issues at diwaniyyas. In 2005, it became the first Gulf state to extend the franchise to women.

The Iraqi invasion had interrupted a struggle between Kuwait's democracy activists and the rulers but it soon resumed outside the country. As international forces gathered, activists called for Al Sabah to promise to restore the national assembly and civil liberties after liberation. Their call fell on receptive ears in Washington, where the Bush administration was trying to persuade the American public that the forthcoming war was not merely about oil but high principles such as promoting democracy. Consequently, once Kuwait was liberated, Washington urged Al Sabah to restore constitutional government and to hold elections. On 7 April 1991, Emir Jabir announced that elections would be held but did not specify when they would take place, implying that he might renege on his pledge, but pressure from local forces and Washington was too powerful to resist and he

announced elections for October 1992. The outcome of the bal-
lot showed a fairly even division among Islamist, secular and
royalist factions.

Political dynamics under the restored constitution reflected
the country's social, ideological and sectarian trends. There are
no political parties, but distinct tendencies express the views and
interests of different segments of the population. The Islamists
have been the most successful tendency, winning between
14 and 19 seats (from a total of 50) in the four national elections held between 1992 and 2006. They do not form a cohesive
bloc because they are divided into three rival associations: the
Islamic Constitutional Movement, which is the local branch of
the Muslim Brotherhood; and two separate Salafi associations
that consider themselves more puritanical than the Brothers. It
is true that they concur on deepening the role of Islam in law
and public life, so they were able to join forces to ban fashion
shows and block women's suffrage, but they split over matters
like economic liberalization and foreign investment. The secular
tendency usually wins about eight seats in the national assembly; its positions include support for privatizing the economy
and opposition to the Islamists on matters of morality and censorship. Yet another current with strong support among Kuwaiti
public sector employees, who tend to be less affluent and come
from tribal areas, has taken ten to six seats in recent elections.

Political debate frequently turned into struggles between
the national assembly and the ruling family. In May 1999,
Emir Jabir issued a decree granting women the right to vote but
Islamist and tribal deputies combined forces to override him
and revoked the decree. Six years later, the emir cleared the parliamentary hurdle by getting a handful of tribal deputies to join
liberals, Shi'as and appointed members to vote for legislation
granting women the vote and the right to run for office. The
government then appointed the first woman to the cabinet.

Endemic tensions between the national assembly and the
rulers erupted in April 2006 over a plan to consolidate electoral districts. This took place a few months after the death of
Emir Jabir and a period of uncertainty regarding the succession
because Crown Prince Emir Saad proved too ill to assume power
and Al Sabah were divided over the choice of a new ruler. In
the end, the cabinet deposed Emir Saad and designated Emir
Sabah to be the new ruler, the first time that a constitutionally
established body determined the succession. Emir Sabah proved
an energetic defender of the ruling clan's powers and opposed
the re-districting plan because it seemed likely to strengthen
the liberal bloc. He dissolved the national assembly, but new

elections in June showed strong support for the plan. The new national assembly adopted a more aggressive attitude towards government ministers, subjecting them to intense grilling on their performance. By custom, the prime minister was spared such treatment, but in March 2008 a deputy insisted on questioning the prime minister. Emir Sabah responded by dissolving the national assembly for the second time in two years. When elections were held in May, tribal candidates fared better than rivals from Islamist and liberal groups, but the confrontational tenor of political discourse did not abate. Less than a year later, Emir Sabah again dissolved government and held elections.

While the May 2009 elections resulted in four women gaining seats in parliament, they did not alter the fundamental stalemate in the power struggle between the government, dominated by Al Sabah, and the national assembly. It is noteworthy that the political contest turns on the terms of power sharing under a constitution. Kuwaiti activists are not seeking either the overthrow of Al Sabah or their reduction to figureheads. Moderating factors include Al Sabah's historic role in carving an independent status for Kuwait, a tradition of constitutional monarchy since formal independence in 1961, and pressures for national unity in the face of external threats from Iraq and Iran as well as the daily experience for Kuwaiti citizens of being a minority in their own country.

BAHRAIN

The democratic example set by Kuwait stimulated renewed demands for participation in Bahrain, particularly restoration of the national assembly, which Emir Isa had dissolved in 1975. As the Shi'i majority seethed over sectarian discrimination and political exclusion, the atmosphere was aggravated by economic hardship. Whereas the other Gulf states' economies possessed enough oil reserves to cope with low prices in the 1980s, Bahrain's oil production peaked around 1970 and diversification projects were proving insufficient to meet a growing population's needs for employment and housing. As long as Emir Isa ruled, backed up by his powerful brother Sheikh Khalifah as prime minister, the government refused to relax its autocratic rule. The political stalemate lasted until Emir Isa's death in 1999 and the accession of his son Hamad, who seemed prepared to forge a more liberal path for Bahrain.

Pressure for a political opening grew in 1992 when Sunni and Shi'i clerics drafted a petition requesting restoration of the constitution and elections to the national assembly. Emir Isa agreed to meet with some of the activist clerics but rejected the petition's demands. The opposition then organized a campaign to get thousands of Bahrainis behind their cause in order to increase pressure on the emir. Leaders of secular and religious currents, both Shi'i and Sunni, drafted a document that gained support from all political currents, including the demand that women obtain the right to vote and hold elected office. In autumn 1994, copies of the petition circulated around the country. The government responded by arresting and exiling opposition leaders. Demonstrations erupted in January 1995 and continued intermittently for the rest of the year. Protestors committed attacks on expatriate Asian labourers, blamed for stealing jobs. Security forces, in large measure recruited from Pakistan and Jordan, arrested thousands and threw them in jail, where many underwent torture. To justify the draconian response, the authorities claimed that extremists were plotting to carry out terrorist attacks and that Iran was hatching a conspiracy to overthrow the government. In addition to force, the rulers resorted to bureaucratic devices to rein in clerical activism.

In 1996, a Higher Council of Islamic Affairs was established to supervise the appointment of Shi'i clerics to mosques and to manage mosque finances. Clerics resisted the assertion of direct control over Shi'i institutions and they boycotted mosques under government supervision. Moreover, activists remained committed to restoration of the national assembly in addition to demanding curbs on corruption and solutions to high unemployment. Emir Isa's attempt to placate democratic demands by expanding the Consultative Council (founded in 1993) was unsuccessful at stemming the cycle of protests and repression that roiled the country for the rest of the decade.

In March 1999, Emir Isa died and his son Hamad became the new ruler. He declared his intention to initiate sweeping political changes: granting amnesty to political prisoners; closing the notorious State Security Courts that presided over the machinery of political repression; organizing elections to municipal councils; and allowing women to run for parliament. Emir Hamad drafted a new national charter that expanded the scope of press freedom and political association, legalized trade unions, and abolished the State Security Law and State Security Court. On the other hand, the national charter created an appointed body, the Consultative Council, diluting the political weight of the elected national assembly, and reserved to the ruler control over the budget and authority over government ministers. In February 2001, Bahraini men and women overwhelmingly approved the charter in a national referendum. Political dissidents returned from exile after spending years abroad.

After a promising start, however, Hamad reversed course in February 2002. He issued a revised constitution that changed his title from emir to king, arrogated more extensive powers to the king, and diluted the prerogatives of the elected assembly. He did, however, proceed with plans to hold national elections in October, the first in nearly 30 years. The roster of opposition political organizations competing for seats included two major Shi'i parties. The Accord Party represented a younger generation of Shi'i activists led by Ali Salman. He had studied in an Iranian seminary in the 1980s and returned to Bahrain in 1992. Like other young clerics, he wove social and political messages in his religious sermons.

The second major Shi'i party was the Islamic Action Society, basically a new name for the pro-Iranian Islamic Front for the Liberation of Bahrain, although it eschewed revolutionary rhetoric. The authorities remained suspicious of the Islamic Action Society because of the close ties between its leaders and Iranian clerics. Before the October 2002 election, government officials tried to dilute the Shi'i vote by redrawing districts and placing restrictions on opposition candidates to hamper their campaign.

The prospect of elections presented opposition leaders with a dilemma. King Hamad refused to return to the more liberal 1973 constitution that allotted more authority to the national assembly. Consequently, activists debated whether they should participate in the elections, thereby lending legitimacy to the government, or boycott them. The Accord Party's leaders split, with the majority deciding to field a slate of candidates. The boycotters left to form a new organization called The Truth. During the campaign, a secret document surfaced that sketched Al Khalifah's strategy of naturalizing foreign Sunnis to dilute the country's Shi'i majority. The Accord Party won 17 seats (from a total of 40) but its secular Sunni allies failed to win a single seat, leading to allegations of fraud to prevent the emergence of a cross-sectarian political coalition. Pro-government Sunni Islamists won 22 seats. The vote also resulted in the election of Bahrain's first female parliamentary representative. For the Consultative Council, King Hamad appointed 20 Sunnis, 18 Shi'as, one Christian and one Jew. The most recent national elections, in autumn 2010 took place in the context of persistent government pressure on the opposition Accord and Truth Parties, including detentions and censorship. In spite of heavy-handed measures, the Accord Party added a seat to its delegation. By contrast, the Sunni Islamist tendency declined to about half a dozen seats, giving way to a cluster of independent pro-business candidates notable for their opposition to the sort of morality legislation that would diminish pleasure-seeking tourists from nearby Saudi Arabia.

The obstacles standing in the way of a liberal political order in Bahrain stem from domestic and foreign factors. The sectarian divide between the Sunni Al Khalifah and the Shi'i majority colours the way democratic demands are perceived. The rulers view the Shi'i population as a threat to their rule, not just because of their numerical superiority but also because they suspect them of loyalty to clerics in Iran and Iraq.

To bolster the Sunni minority, the government has facilitated naturalization for several thousand Sunni Arabs and Pakistanis serving in the military and security forces from which Shi'as are largely excluded. Bahrain's economic dependence on Saudi Arabia for oil and tourism, which leapt after completion of the King Fahd Causeway in 1986, means it must take into consideration Riyadh's chilly attitude towards democracy in the neighbourhood. In the meantime, unemployment remains at high levels for the Shi'i majority, who must cope with daily life without the sort of welfare benefits provided in the other Gulf countries (public health, subsidized housing), spurring protests against expatriate workers hired at low wages. Internal pressures for representative government are not likely to abate given the sectarian element in politics and Bahrain's economic problems, which fall hardest on the Shi'i majority.

QATAR

The early 1990s mood of reform spread from Kuwait, Bahrain and Saudi Arabia to Qatar. Using the device of a petition that straddled the line between request and demand, some 50 eminent Qataris called on Emir Khalifah to open up political life. The December 1991 petition sought free speech and clarification of citizens' political and legal rights. It also urged the emir to create a consultative council to give citizens a share in legislation. Finally, it called for the drafting of a new constitution to provide a foundation for democratic institutions and rights.

Emir Khalifah saw no need to change the basis of Al Thani authority as Qatar's revenues from oil and gas sufficed to support generous social benefits for the country's small population. The petitioners lacked a broad social base, so the emir simply ignored the petition. It turned out, however, that the emir's son Hamad was dissatisfied with his father's conservative approach to developing the country and in June 1995, he seized power in a bloodless *coup d'état*. In order to firm up his position, Emir Hamad curried support from younger members of Al Thani and from the United States by announcing his intention to steer Qatar down a liberal path.

The political experiment began with the chamber of commerce. The ruler had always appointed its members, but in 1998 Emir Hamad decided to make it an elected body. The following year, Qatar had its first elections for municipal councils. The elections were a major step forward for Qatari women, who for the first time enjoyed the right to vote and run for office. Six women ran for seats on the councils but fell short. One woman did win a seat in the 2003 election. Emir Hamad did not design the municipal councils to govern but to advise the Ministry of Municipal Affairs and the Ministry of Agriculture on matters such as public hygiene. The councillors chafed at their limited advisory role but Emir Hamad held firm while allowing elections in 2003 and 2007.

In July 1999, Emir Hamad appointed a committee to work on a new constitution. The committee took three years to complete its task, producing a draft constitution that confirmed the emir's control over essential matters like oil and natural gas revenues and the national budget. It took a step towards representative government by establishing an Advisory Council to be comprised of 30 elected members and 15 members appointed by the emir. A referendum in April 2003 gave overwhelming approval to the constitution. The emir enacted the constitution in June 2004, but delayed the date of its coming into effect until June 2005. Even then, he postponed holding elections for the Advisory Council time and again, implicitly abandoning the promise of moving towards democracy. The stalling of Qatar's political opening gave the impression that Emir Hamad's initial pronouncements were merely a tactic to allow him to consolidate power rather than a commitment to fundamental change.

The emir's commitment to promoting a more liberal social climate proved more genuine. The government abolished the Ministry of Information, which had imposed strict limits on the press. In 1996, Emir Hamad funded the establishment of Al Jazeera satellite television station. Its candid treatment of regional politics shook up the mass media throughout the Arab world and inspired the establishment of other satellite stations that replicated its style if not its substance. In an effort to leap to the forefront of higher education in the region, Qatar invited American universities to establish branch campuses. The roster of prestigious schools included Carnegie Mellon University, Georgetown University and Cornell University, all of which Qatari citizens could attend for free. Emir Hamad also sought to frame modern roles for Qatari women. His wife Sheikha Muza represented a new model for Qatari women to assume a larger role in public life, breaking with the custom of Gulf rulers to keep female relatives out of the limelight. She became the chair of the Qatar Foundation, established to promote education and community development. In 2003, Hamad appointed the first female cabinet member as minister of education.

Apart from Emir Hamad's 1995 coup, Qatar enjoyed a calm political scene, in part because its population is homogeneous, in contrast to the mix of Sunnis and Shi'as in Bahrain and Kuwait. Furthermore, Qatar does not have an active Islamist movement. Al Jazeera's coverage of such movements is sympathetic, and the famous Egyptian Islamist Sheikh Yusuf al-Qaradawi has resided in Doha for many years. His televised sermons and speeches focus on regional issues like Palestine and the American invasions of Afghanistan and Iraq, but he is silent on Qatari affairs, as is Al Jazeera.

The official religious institution is not a potential source of dissent either. Only a small number of religious personalities are Qatari nationals. For decades, the government has employed preachers and prayer leaders from other Arab countries, primarily Saudi Arabia, Egypt, Yemen and Syria. They are just as vulnerable to deportation as other expatriate workers and therefore prefer to stay on the good side of the authorities. Finally, general social unrest is unlikely as Qatar's oil and gas wealth affords the small number of citizens, around 250,000, with one of the highest standards of living in the world. Benefits extend beyond the usual rentier menu of free medical care and education, to housing allowances for civil service employees (over 90 per cent of Qataris in the workforce have jobs in the public sector), marriage stipends for men who marry Qatari women, and free land for investment. Qatar's perennial source of instability, rivalry among branches of Al Thani, was addressed by an article in the 2005 constitution that limited succession to Emir Hamad's male heirs.

OMAN

The post-war wave of political reform also touched Oman. Sultan Qabus had already taken a step towards consulting the public on development issues when he established the State Consultative Council as an advisory body in 1981. Its 45 members appointed to two-year terms came from the ranks of government officials and the private sector as well as tribesmen nominated by district governors. In 1991, the sultan began a modest experiment with representation by dissolving the State Consultative Council and replacing it with the similarly named Consultative Council, which was intended to bring together cabinet members and ordinary Omanis. Members of the new body were selected by the sultan from nominees put forth by limited electorates of 500 voters in each province. The sultan also chose the president of the council, which was divided into committees on the economy, local development, health, legal affairs and education. Each committee advised the relevant cabinet minister. In addition, the Consultative Council reviewed laws drafted by the Council of Ministers and had the right to propose amendments before laws went to the sultan for his disposition.

In November 1996, Sultan Qabus issued a Basic Law, similar to a constitution in that it defined government institutions and their powers. The Basic Law created the Council of Oman, a two-chamber body comprised of the existing Consultative Council and the newly established Council of State. Members of the latter are appointed by the sultan to four-year terms and generally come from the ranks of government officials, military officers and merchants. The Council of Oman's function is restricted to technical, economic and administrative matters. The Basic Law also includes articles pertaining to succession that restrict the sultanate to descendants of Turki ibn Said and establish a Ruling Family Council to designate a successor three days after the throne becomes vacant. If the Council does not select a successor, then the Defence Council is to confirm the sultan's choice. The Defence Council includes members of the police, the armed forces, the royal guard and internal security. In 1997, Sultan Qabus declared that he had arranged the succession and recorded his wishes in sealed envelopes.

Since the promulgation of the Basic Law, the electorate has steadily expanded. In 1997, it rose to 51,000, including 5000 women, making it the first time that Omani women could vote in elections and run for seats on the Consultative Council. The electorate was further enlarged in 2000 to 175,000 Omanis, of whom 30 per cent were women. Three years later, universal suffrage was achieved. The 2003 and 2007 elections under universal suffrage were notable for low voter participation, with about one-third of eligible voters registering in 2003 and fewer than half in 2007. A ban on public assembly during the campaign may have caused apathy, especially among younger Omanis. Women were eligible to run in both elections, but won no seats. On the other hand, the 70-member Council of State in 2007 included 14 women.

Sultan Qabus's gradualist approach to introducing representative institutions may be viewed as an extension of his early efforts to integrate Oman's diverse communities into a cohesive political system, starting with suppression of the Dhufar rebellion. He succeeded in achieving a remarkable level of stability, especially in the light of Oman's long history of regional, tribal and dynastic strife. On the other hand, Oman was not immune to modern forms of political unrest that permeated the region. For instance, in May 1994, an anonymous leaflet in Muscat condemned the decision to establish relations with Israel. The authorities responded by arresting more than 400 people suspected of sympathy with the Muslim Brotherhood. The government put around 150 individuals on trial. Some of the defendants were businessmen and government officials, but for the most part they were younger, university-educated folk from various parts of the country. It is noteworthy that both Ibadis and Sunnis were among the defendants. The implication of their mixed social and religious composition is the emergence of a common Omani political culture cutting across historical lines of identity, at least among educated youth.

The trial concluded with sentences ranging from three to 20 years, but Sultan Qabus issued a general pardon in 1995. Indications of residual Ibadi political impulses surfaced in 2005 after authorities came across a truck loaded with explosives near the Yemen border. A wave of arrests in Muscat and the interior swept up around 300 suspects. Investigators then brought charges against 31 defendants, all of them Ibadis, including religious officials and students from Sultan Qabus University's colleges of education and Islamic studies. The defendants were found guilty of belonging to an illegal group dedicated to reviving the Ibadi imamate and received sentences between seven and 20 years. As in the previous political trial, Sultan Qabus pardoned them.

Oman's political future is clouded by declining oil production that set in after 2000. For a number of years, high prices buffered the budget, but with half the population under 20 years old, time is not on the side of a rentier political bargain. Government planners began to invest in tourism and industry to wean the economy from dependence on oil. They have also tried to increase Omani participation in the labour force, reversing the rising tide of expatriate workers whose numbers grew from under 10 per cent in 1970 to two-thirds by 1980. Five-year plans in 1995 and 2000 set goals for nationals to comprise a larger share of the workforce and to increase women's participation. In the public sector, Omanis began to fill more positions in ministries and banks, but the private sector continued to rely on expatriates for the same reasons as in other Gulf states: higher qualifications, lower wages to expatriates and easier dismissal.

THE UNITED ARAB EMIRATES

During the 1990s, political dynamics in the UAE remained untouched by pressures for political participation felt in the rest of the region. Between Abu Dhabi's willingness to share its huge oil wealth and Dubai's impressive strides towards economic diversification, their citizens enjoyed some of the highest standards of living in the world while citizens of the less well-endowed emirates found opportunities to work in the two wealthy ones. In 2005, however, the steps taken in Bahrain, Qatar and Oman towards representative government spurred the UAE to establish an electoral college to vote for 20 of the 40 seats on the Federal National Council, leaving the balance to appointment by the emirs. The modest nature of the initiative was evident in the decision to restrict the size of the electoral college to 7,000 members out of a population of 400,000. Lacking agitation for elections and political freedoms, politics continued to be largely a contest between Abu Dhabi and Dubai over the perennial question of federal versus emirate-level authority.

In 1996, the emirates agreed to make the 1971 provisional constitution permanent. One sign of its implementation was Dubai's merging of its militia with federal Union Defence Forces. Otherwise, the emirates continued to enjoy a high degree of autonomy. The federation did not develop common policies on ports, energy, finance or foreign relations. Nor was there a political mechanism to plan economic development for the entire federation. Instead, rising economic inequality spurred

9. Abu Dhabi Skyline.

labour migration from Ra's al-Khaima and Fujaira to the wealthy emirates and the conversion of Sharjah and Ajman into bedroom commuter satellites of Dubai.

Abu Dhabi's new oil finds in the 1970s and 1980s revised upward calculations of its reserves to 8 per cent of the world's total supply of oil. During the 1990s, rapid economic growth turned the UAE into one of the wealthiest countries in the world in terms of per capita income. Abu Dhabi's oil reserves are enough to last for 100 years at 2,000 levels of output. Nevertheless, its leaders decided to diversify the economy by combining capital, Western technology and regional labour in joint ventures: aerospace maintenance and parts manufacturing, shipbuilding and weapons systems. Luxury real estate and tourism for Gulf nationals developed at a more deliberate pace than in Dubai.

In the first decade of the twenty-first century, Dubai emerged from relative obscurity to become known as a glitzy city-state perched on the edge of Arabia. Slender skyscrapers, man-made residential islands in the shape of palm trees, and indoor ski slopes made Dubai a global brand for conspicuous consumption and leisure. The whimsical image was part of a serious strategy to wean the emirate from dependence on oil by developing heavy industry using cheap energy and seeking overseas investment opportunities. Dubai's Al Maktum rulers were determined to develop an economic foundation that would enable them to keep Abu Dhabi at arm's length.

The new strategy took shape during the Iran–Iraq war, when turmoil in the oil markets and attacks on tankers signalled the need for economic diversification. The first step in that direction was an extension of Dubai's historical strength in providing facilities for regional trade rooted in the assumption that superior infrastructure attracts business. The dredging of Dubai Creek at the beginning of the 1960s was an early example. A more recent case was the construction in the 1970s of the enormous Port Jebel Ali facility, one of the world's largest, and a nearby dry dock for ship repair. The success of those initiatives prompted increased investment in roads, ports and airports. Dubai was able to boost its role from a regional commercial hub to a global one.

A second diversification strategy sought direct foreign investment. Dubai dodged a federal UAE law banning foreign-owned enterprises by establishing free trade zones that it declared exempt from federal regulations. The first such free zone at Port Jebel Ali, set up in 1985, offered freshly installed infrastructure, office buildings and subsidized utilities to lure foreign companies. Twenty years later, more than 200 companies from Europe, North America, Asia and the Middle East had offices there employing 40,000 workers. Total investment amounted to more than $6 billion in 2002. Dubai tweaked the model in the early 2000s by creating free zones dedicated to specific sectors. Media City became a centre for satellite television and news services; Internet City attracted Asian, European and American high technology companies. In 2007, 800 companies with 10,000 workers were operating in Internet City. There followed free zones for health care, higher education and finance. Neighbouring emirates Sharjah and Ra's al-Khaima likewise created free zones to attract foreign investment.

Luxury tourism and real estate in Dubai were intended to broaden the pillars of diversification and foreign investment. Construction of glamorous hotels got under way in the 1990s. The completion of the dhow-sail shaped Burj al-Arab in 1999 gave Dubai a visual emblem; a tourist board promoted vacations to audiences in Asia, Europe and North America. The warm and sunny Gulf winters along with the permissive atmosphere towards bars and clubs helped fill new hotels. Attractions included desert excursions and blockbuster sporting events and musical entertainment. In 20 years, annual tourist traffic increased from around 500,000 to over 5 million visitors. Expensive real estate projects lured foreign investment, thanks in part to legal reform allowing exceptions to federal law prohibiting foreign property ownership. Overall, Dubai's diversification strategy worked in terms of shifting the emirate's economic activities from oil to trade and foreign investment. By 2007, oil accounted for less than 10 per cent of gross domestic product. On the other hand, Dubai did not escape dependence on external factors, as became clear when the 2008–9 global recession brought the construction and real estate frenzy to a halt.

Dubai's economic success was partly a function of the ability of its ruling family, Al Maktum, to divide responsibilities among its members. When Sheikh Rashid died in 1990, power passed smoothly to his eldest son Sheikh Maktum, who had been crown prince since 1964. His more dynamic younger brother Sheikh Muhammad soon emerged as the central figure in managing the emirate's affairs and he became identified with the diversification strategy. Abu Dhabi also benefited from a smooth succession when Sheikh Zayid died in 2004, passing power to his son and long-time heir Sheikh Khalifah. The new crown prince was another of Zayid's sons, Sheikh Muhammed. The peaceful transition was a notable achievement for a clan that suffered many bloody conflicts earlier in its history.

The three smaller emirates continued their record of stability. Since 1900, Ajman has had only four sheikhs from the ruling al-Nu'aimi tribe. Umm al-Qaiwain's Sheikh Ahmad ibn Rashid al-Mualla ruled from 1929 to 1981, and his son Sheikh Rashid succeeded without incident. Fujaira, perched on the Indian Ocean, has enjoyed similar stability under the Sharqi tribe. Meanwhile, in Sharjah, Sheikh Sultan ibn Muhammad continues to rule. In contrast to tranquil successions in the other emirates, Ra's al-Khaima witnessed a power struggle. Sheikh Saqr ibn Muhammad, who came to power in 1948, remained the longest-ruling sheikh in the federation until he died in October 2010 at 92. In this case, the succession was contested between the late ruler's sons Sheikh Saud and Sheikh Khalid, the older brother, who had been the official heir for 30 years until Sheikh Saqr changed the succession and named Sheikh Saud the new heir. Khalid went to live in exile and returned upon his father's death to assert his right to rule, but Saud had used his seven years as crown prince to buttress his position for a future power struggle with his half-brother and seemed poised to remain in control.

Beneath the surface of political calm and economic dynamism, there were potential sources for instability in the Emirates. Their location at the crossroads of Arabia and South Asia and lax immigration and financial controls make it an inviting place for illegal activities. International smuggling rings funnel gold and diamonds between India, the Middle East and Europe; arms dealers coordinate weapons transactions; and criminal syndicates operate prostitution and human trafficking operations. Even more threatening, terrorist organizations like Al Qaeda exploited the informal financial sector to transfer funds to operatives planning the 11 September attacks on the United States. When the Emirates' passive role in facilitating those attacks came to light, the authorities adopted measures to clamp down on suspicious financial activities. Moreover, after 11 September, the Emirates adopted strict measures to silence Islamist activists. Mosque preachers received instructions to restrict themselves to theological matters and to refrain from mentioning politics. Newspaper columnists known for their Islamist views were censored. These measures targeted political extremists, but other sordid activities like prostitution and human trafficking were barely affected.

The Emirates' dependence on expatriate labour, or more precisely the abuse of foreign workers, became an additional source of concern. Dubai has the largest proportion of expatriates: its total population is around two million, of whom fewer than 100,000 are citizens. The assumption that expatriate workers, grateful for higher wages than imaginable at home, would not endanger stability was dented by strikes and demonstrations against miserable working and living conditions between 2005 and 2007. Workers blocked traffic on major highways and in one incident destroyed machinery and vehicles, an indication that the rentier bargain works for citizens in the short run but may require modification for long-term viability.

CONCLUSION

The first half of 2011 was an eventful time for the Gulf. Osama bin Laden was killed by US forces at his hideout in Pakistan. The Arab Spring touched off a new round of protest and repression in Bahrain and inspired Saudi women to mount the first campaign for the right to drive in 20 years. The Iraqi government is thinking of extending the presence of US forces past the current deadline of December 2011. Such events are reminders that a history textbook's final chapter is soon outdated. However, taking a long view of the Gulf's history, we can discern both the persistence of perennial patterns, albeit reshaped by modern forces, and sharp ruptures wrought by those forces. Three deeply ingrained tendencies in the Gulf stand out for their endurance throughout centuries of change. First, migration remains a conspicuous facet of life, but patterns of movement have shifted in the hydrocarbon era. No longer do tribal sections, like the Utub founders of Kuwait and Bahrain, or traders, like the early twentieth-century Iranian merchants who crossed the waters to Dubai, relocate to improve their fortunes. Citizens of the Gulf Cooperation Council (GCC) states stay put in order to enjoy the privileges afforded by the rentier bargain, and the mobile population is the vast expatriate labour force. Second, the Gulf's population is more polyglot than ever, thanks to the influx of Asian, Middle Eastern and Western workers. The historical language groups are presently outnumbered by the wave of workers from Bangladesh, Pakistan, India, Thailand and the Philippines. Young Arab Emiratis frequently speak Hindi and English while tri-lingual radio stations broadcast programmes in Arabic, Hindi and Malayalam (the language of India's Kerala state). Third, the Gulf has an important role in trading networks. In ancient times, its merchants and sailors exchanged goods with nearby areas of the Middle East and Indus civilization, later expanding their contacts to the entire Indian Ocean rim. In modern times, Europe and North America integrated the Gulf into the global capitalist economy. The twenty-first century may see a return to the Gulf's historic orientation towards Asia. The bulk of expatriate labour already comes from the Indian Ocean rim and South-east Asia, while China, India, Japan, South Korea and Singapore are making strides as trading partners.

10. The Suq al Dijaj in Basra City.

11. Mall of the Pharaohs in Dubai.

12. Arabian Transport, Past and Present.

Material conditions in Gulf vastly different now

In contrast to historical continuities, the physical setting of daily life for today's descendants of yesteryear's nomads, fishermen, pearl divers and date growers has undergone staggering change. One of the clichés about the Gulf in the modern era highlights the breakneck pace of physical transformation and social change, thrusting people from scattered tent encampments and mud-brick villages into spacious homes. The lure of such material comforts as abundant potable water, electricity (at subsidized rates), air conditioning and household conveniences concentrated nomads and villagers in large cities burgeoning with new construction. Hence, the Gulf population is no longer dispersed between roving pastoralists in the desert and sedentary residents of port towns, fishing villages and oases, but is packed into modern cities, along the Arabian side in particular, where residents occupy stately homes and high-rises equipped with colour television sets, computers and electronic gadgets.

In addition to manifest changes in material conditions, the texture of everyday life has been transformed. Previously, kinship ties of clan and tribe played primary roles in assuring one's physical and economic security, but now central government is the guarantor for citizen welfare. Long gone are the days when tribal nomads held the balance of power in Arabia, Iraq and Iran. Mechanized vehicles and airforces tamed them in the early twentieth century, then oil-funded development schemes concentrated them in work camps, towns and cities. On the Arabian side of the Gulf, the modern state and economy remade tribal sheikhs into a stratum of dignitaries acting as political brokers between fellow tribesmen and rulers in return for land deals, jobs, contracts and licences. For ordinary folk, kinship ties remain a valuable resource for business connections, social interaction and affiliation on the sub-national scale, but the political and economic contexts for invoking tribal obligations are products of modern forces even if the ideology of kinship appears primordial to an outsider. Hence, tribalism is still a part of the social fabric but is refashioned to fit the dynamics of modern political structures and economies.

Within the urban setting of the Arab Gulf States, government attention to health and education had direct and indirect effects. Expanded access to modern medical care brought deep cuts in infant mortality rates and a sharp rise in average life span to more than 70 years. In a few decades, these developments combined with high fertility rates to alter the region's demographic profile, so that 60 per cent of the population in GCC countries is now under 25 years old. The population is not only younger but also more educated, as governments built and staffed schools to convert sons of herders, fishers and cultivators into bureaucrats and businessmen. Initially, some families refused to allow girls to attend school, consequently a marked gap in literacy opened between boys and girls, particularly in rural areas. The gender gap eventually closed in elementary and secondary school enrolment as national literacy rates rose to around 90 per cent. Women now outpace men in completing university degrees, but gender still impacts what happens after school. Notwithstanding their preponderance among university graduates, female participation in the labour force is low, ranging from 15 per cent in Saudi Arabia and the UAE to 30 per cent in Qatar and 50 per cent in Kuwait. Such variation runs through the story of how societies have come to grips with the effects of social change on gender roles. In matters of marriage, divorce, custody of children and inheritance, law courts apply rules rooted in Islamic jurisprudence that favour men. Arranged marriage remains the norm, to the discomfort of many young men as well as women. The picture is complicated not only by the contrast between women's high educational attainments and low participation in the workforce, but also the uneven pace of advancement in acquiring political rights. In Kuwait, Bahrain, Qatar and Oman, they have the right to vote and run for office in political systems notable for government limits on the sway of elected representatives.

Notwithstanding substantial variation in political and social life from one country to another, it is true that in a couple of generations, the population of the Gulf has become better educated and more affluent than any in the history of the region. The young in particular are attuned to cosmopolitan tastes in consumption and leisure that show more in common with youth cultures in the West than the ways of the forefathers. With plenty of money and access to the global marketplace in glittering malls – the public squares of the twenty-first century Gulf city – consumption is a common pastime rather than a matter of survival in a harsh environment. Not all Gulf nationals can afford to shop at high-end designer boutiques, but the new bazaars include discount stores stocked with affordable, mass-produced wares from Asia. While scarcity and hunger are distant historical memories, affluence has spawned the ills of over-consumption as gauged by the rising incidence of obesity-related illnesses like diabetes and hypertension.

In the framework of urbanization under national governments, social change has been shaped by rulers' political visions. Iran under the Pahlavi monarchy was bent on transforming a polyglot population – Persians, Arabs, Kurds, Baluchis, Azeris, Turcomen and others – into a uniform, mass-educated body of Persian speakers committed to mobilizing energies to make their nation an industrial and military power. The Islamic Republic erased the Western imprint on Iranian modernity but did not jettison aspirations for a common national identity, or for economic and technical progress requiring an urban, universally-educated, but now virtuous, population. Iraq had a more consistent trajectory of social change even in the midst of post-revolutionary instability, striving for national unity and economic development under a secular banner. Eight years after the American invasion, it remains too early to discern when a stable order will emerge and how it may encompass Kurds and Arabs, Sunnis and Shi'is.

In Saudi Arabia, the fusion of monarchy and religious doctrine is half-way through its third century, but the terms of that fusion have tilted in favour of royal power, allowing for modest inroads against Wahhabi norms in order to foster conditions for prosperity when oil revenues inevitably decline. Nevertheless, the centrality of religious legitimacy for the dynasty seems to set limits on social change (with respect to gender segregation, for example), sowing tension between purity and pragmatism. The smaller Gulf States have adopted an approach in tune with the rulers' instincts for sustaining dynastic power by combining conservative values with forward-looking economic policies. Pressure for conforming to conservative ways arises from the

Gulf's centrality for trade & communication

experience of living as a small, privileged minority in a sea of foreign guest workers.

Underlying shifts in daily life and culture is the political transformation generated by the Gulf's incorporation into a global order dominated by the West. As impressive as imperial power was in the pre-modern era, it rested lightly on societies and economies at the periphery of empires, which is where the Gulf shores sat in relation to Mesopotamian and Persian rulers, be they ancient or medieval. The ascent of Western powers to global dominance ended the cyclical rise and fall of sheikhdoms and kingdoms by endowing on clans that happened to be ruling in the early 1800s the privileged status of treaty partner with Great Britain. Today's smaller Arab Gulf States preserved independence against the appetites of ambitious neighbours because of British guarantees, whether formal or implicit. In addition to consolidating the independence of ruling clans, delineating national boundaries, and assembling Iraq from Ottoman debris, *Pax Britannica* amplified the power of sheikhs *vis-à-vis* townsmen and tribesmen, supplying the diplomatic, financial and military resources to turn sheikhs into rulers.

Brit still has guarantees

For example, fleets and consuls dispatched by the Government of India intervened in power struggles between the cosmopolitan Al Bu Said at Muscat and the insular tribal and Ibadi forces of inner Oman to shore up the former. As the Ottoman Empire collapsed, thanks in part to its defeat at British hands in the First World War, and Iran's Qajar dynasty faded, London eyed the Gulf as its exclusive sphere of influence, one reason why it presumed the authority to draw national boundaries at the northern end and to set firm limits on Saudi expansion in that direction. From the Iranian shore, British officials warily observed Russia's assertions in Iran's northern provinces before the First World War and then coped with a resurgent national government afterward, yet retained influence through control over the oil concession.

The underlying rationale for British – and previous Portuguese and Dutch – interest in Gulf affairs stemmed from its place in trade and communications between the Indian Ocean and the Mediterranean. Merchandise and modes of communication varied over time – spices or silk, sailing with the monsoon or steaming under coal power. In the mid-1800s, the Gulf economy, and the fortunes of its population, became more tightly woven into global trade thanks to rising demand for pearls. London's strategic interests evolved after the First World War due to the spread of aviation, prompting a search for airstrips and bases that added a fresh source of revenue for Arab treaty sheikhs facing impoverishment due to the collapse of the pearling industry. Then came the rush

London tries to get on to...

for oil concessions, a symptom of the global industrial economy's appetite for hydrocarbon fuel. The accumulation of oil revenues made possible the construction of modern governing institutions: ministries, security forces, education systems and the like.

In the half-century between 1930 and 1980, the growth of the state turned sheikhs into rulers who adopted a common strategy to retain the loyalty of their populations, namely, spreading the fruits of oil wealth through social welfare benefits and economic privileges. There is, of course, more to national politics than allocating oil revenues, as evidenced by pressures for representation and participation. Variation in the sheikhdoms' populations and the history of their relations to ruling clans accounts for a spectrum of political dynamics, from the pattern of contestation and consultation in Kuwait to the hostile stalemate in Bahrain between Sunni rulers and Shi'i majority. The question looming over the Gulf in 2011 is whether the kind of popular movements that forced out the presidents of Tunisia and Egypt would bring about fundamental political changes. In January–February 2011, Iran and Bahrain witnessed bouts of protests and unrest, but both governments have abundant experience and previous success in thwarting democratic demands.

To sum up the present outlook, it helps to imagine three levels of political dynamics, the global, the regional and the national. At the global level, for the past 200 years, there has been a single dominant external power (first Britain, then the United States) that plays a conservative role, striving to preempt struggles among local rulers and to prop them up against domestic challenges. The United States became the dominant power in the 1970s and escalated its military involvement in the 1990 Kuwait crisis and the 2003 invasion of Iraq. Whether it possesses the resources to project force in distant waters in the wake of the immense economic crisis that overtook it in the autumn of 2008 and had not abated three years later remains to be seen. It is well to recall that Great Britain withdrew after 150 years of supremacy because of a bankrupt treasury, not because of military defeat. In the short term, Washington is committed to standing by friendly governments and to confronting Iran over its nuclear programme. A military conflict between the United States or Israel and Iran would have unpredictable consequences. It might be contained, but it might also spread to Iraq and the GCC states. If Iran were to acquire nuclear weapons, the region could become the scene of nuclear proliferation.

At the regional level, Iraq and Iran are the two leading powers by virtue of size, population and resources. Moreover, their respective conceptions of their significance as heirs of ancient political traditions, combined with historic Arab–Persian rivalry, fuel a contest for supreme influence in the Gulf, without regard for ideological outlook: pro-Western monarchy, Arab nationalist Baathist republic or revolutionary Islamic republic. Saudi Arabia is a recent entry in the contest, possessing not only the largest oil reserves but prestige as the guardian of Islam's holy places. Compared to Iran and Iraq, its military forces are modest. Indeed, even when Riyadh joined the rest of the Gulf Arab States to form the GCC, their combined military power was not sufficient to offer credible deterrence. Their dependence on Washington for a security shield is reminiscent of the shelter nineteenth-century Arab sheikhdoms found under the British umbrella. Within the GCC, inherited political tensions complicate relations, as between Bahrain and its former possession Qatar, and between Saudi Arabia and the UAE (recall the Buraimi dispute). All of this is to say that the Gulf's political dynamics are as fluid and complex as those of any multi-polar region.

At the national level, the political systems in the GCC states largely rest on the durability of the rentier bargain wherein governments provide basic necessities to citizens in return for loyalty and obedience. How long the oilfields will last varies from one country to another. Bahrain's are just about exhausted; Oman's no longer suffice to support the rentier bargain. Kuwait, Qatar and UAE have small enough populations relative to their reserves to sustain the bargain for several decades. Saudi Arabia occupies an intermediate position. In all cases, diversification strategies have shown promise but not reached the point where rulers and citizens can look to oil-poor futures with confidence. Then there is the related issue of dependence on expatriate labour, which is affordable only as long as oil revenues can pay for it. The GCC states have not yet meshed education systems and workforce training programmes with private sector enterprises to put their economies on a firmer basis by making it possible for citizens to replace expatriates. One wonders how long cheap, abundant fossil fuels can support what is by far the largest population in the history of the Gulf, one that consumes the region's scarcest resource, water, on a scale unimaginable 50 years ago. Finally, the constellation of political forces in each country is dynamic. For all the effectiveness of generous welfare policies at winning loyalty, obedience and acquiescence to dynastic rule, politics is never static, and yesterday's favours may be forgotten in the light of today's economic distress or demands for representation and rights. Hence, the intersection of local and global politics with diminishing resources is bound to keep states and societies in tension for years.

NOTES

INTRODUCTION

1   For a concise overview on the question of naming the Gulf, see Bosworth, C. Edmund, 'The Nomenclature of the Persian Gulf', in Alvin J. Cottreell et al. (eds), *The Persian Gulf States: A General Survey* (Baltimore, 1980), pp. xvii–xxxiv.

CHAPTER 4

1   Saint Augustine, *The City of God* (New York, 1958), pp. 88–9.

CHAPTER 5

1   Lord Lansdowne cited in Busch, Briton Cooper, *Britain and the Persian Gulf, 1894–1914* (Berkeley, 1967), p. 256.
2   Lord Curzon cited in Fisher, John, *Curzon and British Imperialism in the Middle East, 1916–1919* (London, 1999), p. 100.

CHAPTER 8

1   Mahdavi, Hossein, 'The pattern and problems of economic development in rentier states: The case of Iran', in Michael Cook (ed.), *Studies in the Economic History of the Middle East* (London, 1970).

CHAPTER 9

1   Machiavelli, Niccolo, *The Prince and the Discourses* (New York, 1940), p. 21.

BIBLIOGRAPHY

Abdullah, Thabit, *Merchants, Mamluks, and Murder: The Political Economy of Trade in Eighteenth Century Basra* (Albany, NY, 2001).

Abrahamian, Ervand, *Iran between Two Revolutions* (Princeton, NJ, 1982).

Abu-Hakima, Ahmad Mustafa, *History of Eastern Arabia, 1750–1800: The Rise and Development of Bahrain and Kuwait* (Beirut, 1965).

—— *The Modern History of Kuwait, 1750–1965* (London, 1983).

Al-Khalifa, Sheikh Abdullah Bin Khalid, 'The Utoob in the eighteenth century', in Abdullah bin Khalid al-Khalifa and Michael Rice (eds), *Bahrain through the Ages* (London, 1993).

Al-Qasimi, Sultan ibn Muhammad, *The Myth of Arab Piracy in the Gulf*, 2nd ed. (London, 1988).

Al-Rasheed, Madawi, *A History of Saudi Arabia* (Cambridge, 2002).

Al-Tajir, Mahdi Abdalla, *Bahrain, 1920–1945: Britain, the Shaikh and the Administration* (London, 1987).

Allen, Calvin, 'The state of Masqat in the Gulf and East Africa, 1785–1829', *International Journal of Middle East Studies* xiv/2 (1982), pp. 117–27.

Anscombe, Frederick F., *The Ottoman Gulf: The Creation of Kuwait, Saudi Arabia, and Qatar* (New York, 1997).

Arjomand, Said Amir, *After Khomeini: Iran under His Successors* (Oxford, 2009).

Avery, Peter, 'Nadir Shah and the Afsharid Legacy', in Peter Avery, Gavin Hambly and Charles Melville (eds), *The Cambridge History of Iran. Vol. 7: From Nadir Shah to the Islamic Republic* (Cambridge, 1991), pp. 3–62.

Awad, Abdul Aziz M., 'The Gulf in the seventeenth century', *Bulletin of the British Society for Middle Eastern Studies* xii/2 (1985), pp. 123–34.

Balfour-Paul, Glen, *The End of Empire in the Middle East: Britain's Relinquishment of Power in her Last Three Arab Dependencies* (Cambridge, 1991).

Barendse, R.J., 'Trade and state in the Arabian seas: A survey from the fifteenth to the eighteenth century', *Journal of World History* xi/2 (2000), pp. 173–225.

Bathurst, R.D., 'Maritime trade and Imamate government: Two principal themes in the history of Oman to 1728', in Derek

Hopwood (ed.), *The Arabian Peninsula: Society and Politics* (Totowa, NJ, 1972).

Beblawi, Hazem, 'The rentier state in the Arab world', in Hazem Beblawi and Giacomo Luciani (eds), *The Rentier State* (London, 1987).

Bethencourt, Francisco, *Portuguese Oceanic Expansion, 1400–1800* (Cambridge, 2007).

Bulloch, John, *The Gulf: A Portrait of Kuwait, Bahrain and the United Arab Emirates* (London, 1984).

Burrell, R.M., 'Britain, Iran and the Persian Gulf: Some aspects of the situation in the 1920s and 1930s', in Derek Hopwood (ed.), *The Arabian Peninsula: Society and Politics* (Totowa, NJ, 1972).

Carter, Robert, 'The history and prehistory of pearling in the Persian Gulf', *Journal of the Economic and Social History of the Orient* xlviii/2 (2005), pp. 139–209.

Cole, Juan R.I., 'Rival empires of trade and Imami Shi'ism in eastern Arabia, 1300–1800', *International Journal of Middle East Studies* xix/2 (1987), pp. 177–203.

Commins, David, *The Wahhabi Mission and Saudi Arabia* (London, 2006).

Cook, J.M., 'The rise of the Achaemenids and establishment of their empire', in Ilya Gershevitch (ed.), *The Cambridge History of Iran, Vol. 2: The Median and Achaemenian Periods* (Cambridge, 1968–1991).

Cottrell, Alvin J. et al. (eds), *The Persian Gulf States: A General Survey* (Baltimore, MD, 1980).

Crone, Patricia, *God's Rule: Government and Islam, Six Centuries of Medieval Islamic Political Thought* (New York, 2004).

Crystal, Jill, *Oil and Politics in the Gulf: Rulers and Merchants in Kuwait and Qatar* (Cambridge, 1990).

——— *Kuwait: The Transformation of an Oil State* (Boulder, CO, 1992).

Daryaee, Touraj, 'The Persian Gulf trade in late antiquity', *Journal of World History* xiv/1 (2003), pp. 1–16.

——— 'The Persian Gulf in late antiquity: The Sasanian era (200–700 CE)', in Lawrence G. Potter (ed.), *The Persian Gulf in History* (New York, 2009).

Davidson, Christopher M. *The United Arab Emirates: A Study in Survival* (Boulder, CO, 2005).

——— *Dubai: The Vulnerability of Success* (New York, 2008).

——— *Abu Dhabi: Oil and Beyond–Power and Politics in the Gulf* (New York, 2009).

Davies, Charles, *The Blood-red Arab Flag: An Investigation into Qasimi Piracy, 1797–1820* (Exeter, 1997).

Disney, A.R., *A History of Portugal and the Portuguese Empire from the Beginnings to 1807*, 2 vols (Cambridge, 2009).

Eickelman, Dale, 'From theocracy to monarchy: Authority and legitimacy in inner Oman, 1935–1957', *International Journal of Middle East Studies* xvii/1 (1985), pp. 3–24.

Farah, Talal Toufic, *Protection and Politics in Bahrain, 1869–1915* (Beirut, 1985).

Floor, Willem, *The Persian Gulf: A Political and Economic History of Five Port Cities, 1500–1730* (Washington, DC, 2006).

―――― *The Persian Gulf: The Rise of the Gulf Arabs—The Politics of Trade on the Persian Littoral, 1747–1792* (Washington, DC, 2007).

―――― 'The Dutch and the Persian silk trade', in Charles Melville (ed.), *Safavid Persia* (London, 2009a).

―――― 'Dutch relations with the Persian Gulf', in Lawrence G. Potter (ed.), *The Persian Gulf in History* (New York, 2009b).

Foley, Sean, *The Arab Gulf States: Beyond Oil and Islam* (Boulder, CO, 2010).

Gause, F. Gregory, *Oil Monarchies: Domestic and Security Challenges in the Arab Gulf States* (New York, 1994).

―――― *The International Relations of the Persian Gulf* (Cambridge, 2010).

Ghabra, Shafeeq N., 'Balancing state and society: The Islamic movement in Kuwait', *Middle East Policy* v/2 (1997), pp. 58–72.

Hathaway, Jane, *The Arab Lands under Ottoman Rule, 1516–1800* (London, 2008).

Heard-Bey, Frauke, *From Trucial States to United Arab Emirates: A Society in Transition* (London, 1996).

Hegghammer, Thomas, *Jihad in Saudi Arabia* (Cambridge, 2009).

Herb, Michael, 'A nation of bureaucrats: Political participation and economic diversification in Kuwait and the United Arab Emirates', *International Journal of Middle East Studies* xli/4 (2009), pp. 375–95.

Hinds, Martin, 'The first Arab conquests in Fars', *Iran* xxii (1984), pp. 39–53.

Holden, David and Richard Johns, *The House of Saud: The Rise and Rule of the Most Powerful Dynasty in the Arab World* (New York, 1981).

Holt, P.M., *Egypt and the Fertile Crescent, 1516–1922: A Political History* (Ithaca, NY, 1966).

Hourani, George Fadlo, *Arab Seafaring in the Indian Ocean in Ancient and Early Medieval Times* (Princeton, NJ, 1951).

Hoyland, Robert G., *Arabia and the Arabs: From the Bronze Age to the Coming of Islam* (London, 2001).

Ismael, Jacqueline S., *Kuwait: Social Change in Historical Perspective* (Syracuse, 1982).

Jones, Toby Craig, *Desert Kingdom: How Oil and Water Forged Modern Saudi Arabia* (Cambridge, MA, 2010).

Kamrava, Mehran, 'Royal factionalism and political liberalization in Qatar', *Middle East Journal* xiii/3 (2009), pp. 401–20.

Keddie, Nikki, *Modern Iran: Roots and Results of Revolution* (New Haven, CT, 2003).

Kelly, J.B., *Eastern Arabian Frontiers* (New York, 1964).

―――― *Britain and the Persian Gulf 1795–1880* (Oxford, 1968).

Kennedy, Hugh, *The Prophet and the Age of the Caliphates* (London, 1986).

Khuri, Fuad Ishaq, *Tribe and State in Bahrain: The Transformation of Social and Political Authority in an Arab State* (Chicago, IL, 1980).

Kostiner, Joseph, 'Shi'i unrest in the Gulf', in Martin Kramer (ed.), *Shi'ism, Resistance and Revolution* (Boulder, CO, 1987).

Lambton, Ann K.S., *Qajar Persia: Eleven Studies* (Austin, TX, 1987).

Landen, Robert G., *Oman since 1856; Disruptive Modernization in a Traditional Arab Society* (Princeton, NJ, 1967).

―――― 'The changing pattern of political relations between the Arab Gulf and the Arab provinces of the Ottoman Empire', in B.R. Pridham (ed.), *The Arab Gulf and the Arab World* (London, 1988).

Lawson, Fred, *Bahrain: The Modernization of Autocracy* (Boulder, CO, 1989).

Lienhardt, Peter, *Shaikhdoms of Eastern Arabia* (New York, 2001).

Lightfoot, Dale R., 'The origin and diffusion of *qanats* in Arabia: New evidence from the northern and southern peninsula', *The Geographical Journal* clxvi/3 (2000), pp. 215–26.

Litvak, Meir, *Shi'i Scholars of Nineteenth-century Iraq: The 'Ulama' of Najaf and Karbala* (Cambridge, 1998).

Louër, Laurence, *Transnational Shia Politics: Religious and Political Networks in the Gulf* (New York, 2008).

McLachlan, Keith, 'Oil in the Persian Gulf area', in Alvin Cottrell (ed.), *The Persian Gulf States: A General Survey* (Baltimore, CO, 1980).

Macris, Jeffrey R., *The Politics and Security of the Gulf: Anglo-American Hegemony and the Shaping of a Region* (Abingdon and New York, 2010).

Mahdavi, Hossein, 'The pattern and problems of economic development in rentier states: The case of Iran', in Michael Cook (ed.), *Studies in the Economic History of the Middle East* (London, 1970).

Mallat, Chibli, 'Muhammad Baqer as-Sadr', in Ali Rahnema (ed.), *Pioneers of Islamic Revival* (London, 1994).

Marr, Phebe, *The Modern History of Iraq* (Boulder, CO, 1985).

Masters, Bruce, 'Semi-autonomous forces in the Arab provinces', in Suraiya N. Faroqhi (ed.), *The Cambridge History of Turkey*, Vol. 3 (Cambridge, 2006).

Matthee, Rudi, 'Boom and bust: The port of Basra in the sixteenth and seventeenth centuries', in Lawrence G. Potter (ed.), *The Persian Gulf in History* (New York, 2009).

Mughni, Haya, *Women in Kuwait: The Politics of Gender* (London, 1993).

Naji, Kasra, *Ahmadinejad: The Secret History of Iran's Radical Leader* (Berkeley, CA, 2008).

Newman, Andrew J., *Safavid Iran: Rebirth of a Persian Empire* (London, 2006).

Niblock, Tim with Monica Malik, *The Political Economy of Saudi Arabia* (London, 2007).

Nieuwenhuis, Tom, *Politics and Society in Early Modern Iraq: Mamluk Pasha, Tribal Shaykhs and Local Rule between 1802 and 1831* (The Hague, 1982).

Omar, Farouk, 'Urban centres in the Gulf during the early Islamic period: A historical study', *Bulletin of the British Society for Middle Eastern Studies* xiv/2 (1987), pp. 156–61.

Onley, James, *The Arabian Frontier of the British Raj: Merchants, Rulers, and the British in the Nineteenth-century Gulf* (New York, 2007).

Owtram, Francis, *A Modern History of Oman: Formation of the State since 1920* (London, 2004).

Ozbaran, Salih, 'The Ottoman Turks and the Portuguese in the Persian Gulf, 1534–1581', *Journal of Asian History* vi/1 (1972), pp. 45–87.

Perry, John R. *Karim Khan Zand: A History of Iran, 1747–1779* (Chicago, IL, 1979).

——— 'The Zand dynasty', in Peter Avery, Gavin Hambly and Charles Melville (eds), *The Cambridge History of Iran. Vol. 7: From Nadir Shah to the Islamic Republic* (Cambridge, 1991).

Peterson, J.E., 'Tribes and politics in Eastern Arabia', *Middle East Journal* xxxi/3 (1977), pp. 297–312.

——— *Oman in the Twentieth Century: Political Foundations of an Emerging State* (London, 1978).

——— *The Arab Gulf States: Steps toward Participation* (New York, 1988).

——— 'The Arabian peninsula in modern times: A historiographic survey', *American Historical Review* xcvi/5 (1991), pp. 1435–49.

Potter, Lawrence G., 'The consolidation of Iran's frontier on the Persian Gulf in the 19th century', in Roxanne Farmanfarmaian (ed.), *War and Peace in Qajar Persia: Implications Past and Present* (New York, 2008).

——— (ed.), *The Persian Gulf in History* (New York, 2009).

Potts, Daniel T., *The Arabian Gulf in Antiquity*, 2 vols (Oxford, 1990).

Ramazani, Rouhollah K. and Joseph A. Kechichian, *The Gulf Cooperation Council: Record and Analysis* (Charlottesville, VA, 1988).

Rathmell, Andrew and Kirsten Schulze, 'Political reform in the Gulf: The case of Qatar', *Middle Eastern Studies* xxxvi/4 (2000), pp. 47–62.

Risso, Patricia, *Oman and Muscat: An Early Modern History* (New York, 1986).

——— *Merchants and Faith: Muslim Commerce and Culture in the Indian Ocean* (Boulder, CO, 1995).

——— 'Cross-cultural perceptions of piracy: Maritime violence in the western Indian Ocean and Persian Gulf region in a long eighteenth century', *Journal of World History* xii/2 (2001), pp. 293–319.

Shamlan, Sayf Marzuq and Peter Clark, *Pearling in the Arabian Gulf: A Kuwaiti Memoir* (London, 2000).

Soucek, Svat, *The Persian Gulf: Its Past and Present* (Costa Mesa, CA, 2008).

Stern, S.M., 'Ramisht of Siraf, a merchant millionaire of the twelfth century', *Journal of the Royal Asiatic Society of Great Britain and Ireland* (1967), pp. 10–14.

Sweet, Louise, 'Pirates or polities? Arab societies of the Persian or Arabian Gulf, 18th century', *Ethnohistory* xi/3 (1964), pp. 262–80.

Teitelbaum, Joshua (ed.), *Political Liberalization in the Persian Gulf* (New York, 2009).

Tétreault, Mary Ann, *Stories of Democracy: Politics and Society in Contemporary Kuwait* (New York, 2000).

——— 'The political economy of Middle Eastern oil', in Deborah J. Gerner and Jillian Schwedler (eds), *Understanding the Contemporary Middle East*, 3rd ed. (Boulder, CO, 2008).

Tilly, Charles, 'How empires end', in Karen Barkey and Mark von Hagen (eds), *After Empire: Multiethnic Societies and Nation-building: The Soviet Union and the Russian, Ottoman, and Habsburg Empires* (Boulder, CO, 1997).

Tripp, Charles, *A History of Iraq*, 3rd ed. (Cambridge, 2007).

Valeri, Marc, *Politics and Society in the Qaboos State* (New York, 2009).

Vassiliev, Alexei, *A History of Saudi Arabia* (London, 1998).

Whitcomb, Donald, 'The archaeology of al-Hasa oasis in the Islamic period', *Atlal: Journal of Saudi Arabian Archaeology* ii (1978), pp. 95–113.

Whitehouse, David, 'Maritime trade in the Gulf: The 11th and 12th centuries', *World Archaeology* xiv/3 (1983), pp. 328–34.

Wilkinson, John C., *The Imamate Tradition of Oman* (Cambridge, 1987).

Wilson, Arnold Talbot, *The Persian Gulf: An Historical Sketch from the Earliest Times to the Beginning of the Twentieth Century* (Oxford, 1928).

Winder, R. Bayly, *Saudi Arabia in the Nineteenth Century* (New York, 1965).

Yergin, Daniel, *The Prize: The Epic Quest for Oil, Money and Power* (New York, 1991).

Zahlan, Rosemarie Said, *The Creation of Qatar* (London, 1979).

——— *The Making of the Modern Gulf States: Kuwait, Bahrain, Qatar, the United Arab Emirates, and Oman* (London, 1989).

INDEX

Abbas, Shah (Safavid), 40–44, 46, 49

Abbasid dynasty, 23, 25–29

Abdulaziz ibn Abd al-Rahman 'Ibn Saud' (Saudi Arabia), 100–101, 106, 134–137, 139–141, 146, 150, 153, 161, 179

Abdullah al-Salim, Sheikh (Kuwait), 148–149, 184–185

Abdullah ibn Abdulaziz, Crown Prince/King (Saudi Arabia), 181, 216, 274, 276–277

Abdullah ibn Ahmad, Sheikh, (Bahrain), 102, 108

Abdullah ibn Faisal, Emir (Saudi Arabia), 94–95, 269

Abdullah ibn Jabir, Sheikh (Kuwait), 108

Abdullah ibn Jiluwi, Emir (Saudi Arabia), 136, 153

Abdullah ibn Qasim, Sheikh (Qatar), 106, 150, 188

Abdullah ibn Sabah, Sheikh (Kuwait), 66–67, 107

Abu Dhabi, 16, 68, 74, 77, 79, 84–87, 97, 103, 105, 139, 152–154, 158, 161–162, 189–191, 193, 197, 202, 208–211, 237–238, 287–288, 290

Abu Musa, 160, 192–193, 218–219

Achaemenid Empire, 14–15

Afrasiyab Clan (Iraq), 44–46, 56

Agha Muhammad Khan (Qajar), 54–55

Ahmad al-Jabir, Sheikh (Kuwait), 146–148

Ahmad ibn Ali, Sheikh (Qatar), 188–189, 213

Ahmad ibn Khalifah, Sheikh (Bahrain), 67, 101

Ahmad ibn Rashid, Sheikh (Umm al-Qaiwain), 152, 290

Ahmad ibn Said, Sayyid (Oman), 69

Ahmadinejad, Mahmud, 266–268

Ajman, 74, 79, 152, 193, 208, 237, 288, 290

Algiers Agreement, 218–219, 232

Ali ibn Abdullah, Sheikh (Qatar), 188

Ali ibn Abi Talib, 18, 21–23

al-Allawi, Ayad, 253, 257–258

Anglo-Iranian Oil Company (AIOC), 124–126, 127, 142, 148, 150, 166

Anglo-Persian Oil Company (APOC), 118–119

Aramco, 138–139, 143, 148, 161

Arif, Abd al-Rahman, 176–177

Arif, Abd al-Salam, 173, 175–176

Ashura, 22, 28, 58, 144, 230
al-Awda, Salman, 269, 271
Azzan ibn Qais, Sayyid
	(Oman), 89, 95

Baath Party, 149, 166–167,
	173, 175–178, 184, 217,
	219, 227, 231, 257
Babi Movement, 112–113
Badr ibn Saif, Sayyid (Oman),
	71
Baghdad Pact, 127, 133, 169,
	173–174
Bahrain, 2, 4, 6, 8–9, 13–14,
	16–17, 27–28, 30–31,
	33, 36–38, 40, 42,
	47–49, 51, 53, 60,
	66–68, 72, 74, 77–78,
	80–84, 87, 92–93, 95,
	101–107, 112, 123–124,
	137, 140–146, 149–152,
	154, 156, 163–164,
	186–189, 192–193,
	197–198, 202–204, 207,
	210–214, 220, 227–229,
	234–235, 238, 250–251,
	279–282, 284, 287, 292,
	295, 298–99
Bahrain Petroleum Company
	(BAPCO), 142,
	144–145, 187
al-Bakr, Ahmad Hasan, 177,
	217, 231
Baluchis, 12, 69, 117, 142,
	159
Bandar Abbas, 3, 29–30, 41,
	44, 50, 58–59, 70–71,
	87, 89–90, 110, 113
Bandar Rig, 59–60, 67
Bani-Sadr, Abol Hasan, 227,
	241, 266
Bani Yas, 68, 85–86, 105, 161
Banu Ka'b, 57, 61
Banu Khalid, 38, 50, 62–64,
	66

Basic Law (Oman), 285
Basic Law of Government
	(Saudi Arabia),
	270, 274
Basra, 24–26, 33, 36–38,
	42–46, 50–54, 56–62,
	66–67, 69, 71, 81–82,
	99, 105, 107–108,
	110, 118, 121,
	127–129, 131–133,
	175, 218, 238,
	257, 259
Bazargan, Mehdi, 226
Britain, 1, 55, 71–74, 76,
	78–85, 87, 90–92, 94,
	96, 104–106, 110, 114,
	116–121, 123, 125,
	127–128, 130–134,
	136–137, 145, 153,
	159, 161–162, 164–166,
	194–197, 204, 208, 230,
	255, 262, 297–98
British Political Agent, 91,
	141, 143, 150, 156–157,
	188, 190
British Resident, 78, 80, 86,
	89, 94–95, 103–105,
	108–109, 123, 151, 160,
	191–192
Al Bu Said, 68–72, 81–82,
	87–92, 94
Buraimi, 71, 84–85, 88–89,
	92–95, 191
Buraimi dispute, 158–159,
	161–162, 179, 194
Bush, George H.W., President,
	245–248, 277
Bush, George W., President,
	252, 254–256, 259, 265,
	273
Bushehr, 3, 16–17, 59–60,
	69–71, 78, 80, 82,
	94–95, 107, 110, 113,
	265, 268
Buyid dynasty, 28–29

Canning Award, 88
Carmathians, 26–28, 31, 49
Constitution
    Bahrain, 211–212,
        280–281
    Iran, 227, 243, 263
    Iraq, 128–130, 177, 217,
        258–259
    Kuwait, 147, 184–186, 214,
        248, 277–279
    Oman, 205, 285
    Qatar, 212, 282–284
    Saudi Arabia, 179–181
    United Arab Emirates, 193,
        208, 210–211, 238, 287
Constitutional Revolution
    (Iran), 115–117
Cox, Percy, 91, 129, 139
Curzon, Lord, 91, 109–110

Dammam, 77, 89, 102–103,
    144, 215–216, 230
D'Arcy Concession, 118
Daud Pasha, 58, 97–98
Da'wa Party, 177–178, 210,
    227, 231, 235, 256, 258
Dhahran, 77, 138, 215, 230,
    251
Dhahran air base, 180–181
Dhiyab ibn Isa, Sheikh (Abu
    Dhabi), 84
Dhufar, 90, 151, 195–196,
    204–208, 218, 220, 223,
    286
Dhufar Liberation Front,
    195–196
Dilmun, 13–14
al-Dir'iyya, 62–65, 73, 92
Doha, 77, 105–106, 150–151,
    161, 284
Dubai, 6, 70–71, 77, 79,
    83–85, 87, 113, 143,
    151–156, 163, 189–193,
    207–211, 227–228,
    237–238, 251, 287–292

Dutch East India Company,
    32–34, 41–44, 47,
    50–51, 53, 59–61,
    117

Eastern Province (Saudi
    Arabia), 137–139, 179,
    198, 230
Education, 204
    Bahrain, 143–144
    Dubai, 155–156
    Iran, 113, 125
    Iraq, 98, 218, 254, 256
    Oman, 207
    Qatar, 151, 284
    Saudi Arabia, 180, 182,
        215, 243–244, 276–277
Elections
    Bahrain, 212, 280–282
    Iran, 227, 241, 263–264,
        266–268
    Iraq, 248, 254, 256,
        272–273
    Kuwait, 147, 185, 212, 214,
        236–237, 248, 277–279
    Oman, 285–286
    Qatar, 283
English East India Company,
    59, 61, 71–72

Fahd ibn Abdulaziz, King
    (Saudi Arabia), 181,
    216, 243, 247, 269–270,
    274, 276
Faisal ibn Abdulaziz, King
    (Saudi Arabia), 140,
    167, 179–184, 200, 230,
    243
Faisal ibn Hussein, Emir/King
    (Iraq), 128–131
Faisal ibn Turki, Emir (Saudi
    Arabia), 93–95,
    102–103
Faisal ibn Turki, Sayyid
    (Oman), 90–92

Fath Ali Shah (Qajar), 55
Fatimid dynasty, 26–28
France, 55, 70–72, 78, 82–83,
    91, 128, 235, 253, 262,
    265
Friendly Convention, 1861,
    (England and Bahrain),
    103
Fujaira, 86, 193, 208, 238

General Treaty of Peace with
    the Arab Tribes, 74,
    78–79
Ghalib ibn Ali al-Hinai, Imam
    (Oman), 158–159,
    194
Green Revolution, 268
Gulf Cooperation Council
    (GCC), 1, 208, 234,
    251, 262, 264
Gulistan, Treaty of, 55
Gwadar, 70, 90

Hamad ibn Isa, Emir/King,
    r. 1999– (Bahrain),
    279–281
Hamad ibn Isa, Sheikh, r.
    1932–1942 (Bahrain),
    141–144
Hamad ibn Khalifah, Emir
    (Qatar), 283–284
Hamad ibn Said, Sayyid
    (Oman), 69–70
Hamud ibn Azan, Sayyid
    (Oman), 88
al-Hasa, 2, 7–8, 13, 16–17, 24,
    27–28, 31, 38, 40, 45,
    50, 62–64, 66–67, 77,
    83, 92–96, 100–103,
    105, 108, 120, 134,
    136–137, 139, 141, 145,
    150, 153, 159, 161–162
Hasan ibn Rahma, Sheikh
    (Ra's al-Khaima),
    73–74

Hasan Pasha (Baghdad), 46,
    56–57
Hashemite Kingdom of Hijaz,
    134–135
al-Hawali, Safar, 269, 271
Higher Executive Committee
    (Bahrain), 144–145
Hormuz Kingdom, 29–31, 32,
    35–36, 38, 40, 42–43,
    46, 48, 67
Hormuz Strait, 1, 3, 7, 17, 33,
    67, 70, 72, 77, 82, 123,
    239
Hussein ibn Ali, Imam, 21–23,
    28, 64
Hussein, Sharif, 128, 134

Ibadi, 24, 28, 31, 33, 46–47,
    53, 68–69, 87–92,
    156–159, 162, 194,
    205–206, 286, 297
Il-Khan dynasty, 29, 39
Iran, 1, 3–4, 7, 9, 14–17,
    21, 23, 28–30, 32–33,
    37–43, 48–55, 58–61,
    76–78, 80, 83, 89, 99,
    102–104, 111–117,
    121–127, 131, 133,
    141–142, 148, 153,
    160, 164, 168–172,
    174, 176–177, 179,
    185, 192–194, 197–199,
    201–202, 205, 207–208,
    218–227, 229–242,
    251–252, 255–259,
    260–269, 271, 292, 295,
    296–98
Iran–Iraq War, 231–234,
    238–241
Iranian Revolution, 223–231,
    234–235, 238
Iraq, 20, 22–23, 25–26, 28–29,
    32–33, 36–37, 39–40,
    43–46, 48–51, 53,
    56–58, 64, 98–100,

121–123, 127–134, 139,
147–149, 164–168,
171–178, 183, 196–202,
204, 207–208, 217–221,
224, 227–229, 231–233,
235, 237–241, 244, 260,
262, 269, 275, 292,
296, 298
Iraq Petroleum Company,
128, 130, 132, 154,
173–174, 176, 217,
220
Iraqi Communist Party, 173,
175, 178
Iraqi National Accord, 253,
257
Isa ibn Ali, Sheikh (Bahrain),
83, 103–105, 141
Isa ibn Salman, Sheikh
(Bahrain), 186,
211–212, 279–280
Ismail, Shah (Safavid), 39

Jabir ibn Abdallah, Sheikh
(Kuwait), 107
Jabir ibn Mubarak, Sheikh
(Kuwait), 110
Jabir ibn Sabah, Emir
(Kuwait), 214, 235–237,
248, 277–278
al-Ja'fari, Ibrahim, 258
Al Jazeera, 283–284
Juhaiman al-Utaibi, 229–230

Kalba, 86, 152–153
Karim Khan Zand, 54–55, 60,
67, 160
Kerbala, 22–23, 43, 58, 64, 98,
112, 227–228, 260
Khalid ibn Abdulaziz, King
(Saudi Arabia), 181, 216
Khalid ibn Muhammad,
(Sharjah), 192, 209
Al Khalifah, 66–68, 71, 97,
101–102, 104–105,

140–143, 186–187,
211–212, 228, 282
Khalifah ibn Hamad, Sheikh
(Bahrain), 279
Khalifah ibn Hamad, Sheikh
(Qatar), 188–189, 213,
282
Khalifah ibn Shakhbut (Abu
Dhabi), 79, 84–85
Khalifah ibn Zayid, Sheikh,
d. 1945 (Abu Dhabi),
86–87
Khalifah ibn Zayid, Sheikh,
r. 2004– (Abu Dhabi),
191, 290
al-Khalili, Muhammad, Imam
(Oman), 157–158
al-Khalili, Said ibn Khalfan,
88–89
Khamenei, Ali, 226, 242,
263–264, 268
Kharg Island, 4, 59–61, 233
Kharijites, 21–22, 24, 31
al-Kharusi, Salim, Imam
(Oman), 92, 157
Khatami, Muhammad,
263–266
Khobar, 77, 230, 271, 274
Khomeini, Ruhollah,
170–171, 221–228,
231, 235, 240–242,
261
Khuzistan, 123, 174, 218
Kirkuk, 132, 174, 176, 259
Kurdish Democratic Party,
254
Kurds, 56, 128–129, 176–177,
218–219, 226, 241, 246,
254, 257, 296
Kuwait, 1, 4, 9, 13, 54, 66–67,
77, 80, 82–83, 95–96,
101, 106–110, 120, 129,
133, 139, 145–150,
163–165, 168, 175–176,
184–187, 193, 201–202,

204, 207, 213–214,
228–229, 234–236,
238–40
Kuwait Crisis, 1990, 244–248
Kuwait Oil Company,
147–148, 214

Labour, expatriate, 12, 143,
149, 167, 182, 186–187,
199–200, 203, 207, 211,
215–216, 240, 244, 276,
287, 291–292, 299
Labour movements, 122, 131,
133, 139, 142–147,
150–151, 156, 163, 179,
182, 186–187, 212
bin Laden, Osama 255,
271–273, 292
Land reform, 170, 178
Lansdowne, Lord, 109
Liberation Movement of Iran,
171, 224–226, 260
Lingah, 3, 6, 78, 85, 87, 113,
160, 211
Liwa, 84–86, 161

Al Madhkur, 59–60, 67, 113
Mahdi Army, 257–258, 260
Majid ibn Ahmad, Sayyid
(Oman), 88, 90
Majles movements, 146–148,
154–155
Al Maktum, 85, 87, 155–156,
288, 290
Maktum ibn Buti, Sheikh
(Dubai), 84
Maktum ibn Hasher, Sheikh
(Dubai), 87
Maktum ibn Rashid, Sheikh
(Dubai), 290
al-Maliki, Nuri, 258
Mamluk pashas, 57–58, 64,
97–98
Manama, 77, 102, 123, 141,
143

Maritime Peace in Perpetuity,
Treaty of, 79
Midhat Pasha, 95, 98–101,
108
Mir Muhanna, 60–61
Mir Nasir, 60
Mohammerah, 107–110,
123
Mojahedin, 222–223, 241,
260
Moresby, Treaty of, 81
Al-Mualla, 290
Mubarak ibn Jabir, Sheikh
(Kuwait), 108–110,
136
al-Mudarrisi, Hadi, 228,
234–235
al-Mudarrisi, Muhammad
Taqi, 228
Muhammad Ali Pasha, 65,
92–94, 98, 165
Muhammad Ali Shah (Qajar),
115–116
Muhammad ibn Abd
al-Wahhab, 62–64, 93
Muhammad ibn Abdullah,
Sheikh (Bahrain),
102–103
Muhammad ibn Khalifah,
Sheikh, d. 1772
(Bahrain), 66
Muhammad ibn Khalifah,
Sheikh, r. 1834–1842,
1849–1868 (Bahrain),
102–103
Muhammad ibn Rashid
(Dubai), 290
Muhammad ibn Rashid, Emir
(Hail), 95
Muhammad ibn Saud, Emir
(Saudi Arabia), 63
Muhammad ibn Thani,
Sheikh (Qatar), 105
Muhammad Reza Shah,
125–127, 164, 168–172,

174, 184, 192, 197,
202, 218, 220–225
Musaddiq, Muhammad,
126–127, 165–166, 169,
171, 226
Muscat, 42, 47, 51, 64, 69–71,
78, 81–82, 86–92,
156–157, 196,
205–206, 228, 238,
286, 297
Muslim Brothers, 122
Muslim Brothers, Kuwait, 236
Muzaffar al-Din Shah (Qajar),
115

Nadir Khan/Shah, 52–55, 60,
69
Al Nahayyan, 152, 190
Najaf, 22, 43, 58, 99, 115,
171, 178, 221, 227–228
Nasir al-Din Shah, 112–114
Nasir ibn Murshid, Imam
(Oman), 47
Nasser, Gamal Abdul, 133,
140, 151, 156, 162,
165–167, 172–173,
175, 178–180, 183,
188, 191–192, 194,
199, 269
National Front (Iran), 169,
171, 223–224
Nizwa, 28, 46, 69, 83, 158
Non-Alienation Bond,
(Anglo-Kuwaiti),
109
Al-Nu'aimi, 290
Nuclear power
Iran, 1, 265–268, 298
Iraq, 175, 231–232, 246,
252, 254

Obama, Barack, President
260, 268
October 1973 War, 198,
200–202, 214

Oil, 1, 117–119, 122–124,
126–128, 130, 132,
137–140, 142–152,
154–156, 158–163,
167–174, 176, 179,
181–182, 184, 186,
188–191, 193, 195,
197–206, 208–217,
220, 223, 230,
232–240, 243,
245, 250, 253, 258,
261, 263, 267, 270,
275–277, 279,
282–284, 286–290,
294, 296–99
Oman, 1, 3, 7–8, 13–17, 21,
24, 28–29, 31–33,
35–36, 46–47, 50, 53,
59, 67–69, 71–73, 79,
81–85, 87–91, 94–95,
102, 113, 120–121,
156–159, 162, 165, 179,
194–196, 198, 204–208,
218–220, 234, 238,
285–287, 295, 297
Organization of Petroleum
Exporting Countries
(OPEC), 168, 201–202,
234, 238, 248
Ottoman Empire, 32–33,
37–41, 43–46, 48–61,
65–66, 76, 78, 80,
82–83, 93–103,
105–108, 117, 120, 129,
161

Pahlavi dynasty, 12–27,
169–172, 220–226
Patriotic Union of Kurdistan,
254
Pearling, 1, 2, 4, 6–7, 11, 13,
42, 66, 77, 79, 81, 84,
85–86, 120–122, 140,
142–143, 145, 147–148,
150–152, 154–156, 297

Piracy, 3, 70–74, 78–79, 101
Portugal, 1, 5–6, 12, 32–38,
       42–44, 46–47, 50

Qabus ibn Said, Sultan
       (Oman), 196, 204–208,
       238, 285–286
Qais ibn Ahmad, Sayyid
       (Oman), 69–70
Qajar confederation, 52,
       54–55
Qajar dynasty, 55, 58, 70, 76,
       78, 80, 82, 87, 89, 99,
       103, 111–117, 122–123,
       160
Qasim, Abd al-Karim,
       173–175, 178, 219
Qasimi, 68–74, 84–87, 113,
       160, 191–193
Qasim ibn Muhammad,
       Sheikh (Qatar), 86, 100,
       105–106
Qatar, 9, 16, 66–67, 77, 80,
       83, 86, 100–101, 103,
       106, 108, 139, 150–152,
       156, 161–164, 179,
       188–190, 192–193, 197,
       200, 202–203, 207,
       211–213, 234, 247, 251,
       282–284, 287, 295, 299
Qatif, 27, 89, 100, 228
Al Qaeda, 254, 265, 272–274,
       291
Al Qaeda in the Arabian
       Peninsula (AQAP), 274
Al Qaeda in Mesopotamia,
       258–260
Qeshm Island, 3, 30, 47,
       70–71, 78, 85, 123
Qizilbash, 39–40, 54

Rafsanjani, Ali Akbar, 226,
       242, 261–263, 266, 268
Rahma ibn Matar, Sheikh
       (Ra's al-Khaima), 70

Ra's al-Khaima, 68–74, 77, 79,
       85–87, 92, 152–154,
       160, 190–193, 208, 210,
       220, 237, 288–290
Al Rashid, 86, 95–96,
       100–101, 110, 134–135
Rashid ibn Ahmad, Sheikh
       (Umm al-Qaiwain), 290
Rashid ibn Humaid, Sheikh
       (Ajman), 152
Rashid ibn Maktum, Sheikh
       (Dubai), 87
Rashid ibn Said, Sheikh
       (Dubai), 189, 191, 211,
       290
Rentier bargain, 149–150,
       186, 203, 206, 211–212,
       284, 287, 291–292, 299
Reza Khan/Shah, 123–124,
       127, 153, 160
Russia, 1, 41, 50, 52, 55–56,
       78, 93, 97, 109–111,
       114–118, 197, 253, 262,
       265, 267, 297
Rustaq, 47, 69–70, 90

Saadabad Pact, 131, 174, 177
Al Sabah, 66–67, 107–108,
       139, 145–149, 184–185,
       213–214, 219, 228, 237,
       246, 248, 277–278
Sabah ibn Ahmad, Emir
       (Kuwait), 278–279
Sabah ibn Jabir, Emir
       (Kuwait), 66
Sabah ibn Salim, Emir
       (Kuwait), 185, 213–214
Saddam Hussein, 73, 177,
       207, 217, 229, 231–232,
       240, 245–247, 249–261,
       266, 272–274
al-Sadr, Muhammad Baqir,
       178, 219, 231
al-Sadr, Muqtada, 257–260
Safavid dynasty, 32–33, 37–50

al-Saffar, Hasan, 228, 230, 238
Sahwa, 269–272, 275
Said ibn Ahmad, Sayyid
   (Oman), 69
Said ibn Maktum, Sheikh
   (Dubai), 152, 155, 191
Said ibn Sultan, Sayyid
   (Oman), 71–72, 81–82,
   87–88, 93, 102
Said ibn Tahnun, Sheikh (Abu
   Dhabi), 85
Said ibn Taimur, Sultan
   (Oman), 157–159,
   194–196, 206
Saif ibn Sultan II, Sayyid
   (Oman), 47, 68–69
Saif ibn Sultan, Sayyid
   (Oman), 47
Saljuk dynasty, 28–30, 52, 57
Salman ibn Ahmad, Sheikh
   (Bahrain), 102
Salman ibn Hamad, Sheikh
   (Bahrain), 143–144,
   186
Saqr ibn Muhammad, Sheikh
   (Ra's al-Khaima),
   192–193, 290
Saqr ibn Sultan, Sheikh
   (Sharjah), 191–192, 209
Sasanian Empire, 8, 16–17,
   20–21
Saud ibn Adulaziz, King
   (Saudi Arabia),
   139–140, 179–182
Saud ibn Faisal, Emir, 95
Saud ibn Saqr, Sheikh (Ra's
   al-Khaima), 290
Saudi Arabia, 77–78, 80,
   84–85, 102, 106,
   120–121, 134–140,
   144, 146–150, 156,
   158, 161–164, 167–168,
   178–184, 187, 190,
   192–194, 197–204, 207,
   213–216, 219, 228–229,
   233–235, 238–239, 243,
   245–247, 249–251, 262,
   269–277, 282, 284,
   295–296, 299
Saudi emirate, 62–65,
   92–96
Shakhbut ibn Dhiyab, Sheikh
   (Abu Dhabi), 84
Shakhbut ibn Sultan, Sheikh
   (Abu Dhabi), 152–153,
   161, 190–191
Shariati, Ali, 222–224, 227
Sharjah, 13, 68, 74, 77–79,
   85–86, 88, 121,
   152–155, 160, 190–194,
   208–209, 228, 238,
   288–290
Shi'ism
   Ismaili, 23–24, 26–28, 49
   Twelver, 23, 28, 38–40,
      48–49, 52, 58, 222, 227
Shirazi movement, 228, 230,
   234, 238
Shirazi, Muhammad, 228
Sib, Agreement of, 157–158
Silk trade, 29, 33, 38, 40–41,
   43–44, 50
Siraf, 3, 17, 25, 28–29
Slave trade, 78, 80–83, 88,
   90–91, 155
Sohar, 69–70, 88, 90
Soviet Union, 123, 125,
   164–166, 172–173, 176,
   196–198, 204, 210, 220,
   226, 233–234, 236–237,
   239, 244–245, 272–273
Sultan ibn Abdulaziz, Prince
   (Saudi Arabia), 181, 276
Sultan ibn Ahmad, Sayyid
   (Oman), 69–71
Sultan ibn Muhammad,
   Sheikh (Sharjah), 209,
   290
Sultan ibn Saif II, Sayyid
   (Oman), 47, 68

Sultan ibn Saqr, Sheikh (Ra's al-Khaima), 73–74, 79, 86, 88
Sultan ibn Saqr, Sheikh (Sharjah), 153
Sunni, 21, 24, 27–28, 30–31, 39, 48, 53, 98, 104, 107, 122, 128–129, 135, 140–142, 144–145, 178, 186–187, 206, 227–229, 235, 257–259, 265, 280–282, 298
Supreme Council for Islamic Revolution in Iraq (SCIRI), 229, 257–259
Suq al-Manakh, 236–237

Tahmasp, Shah (Safavid), 39–49
Taimur ibn Faisal, Sayyid (Oman), 92, 156–157
Talib ibn Ali, Imam (Oman), 158, 194
Tanzimat era, 97–100, 108
Al Thani, 105–106, 150–151, 188, 213, 282–284
Thuwaini ibn Said, Sayyid (Oman), 88–89
Tobacco protest, 114–155
Trucial Oman, 152, 154–155
Trucial Oman Levies/Trucial Oman Scouts, 154–155, 162, 194, 209
Trucial Sheikhdoms, 83, 94–95, 104, 106, 139
Trucial States, 83–87, 152–156, 160, 179, 189–194
Trucial States Council, 156, 189, 208
Tudeh Party, 164, 169, 171
Tunb Islands, 160, 192–193, 218–220
Turkey, 123, 127–129, 131, 133, 233, 246

Turki ibn Abdullah, Emir (Saudi Arabia), 92–94, 102
Turki ibn Said, Sayyid (Oman), 90, 285
Turkmanchai, Treaty of, 111

Umayyad dynasty, 21–25
Umm al-Qaiwain, 74, 79, 83, 152, 193, 208, 210, 238, 290
United Arab Emirates, 208–211, 287–291
United Nations, 162, 194–195, 240, 245–246, 252–253, 255–257, 262, 267–268
United States, 1, 88, 118, 121, 125–127, 137, 164, 166, 168–170, 172, 177, 179–181, 193, 197–202, 208, 212, 218, 220, 223, 225–226, 233–235, 239–240, 242–247, 249–256, 259, 262, 264–274, 283, 291, 298
Uqair Conference, 139, 146
Utub, 66, 107, 145, 148, 292

Wahhabism, 62–65, 92–93, 95–96, 134–136, 138, 140, 159, 164, 181–182, 229–230, 247, 269–270, 275, 296
Women, 11, 218, 287
  dress
    Iran, 125, 227
    Kuwait, 236
  legal rights
    Iraq, 174, 217
    Saudi Arabia, 275–277
  political participation
    Bahrain, 212, 280–281

Iran, 170
Kuwait, 277–279
Oman, 285–286
Qatar, 283–284
Saudi Arabia, 270, 275

Yariba Imamate, 32, 47,
    68–69, 87

Zanzibar, 47, 70, 73, 81–82,
    87–90, 207

Zayid ibn Khalifah, Sheikh
    (Abu Dhabi, r.
    1855–1909), 85–87, 103
Zayid ibn Khalifah, Sheikh
    (Abu Dhabi, r.
    1966–2004), 190–191,
    193, 210, 290
Zubara, 66–68, 102, 105,
    150, 193
Zuhab, Treaty of, 46, 50,
    58